Lethal Force and New Zealand Police

Richard S. Shortt

Lethal Force and New Zealand Police

The History, Law, Practice and Reality of Lethal Force Use by a Well-Armed and Capable National Police Service

Springer

Richard S. Shortt
Canberra, Australia

ISBN 978-3-031-05268-2 ISBN 978-3-031-05269-9 (eBook)
https://doi.org/10.1007/978-3-031-05269-9

This Springer imprint is published by the registered company Springer Nature Switzerland AG
The registered company address is: Gewerbestrasse 11, 6330 Cham, Switzerland

Preface

During the early stages of the global Covid-19 pandemic and accompanying lockdowns which saw millions confined to their homes, the author looked for home-based intellectual distractions to help wile away his enforced inactivity. One such distraction was to reconsider a 20-year-old research paper he had completed into the armed response model best suited to the New Zealand Police, the organisation within which he had had a long career. It was during this reconsideration that he read the book by Peter Squires and Peter Kennison *Shooting to Kill? Policing, Firearms and Armed Response* (2010) that discussed, in a wide-ranging fashion, the use of lethal force by Police in the United Kingdom.

That book caused the author to search for something similar addressing the environment in Aotearoa New Zealand, and to his surprise he found nothing similar existed. There were a number of academic papers (like his own from 2000) which touched on aspects of lethal force use, but nothing that presented a comprehensive overview and discussion of the various elements that comprise the subject. What had been planned as a simple reconsideration of models of armed response grew into this book examining the history, law, practice and reality of lethal force use by New Zealand Police.

In particular, as the initial work progressed, four facts emerged from the environment in Aotearoa New Zealand that struck the author as incongruent.

The first was the much-lauded traditional view that the New Zealand Police was a routinely unarmed police service, one of very few in the world today. The author, during his 34 years of service, knew this was partly true, but also inaccurate. He had on many occasions undertaken duty while armed and had witnessed both first-hand and in the media increasing evidence of the NZP resorting to the carriage and use of firearms. His own research paper, from 2000, had indicated that the old model of firearms deployment was under pressure and likely no longer fit for purpose.

The second and third elements that struck the author was that Aotearoa New Zealand had abolished the judicially imposed death penalty in 1989, and had then enacted a Bill of Rights in 1990 that enshrined a right of not being unlawfully deprived of life, except in limited circumstances.

Finally, the fourth fact was that in a country with no death penalty, an enshrined right to life and a routinely unarmed police service, 61 people were shot at by Police between 2000 and 2019, with 23 of them receiving fatal wounds.[1] Furthermore, when comparing the rate of *fatal* shootings by police between Australia (a country where police officers always carry a pistol when on duty) and Aotearoa New Zealand (a country where firearms are now carried in police cars, to be accessed when needed by an officer) for the years 2010–2019, it was discovered that New Zealand Police killed more people per 100,000 citizens than their Australian counterparts during those years (refer to Chap. 8 for further details).

Individually, all of those issues were worthy of more detailed examination and discussion. But, rather than tackling each in isolation, the author felt it was an opportunity to delve back into history to outline what relationship New Zealand Police had with firearms and lethal force, as well as considering the contemporary environment where use of lethal force by Police has increased in recent years. The use of lethal force against Police, and in general society, also warranted commentary as the author considered it was not possible to fully appreciate the environment surrounding the use of lethal force by Police without that wider context.

This book is the result. As set out in greater detail in Chap. 1, it is broken into three parts to help provide the history, context, contemporary situation/evidence and what may be required in Aotearoa New Zealand's future to help mitigate and manage both the use of lethal force and the perception of the New Zealand Police as the only authority permitted by law to resort to such a drastic measure on behalf of society and the state.

The author hopes this book is not an end point. He hopes that some readers will consider it a start point for their own research, analysis and publication. The taking of a life by Police or the taking of a police officer's life are too important not to be the subject of rigorous scrutiny, debate and knowledge in a land that has taken away the right of the state to impose a judicial death sentence and which purports to cherish the lives of all citizens.

Canberra, Australia — Richard S. Shortt

[1] In the book, the author's definition for the "use of lethal force" includes any situation where a police officer decides to fire a firearm loaded with live ammunition at another person, knowing that it is likely the person could die as a result. This is an expanded definition of use of lethal force and, therefore, includes times when police bullets miss the person being shot at (12 such occasions occurred between 2000 and 2019) and situations where a non-fatal injury resulted from the bullet(s) hitting the person shot at (28 such occasions occurred between 2000 and 2019). The author explains his reasons for promoting the use of this definition when others might argue that lethal force only applies when a person dies as a result of the actions of an armed police officer.

Acknowledgements

In completing the book, I am indebted to the following individuals and organisations for the support I received that meant I could achieve my goal.

My special thanks go to three people, firstly, Thomas, my son and unpaid – but loyal – research assistant in Aotearoa New Zealand. His repeated trips to the National Library were invaluable. Secondly, my beloved companion, Leonie Mack, whose reading of my drafts and feedback helped me see the "wood from the trees". Finally, Dr. Garth Den Heyer, who put me in touch with my publisher without whom the entire exercise would have been a great time-filler, but nothing more.

My special thanks also go to all of the academics, journalists, writers and organisations who permitted me to use their published material in preparing and finalising this book. In particular, the Independent Police Conduct Authority. Without all of their kind heartedness and understanding, much would have been left unsaid within this work.

Finally, many thanks go to Springer Nature for their support in bringing the project to a successful conclusion.

Contents

Part I Law, Oversight and Context Regarding Lethal Force

1 "Armed Police, Drop Your Weapon!" Introduction ... 3
Introduction ... 3
Bibliography ... 10

2 The Law and Morality Regarding the Use of Lethal Force ... 13
The Moral Dimension ... 19
Bibliography ... 21

3 Oversight of New Zealand Police Use of Lethal Force ... 23
Pre-1989 ... 23
Post-1989 ... 24
Independent Investigation and Growth ... 27
Transformation ... 29
The Present Day ... 31
PCA and IPCA Reporting on Shootings by Police ... 33
PCA/IPCA Decisions Regarding Shootings ... 39
Satisfaction with the IPCA ... 42
Bibliography ... 44

4 New Zealand Police and Firearms ... 47
Bibliography ... 71

5 Policies, Procedures, Equipment, Training, Tactics and Specialist Groups ... 75
Policies and Procedures ... 75
Equipment ... 84
Training ... 86
Tactics ... 92
Specialist Units ... 97
Armed Offenders Squad (AOS) ... 97
Special Tactics Group (STG) ... 99
Bibliography ... 103

6 Use of Force: Reviews, Reports and Changes 107
Staff Safety Project (1998) 108
"Are the New Zealand Police on Target?": An Investigation of Alternative Models of Police Response to Dangerous and Unlawful Firearms Incidents (2000) 110
A Strategic Evaluation of the New Zealand Police Position Concerning the Use of Force When Responding to Potentially Violent Situations: A Review of Best Practice, Policy and Training (2001) 114
Review of Access and Availability of Firearms for New Zealand Police (2010) 118
Bibliography 128

Part II Reality of Lethal Force Use – 2000–2019

7 Use of Lethal Force Against New Zealand Police and the Risks Faced 133
Fatal and Non-fatal Shootings of Law Enforcement Officers 141
Perception of Risk 149
Bibliography 153

8 Use of Lethal Force by New Zealand Police 157
Shootings: 2000–2019 157
Who Was Shot and Who Shot Them? 159
Why Were They Shot? 159
Mental Illness 162
What Were the Weapons Involved on Both Sides? 163
What Distances Were Involved? 167
Where and in What Circumstances Did the Shootings Occur? 168
Were Any of the Shootings the Subject of Adverse Comment by the IPCA? 172
Bibliography 174

9 Seven Case Studies 177
Stephen Bellingham: Fatally Shot 2007 177
Halatau Naitoko: Fatally Shot 2009 181
Lachan Kelly-Tumarae: Fatally Shot 2011 186
Adam Morehu: Fatally Shot 2013 189
David Cerven: Fatally Shot 2015 192
Jerrim Toms: Fatally Shot 2018 194
Astin Hooper: Fatally Shot 2019 197
Bibliography 201

Part III Observations and Suggestions Regarding the Future

10 Observations Regarding the Use of Lethal Force 205
The Gun Culture of the Society 206
The Standards of Firearms Training 215
The Extent of Militarisation 217
Bibliography 225

11 Use of Lethal Force Law, Governance, Policy and Procedure 229
Independent Police Conduct Authority 229
Police Policy, Practice and Governance 231
Use of Lethal Force Legal Matters 235
Bibliography 238

12 Conclusion: Where to from Here? 239
Bibliography 244

Index 245

About the Author

Richard S. Shortt The author joined the New Zealand Police in 1977. He worked as a uniformed constable, detective, sergeant, senior sergeant and inspector across a range of policing environments from major cities to rural stations until 2001. During the last decade of his career (2001–2011), the author undertook two secondments to other New Zealand Government departmental roles. The first was as a national security advisor with the Department of the Prime Minister and Cabinet (DPMC), and the second was with the New Zealand Security Intelligence Service (NZSIS) leading the newly formed Combined Threat Assessment Group. On returning to New Zealand Police in 2008, the author joined the newly created Organised and Financial Crime Agency, New Zealand, focused on combatting serious and organised crime through inter-agency collaboration, before his retirement in 2011.

While an operational police officer, the author carried firearms as a personal protection officer, detective, and uniformed officer. In the 1990s, he joined an Armed Offenders Squad (AOS) as the second-in-charge and responded to callouts to firearms-related events for 5 years before transferring on promotion to the Royal New Zealand Police College as an inspector where he coordinated, among other courses, the AOS qualifying course for 3 years.

During his police service, he gained a Diploma in New Zealand Policing, a Master of Public Management degree, and, following retirement, a PhD from Charles Sturt University in Australia. The author now lives in Australia.

Abbreviations

9/11	11 September 2001, terrorist attacks in New York and Washington DC, and the crashing of a hijacked aircraft in Pennsylvania, United States of American
AC	Armed Constabulary
AOS	Armed Offenders Squad
ART	Armed Response Team
ARV	Armed Response Vehicle
ATS	Anti-Terrorist Squad (note: subsequently renamed the STG)
CIB	Criminal Investigations Branch
IPCA	Independent Police Conduct Authority (note: 2007 to the present)
NCO	Non-Commissioned Officer (note: sergeant or senior sergeant)
NorthComm	Northern Communications Centre
NZCF	New Zealand Constabulary Force
NZL	New Zealand Law
NZP	New Zealand Police
PCA	Police Complaints Authority (note: 1989–2007, then the IPCA)
PITT	Police Integrated Tactical Training
RNZ	Radio New Zealand
RNZPC	Royal New Zealand Police College
SSTT	Staff Safety Tactical Training
STG	Special Tactics Group
TENR	Threat Exposure Necessity Response threat assessment model
TO	Tactical Option(s)
TOF	Tactical Options Framework
TOR	Tactical Options Reporting
TVNZ	Television New Zealand
USA	United States of America
VIP	Very Important Person(s) (incl. dignitaries and political high-office holders)

Part I
Law, Oversight and Context Regarding Lethal Force

Chapter 1
"Armed Police, Drop Your Weapon!" Introduction

Introduction

The title of this chapter uses the phrase taught to the author when being trained in the use of police firearms and quite likely to have been shouted at people subsequently shot by police through to the current day. The phrase (or words to that effect) may have been repeated a number of times or spoken just once. In some situations, due to urgency, danger or just the speed of events, the phrase may not have been used at all. The phrase is intimately linked to the use of lethal force by police.

The importance of research regarding the use of police firearms, or, put another way, the use of lethal force, has in the author's view become all the more relevant in times when allegations of bias have become commonplace in respect of police. No other act on the part of police comes with an often "copper-clad" inability to reverse the outcome through litigation or negotiation. It was, in 22 instances in Aotearoa New Zealand between 2000 and 2019, quite irreversible.

In Aotearoa New Zealand,[1] the relevance of research into the use of lethal force is encapsulated in Section 8 of the *New Zealand Bill of Rights Act 1990* (NZL) (New Zealand Government, 1990), which states:

> **Right not to be deprived of life**
> No one shall be deprived of life except on such grounds as are established by law and are consistent with the principle of fundamental justice. (ibid.)

Aotearoa New Zealand gave even earlier voice to the right to life when it abolished the death penalty from its statutes. It was removed in 1961 for all crimes except treason and then in 1989 for all crimes with the passing of the *Abolition of the Death Penalty Act 1989* (NZL) (New Zealand Government, 1989).

[1] "Aotearoa New Zealand" is the combination of the Māori and English language names for New Zealand. It is not the country's official name, but will be used by the author when referring to the country in this work.

R. S. Shortt, *Lethal Force and New Zealand Police*,
https://doi.org/10.1007/978-3-031-05269-9_1

However, while judges can no longer impose a death sentence on behalf of the state, police officers – agents of the state or to use the language of the *Policing Act 2008* (NZL) "… an instrument of the Crown …" – can take a citizen's life and are justified by law in doing so. In Aotearoa New Zealand, the *Crimes Act 1961* (NZL), sections 39–41, and 48, cover the use of force by Police (and others) and in particular the use of force by Police that may be "intended or likely to cause death or grievous bodily harm" (New Zealand Government, 1961). Greater detail and discussion will be provided regarding these sections later in this book.

Some, having read the above commentary, may ask whether Police should have firearms and should be able to shoot people? These are great questions. They resonate not only on the legal level but also on the moral level and within society generally, as has been seen with protests about Police shootings in the USA over a number of years and particularly during 2020 (e.g. the shootings of Jacob Blake in Kenosha, Wisconsin (2020), and Marcellis Stinnette in Waukegan, Illinois (2020)). Even in Aotearoa New Zealand, there was opposition to Police having and using firearms, for example, see the article titled "NZ police should not have guns" in the *Otago Daily Times* (4 June 2020).

It is also useful, from time to time, to reflect on questions like "Why do police have firearms?" and "Why does Aotearoa New Zealand, avowing as it does to respect the right to life and to not impose death penalties, allow police officers to take lives?". And, "How does New Zealand Police govern and manage its use of lethal force?". To some, it may seem self-evident why police have firearms and use them, but to others, it may seem contradictory. It is hoped this book will provide answers to those questions and cause readers to ponder the issue further, perhaps removing the contradiction they experience.

The author is not a lawyer, nor a philosopher, but legal minds and philosophers have considered those very questions, for example, Seumas Miller, an Australian philosopher, who explored the topic in his book on the ethics of the use of lethal force by the police and military (Miller, 2016), and the Independent Police Conduct Authority (Aotearoa New Zealand) which investigates police shootings and determines whether legal justification is found. More will be presented on these topics in both Chaps. 2 and 3.

This book is part history lesson and part contemporary commentary on the New Zealand Police and their use of lethal force. It takes the reader on a journey from the mid-1800s when policing first appeared in the colony of Aotearoa New Zealand through to the 2020s where the country can boast to have – in the author's opinion – a well-trained, well-equipped, well-armed police service that seeks to serve all citizens "… without favour or affection, malice or ill-will …" as stated in the oath that all constables entering the service take (New Zealand Government, 2008, p. 17).

The author's original interest in this topic arose via two distinct pathways. The first was his time spent as a member of the New Zealand Police between 1977 and 2011. During those years, he was trained in the use of firearms and carried them on many occasions in a variety of roles, including as a member of an Armed Offenders Squad (AOS). The second pathway was research he undertook in 1999–2000 with regard to a Master of Public Management degree resulting in his thesis entitled "Are the New Zealand Police on Target? An Investigation of Alternative Models of Police Response to Dangerous and Unlawful Firearms Incidents" (Shortt, 2000). That work examined the firearms deployment policy of the New Zealand Police and contrasted it with the approaches taken in Australia (a "routinely armed"[2] set of Police services) and the UK – excluding Northern Ireland (a "routinely unarmed" set of constabularies). At the time of the research, New Zealand Police identified itself (in fact, still does) as being a "routinely unarmed" police service.

Building on from those two pathways, this book arose from more recent research by the author that initially sought to determine if there had been any change in the New Zealand Police's firearms deployment practices and number of people or police being shot since the original research was completed in 2000. However, as the work unfolded, it refocused into a more detailed examination of the environment surrounding the use of lethal force by Police in Aotearoa New Zealand, using the circumstances regarding the shootings by Police that occurred between 2000 and 2019 (as detailed in Chap. 8) as contextual examples of that environment. The work also broadened to include examination of the risks faced by police officers from the illegal use of firearms within society.

Inspiration for the refocus also came, it must be acknowledged, from reading Peter Squires and Peter Kennison's excellent work *Shooting to Kill? Policing, Firearms and Armed Response* (Squires & Kennison, 2010), detailing the lethal force situation in the UK.

This book will canvas the law on use of force in Aotearoa New Zealand and the history of New Zealand Police involvement with firearms including the organisation's policies, procedures and training with regard to the use of lethal force. It will discuss the specialist Police units that can be called upon to help officers resolve dangerous events and will comment on the types of weapons and equipment that modern police officers have available to them. The book will also comment on the oversight afforded to Police use of firearms by the Police Complaints Authority (PCA) and its successor the Independent Police Conduct Authority (IPCA), to provide context for the closer examination of 43 publicly available reports on shootings by Police that form a substantial element of Part II of the book.

Because policy and policy changes do not come about in a vacuum, the book revisits and comments on historic reports from the late 1990s to the mid-2000s regarding New Zealand Police that had an impact upon the way use of force was considered and how firearms were deployed. The same chapter also includes comment upon the most recent and substantive policy shift, namely, the placing of Police firearms in all operational response vehicles which occurred over the period 2010–2012.

As mentioned, Part II of the book looks in detail at 43 instances where police officers used firearms to kill or injure people during the course of their duties. These reports, issued by the PCA and its successor the IPCA, provide the most detailed

[2] The terms "routinely armed" and "routinely unarmed" are explained in greater detail later in this chapter. Hendy (2012), p. 10, also provides a useful description.

and authoritative publicly available accounts of those shooting events which occurred between 2000 and 2019. Part II of the book also considers the risks faced by police officers from the illegal use of firearms and from violence being used against them as they go about their duties.

Finally, in Part III, the book will present a set of observations made by the author as a result of immersing himself in the research and a set of suggestions about what Police, the IPCA and government should now be considering when it comes to the issue of use of lethal force in the 2020s and beyond.

A detailed outline of the book and its parts follows:

Part I sets the scene for the reader regarding the policing environment in Aotearoa New Zealand.

Chapter 1 describes the rationale behind this book and what it seeks to achieve.

Chapter 2 examines in brief the law in Aotearoa New Zealand concerning the use of force, particularly by police, and what it means for every day citizens and police officers.

Chapter 3 describes the mechanisms used in Aotearoa New Zealand to oversight and investigate the police use of force and in particular the use of deadly or potentially deadly force. It details the background and development of the primary organisation responsible for this work, the IPCA.

Chapter 4 details the history and context of firearms use by New Zealand Police from the mid-1800s until the early 2020s.

Chapter 5 describes and discusses the New Zealand Police's policy, procedure, equipment, tactics, training and specialist firearms units.

Chapter 6 revisits and reviews four earlier research papers and projects undertaken regarding the use of force and deployment of firearms by New Zealand Police. These documents helped shape the current use of force and firearms policy, procedures, guidelines, training and deployment of police firearms in Aotearoa New Zealand.

Part II examines the risks faced by police officers and analyses 43 publicly available reports into shootings by Police occurring between 2000 and 2019. It also presents seven detailed case studies of shootings by Police that draw attention to important aspects of the use of lethal force environment.

Chapter 7 presents data and commentary on lethal force use *against* New Zealand Police and the risks of death and serious injury, both from an historical perspective and in more contemporary times. The chapter includes how Police have responded to the risks.

Chapter 8 presents commentary on the civilians killed as a result of lethal force use *by* New Zealand Police. The chapter is broken into subsections summarising:

8.1 Who were the subjects of the shootings, and who were the police officers who shot them?

8.2 Why did these shootings take place, and how did the police come to be involved in them?

8.3 What weapons were involved in the shootings, on all sides?

8.4 What distances were involved on the shootings?
8.5 Where did these shootings occur, were they inside structures or outside, or did they involve a vehicle or other means of transport?
8.6 Were any of the shootings the subject of adverse comments by the IPCA?

Chapter 9 presents a series of 7 case studies drawn from the 43 PCA/IPCA reports reviewed. Each contains critical comment from the PCA/IPCA about Police, despite each case resulting in a "justified" shooting outcome. These case studies will illustrate where the PCA/IPCA found concerns with Police and draw out some common areas where police officers did not maintain "best practice" standards. The chapter does not set about relitigating the events that took place, but aims to identify common themes or points that are greater than just the findings arising from any one individual shooting.

Part III looks at what can be learned from these events and from the way the Police use lethal force and how it is overseen by the IPCA.

Chapter 10 sets out observations the author thinks have been highlighted by the research and assessment of the 43 shootings.

Chapter 11 looks back at the law on use of force and Police policy and procedures, discussing whether there is a need for adjustment or new law. It covers what the author describes as the "soft" side of the environment, including issues regarding the IPCA, Police policy, practice and governance and use of force legal consequences.

Chapter 12 contains concluding comments and discusses alternative options for New Zealand Police, the IPCA and government regarding use of lethal force, including firearms deployment, and comments on the obligations that all parties have to minimising the deaths of citizens at the hands of an "instrument of the Crown".

With regard to some of the data and detail used in this book, it is acknowledged the sample sizes for the analysis and discussion in Chaps. 7, 8 and 9 are small. For example, just 43 publicly available reports on shootings by Police and 4 brief profiles on Police deaths and injuries – supported by what media reporting could be found – stretched out over two decades. Some may view these small samples as positive indicators of policing in Aotearoa New Zealand. Others, perhaps families and friends of those shot (and particularly those killed), may have a different perspective born out of grief and loss.

The death of a person leaves a hole in many lives. It leaves many things unsaid, unfinished and unfathomable. Loss of life is irreversible. The act of taking a life cannot be undone by the taker; it cannot be overturned on appeal to a higher court. It is an incredibly final outcome. That finality makes examination of this topic all the more important.

The ripples from a shooting extend over a wide array of people, communities and organisations, and, once a trigger is pulled – in the milli-second that it takes – the bullet cannot be put back in the gun. That slight flexing of a finger has serious consequences. Shootings by, or of police, are therefore – in the author's view – most worthy of multiple forms of examination and review. Not just investigative, legal and forensic examinations as are undertaken by Police, the IPCA or coroners but also from a social science perspective with the objective being to identify how they can be avoided or their frequency minimised, if in fact they can be any more than they already are.

What this book will not do is attempt to relitigate the circumstance surrounding the shooting events or the recommendations and findings of the review authorities. The investigations and reviews undertaken by the police, PCA and IPCA have been completed by highly qualified individuals and teams. They had access to those involved, to scenes, to evidence gathered and to police files. In a number of instances, this included people who had survived being shot.

What this work does set about doing that is different to the work of the Police and the PCA and IPCA is to aggregate the data from the killing or wounding of police officers, and the data from the 43 events involving a death or injury by Police, into consolidated data sets. In doing so, the author sought to look not at individual instances (however, some will be highlighted as examples), but instead look across all of the publicly reported instances over a significant 20-year period of time to examine if anything can be determined from such an examination.

As mentioned earlier, this research has used as its primary sources the publicly available reports and information from websites, both official government agency sites and news media, including the IPCA. The New Zealand Police site, for example, supplied data, reports, profiles and summaries of each shooting of Police. The IPCA site provided 43 reports on shootings by Police from the moment the police became aware of/involved in an incident, right through to when the shot(s) were fired and what action was then taken by Police to assist the person that had been shot. The data, profiles, reports and media reporting – short of examining the actual police files – are the most publicly accessible descriptions available concerning each of the uses of lethal force. Some Official Information Act requests were lodged with the New Zealand Police to fill gaps in the data.

Due to the Covid-19 global health pandemic, there was no opportunity for face-to-face discussions or interviews with specific people related to the work given the author was based in Australia.

Unfortunately, with regard to the PCA/IPCA reporting, while often quite similar in structure and content, they are not based on a standard template that ensured standardised data across all investigations, nor did they always contain data the author had hoped to find. For example, some early reports did not clearly confirm how many shots were fired and what their individual trajectories were; most provided no indication of the ethnicity of the person shot, and in some reports, it was challenging to discern what distances were involved between the police officer(s) who fired and the subject of the shooting. More will be said on this aspect later in Chaps. 8 and 10.

These 43 instances do not represent every occasion when police armed themselves, responded to incidents and confronted people. There were many thousands of those over the 20 years. For example, Police reporting from 2012 to 2019 shows that police officers presented firearms at people on 2710 occasions. By 2019, Police were reporting that there were 4860 events where tactical options were used,[3] with 343 involving the deployment of firearms. At those 343 deployments, "98% … involved only a presentation" of a firearm, with there being just "… eight firearms discharges … three resulting in fatal injuries, three in non-fatal injuries, [while] two missed" (New Zealand Police, 2021, p. 9 & 23).

Thankfully, the figures reveal the vast majority of armed police responses were resolved without police firing a shot. There will be wider exploration of Police tactical options reporting to show the number of time police officers have deployed and used firearms later in this book.

However, when shots miss or are not fired, as highlighted by Squires and Kennison (2010), there are no media frenzy and no independent investigation. In the author's opinion – adopting the approach from the world of occupational health and safety – those "near-miss" events should also form part of the research undertaken by Police services, oversight organisations and academia when considering the use of force, particularly lethal force, by agents of the state.

Those events may well hold important lessons about why a small number of events end in tragic circumstances and many, many others do not. The data required for such research, however, sits within Police organisations and would be challenging to amass, and there is currently no legislative requirement for oversight agencies – like the IPCA – to investigate and report on near-miss situations when it comes to police deployment of firearms.

In this work, the author adopts the practice of referring to "the use of lethal force" rather than just writing about firearms and shots fired or shootings. Furthermore, the author takes the position that use of lethal force occurs when a police officer pulls the trigger of their weapon while aiming at and intending to shoot another person with live ammunition (as opposed to training scenarios using non-lethal simulation ammunition). It is immaterial if the shot(s) miss, kill or wound; those outcomes are down to the physics of firearms use and luck.[4] A deliberately fired warning shot, however, is not considered a use of lethal force, as there was no intention to shoot another person, nor is an unintentional discharge of a firearm through careless handling considered a use of lethal force.

The missed shots (and the people shot but not killed by police) take on even greater significance when it is recognised that police are not trained to shoot to wound. Police are trained to shoot to incapacitate a person who is a threat to themselves or another. The aiming point for this is "centre mass" – the torso – which contains most of the vital organs needed for life (Author's personal experience as a New Zealand police officer) (note: "incapacitation" is also the term used in the

[3] Tactical options are deemed by New Zealand Police to include use of restraint holds, physical grappling, use of handcuffs, batons, OC spray, taser and firearms.

[4] The author suggests there are in fact six outcomes that can arise from use of lethal force. They are missing the intended person with the bullet harmlessly hitting the ground, a miss with the bullet striking a vehicle or structure that was not the intended target, hitting the intended person with fatal consequences, hitting the intended person with non-fatal consequences or hitting an unintended person with either a fatal or a non-fatal consequence.

UK – e.g. see Squires and Kennison (2010)). Therefore, every shot fired by a police officer at another person – with the intention of incapacitating – is highly likely to result in a catastrophic injury or death.

An even more stark perspective on surviving a police shooting is the fact some police – in particular members of the Special Tactics Group (STG) – are trained to shoot directly at a person's head in situations of extreme and dire need such as hostage takings, terrorist events or when a person is wearing bullet-resistant protection and only such a shot will ensure the serious threat they pose is stopped (Independent Police Conduct Authority, 2014). More will be written about this approach in later chapters.

Add to all of this is the additional fact that police are trained to fire – if necessary – multiple shots to ensure the threat they face has indeed been incapacitated (Author's personal knowledge and experience). Even though the first shot may have killed or mortally wounded the other person, officers may fire more shots until they see an effect they identify with incapacitation – often evidenced by the person falling to the ground, dropping their weapon or movement stopping (IPCA police shooting reports 2000–2019). Thus, surviving being shot at by Police is a substantial achievement, but one down to physics and luck, rather than the intent of the officer doing the shooting.

Finally, before moving to the body of this work, it is useful to appreciate that the New Zealand Police has for many decades considered itself (and been considered by others – e.g. see Squires & Kennison, 2010) as one of the few police organisations globally to be "routinely unarmed"; the others include England, Scotland, Norway and the Irish Republic (Eire). That is to say officers on duty, either in uniform or in civilian clothing, do not as a matter of course carry a firearm on their person or even in the vehicles they use (Hendy, 2012, p. 8; New Zealand Police, 2021; Shortt, 2000).

That does not mean the New Zealand Police is an unarmed police service. That has never been the case. It is armed, and the author maintains that today it is routinely so, although some may argue instead that it is semi-armed (Hendy, 2012, p. 14). The firearms capability of the New Zealand Police will be discussed in greater detail in later chapters.

Bibliography

Balchin, J. (2020, June 4). *Otago daily times*. Retrieved from odt.co.nz: https://www.odt.co.nz/opinion/NZ police should not have guns.

Hendy, R. (2012). *The strategic impact of routine arming that New Zealand Police*. School of Government, Victoria University of Wellington.

Independent Police Conduct Authority. (2014). *Fatal Police shooting of Antony Ratahi*. Independent Police Conduct Authority.

Miller, S. (2016). *Shooting to kill: The ethics of police and military use of lethal force*. Oxford University Press.

New Zealand Government. (1961). *Crimes Act 1961 (NZL)*. New Zealand Government.

New Zealand Government. (1989). *Abolition of the Death Penalty Act 1989*. New Zealand Government.

New Zealand Government. (1990). *New Zealand Bill of Rights Act 1990*. New Zealand Government.

New Zealand Government. (2008). *Policing Act 2008*. New Zealand Government.

New Zealand Police. (2021, July 12). *Tactical Options 2019 Annual Report*. Retrieved from police.govt.nz: https://www.police.govt.nz/sites/default/files/publications/annual-tactical-options-research-report-8.pdf

Shortt, R. S. (2000). *Are the New Zealand Police on target? An investigation of alternative models of Police response to dangerous and unlawful firearms incidents*. Victoria University.

Squires, P., & Kennison, P. (2010). *Shooting to kill? Policing, firearms and armed response*. Wiley.

Chapter 2
The Law and Morality Regarding the Use of Lethal Force

Given, as previously outlined, Aotearoa New Zealand has protections safeguarding the right to life and has abolished the death penalty, how is it that between 2000 and 2019 21 citizens and 1 foreign national were shot and killed by agents of the state? What enables Police to act in this way?

Let's commence this discussion with how New Zealand Police (the national Police service for Aotearoa New Zealand) are established and empowered. The *Policing Act 2008* (NZL) (New Zealand Government, 2008) establishes the organisation and sets the legislative parameters within which it operates. The Act sets out the role and functions of the New Zealand Police and – importantly – establishes constabulary independence from political interference in the command and control of Police operational activities (Ibid., s.30(4)).

The Act expands on independence (and other matters) in the six principles upon which it is based; they state:

- Principled, effective, and efficient policing services are a cornerstone of a free and democratic society under the rule of law:
- Effective policing relies on a wide measure of public support and confidence:
- Policing services are provided under a national framework but also have a local community focus:
- Policing services are provided in a manner that respects human rights:
- Policing services are provided independently and impartially:
- In providing policing services every Police employee is required to act professionally, ethically, and with integrity. (ibid., s. 8).

Later in the Act, in sections 28 and 29, it also establishes that the commissioner of police is responsible for developing and promulgating to staff "general instructions" (New Zealand Government, 2008). These, and any "Commissioner's circulars; and applicable local orders", must be obeyed by Police employees and guide them in the discharge of their official duties (Ibid., s.30(1)). Official duties are summarised in the Act under the heading "Functions of Police", at section 9 of the Act. They are:

- Keeping the peace.
- Maintaining public safety.
- Law enforcement.
- Crime prevention.
- Community support and reassurance.

R. S. Shortt, *Lethal Force and New Zealand Police*,
https://doi.org/10.1007/978-3-031-05269-9_2

- National security.
- Participation in policing activities outside New Zealand.
- Emergency management.

The *Policing Act 2008* (NZL) is, however, silent on the use of force by members of the New Zealand Police with just two exceptions. Both relate to the taking of identifying particulars from persons who are in custody or detained by way of summons. This deals with things like taking fingerprints or obtaining a photograph; however, no wider explanation is provided. There is no reference in the Act to using force (particularly lethal force) to protect police or others, to make arrests or to bringing to a close an event that may be creating a danger to the community. For that, we must move to another enactment, the *Crimes Act 1961* (NZL).

The law regarding the serious use of force by one person against another is covered in the *Crimes Act 1961* (NZL). Less serious interactions are covered by the *Summary Offences Act 1981* (NZL). For the purposes of this discussion, the focus is on the *Crimes Act* and the provisions concerning the use of physical force by one person against another.

The sections most relevant to this work and Police are those contained in Part 3 of the Act entitled "Matters of justification or excuse" (*Crimes Act, 1961,* (NZL)) and in particular sections 39, 40 and 41. The three sections deal with "force used in executing a process [under law] or in arrest" (s. 39), "preventing escape or rescue" of an arrested person or sentenced prisoner (s. 40) and "prevention of suicide or certain offences" (s. 41).

When it comes to New Zealand Police, section 39 specifically states:

> … that **justification or protection** [from criminal responsibility] shall extend and apply to the use by him or her of **such force as may be necessary to overcome any force used in resisting such execution or arrest**, **unless** the sentence, warrant, or process can be executed or the arrest made **by reasonable means in a less violent manner**: provided that, except in the case of a **constable** or a person called upon by a constable to assist him or her, this section shall not apply **where the force used is intended or likely to cause death or grievous bodily harm**. [emphasis added] (*Crimes Act, 1961, s. 39* (NZL)).

Section 39 is, therefore, the foundational basis in law for police officers to use force, including lethal force, to effect an arrest if that arrest is being resisted and there is no reasonable and less violent means of overcoming the resistance.

Sections 40 and 41 (*Crimes Act, 1961,* (NZL)) also provide an authority to use force, but neither section contains the "… intended or likely to cause death or grievous bodily harm" caveat applied in section 39. The caveat signifies for New Zealand Police an important acknowledgement – from the lawmakers of the country – that there will be occasions when police officers have to use force and may even have to use deadly force in order to undertake their functions as set out in the *Policing Act 2008* (NZL).

In the Independent Police Conduct Authority's commentary on section 40, for example, the Authority[1] comments that the section "allows the use of force, including lethal force, to prevent an escape" (Independent Police Conduct Authority, 2021, p. 22). However, the Authority makes the point that the section "… is silent as to the circumstances in which [force] will be justified" (Independent Police Conduct Authority, 2021, p. 22). The section of the Act simply states "…such force as may be necessary to prevent the escape of [someone who] takes to flight in order to avoid arrest" (ibid.). In an effort to clarify the situation, the Authority's view is that:

> … the primary purpose of an officer using force under section 40 is to take the fleeing or escaping offender into custody, and the proportionality of his or her force should be assessed against two factors:
>
> (a) the seriousness of the offence for which the person is to be apprehended (and the consequent public interest in detaining them in order to bring them to justice); and,
> (b) the likelihood and degree of risk the offender poses if escape is not prevented. (ibid.)

Unfortunately, the Authority concedes that at this time, there is no "direct legal authority" on how to interpret the section's contents (ibid.).

The above commentary regarding section 40 contrasts with the situation regarding section 41. That section of the *Crimes Act 1961* (NZL) permits the use of force "… as may be reasonably necessary in order to prevent the commission of suicide, or the commission of an offence which would be likely to cause immediate and serious injury to the person or property of any one …" (New Zealand Government, 1961). In this case, the Authority was able to call upon case law from the Court of Appeal, namely, *Russo v R,* where it was "held that the necessity to use force was to be assessed by reference to the reasonableness of the belief", essentially an objective test about the belief and not a subjective test regarding the "actual belief of the officers concerned" (ibid., pp. 22–23).

The Authority went on to comment about sections 40 and 41:

> The Authority believes that the test in *Russo* is more applicable to section 40 than the test in *Haddon* [a case also from the Court of Appeal dealing with a use of force where the subjective test was applied]. That is because, like section 41, section 40 justifies the use of force for preventive rather than defensive reasons (although there is obviously some overlap between the two) … (Independent Police Conduct Authority, 2021, p. 23).

Ultimately, it will take case law to clarify the situation, irrespective of the Authority's view. However, in the absence of any such court ruling, when determining justification on the part of a police officer, it is the Authority's opinion that is relied upon and which is on display above. The Authority continued to raise the issue of the need for clarity related to section 40 (and section 39) in its 2020 briefing to the new minister taking over following that year's general election (Independent Police Conduct Authority, 2020a, pp. 18–19).

---

[1] The institution of the Independent Police Conduct Authority is headed by a person who bears the title "the Authority". The IPCA can at times also be referred to – institutionally – as the Authority. To avoid confusion, the author will use "IPCA" or "Independent Police Conduct Authority" when making institutional references and "the Authority" when referring to statements, findings or decisions attributed to the head of the organisation.

The other significant – perhaps most significant – *Crimes Act 1961* (NZL) section to consider in the context of Police use of force is "Section 48: Self-defence and defence of another" (*Crimes Act, 1961,* (NZL)). That section was quoted by the PCA/IPCA as the justification (or part of the justification) for police use of firearms in all 43 of the shooting cases reviewed for this work.

The section states:

> Every one is justified in using, in the defence of himself or herself or another, such force as, in the circumstances as he or she believes them to be, it is reasonable to use (Ibid., s. 48).

The claim of self-defence as a justification for the use of lethal force is common to both Aotearoa New Zealand (Stuff.co.nz, 2009) and the UK according to Squires and Kennison who mention and discuss it in various parts of their book (Squires & Kennison, 2010).

The use of force protections detailed above do not provide for carte blanche application of lethal force by police, however, as section 62 of the *Crimes Act 1961* (NZL) deals with the issue of excess use of force, stating:

> Every one authorised by law to use force is criminally responsible for any excess, according to the nature and quality of the act that constitutes the excess.

Therefore, any suggestions of excess use of force by a constable can be reviewed under law using section 62 as the foundation, and, if the constable is found to have used excess force, other provisions of the *Crimes Act 1961* (NZL) regarding use of force can then be considered with regard to the officer's actions.

The review and oversight of shootings by police, both fatal and non-fatal, occur through five avenues. The first is the homicide, or serious crime investigation, undertaken by Police when one of their own shoots someone. Those investigations also provide the information and data that the Independent Police Conduct Authority uses as the foundation for their investigations – more on this later. The Police investigations should be both thorough and impartial. The IPCA has commented on occasion about the perceived lack of impartiality (e.g. see the IPCA report into the shooting of Stephen Bellingham, in 2007), but the Authority has never substantially criticised any Police investigation and on occasions has noted the thorough nature of them.

As a result of the Police investigations, reaching a point where senior investigating officers have formed a view on whether criminal charges should be considered, the second and third avenues of review occur. These involve referring the evidence and conclusions to internal Police lawyers, and/or independent Crown Law Office lawyers,[2] in order to validate or challenge the conclusions reached by the investigatory team.

---

[2] "...the Crown Law Office operates as a government department with the Solicitor-General as its Chief Executive. The office has more than 70 legal staff ..." the office provides Police with independent legal advice on serious or potentially controversial matters (www.crownlaw.govt.nz) (Author's personal knowledge).

The fourth review mechanism is the IPCA (formerly known as the Police Complaints Authority (PCA)). Under the model of independent oversight and investigation now used, IPCA investigators become involved with the Police investigation at a very early stage. For example, in respect of the fatal shooting of Shayne Sime, the Authority's report stated:

> 98. As required under section 13 of the Independent Police Conduct Authority Act 1988, the Police notified the Authority on 29 June of the shooting of Shayne Richard Sime. [note – Sime was shot late on the evening of 28 June].
> 99. The Authority commenced an investigation in accordance with the Act … The investigation was separate from and independent of any Police criminal and disciplinary investigations.
> 100. The Authority's investigator attended the initial Police investigation briefings, visited the scene at Wadhurst Place, monitored the Police investigations throughout and reviewed documentation produced by the Police investigation team and ESR.[3] Interviews were separately conducted with the AOS Commander and Incident Controller. (Independent Police Conduct Authority, 2010, p. 25).

The fifth review mechanism is via the law courts, including both criminal and coronial courts. By way of notable example, one fatal shooting case, involving Steven Wallace, in 2000, involved all of the mechanisms coming into play (Independent Police Conduct Authority, 2009).

In that case, the Police investigation recommended no charges be laid against the officer who fired the fatal shots at Wallace. This was, as described in the IPCA public report, "… reviewed by both the Crown Solicitor in Wellington [Crown Law Officer lawyer] and the Deputy Solicitor General, both of who agreed with Detective Inspector Pearce's findings" (Independent Police Conduct Authority, 2009, p. 15). The Wallace family, however, disputed those decisions and launched a private prosecution process through the criminal courts charging the police officer with murder (ibid.). The case made its way through the lower court system and was ultimately heard before a justice and jury in the Wellington High Court in 2002 (ibid., p. 16). The jury found the officer acted in self-defence and he was acquitted of the charge (ibid.). During this time, an inquest had been opened in the Coroner's Court, and – although adjourned during the criminal trial – it subsequently resumed (ibid.).

The coroner's finding was delivered in 2007, and the IPCA reported the results as:

> Wallace died of gunshot wounds he received when shot by armed Police … individually and collectively all three officers [the sergeant and the two armed constables at the scene] had demonstrated poor decision-making and a lack of leadership in the handling of this incident, but [the coroner] declined to make any recommendations as this was a matter of performance and not an issue of adequacy of policy or procedure. (ibid., p 17).

In a statement by the police commissioner, following the coronial findings being announced, the criticism was dismissed, and the commissioner "… commended the three officers for their professionalism and dedication" (ibid.).

---

[3] "ESR is a Crown Research Institute that provides science services and research capability across a number of science disciplines …" it is the primary provider of specialist forensic support to the New Zealand Police in dealing with crime scenes and exhibits retrieved during investigations (www.esr.cri.nz) (Author's personal knowledge).

During the Police investigation, the court case and the coronial enquiry, the IPCA had also been following the case and had placed its own activity on hold until:

> 3. … the Coroner's inquest had been conducted and the findings had been released.
> 5. In later 2007, the Coroner delivered his verdict into Steven's death and, following a request from the Wallace family, the (now) Independent Police Conduct Authority recommenced it independent investigation under section 12(1)(c) of the Act.
> 6. During its investigation, the Authority interviewed more than 50 people including Police officers, civilian witnesses, and expert witnesses. The Authority's investigators also examined the Police criminal investigation files, the transcripts of evidence from the depositions hearing [initial hearing before a full trial is undertaken] and the trial of Senior Constable Abbott, and the Coroner's findings. (Independent Police Conduct Authority, 2009, p. 3).

Ultimately, the IPCA concluded in their report that "… it is not open to the Authority to review the jury's verdict …"; therefore, the shooting was confirmed by it as justified. The Authority did, however, direct its attention to a number of the issues that arose before the shooting and about "… the interactions of the Police and the Wallace family" (ibid., p. 20).

The Wallace case was unique in Aotearoa New Zealand for the fact that it illustrated all of the review mechanisms related to a concern associated with s. 62 of the *Crimes Act 1961* (NZL) in play and how each interacted with the others.

Returning now to the general commentary on how excess use of force by a police officer could be actioned, the legal options range from taking no action where a justification defence has been established (see commentary below regarding s. 48) to prosecution for a common assault (e.g. a finding of a minor use of force) right through to and including the most serious outcome, a charge of murder involving "… the killing of a human being by another, directly or indirectly, by any means whatsoever" (*Crimes Act, 1961, s. 158* (NZL)).

Having considered the legal provisions that allow use of force, and the potential consequences of doing so, it is time to discuss the legal defences open to those who shoot someone.

Under the *Crimes Act 1961* (NZL), the primary defence relied upon in very serious cases (e.g. involving death or grievous bodily harm), section 48 and the claim of self-defence comes into consideration. The test applied when considering a self-defence claim by a police officer is a subjective one. In other words, the test is whether or not *what the police officer thought* was reasonable force, given the situation they faced, was in fact reasonable for them to use. It is not an objective test which would see the police officer's actions being considered by people based on *what others thought* would have been reasonable. It is, therefore, a defence or justification that does not allow for "second-guessing" by another who was not involved in the event (Independent Police Conduct Authority, 2020b, p. 17).

Furthermore, as discussed by the Authority in the report concerning the shooting of a man named Ineson (Independent Police Conduct Authority, 2020b), the threat posed by the person who is shot does not need to "be imminent" before force can be used (ibid., p. 18). However, in considering section 48, "imminence is highly relevant to the assessment of the reasonableness" of the force used (ibid.). The Authority explained the situation thus:

> The courts have said that the consideration of what is reasonable force in the context of defending yourself and others *'must depend upon the imminence and seriousness of the threat and the opportunity to seek protection without recourse to the use of force'* [*R v Wong [1990]* 2 NZLR 529, at 536]. While imminence has a temporal context, it can mean *'about to happen'* or *'soon to happen'* rather than *'immediate'*. We must consider that in the context of the rapidly unfolding events that confronted the officers. (Italics in original) (Independent Police Conduct Authority, 2020b, p. 18; Stuff.co.nz, 2009).

Self-defence under s. 48 can be claimed by any person who uses force against another person. It is not restricted to police officers. What the justification does not take into account, however, are the circumstances that pertain specifically to a police officer rather than to a member of the general public.

Those circumstances, it is contended, are that police officers receive specific training in how to respond to and manage dangerous events; police officers are specially equipped with a range of both "less-than-lethal" force options (e.g. taser, OC spray, empty hand self-defence) and "lethal" (or potentially lethal) force options (e.g. a baton or firearm); police officers can also call upon other police officers to assist; and police officers can call upon specialised help over and above what their own training and equipment provide (e.g. police dogs and their handlers, police helicopters, tactical support units like the AOS and the STG or the Police Negotiation Team (PNT)).

For want of all-encompassing terms to encapsulate the above resources, the terms "tactics" and "tactical options" will be used. Tactics describes the training in how to approach, cordon, contain, manage and speak to a person deemed a danger, while tactical options include all of the various "tools" a police officer can call upon as described above.

The law itself, however, is silent on tactics and tactical options and makes no requirement for consideration of their use. The law sets out a simple statement that will apply to any person who uses force, be they an ordinary citizen or a trained, experienced, well-armed and supported police officer.

The two pieces of legislation discussed above, the *Policing Act 2008* and the *Crimes Act 1961* (NZL), therefore, set the legal framework within which New Zealand Police operate. As officers of the state, empowered by the *Policing Act 2008* (NZL), they may use force of various types and levels in order to safely and efficiently deal with a myriad of situations on behalf of society, and provided they are found to have acted lawfully, they may even take the life of another. Below the legislative mandates sit a suite of Police instructions and guidelines which set out to shape how police officers go about their duties and use the powers entrusted to them. Those instructions and guidelines will receive more commentary in Chap. 5 under the section dealing with policies and procedures among other things.

The Moral Dimension

Beyond the law, there is a further dimension regarding Police use of force that is not often discussed, namely, the moral aspect of such action. This section will briefly consider the moral aspect of using lethal force using one philosopher's perspective.

According to Seumas Miller in his book *Shooting to Kill: The Ethics of Police and Military Use of Lethal Force*, there have been many philosophical considerations regarding the moral justification for killing in personal self-defence. However, it seems that less has been written about the justification for police use of lethal force (Miller, 2016).

In the case of police officers, Miller contends that there is a moral justification on two counts. Firstly, there is the justification provided by the right to self-defence against another who poses a threat of serious injury or death which extends to the justification to use lethal force to protect the life of another (Miller, 2016, p. 15), and secondly, he describes a police officer's justification for the use of lethal force as:

> … to some extent role-specific. Both police officers and military combatants evidently have a moral duty to put themselves in harm's way to protect others … Moreover, the moral justification for police and military use of lethal force appear to be, in part , institutionally based. Thus police, under some circumstances, have an institutionally based moral duty to use lethal force to uphold the law …. (Miller, 2016, p. 2).

For police officers, the basis of the institutional justification argument arises from their belonging to New Zealand Police which is charged by society with carrying out particular actions on behalf of the social collective. In Aotearoa New Zealand's case – as discussed earlier – this is confirmed by the *Policing Act 2008* (NZL) and the particular functions of maintaining public safety and law enforcement and, importantly, through police officers taking the constable's oath[4] which confers constabulary powers on each officer (New Zealand Government, 2009).

As a social institution, Miller sees the New Zealand Police as delivering what he terms to be "collective goods" on behalf of the whole community. Collective goods, in his description, have three properties. Firstly, they are "produced, maintained or renewed by means of joint activity of members of organisations" – in the case of police, the delivery of the functions required of New Zealand Police as per the *Policing Act 2008* (NZL). Secondly, the collective goods must be "available to the whole community", and thirdly, the collective goods ought to be produced (or maintained or renewed) and "made available to the whole community, since they are desirable goods and ones to which the members of the community have an (institutional) joint moral right" (Miller, 2016, p. 85).

New Zealand Police – as the national and only police service in the country – delivers "collective goods" to all parts of the land; furthermore, it is evident from community support for New Zealand Police (e.g. 79% of surveyed citizens in the 2018/2019 Satisfaction Survey report trust and confidence in Police) that the "collective goods" the institution delivers are in fact desired and ones to which – it is

[4]The oath reads: "I [name], swear that I will faithfully and diligently serve Her (or His) Majesty [specific name of the Sovereign], Queen (or King) of New Zealand, her (or his) heirs and successors, without favour or affection, malice or ill-will. While a constable I will, to the best of my power, keep the peace and prevent offences against the peace, and will, to the best of my skill and knowledge, perform all the duties of the office of constable according to law. So help me God". (An affirmation form of the same words exists for those who do not align with a religious belief system.)

contended – the community has a moral right, namely, peace, maintenance of public safety, law enforcement, crime prevention, community support and disaster response.

Miller expands upon his institutional argument by determining that such arrangements also impose both "moral rights and duties" on institutional members to do things that they did not have to do before joining the institution. He labels these as "special moral rights and duties" which for a police officer entails the "collective good of aggregate human security" (Miller, 2016, pp. 85–86). He explains it thus.

> For example, police officers may have an institutional and, indeed now, moral duty to put themselves in harm's way in a manner and to an extent (e.g., by arresting armed and dangerous offenders) across the entire community (jurisdiction) that is not morally required of ordinary citizens, and that was never morally required of anyone prior to the establishment of police organisations .... (ibid. p. 86).

Miller balances the justification for the use of lethal force against three principles – *imminence*, *necessity* and *proportionality* (Miller, 2016, p. 18). In his argument concerning these principles, the moral justification for the use of lethal force comes if the threat to one's life (or the life of an innocent other(s)) is *imminent*, it is *necessary* to use the force to save one's own life (or that of the other(s)) and the use of force is not *disproportionate* to the threat posed.

In Miller's description of when lethal force is deemed to be morally justifiable, parallels can be seen with the wording and application of s. 48 of *the Crimes Act 1961* (NZL), and, as will be seen later in this work, it aligns closely to the Police policy and procedural requirements concerning use of firearms. It also bears resemblance to the considerations taken into account by the IPCA when it conducts an investigation into a shooting by police.

Through Miller's work, it can be seen a case can be made for there to be not just a legal basis for justificating the use of force, and lethal force, but also a moral justification based on a police officer's role, their oath of office and their membership of a police institution.

Bibliography

Independent Police Conduct Authority. (2009). *Report on the shooting of Steven Wallace*. Independent Police Conduct Authority.

Independent Police Conduct Authority. (2010). *Public report into police shooting of Shayne Richard Sime*. Independent Police Conduct Authority.

Independent Police Conduct Authority. (2020a). *Briefing to incoming minister 2020 general election*. Independent Police Conduct Authority. Retrieved from ipca.govt.nz

Independent Police Conduct Authority. (2020b). *Fatal shooting of Donald Ineson to defend others legally justified*. Independent Police Conduct Authority.

Independent Police Conduct Authority. (2021). *Non-fatal police shooting on motorway north of Auckland justified*. Independent Police Conduct Authority.

Miller, S. (2016). *Shooting to kill: The ethics of police and military use of lethal force*. Oxford University Press.

New Zealand Government. (1961). *Crimes act 1961*. New Zealand Government.

New Zealand Government. (2008). *Policing Act 2008*. New Zealand Government.
New Zealand Government. (2009). *Policing (Constable's oaths validation) Amendment Act 2009*. New Zealand Government.
Squires, P., & Kennison, P. (2010). *Shooting to kill? Policing, firearms and armed response*. Wiley.
Stuff.co.nz. (2009, January 31). Police instructions concerning the use of firearms. Retrieved from stuff.co.nz: https://www.stuff.co.nz/the-press/news/our-communities/51427/Police-instructions-concerning-the-use-of-firearms

Chapter 3
Oversight of New Zealand Police Use of Lethal Force

Pre-1989

Until 1989, Police were both the "trigger-pullers" and investigators when it came to shootings by police officers. That is not to say the officer involved in the shooting was part of the investigation, quite the contrary. The homicide or serious injury investigation was undertaken by officers viewed as distanced from the place where the shooting occurred, likely coming from another Police district entirely. There was, however, no independent oversight or review, unless the Police file concerning the shooting was passed to the Crown Law Office for an opinion regarding what had been concluded or a complaint had been made to the Ombudsman[1] (Police Complaints Authority, 2007a, p. 10). And, as the much later Commission of Inquiry into Police Conduct confirmed in 2007, independence of enquiry (or, put another way, avoidance of conflict of interest) is both of great importance and still an issue for Police (Bazley, 2007, pp. 103–104).

During those earlier years, if a police officer shot and killed a person, a homicide investigation would be launched. That work would unfold in exactly the same manner as any other homicide investigation with a team of detectives, led by a senior detective, enquiring into the circumstances of what took place. In theory, at least, the enquiry could result in a charge of murder being laid, though none ever was by Police. Alternatively, to allay public concerns, Police could seek a review of the conclusions reached about criminal liability from the Crown Law Office to determine if the right legal view had been reached by the investigators with regard to the evidence and the law (Author's personal knowledge).

[1] "The Ombudsman helps New Zealanders deal with public sector agencies. They handle complaints, undertake investigations and inspections, and encourage good administration" (www.ombudsman.parliament.nz).

R. S. Shortt, *Lethal Force and New Zealand Police*,
https://doi.org/10.1007/978-3-031-05269-9_3

If the shooting did not result in a fatality, a serious crime investigation would instead be applied to the situation, again using a team of detectives, to determine if any crime had been committed by police, for example, attempted murder or wounding with intent.

At the same time as the detective-led investigation, another purely "in-house" Police enquiry would be carried out to determine if Police policy, procedure and practice guidelines (in particular General Instructions) had been adhered to at all stages of the event leading up to the use of lethal or potentially lethal force (Author's personal knowledge). That "in-house" enquiry could result in sanctions being taken by Police against a police officer, or officers, including supervisors and commissioned officers, if serious breaches were uncovered. These sanctions ranged from "counselling" by a more senior police officer to adverse reports on personnel files, fines or even consideration of terminating the employment of those concerned (Author's personal knowledge).

Furthermore, depending on the circumstances of a shooting, and the personalities involved at senior levels within New Zealand Police, additional reviews could be undertaken. For example, in 1999, following the fatal shooting of a man in Helensville, north of Auckland, the author was engaged by the then district manager (later re-titled district commander) to undertake a third enquiry focused on the staff safety dimension. The audit ran in parallel to both the homicide investigation and the Police Complaints Authority enquiry. The district manager concerned had led a substantial, organisation-wide, Staff Safety Review and was keen for a "staff safety" eye to be run over the events that had occurred.

By the late 1980s, considerable political and social change was sweeping Aotearoa New Zealand. Debates and changes to legislation were underway across a diverse range of issues. Some arose from events that had occurred earlier in the decade, for example, the Springbok rugby tour of 1981 which had given rise to numerous complaints against police for excessive use of force, while others arose due to a new government taking office with an agenda for social and structural change. Not only was an independent oversight mechanism regarding Police being debated as of 1985 (Bazley, 2007, p. 168), in 1989 the death penalty was finally abolished from the statute books (New Zealand Government, 1989), and, a year later, a Bill of Rights for all citizens was introduced (New Zealand Government, 1990).

Post-1989

The legislation establishing formal external review of policing in Aotearoa New Zealand was introduced and passed by Parliament in 1988 and was titled the *Police Complaints Authority Act 1988* (NZL). The PCA (as it was then known) became operational on 1 April 1989 (Bazley, 2007, p. 166). Its creation fitted in well with the shift towards socially responsible government occurring in Aotearoa New Zealand at that time. The Act set the functions of the organisation as:

12 Functions of Authority

(1) The functions of the Authority shall be –

(a) to receive complaints–

(i) alleging any misconduct or neglect of duty by any member of the Police; or
(ii) concerning any practice, policy, or procedure of the Police affecting the person or body of persons making the complaint in a personal capacity:

(b) To investigate of its own motion, where it is satisfied that there are reasonable grounds to carry out an investigation in the public interest, any incident involving death or serious bodily harm notified to the Authority by the Commissioner under section 13 of this Act:
(c) To take such action in respect of complaints, incidents, and other matters as is contemplated by this Act.

(2) In the course of taking action in respect of any complaint the Authority may investigate any apparent misconduct or neglect of duty by a member of the Police, or any Police practice, policy, or procedure, which appears to the Authority to relate to the complaint, notwithstanding that the complaint itself does not refer to that misconduct, neglect, practice, policy or procedure.
(3) Nothing in subsection (1) of this section shall authorise the Authority to investigate any matter relating to the terms and conditions of service of any person as a member of the Police. (New Zealand Government, 1988a)

The PCA and the Authority (as the new organisation and the person leading it were now referred to) were in fact just one person who assumed the role until they either chose to resign or attained the age of 72 years (New Zealand Government, 1988a). This person was appointed by the Governor-General – based on a recommendation from the House of Representatives – and was to be an individual who was "... qualified as a barrister or solicitor of the High Court ... and possess[ing] suitable legal experience for the task" (ibid.); however, the Act also spoke of a Judge holding the office and went on to explain that such a person would not lose any of their "... tenure of judicial office, rank, title, status, precedence, salary, annual or other allowances, or rights or privileges as a Judge (including matters relating to superannuation and, for all purposes, service by a Judge as the Authority shall be taken to be service as a Judge" (ibid., s. 4(4)). Hence, it was unsurprising that a Judge, albeit retired, was chosen to be the initial "Authority" and that ever since a Judge or retired Judge has filled the role (Independent Police Conduct Authority, 2021a).

The PCA, however, had no in-house investigative support and relied upon investigations undertaken by the Police who had the personnel and experience to do complex and often time-consuming activity (Den Heyer & Beckley, 2013). It turned out that providing the oversight required proved to be a challenging task and also allowed for continuing disquiet regarding the degree of independence the PCA had in undertaking the reviews that formed the basis of the organisation's work (ibid., p. 211). Also, notably, under the legislation, the PCA was "not empowered to investigate complaints alleging criminal misconduct or to prosecute alleged offending. Nor could the PCA determine the guilt or innocence [of police officers] in criminal cases" (Bazley, 2007, p. 169).

One enlightening description of what the PCA oversight role entailed was given during the 2004–2007 Commission of Inquiry into Police Conduct, by counsel representing the PCA:

> Mrs Brown complains to the Police about a burglary of her house by a third party.
>
> Then (being dissatisfied about the Police handling of the matter) she complains about that ... The first complaint is for the Police to [handle]. The second is for the PCA (or the Police under its oversight).
>
> In the second example, Mrs Brown complains to the Police about a sexual assault on her by a member of the Police. This complaint has two dimensions – one of criminal offending (to be investigated by the Police), and the second of Police misconduct (to be investigated by the PCA). The two dimensions will obviously overlap to some extent, but it is only the complaint to the extent that it alleges misconduct on the part of the Police which the PCA is empowered to investigate. (Bazley, 2007)

Importantly, in terms of this book, Section (1)(b) of the Act required the Authority to consider investigating any incident involving death or serious bodily harm notified to the Authority by the commissioner under section 13 of the Act. That section required the police commissioner to notify the Authority via a "written notice setting out particulars of the incident" of all instances where a police officer "acting in the execution of the member's duty causes, or appears to have caused death or serious bodily harm was caused" (New Zealand Government, 1988a).

Clearly, Parliament had decided that such events were of such substantive importance that they required an unequivocal direction to the commissioner to report them rather than leaving it to a commissioner's discretion as to whether a death or injury was deemed worthy of reporting. However, there remained discretion on the part of the Authority as to whether an independent investigation was undertaken with the requirement for any such action to be based on "reasonable grounds ... [and] ... in the public interest"; thus, in theory at least, not all reports would necessarily result in an independent investigation above and beyond the Police's own.

Despite creation of the new entity, disquiet persisted regarding the perceived lack of investigative independence, potentially fuelled by the discussion detailed above. The disquiet was also viewed as impacting the New Zealand Police who had hoped the PCA would enhance public approval of them and the work they did (Samkin et al., 2010).

Organisational legitimacy and public approval, as Samkin et al. discussed in their paper regarding New Zealand Police, were viewed by Police as crucial to their work given the public of Aotearoa New Zealand were the primary avenue for information regarding crimes and offending (Samkin et al., 2010, p. 24). Furthermore, legitimacy and competency were considered traits that helped an organisation like New Zealand Police deliver "socially constructed standards of quality and desirability as well as perform in accordance with accepted standards of professionalism" (ibid., p. 25).

Independent Investigation and Growth

In June 2000, following 12 years of PCA activity, the Minister of Justice commissioned a review of the PCA (Gallen, 2021, p. 9). The work undertaken by Sir Rodney Gallen – a former Court of Appeal Judge – ran for 5 months. The primary rationale for the review, as set out in Sir Rodney's report, was "a rise in criticism of the Authority substantially directed, not at the Authority as such, but at its reliance upon police investigations of complaints against police" (ibid., p. 6). That reliance had given rise to a "perception" there was neither independence nor appropriateness in the situation (ibid.).

Coincidentally, in April 2000, perhaps the most high-profile challenge regarding the independence and functioning of the PCA arose with the fatal shooting of Stephen Wallace by a police officer (for greater detail, refer to Chap. 4). The concerns raised as a result of the Wallace shooting included the probable time the PCA would take to complete its report and the fact that yet again Police "were effectively investigating one of their own which the media argue[d] did not inspire confidence in the process" (Samkin et al., 2010, p. 28). Unfortunately, history was to show, for a range of administrative and legal reasons, the concern regarding length of time for a report was valid.

The Independent Police Conduct Authority (IPCA) (the name change having occurred in 2007) report into Wallace's shooting was not released until March 2009, almost a decade after the event. It must be pointed out that the extraordinary time delay in the case was the exception, not the rule.

Interestingly, Sir Rodney's report established no formal link between the review process and the Wallace shooting, other than timing (Gallen, 2021). But, it is felt by the author that the commentary unfolding around the Wallace shooting was unlikely to have escaped the attention of the reviewer given its direct relevance to his work. And, within the final report, a reference was made which – to the author's eye – was a direct reference to one of the substantive issues arising out of the Wallace shooting:

> 21.6.6 In certain high profile cases, a police officer's safety or that of his family may be put at risk if material were disclosed in an inappropriate way. *Such a situation occurred recently* where the news media voluntarily accepted the undesirability of publishing the name of a police officer. One newspaper however did not see the necessity of conforming to this principle taking the view it was outweighed by other considerations …". (Italics added) (Gallen, 2021, p. 58)

As Gallen gathered information for his review, he noted that there were – both domestically and internationally – calls for the provision of independent investigative capability within oversight organisations such as the PCA (Gallen, 2021, pp. 46–49). Gallen's report and his recommendations were presented to the Minister of Justice in October 2000. The key recommendations were summarised by the minister as being:

- The Authority should have enhanced investigative capacity of its own, independent of the Police
- The Authority should no longer be a Crown entity but an Officer of Parliament

- The Authority should no longer consist of one person, but three: a current or former judge, a Māori member, and a lay person representing the community
- That the status quo should be retained with regard to the secrecy of the Authorities investigations, both in relation to the material obtained on investigation and to the release of the ultimate decision. (Minister of Justice, 2021)

The recommendations were then considered by the Cabinet which determined a number of outcomes would occur. These included:

- Provision of an independent investigative capacity of six independent investigators – whose focus would be the most serious cases such a *death and serious bodily harm which appear to have been caused by police*
- A name change to the Independent Police Complaints Authority (IPCA)
- Continuance of the Authority as a Crown Entity
- Expanding the Authority to consist of three members – a chair who holds or has held judicial office, and two Deputies (Italics added). (ibid.)

This resulted in the Independent Police Complaints Authority Amendment Bill being introduced to the House of Representatives in December 2002 (Bazley, 2007). However, it was to be 5 years before the *Independent Police Conduct Authority Act 2007* (NZL)[2] came into being in November 2007 (New Zealand Government, 1988b). The reason for the delay between 2002 and 2007 was a major scandal that put Police accountability front and centre of public and government attention.

In January 2004, while the Wallace shooting enquiries were underway (both Police and PCA), and the Gallen review findings were being contemplated and moved towards implementation in the parliament, the next challenge for Police and the PCA arose. It came in the form of a headline proclaiming "Police Raped Me" concerning a very senior police officer and some of his colleagues and included serious allegations of rape and sexual misconduct. New Zealand Police were again thrust into a spotlight that challenged organisational legitimacy and competency, along with the independence of the PCA (Samkin et al., 2010, p. 29). The revelations resulted in the founding of a Commission of Inquiry into Police Conduct by the Prime Minister and a subsequent 3-year-long examination led by Dame Margaret Bazley (ibid.).

As the commission worked through its enquires and hearings, Bazley also delved into a set of suggestions produced by the New Zealand Police in late 2005 regarding further alterations to the structure of the PCA and the way it investigated complaints (Bazley, 2007, pp. 189–192). The suggestions included:

> … primary responsibility for resolution of serious complaints would shift from New Zealand Police to the PCA, which would be able to make use of its power under section 27 of the PCA Act to investigate the complaint itself, and make recommendations as to the appropriate outcome. It would also enable the PCA to assume oversight of the investigation of less serious complaints. The police acknowledged in their proposal that the changes may need further policy work and that their proposal would require substantial increase in PCA resources. (ibid.)

[2] Of note is the name change from the originally proposed Independent Police *Complaints* Authority to the Independent Police *Conduct* Authority. This was as a result of the Commission of Enquiry into Police Conduct (2004–2007).

By the time those suggestions were put, the Bill seeking amendments to the PCA (arising out of Sir Rodney Gallen's work) was already making its way through the parliamentary process.

The Police explained their reasons for making such expansive suggestions were that the PCA had become more of a reviewing body of Police investigations and that this gave rise to a perception that there was no independence in the oversight process (ibid.). Police also wanted sections 32 and 25 of the PCA legislation repealed so that information discovered during PCA investigations could be used for a range of purposes including in criminal and disciplinary proceedings (Bazley, 2007, pp. 189–192).

The concern regarding the perception of independence was also separately raised by an expert witness to the Commission of Inquiry and a number of the sexual misconduct complainants who had approached the commission (ibid., p. 190).

The commission and the New Zealand Police Association did not support all of the suggestions made by the Police, both feeling that the Police had the best expertise and resources to conduct serious and complex criminal investigations (ibid.).

Initially, as mentioned, the PCA did not have any investigative capability, but – as a consequence of Gallen's review – by November 2003, that situation had changed, and a small team of investigators and reviewers were supporting the Authority in their work. By 2005, that support consisted of "… a Deputy Authority, and a staff of four investigators and six reviewing officers and three administrative staff" (Bazley, 2007, pp. 174–175). The practice by then was for an investigating officer to be assigned "in appropriate cases" (ibid., p. 174) with a role described as "… 'active monitoring' … the PCA investigator actively endeavours to ensure that the Police investigation is timely, thorough, and in accordance with best practice" (ibid.).

Transformation

Change for the PCA – as it was still known – was on its way. In February 2007, Justice Lowell Goddard QC, a former High Court Judge, was appointed as the first woman to hold the position of chair of the expanded Authority.

One of Goddard's first actions was to announce an internal review of "organisational structure and operating strategy" (Police Complaints Authority, 2007b). Goddard was aware that the new Act for her new organisation was awaiting Royal Assent and that the workload for her organisation had been increasing for a number of years with the result that a backlog of complaints existed (ibid., p. 4). The review was focused on addressing that backlog, but also on preparing the organisation for the new staff promised by the minister as a result of Gallen's review and the Bazley-led Commission of Inquiry (ibid.). Goddard stated that she was "committed to overcoming the two major issues confronting the Authority: the public perception that the PCA is not truly independent of the Police … and an apparent lack of timeliness on the part of the Authority in reviewing … investigations and in issuing reports" (ibid.).

Subsequently, in the 2007 redrafted legislation for the now named Independent Police Conduct Authority (IPCA) (New Zealand Government, 1988b), the functions of the organisation were redefined as:

- receive and consider complaints (i) alleging misconduct or neglect of duty by any member of Police or (ii) concerning any Police practice, policy or procedure affecting the complainant; or
- Investigate incidents in which a member of Police (acting in the execution of his or her duty) causes or appears to have caused death or serious bodily harm. (Independent Police Conduct Authority, 2008, p. 4)

Following the legislative and organisational changes affecting the IPCA, Goddard's opening statement in the organisation's Statement of Intent for the years 2010/2011–2012/2013 (Independent Police Conduct Authority, 2010, p. 3) best encapsulates the Authority's view, and no doubt that of the Government, on what the organisation's role was in Aotearoa New Zealand:

> All New Zealanders should expect to live in a safe and just society and, to that end, society requires an accessible and trusted justice system, and effective constitutional arrangements. The Independent Police Conduct Authority … is part of the wider justice sector that seeks to create this society. Accordingly, the expectations of the Government and the public are that the IPCA will contribute toward achieving those outcomes. The IPCA aims to contribute to a safe and just society by helping to ensure the public can have absolute confidence in the New Zealand Police. (ibid.)

Meanwhile, on the structural side, the Authority established "investigating teams comprising team leaders, investigators, and analysts" within the organisation and also recruited four further investigators taking the total compliment to nine (Independent Police Conduct Authority, 2009, p. 11). The investigative teams were viewed by Goddard as "result[ing] in a strengthened public confidence in the independence of the Authority" (ibid. p. 12).

The policy followed by the IPCA in recruiting investigators was to select people with strong backgrounds in criminal investigations, meaning that all of the organisation's investigators were either former Aotearoa New Zealand or Commonwealth country police officers. The Authority frankly acknowledged the approach may have given rise to disquiet and belief that the independence of the organisation and the Authority were at risk, but it was felt within the IPCA that independence and credibility of its work would be at greater risk without adequate investigative expertise (Independent Police Conduct Authority, 2009, p. 6).

To facilitate working relationships with Police in the case of parallel investigations (which were almost certain to occur in fatal or non-fatal shootings), a "protocol for cooperation" was entered into between the two organisations, but, sadly, this was not made public (Independent Police Conduct Authority, 2008, p. 7).

Goddard's substantial changes – one might even say transformational changes (e.g. see Den Heyer & Beckley, 2013, p. 211) – were in place and operating by early 2009, while Goddard's 5-year term at the helm continued, before finally ending in 2012 (ibid., p. 2).

The evolution of the IPCA did, however, continue under its new Chair, Justice Sir David Carruthers. For example, in the 2012–2013 Annual Report, he noted that "Our updated organisational structure will require increased capability and we plan to evolve towards this within current resource levels and in a financially sustainable way" (Independent Police Conduct Authority, 2013, p. 13). With the report going on to say a little later, "We also continue to operate in a tight fiscal environment and we have been mindful of Government's expectations that we deliver our services within available resource levels" (ibid.). Coded bureaucratic language for "of course you can make changes as long as they do not require more staff or funding", in the author's experience.

The Present Day

Fast forward to 2020–2021, and the IPCA briefing to its incoming minister, following the 2020 general election, revealed a staff of 41 full-time equivalent people, 3 Authority "board members" and the completion of 57 independent investigations (Independent Police Conduct Authority, 2021b, p. 9). The IPCA's briefing paper and website confirmed the use of two teams of investigators and report writers made up of staff with both policing and non-policing backgrounds, with one team covering the Upper North Island (Te Ika-a-Māui) and the second the Lower North and South Island (Te Ika-a-Māui and Te Waipounamu) (Independent Police Conduct Authority, 2021b, c).

With over three decades of activity under its belt, the IPCA identified in its ministerial briefing a number of areas where the environment it worked within, and the laws of Aotearoa New Zealand, could do with reconsideration and possible improvement (Independent Police Conduct Authority, 2021b, pp. 18–22). Of particular relevance to this book were the following points:

- … a lack of clarity regarding Police powers to use force that are contained in sections 39-40 of the Crimes Act 1961. In particular, the sections are silent as to the basis upon which the necessity for the use of force is to be assessed.
- … [referencing s. 40] the Police and the Authority disagree about whether the proportionality [of the force used] is to be assessed against the circumstances that the officer *actually* believed to exist or *reasonably* believed to exist (i.e. whether the officer's belief is to be assessed subjectively or objectively). Nor is it clear what types of circumstance are relevant. Arguably the need to use force should be judged against both the seriousness of the suspected offence and the public interest in bringing the person to justice, and the ongoing risk that the person poses if they are not immediately apprehended. However, it is unsatisfactory that there is no statement of the law to that effect.
- The same problem [as above] had arisen to a lesser extent in relation to section 39 ….
- Because these sections are routinely relied upon by officers on a daily basis, the Authority believes that it is desirable that there be urgent legislative clarification to put the matter beyond doubt.
- *Powers to prosecute (or to refer prosecution decisions to the Crown)*: The Authority does not have the power to prosecute; instead, Police are solely responsible for making such decisions … the downside is that Police may, at times, lack enough objectivity to

> make good decisions, and may not be as adept at striking the correct balance between the critical nature of dealing with conduct issues effectively and being a good employer who protects and supports their frontline staff … options which might include allowing the Authority the power to refer some matters direct to the Crown[3] for decisions on prosecution to be made (such as driving matters, or cases regarding use of excessive force …. (Independent Police Conduct Authority, 2021b, pp. 18–22)

Clearly issues exist which reflect both on the legislation concerning police use of force in Aotearoa New Zealand and on the powers available to the IPCA that enable it to provide a truly independent oversight institution and one that can be trusted by the public.

A contemporary example of those ongoing challenges is provided in a 2021 media article concerning the 2016 police shooting of a man named Stephens (Espiner, 2021). In the report, the family of the dead man were reported to be challenging a coroner's decision to hold a "narrow inquest" into the death and the coroner's decision to accept the IPCA's finding that Stephens was justifiably shot by police (ibid.). The family were reported to be seeking a judicial review of the coroner's ruling and a full inquest into the death, with their legal representatives claiming police involved may not have told the truth to the IPCA and that some police video evidence may have been tampered with (Espiner, 2021).

Interestingly, in light of the comments made by the Authority about the circumstances that justify the use of force to prevent escape or to make an arrest under the *Crimes Act 1961* (NZL) (ss. 39 and 40), Stephens was shot after reportedly:

> … walk[ing] calmly past [a police officer], ignoring L07 completely [police officer's coded reference]. He's only interested in the car. He throws a 2.5 kg weight at the rear windscreen. The weight bounces off but L07 is annoyed … Stephen's takes a weed slasher and smashes the left side windows of the police car and cracks the windscreen. He strikes the car seven times in all. L07 gets back in the police car … he calls 10-10 on the police radio, code for 'immediate assistance' …. (ibid.)

Despite only property damage to the police car, and no attempt to assault the police officer (L07) or two other people who come close to Stephens later in the event, the response escalates to police officers armed with tasers and firearms and results in an officer who has just a year's service advancing to within 5–6 metres of Stephens with a Bushmaster rifle and shooting him twice in the chest when Stephens advanced towards the officer and refused to put down the slasher that he had in his hands (ibid.).

Stephens' death is one of those included in the Chap. 8 review of police shootings between 2000 and 2019.

As at the time of writing, the legal situation in Aotearoa New Zealand remains that the IPCA cannot investigate Police actions unless a death or serious bodily harm has occurred, or a complaint has been made, or a referral from Police has been

[3] Crown Law Office provides legal advice and representation service to the government in matters affecting the executive government, particularly in the areas of criminal, public and administrative law (Crown Law Office, 2021).

made via an MOU between the Police and IPCA (Independent Police Conduct Authority, 2020a, p. 10).

Furthermore, the IPCA cannot prosecute or initiate disciplinary action against a police officer. The Authority is restricted to making recommendations, which can include that "disciplinary action or criminal proceedings be considered or instituted" (Independent Police Conduct Authority, 2021b). However, if the Authority is not happy with the Police response to its recommendations, "the Authority must inform the Attorney-General and the Minister of Police, and, if the Authority considers it appropriate, a copy of their report to the Attorney-General may be sent for tabling in Parliament – via the Attorney-General, who is duty bound to do so" (ibid.). To date, none of these "last resort" actions have occurred.

From the author's review of the Annual Reports, Statements of Intent and the Briefing to the Incoming Minister, it is clear that the workload of the IPCA and its staff continues to climb year by year. In the most recent Annual Report available, that of 2019–2020, the organisation made an extraordinary comment about that very issue:

> The steady increase in complaint volume noted over the last few annual reports has continued but with a sharp 28% rise for this year … For a short period, we were forced to *take the drastic measure of advising complainants we did not have the capacity to deal with their complaints*. Normal business resumed when the Ministry of Justice provided additional funding to employ contract staff. (Italics added) (Independent Police Conduct Authority, 2020a, p. 6)

Sadly, it appears that despite almost yearly advice about complaint volumes rising and resource pressures mounting, the IPCA was left under-resourced to the point it had to publicly admit it was defeated and unable to undertake its statutory role. Such a state of affairs does not bode well for the work the IPCA is required to do and in particular regarding the most serious action an agent of the state can take – the killing or serious injuring of a citizen.

PCA and IPCA Reporting on Shootings by Police

In their 2015–2016 Annual Report, the IPCA made specific reference to the number of shootings by police occurring and the concern that raised for the Authority (Independent Police Conduct Authority, 2016, p. 6). The report stated:

> … reports into those aspects of Police activities are just beginning to emerge. They are, of course, at the highest level of concern for any Police oversight organisation and we are keen to play our part in ensuring that the use of force operates within well understood limits and in the case of ultimate force is always the final tactical option and never the first. (Independent Police Conduct Authority, 2016, p. 6)

This was the first time a concern had been specifically expressed by the IPCA regarding the use of lethal force by police across the period 2000 to 2019 and was a response to the six shootings by police (three fatal and three non-fatal) that occurred within the annual report's timeframe (financial year 1 July 2015–30 June 2016). It possibly also reflected concern regarding the calendar year shooting statistics for 2015 (again, three fatal and three non-fatal) and possibly the IPCA's awareness of the statistics for the first half of the calendar year 2016 (a further one fatal and one non-fatal).

Without doubt, the years 2015 and 2016 were part of a 3-year period, which included 2017, where the number of shootings by police (15 fatal or non-fatal recorded on the IPCA website, while Police Tactical Option Reporting (2020) reported 18 instances of shooting at a person – including 3 instances where the shots missed and 1 occasion where it could not be established if police shots had caused the resulting death) outstripped any other 3 year totals in the 2000–2019 period.

In further commentary regarding shootings by police, the Authority dedicated a subsection of its "2015/2016 Achievements" section to "Police Shooting Cases", stating:

> The Authority independently investigates all incidents where Police discharge firearms in the line of duty and cause injury or death to a person. There have been six Police shooting incidents during the financial year; three fatal and three non-fatal. There were three Police shooting incidents in the previous financial year and the Authority had concluded those investigations.
>
> In some situations the Authority is unable to promptly release its report publicly at the conclusion of the investigation, most notably if there are ongoing criminal proceedings resulting from the incident. This has meant the Authority did not publish any reports in relation to its independent investigations of Police shooting incidents in the 2015/2016 financial year. (Independent Police Conduct Authority, 2016, p. 14)

The commentary was informative as it set out the approach the IPCA took, at that time, to the investigation of use of lethal force by Police, but also leaves open a question about occasions when police officers present and discharge firearms at a person, or in other circumstances where harm might occur (e.g. firing at a fleeing car), but do not hit anyone or cause any injury (i.e. they miss).

Under section 13 of the *Independent Police Conduct Authority Act 1988* (NZL), the commissioner of police has a duty to notify the Authority of any death or serious bodily harm inflicted by a member of the Police in the course of their duties. There is no legal requirement to notify the Authority of any instances where Police miss when shooting at a someone, as outlined above. Furthermore, the Act establishes no requirement for the Authority to consider or investigate any such situation, unless it forms part of a complaint made to it.

One avenue through which such near-miss situations may appear before the Authority is via the memorandum of understanding (MOU) that the IPCA and Police negotiated in 1994 (Independent Police Conduct Authority, 2010, p. 12). The IPCA described the agreement as:

> … cover[ing] instances which may present reputational risk to the Police, including serious offending by a Police officer or Police actions that may have an element of corruption. Under the MOU, such cases are referred by Police to the Authority even when there had not been a complaint from a member of the public or an incident involving a death or serious bodily harm. (Independent Police Conduct Authority, 2020a, p. 8)

Review of a copy of the MOU, posted on the Police website, but undated, reveals no reference to the use of lethal force or to near-miss uses of lethal force. The version posted merely confirms the above statement and further confirms that the commissioner "may notify the Authority of any matter involving criminal offending or serious misconduct by a Police employee, where that matter is of such significance or public interest that it places or is likely to place the Police reputation at risk" and that the Authority "may" act on such notifications (New Zealand Police, 2021a).

If that mechanism does capture near-miss firearms-related events, it is to be commended as each near-miss situation is in fact pure luck on the part of the intended target given the author's understanding of how police officers are trained to use firearms and may well provide a much wider view on the use of potentially lethal force by Police to the Authority.

A year later, further commentary appeared in the IPCA 2017–2018 Annual Report indicating that the Authority had been advised of 12 shootings by Police during the reporting year, 1 fatal and 11 non-fatal. Unfortunately, the author could only discover reports about three of those cases on the IPCA website, one for a fatal shooting and two for non-fatal shootings. The author sought further information from the IPCA about the anomaly, but none was forthcoming.

The following year, 2018–2019, the IPCA Annual Report identified that there were seven shootings by police reported to the Authority during the financial year (1 July 2018–30 June 2019) (Independent Police Conduct Authority, 2019, p. 5). The report went on to describe those shootings as being two fatal and five non-fatal events (ibid., p. 16). The author could only find four reports on the IPCA website for investigations relating to that reporting, while in the 2019–2020 Annual Report, there was no commentary on the number of shootings reported to the Authority or regarding shootings by Police in general (Independent Police Conduct Authority, 2020a).

In exploring the timeliness and quantity of information delivered through IPCA reporting, the author divided the research period of 2000 to 2019 into three timeframes. This was to discover if, as resources came online, timeliness and quantity of information changed. The first period was 2000–2003, when the PCA was a single individual who essentially undertook reviews of Police investigations. The second timeframe was 2004–2010, when the PCA/IPCA began to receive additional resources and independent investigative support. The final timeframe was 2011–2019, when the IPCA was operating teams of investigators, analysts and reviewers.

With regard to the timeliness of investigation and report publication, from the 43 PCA and IPCA investigative reports reviewed for Chap. 8, it was established that the average length of time from the shooting to publication of a report was 21.2 months, with the median time being 18 months; see Fig. 3.1. Thirteen investigations and reports took longer than 2 years from event to publication, with four taking longer than 3 years. Thirteen investigations and reports were completed and released in 12 months or less (ibid.). It needs to be appreciated that timeliness by the PCA/IPCA was impacted by the time taken by Police to complete their enquiries, and occasionally that included time taken to seek legal opinions or for legal proceedings

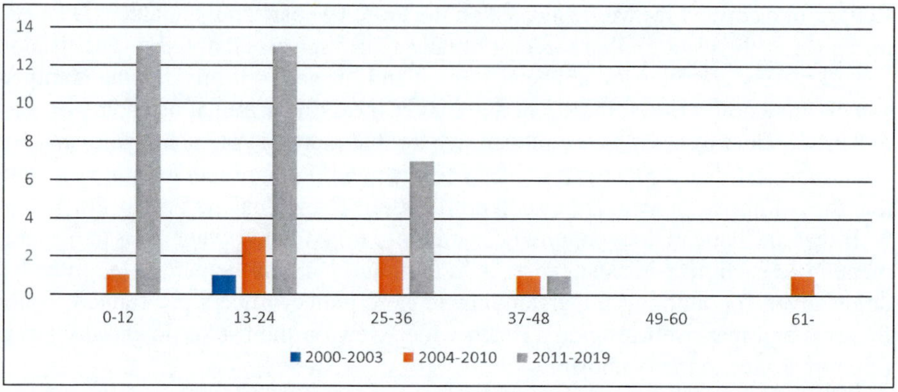

Fig. 3.1 PCA/IPCA reporting times (months) from shooting to public release of report. (Data obtained from PCA/IPCA reports into shootings by Police between 2000 and 2019)

to be completed (e.g. the report into the shooting of Stephen Wallace was published 107 months after the event – almost 9 years later – the longest timeframe in the data set) due to a series of legal actions.

The timeframes outlined contribute, no doubt, to ongoing stress for the families and friends of those shot (particularly when the shooting was fatal) and for the police officer(s) involved and their families and friends. The lag also leaves a question mark over the reputation of the New Zealand Police until the Authority hands down their final recommendations and its view on justification. In terms of contributing to the outcome of a just and trusted justice system and to public confidence in the Police, such delays cannot be viewed as helpful, albeit they may be unavoidable on the part of the Authority.

During research for the book, the author identified there was no easily accessed definitive list of all uses of lethal force by New Zealand Police (applying the author's definition of lethal force). None could be *easily* found on the Police website or in the organisation's public facing corporate documents, and only published reports on shooting investigations were to be found on the IPCA website, which does not provide a definitive list as discussed above. Furthermore, with respect to the IPCA investigative reports, they are published on the website according to the date they were issued, and that can be months or even years after the shooting taking place. Finally, by chance, the author happened upon a "Tactical Options: Supplement – Police Shootings 1916–2020" report appended to the 2019 Tactical Options annual report (New Zealand Police, 2021b).

Of particular interest to the author was the fact the Police report, from the year 2001 onwards, listed a "miss" as a police shooting, which indicated an alignment of sorts between the author's definition of use of lethal force (based on the intention of the police officer) and police's view on what constituted a "police shooting", which appears to still focus on outcomes, but more widely than before.

The most obvious place for such a list, or web-based record, it is posited, is the publicly accessible IPCA website. The record need not provide details which are not already in the public domain (i.e. the name or personal details of the person shot), given the potential for unfinished criminal investigations or prosecutions associated with the use of lethal force. However, the record should detail the date, time, geographic location, gender of the person involved and outcome of the event – for example, "miss", "fatal" or "non-fatal". That would allow the public visibility of the number of uses of lethal force (or intended lethal force), and, ultimately, the IPCA published investigation report should also be linked back to the original reference.

With the IPCA legislation establishing the seriousness with which Parliament takes instances of police officers causing death or serious bodily harm, the lack of such a definitive and authoritative official record is perplexing. The suggestion raised here will be discussed further in Chaps. 10, 11 and 12.

Another publicly visible aspect of the work completed by the oversight authority is the detail provided in the reports released to the public regarding each shooting. While not a measure of the quality of the IPCA's work, the report's content is considered relevant by the author. The reports by the IPCA are the only opportunity citizens[4] have to read in full – beyond any media reporting or releases made by Police – about why an agent of the state took the life of another citizen or nearly did. In a country that has a Bill of Rights enshrining the right to life, and which does not have a death penalty, the reports provide the only independent sources citizens have upon which to base their trust and confidence in the national Police service when it comes to use of firearms and lethal force. The longer a report, the greater the detail that can be provided about the "Who, Where, What, When, Why and How" related to the shooting and, ultimately, to support the conclusions, recommendations and findings signed off by the Authority.

As can be expected from the variety of circumstances encountered when police officers shoot someone, the detail in the reports produced by the IPCA can vary[5]. Of the 43 reports reviewed, 1 was produced by the PCA (2000–2003), while 8 were produced by the IPCA between 2004 and 2010, and the remaining 34 were the product of the IPCA between 2011 and 2019. The reports varied in length/detail from 3 through to 107 pages; see Fig. 3.2.

Curiously, there were two reports consisting of only three pages. The first was issued in November 2012, regarding the non-fatal shooting of a man named Hartley by police in February 2011; the second was issued in October 2013, regarding the

[4] This often includes family and friends of the person who was the subject of lethal force use, who may or may not be briefed more widely by Police or the IPCA, the family and friends of the police officer(s) responsible, other members of the Police and people who may have witnessed or been involved with the use of lethal force in some other way.

[5] The "detail" in the reports referred to in this work is text pages containing information about the shooting, including any appendices on Police policy and procedure. It excludes the cover page, index, back page, blank pages and any page simply explaining what the IPCA and the Authority are and how they work.

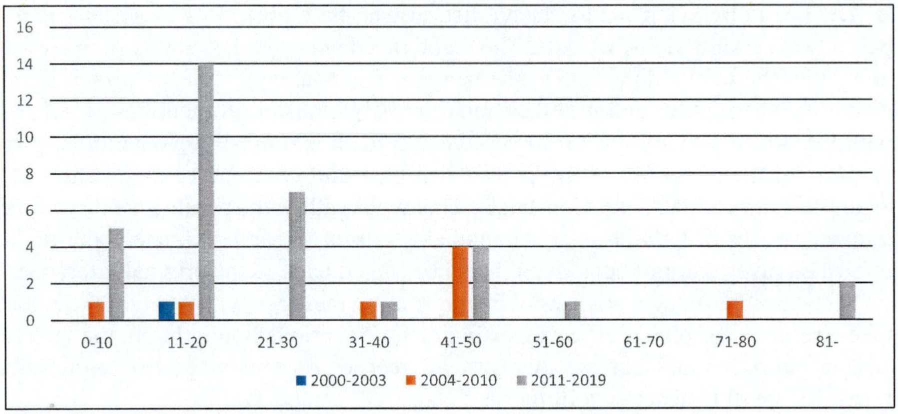

Fig. 3.2 PCA/IPCA public report length (pages). (Data obtained from PCA/IPCA reports into shootings by Police between 2000 and 2019)

fatal shooting of a man named Hussein, by police in March 2011. Each contained an explanatory statement from the Authority that stated:

> NOTE: The Authority has chosen to not produce a full public report in light of its conclusions and in the interests of timely reporting. Police conduct in this case did not raise issues that require a full report in the public interest. This summary report serves as a statement of the facts of the shooting and of the Authority's findings.

The author contends, having read those 2 "summary reports" and 41 other PCA/IPCA reports, 3 pages of detail is insufficient for the Authority to achieve their stated aim of delivering confidence in the New Zealand Police and in its own capability and decision-making. However, the author does acknowledge the Authority's desire to deliver timely findings.

The 43 reports reviewed also varied in respect to the information they contained and their structure. For example, not all reports identified the name of the person shot, with four non-fatal reports referring to an identifying letter (i.e. Mr X) and one non-fatal report just referring to an unnamed male. It is accepted that the use of identifying letters was due to unresolved criminal proceedings taking place at the time of the report's release; however, following completion of those matters, the IPCA could consider reviewing and updating the reports on its website.

The reports did not provide a confirmed ethnicity for the person shot, but it is often commented upon in media and social media reporting. That media and social media reporting can have a direct impact upon the perception of the New Zealand Police. Factual information on ethnicity in IPCA reporting would be beneficial, in the author's view.

Finally, the reports were not always fulsome in recording the number of shots fired by either the person shot by police or the police or on the impact point(s) of shots fired by all involved. These seemingly minor matters do provide additional detail and context regarding the use of lethal force. In general, the differences in report content and style appeared to align with changes in the Authority (i.e. who the person or person(s) fulfilling the role of the "Authority" were) and with the addition of investigative teams.

PCA/IPCA Decisions Regarding Shootings

In all of the 43 shootings reviewed, the PCA or IPCA concluded that the police officer(s) involved were justified in the action(s) taken, under the various sections of the *Crimes Act 1961* (NZL) allowing Police to use force.

As Fig. 3.3 shows, the most common justification determined by the Authority was that of self-defence pursuant to section 48 of the *Crimes Act 1961* (NZL). Thirty-four of the shootings were justified under that section alone, while a further eight shootings were determined to be justified under that section and either section 39 (making an arrest) or sections 39 and 40 (making an arrest and preventing an escape).

While none of the shootings were determined to be unjustified, the Authority was not always praiseworthy of the actions taken by police. In five of the reports issued, the Authority questioned the tactics of the police officers involved and in some cases suggested they should have considered alternative tactical options (e.g. see the shooting reports for Kelly-Tumarae (2013); Morehu (2015); Cerven (2016); Toms (2018); and Hooper (2021)).

Across the 43 reports reviewed, the PCA/IPCA, as well as commenting on the justification for the events reviewed, also made a number of formal findings in respect of the actions of police. The author reviewed the findings and determined that 352 were made that directly related to the shooting of people or the immediate

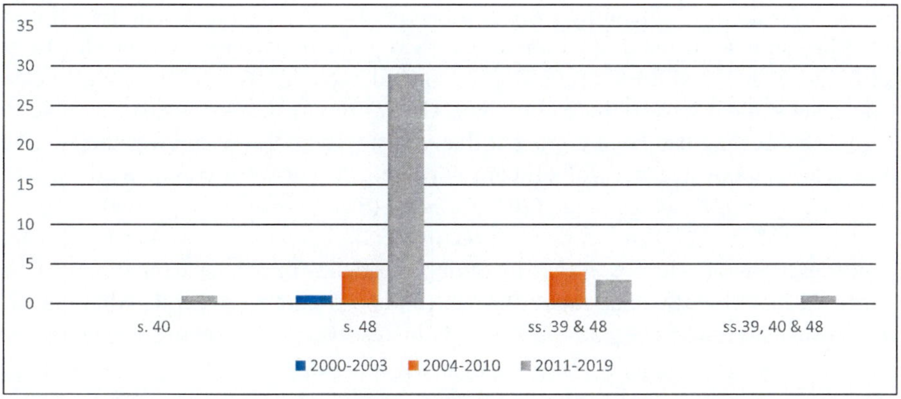

Fig. 3.3 PCA/ICPCA crimes act justification decisions (number of reports) (2000–2019). (Data obtained from PCA/IPCA reports into shootings by Police between 2000 and 2019)

Table 3.1 PCA/IPCA findings analysis for positive or negative commentary (2000–2019)

Area the finding covers	Positive	Negative
Command and control	23	33
Tactics (used)	42	10
Tactical options (chosen, incl. shooting a subject)	111	5
Policy adherence (admin)	25	27
Procedure adherence (admin)	11	13
Training	2	3
Other (i.e. medical assistance given)	42	5

Data obtained from PCA/IPCA reports into shootings by Police between 2000 and 2019

pre-shooting or post-shooting events[6]. The author coded the findings against seven areas listed in Table 3.1, along with whether the finding read in a "positive" or "negative" way concerning the actions of police. Of those findings, 256 were classified by the author as "positive" in nature, while 96 were classified as "negative" in nature.

As can be seen, the three areas with the most positive commentary were Tactical Options, Tactics and Other, while the three areas that had the most negative commentary were Command and Control, Policy adherence and Procedure adherence. Overall, 256 of the findings contained comments assessed as positive regarding Police action, while 96 contained commentary assessed as negative. Three of the finding areas, when negative commentary was particularly noticeable and repeated, were (a) not advising the communications centre that officers had armed themselves, (b) not donning protective ballistic vests when they armed themselves and (c) communications between officers.

Elsewhere, the Authority also made recommendations to Police with regard to how they undertook post-shooting investigations, with, for example, a number of requests for Police to institute a drug and alcohol testing regime for police officers who had shot someone. For example, see the commentary regarding the shootings of Mahdi (2004) and Burton (2006). It seemed like the suggestion for such a process had taken hold when in the Bellingham (2007) report the Authority was able to report that testing had been done, but that was not to be the case. Over the coming years, four more instances of officers not being tested were commented on (see Naitoko (2009); Kelly-Tumarae (2011); Ratahi (2011); and Mr X (2014)).

In consideration of those repeated recommendations, two cases warrant greater consideration. The first was that involving the death of a man named Ratahi, in 2011. In that case, Special Tactics Group (STG) officers were deployed alongside the Armed Offenders Squad (AOS) to help resolve a challenging siege/hostage

[6] For example, a pre-shooting event would include a search for the subject after a report about them was received, and a post-shooting event would include medical treatment offered to the shot person or handling of firearm exhibits.

situation. Following Ratahi being shot and killed by one of the STG officers, the commander of the STG contingent refused to allow any of his team to be alcohol or drug tested (Independent Police Conduct Authority, 2014, p. 26). In the Authority's report, the officer who fired the fatal shot is reported as saying he was willing to have had such testing, and other AOS and STG officers admitted that they had consumed alcohol in the 10 hours before the operation commenced (ibid.). That situation appears to have led to a very quick policy and practice change by Police, as the Authority went on to report that a new 12-hour rule regarding the consumption of alcohol by AOS and STG had been instigated, and a rostering change had also eventuated which meant officers not on-call could partake of alcohol (ibid., p. 29).

However, the second case, involving the shooting of a man labelled "Mr X" at Kerepehi, in 2014, had the Authority again commenting on the fact that the officer involved had refused a breath test when it was requested of him (Independent Police Conduct Authority, 2017, p. 9). Again, as in the 2011 case above, the recommendation must have generated a change in Police practice as ten subsequent IPCA reports were explicit in stating that the officer(s) involved had been tested either for alcohol or for alcohol and drugs (e.g. see reports on the shootings of Shortcliffe (2015); Te Moananui (2015); Hurinui (2015); and Brown (2017) and the shooting at Vinegar Hill (2017)).

Clearly, some tidying up was needed on the part of Police to clarify if the testing was for just alcohol, or both drugs (licit[7] or illicit) and alcohol, as some reports mentioned only alcohol, while others mentioned both substances (e.g. see shooting reports for Smiler (2015) and non-fatal shooting at Nelson (2017)). Such testing was not an unreasonable impost; it is suggested by the author, for two substantive reasons. The first relates to the general advice Police give to civilian firearm owners known as "The Seven Firearms Safety Rules" (New Zealand Police, 2021c). Rule 7 states "Avoid both alcohol and drugs when handling firearms" (ibid.). The second – clearly linked to the first – is that drugs (licit or illicit) and/or alcohol can play a part in affecting the decision-making process a police officer is required to undertake when it comes to assessing risk and selecting appropriate tactics and options and to their ability to safely handle police firearms when under the added pressure of operational stress.

The IPCA was subsequently able to confirm in 2017, in their report into the shooting of a man at Kerepehi, that "… As at 14 February 2017, a new drug and alcohol testing policy was introduced which requires all Police employees who have discharged a firearm during an incident to undergo a drug and/or alcohol testing procedure" (Independent Police Conduct Authority, 2017, p. 9). Good practice appeared to have finally won the day, but still a question mark as to why both substances are not being tested for routinely.

As closing commentary on the above issue, subsequent references to drug and alcohol testing in the IPCA reports issued after 2017 identified that in one

[7] Licit drugs include prescription medications that may impede judgement, motor skills and ability to think quickly and clearly when under pressure. For example, see https://adf.org.au/insights/drugs-and-driving/ and https://www.sciencedirect.com/science/article/abs/pii/S0001457517301744

instance – regarding the non-fatal shooting of a "Mr X" in February 2019 – "All officers who were present at the time Mr X was shot underwent drug and alcohol testing by an external provider" (Independent Police Conduct Authority, 2020b, p. 2), while two other reports issued in 2021 were silent on the issue of drug and alcohol testing. That absence of comment was, hopefully, just another two examples of the non-standard nature of the contents of IPCA reports discussed earlier and not an indication that testing was not taking place.

Again, it is the author's contention that not including such information may adversely impact the trust and confidence citizens have in the IPCA reporting and on New Zealand Police.

Satisfaction with the IPCA

Having mentioned trust and confidence with regard to IPCA reporting, it is appropriate to consider what the organisation discovered when surveying the public and police officers for their views on that topic.

In the IPCA's 2018–2019 Annual Report, the process for assessing complainants and Police satisfaction with the work of the organisation was described thus:

> We measure by way of a telephone survey, the level of satisfaction of complainants and Police officers complained of, with our work performance. A target of 75% satisfaction level has been set. Unless it is inappropriate to do so, following the closure of the case we attempt to survey Police officers, complainants, and victims or next of kin involved in Category 1 [death or serious bodily harm caused by Police] and Category 2 files providing they had had significant[8] contact with staff. However not all parties are able to be contacted or agree to participate once they are spoken to. As part of the survey, participants who do agree to participate are asked to comment on their level of satisfaction relating to their contact with our staff and our investigation and review processes. (Independent Police Conduct Authority, 2019, p. 22)

Table 3.2 shows the survey results for the years 2017–2018 and 2018–2019:

While no numerical split was made to help identify satisfaction with Category 1 matters (deaths and serious bodily harm matters), later in the commentary, the Authority stated "The level of satisfaction with Category 1 investigations was high and met the performance target [75%] …"(ibid., p. 23).

In 2020, the IPCA reported that they had piloted a "replacement satisfaction research programme, utilising a combined quantitative/qualitative survey methodology" (Independent Police Conduct Authority, 2020a, p. 27). Unfortunately, the new methodology "resulted in substantially lower response rates from both complainants and Police personnel, making it difficult to compare with previous years" (ibid.).

The IPCA is an organisation that seeks to contribute towards a trusted justice system and through that to the high level of trust and confidence citizens have in the

[8] Defined by the IPCA as "…two or more substantial, interactions involving direct contact" (ibid)

Table 3.2 PCA/IPCA measure of public satisfaction with the organisation's work (2017–2019)

Measure (75% target)	2017–2018	2018–2019
Satisfaction with contact	84%	89%
Satisfaction with investigation process	74%	78%
Satisfaction with review process	75%	29%
Satisfaction with facilitated resolution process	64%	87.5%

Data obtained from PCA/IPCA annual reports

New Zealand Police. However, despite this lofty goal and being applaudable, the IPCA makes no specific effort to measure or quantify the impact of its work on the public, instead limiting its surveying to complainants, victims (if possible) and police officers. In their own words, the IPCA states:

> The Authority cannot formally measure its individual impact on the level of public trust and confidence in Police; it is but one cog in the overall justice system. The impact of our work can be measured by reference to the visibility and accessibility of the Authority .... (Independent Police Conduct Authority, 2020a, p. 25)

The author does not share that view. Wider public surveys of the perceptions citizens have of the IPCA and its work would surely provide an indication to the organisation on how those not directly involved in its work view it. It seems to the author that a worthy measure is not being addressed. Publishing reports and providing a publicly accessible website are all well and good, but do they have an impact in the wider community? It would be interesting to know.

In summary, since 1989, there have been independent review and, more recently, investigation of uses of lethal force by police officers that kill or injure citizens. Furthermore, as a result of an MOU with New Zealand Police, it seems likely that instances where a police officer has shot at a person but missed them *may* be subject to independent review and investigation, although no IPCA public reports support that proposition. The IPCA has grown over its three decades of operation from a single person "Authority" to an organisation of 41 full-time equivalent staff (a mix of permanent, contract and full-time and part-time roles) with two teams of investigators (Independent Police Conduct Authority, 2020a, p. 11). But, the IPCA still relies heavily on the Police conducting the major part of any investigation and on Police deciding whether or not to pursue criminal charges or disciplinary action against a police officer.

Between January 1990 and December 2019, the data available from Police in their list of shootings identified that 84 people were shot at by police officers in Aotearoa New Zealand (including those instances where shots missed) (New Zealand Police, 2021b).

Since the creation of the Police Complaints Authority in 1989, and through the years of its successor – the Independent Police Conduct Authority – all fatal and non-fatal shootings by police officers have been found to be justified (Independent Police Conduct Authority, 2021a). As far as the author can ascertain, no reports have been publicly published regarding the events where shots were fired but missed their intended targets.

Bibliography

Bazley, M. (2007). *Report of the Commission of Inquiry into Police Conduct – Volume 1*. Commission of Inquiry into Police Conduct.

Crown Law Office. (2021, June 22). *Crown Law Office*. Retrieved from crownlaw.govt.nz: https://www.crownlaw.govt.nz

Den Heyer, G., & Beckley, A. (2013). Police independent oversight in Australia and New Zealand. *Police Practice and Research*, 205–225.

Espiner, G. (2021, June 22). *The untold story of how police shot Shargin Stephens*. Retrieved from stuff.co.nz: https://www.stuff.co.nz/national/300338911/the-untold-story-of-how-police-shot-shargin-stephens?cid=app-iPad

Gallen, R. (2021, June 22). *Review of the police complaints authority.*. Retrieved from natlib.gov.nz.: https://ndhadeliver.natlib.govt.nz/delivery/DeliveryManagerServlet?dps_pid=IE763528

Independent Police Conduct Authority. (2008). *Independent police conduct authority annual report 2007–2008*. Independent Police Conduct Authority.

Independent Police Conduct Authority. (2009). *Annual report 2008–2009*. Independent Police Conduct Authority.

Independent Police Conduct Authority. (2010). *Statement of Intent 2010/11–2012/13*. Independent Police Conduct Authority.

Independent Police Conduct Authority. (2011). *Independent police conduct authority annual report 2010–2011*. Independent Police Conduct Authority.

Independent Police Conduct Authority. (2013). *Independent police conduct authority 2012–2013 annual report*. Independent Police Conduct Authority.

Independent Police Conduct Authority. (2014). *Fatal police shooting of Anthony Ratahi*. Independent Police Conduct Authority.

Independent Police Conduct Authority. (2016). *Annual report 2015–2016 independent police conduct authority*. Independent Police Conduct Authority.

Independent Police Conduct Authority. (2017). *Non-fatal police shooting of Mr X in Kerepehi*. Independent Police Conduct Authority.

Independent Police Conduct Authority. (2019). *Independent police conduct authority annual report 2018–2019*. Independent Police Conduct Authority.

Independent Police Conduct Authority. (2020a). *Independent police conduct authority annual report 2019/20*. Independent Police Conduct Authority.

Independent Police Conduct Authority. (2020b). *Non-fatal shooting following pursuit in Christchurch*. Independent Police Conduct Authority.

Independent Police Conduct Authority. (2021a, June 23). *History*. Retrieved from ipca.govt.nz: https://www.ipca.govt.nz/Site/about-us/History.aspx

Independent Police Conduct Authority. (2021b, June 22). *IPCA briefing to incoming minister 2020 general election*. Retrieved from ipca.govt.nz: https://www.ipca.govt.nz/IPCABriefingtoIncomingMinister-2020.pdf

Independent Police Conduct Authority. (2021c, June 22). *Our people*. Retrieved from ipca.govt.nz: https://www.ipca.govt.nz/Site/about-us/Our-People.aspx

Minister of Justice. (2021, June 18). *Background information on Govt response to Gallen review of PCA*. Retrieved from beehive.govt.nz: https://www.beehive.govt.nz/node/10270

New Zealand Government. (1988a). *Police Complaints Authority Act 1988*. New Zealand Government.

New Zealand Government. (1988b, March 10). *Independent Police Conduct Authority Act 1988*. New Zealand Government.

New Zealand Government. (1989, November 28). *Abolition of the Death Penalty Act 1989*. New Zealand Government.

New Zealand Government. (1990). *New Zealand Bill of Rights Act 1990*. New Zealand Government.

New Zealand Police. (2021a, October 28). *IPCA-Police MOU*. Retrieved from police.govt.nz: https://www.police.govt.nz/sites/default/files/publications/ipca-police-mou.pdf

New Zealand Police. (2021b, July 12). *Annual tactical options research report 8*. Retrieved from police.govt.nz: https://www.police.govt.nz/sites/default/files/publications/annual-tactical-options-research-report-8.pdf

New Zealand Police. (2021c, July 9). *The Seven Firearms Safety Rules*. Retrieved from police.govt.nz: https://www.police.govt.nz/advice-services/firearms-and-safety/firearms-safety/arms-code/seven-firearms-safety-rules

Police Complaints Authority. (2007a). *Police complaints authority statement of intent 2007/08*. Police Complaints Authority.

Police Complaints Authority. (2007b). *Police complaints authority annual report 2006–2007*. Police Complaints Authority.

Samkin, G., Allen, C., & Wallace, K. (2010). Repairing organisational legitimacy: The case of the New Zealand Police. *Australasian Accounting, Business and Finance Journal, 4*(*3*), 23–45.

Chapter 4
New Zealand Police and Firearms

Check for updates

Before getting too involved with policy, procedure and the shootings that form an important element of this book, it is useful for the reader to understand the earlier comment regarding New Zealand Police believing themselves to be a *routinely unarmed* service (New Zealand Police, 2021a) but actually being – in the author's opinion – a well-armed and routinely armed police service. It all comes down to style. Let's begin by looking at the context surrounding policing in Aotearoa New Zealand. What follows is not a complete historical record for New Zealand Police; these exist and are worthy of review by those with intense interest. However, as one historian of policing in Aotearoa New Zealand noted, "Police history is an area grossly neglected by scholarly writers" (Hill, 1986a, p. xvii). This section should instead be considered a "potted-history" drawing upon significant events, times and relevant firearms-related anecdotes.

Many, in fact most, police services[1] around the world issue firearms as a routine item of police officers' equipment. A handgun of some sort in a holster, a rifle or shotgun or semi-automatic weapon in the car or sometimes over the shoulder. In some parts of the world, it is not unusual to regularly see police officers carrying semi-automatic or automatic carbines or sub-machine guns as they go about their duties. In a very small number of instances, police services do not do so. That was the case in Aotearoa New Zealand until 2011, but it has not always been like that.

The historical roots of policing in the country grew out of the arrival of British colonists in Aotearoa New Zealand. Before that time, there were no police as we know them today, nor were there firearms. Maori enforced their own customary laws through customary practice and tribal leaders. Weaponry was based around spears and clubs. In the early 1800s, as interaction between sailors, sealers and whalers increased, firearms (muskets) began to appear in the country and in the hands of locals (both original and recent) as trading between the parties increased (Hill, 1986a, pp. 30–31). Many Māori were quick to appreciate the advantage

[1] Police organisations are known by a variety of descriptors such as "force", "constabulary" or "service". In Aotearoa New Zealand, the descriptor "force" was removed from the Police's title in 1958. The organisation now has the official title of New Zealand Police, with a te Reo (Māori language) translation of Ngā Pirihimana o Aotearoa, and is widely referred to as a service. This work will use the term service when referring to the organisation.

R. S. Shortt, *Lethal Force and New Zealand Police*,
https://doi.org/10.1007/978-3-031-05269-9_4

firearms gave when attacking or defending during intertribal warfare (ibid) (Swinton, 2019, p. 2).

Following the signing of the 1840 Treaty of Waitangi between most Māori Iwi (tribes) and the British Crown, British laws were introduced, and policing began to emerge as the numbers of settlers and other European arrivals (e.g. whalers, sealers, traders, ships crews) increased. Initially, police (mounted troopers) were shifted from the British colonies of New South Wales and Victoria in Australia, while ultimately police were recruited "internally at the 'pakeha' [European] settlements" (Hill, 1986a, pp. 90–92 & 122–128). Hill's two-volume, three-book set – *Policing the Colonial Frontier* (Volume 1, Parts 1 and 2) and *The Colonial Frontier Tamed* (Volume 2) – provide a detailed and most excellent examination of those early years (1767–1867 and 1867–1886) policing the new frontier that was Aotearoa New Zealand. It tells of how relatively "new" developments in civil policing in England and the metropolis of London were factored into the new frontier's police arrangements, as were those of the earlier established Australian colonies.

As a "frontier colony", and post-1840, firearms became a prevalent tool in the hands of many now residing in Aotearoa New Zealand (Shortt, 2000, p. 37). Not only did settlers (particularly those living on isolated farms) have firearms to protect themselves from Māori – who were viewed with suspicion and fear given some of the indigenous people were not impressed with the spread of pakeha (European settlers) into their tribal lands – but also from rogue elements among their own kind. Settlers also used firearms to help gather food through hunting (Swinton, 2019) and to manage livestock. Māori, as mentioned earlier, had also quickly identified the advantage a musket, shotgun or pistol had over traditional weaponry and were now readily supplementing their own arsenals with such weapons. Finally, there were rogue elements within the new migrant pakeha population who saw the use of a firearm as advantageous when engaging in nefarious activities such as plundering others' goods or stealing from gold diggers or gold transportation services. It was, therefore, hardly surprising that early policing in the colony also sought recourse to firearms to help enforce the new laws and expectations of conduct, but also to protect police officers from those who might choose to use a firearm against them.

During those early years, as Hill describes, a variety of policing entities were established around the country in various settlements and locations on an almost "as-needed" basis. It was Governor Grey who established what was termed the "Armed Police Force" system (Hill, 1986b, p. xi), for example, the armed Auckland and New Plymouth police mentioned by Hill (Hill, 1986a, pp. 274–275). These early entities and policing in general within the colony also included Māori members, as is described in one instance where the decision was taken that if a solider was to be detained, "only pakeha [European] police could conduct the arrest" (ibid., pp. 275–276). Furthermore, there was no centralised "ownership" of policing across the land, nor was there a single force or service.

Within these early policing arrangements, a variety of firearms were provided to police officers including flintlock, muzzle-loading, Light Dragoon Horse pistols; 0.32 calibre transitional, muzzle-loading revolvers; 0.733 calibre Paget, muzzle-loading carbines; 0.66 Lovell's, muzzle-loading carbines; and Enfield, muzzle-loading carbines (Osborne, 1990a, 1990b).

The strategic approach to policing in Aotearoa New Zealand during these times was, according to Hill, "… that of imposing order upon a population – both Māori and pakeha – that was perceived by the state to be turbulent and untamed" (Hill, 1986b, p. xi). What followed the Treaty signing was two decades of relative stability with policing establishing "minimal degree[s] of 'order and regularity'" (ibid.) across both settler and Māori communities.

However, by the mid to late 1850s, interracial tensions were building towards a tipping point with Māori (especially on Te Ika-a-Māui (North Island)) recognising the consequences of having their lands settled by the newcomers and particularly when the pakeha population exceeded that of the indigenous people. In the 1860s, those tensions boiled over and escalated into warfare, and the strategic focus for policing shifted to a model of much harsher coercion (ibid.).

Meanwhile, on Te Waipounamu (South Island), the 1860s saw a time of gold rushes and disorder caused by the influx of miners and other "fortune seekers" from around the globe, often from other frontier countries where law and order was rough and ready and enforced through use of firearms.

It has been described as a "difficult time" (New Zealand Police, 2021b), with Hill confirming the creation of several "paramilitarised police forces" (Hill, 1986b, p. xi) using the model of the Australian colony of Victoria, with men from that colony and from the Irish Constabulary being imported to staff them (ibid.).

As stability slowly and painfully returned to the colony in the later part of the 1860s, moves were made to withdraw British military regiments from the land (due to the cost of deploying them) and to turn the myriad of policing entities that now existed into a more centralised organisation. In August 1867, legislation was introduced into the House of Representatives to create a force to be known as the Armed Constabulary (AC). Hill described the institution as "essentially Irish Constabulary in conception, with dashes of Victorian [Australian colony] and Otago [a Te Waipounamu/South Island province] flavouring … in a military direction" (Hill, 1986b, p. 10).

The AC, when first established, were armed with a variety of weapons used by the earlier units it grew out of and so, no doubt, had access to the weapons described by James Belich in his book *The New Zealand Wars* which included "muzzle-loading Enfield rifles … Terry and Calisher carbines and five-shot revolvers – breech-loading and repeating weapons suitable for bush-fighting" (Belich, 1986, p. 214). John Osborne also described the AC as having Adam's 6-shot, double-action, rod ejector revolvers; 0.44 Beaumont Adams, 5-shot, double-action revolvers; Sharps, breech-loading carbines; 0.451 Westley Richards', "Monkey Tail", breech-loading carbines; and 0.577 Storm's, capping, breech-loading carbines (Osborne, 1990a, 1990b). Quite a variety.

In his most descriptive depiction of the AC and their weapons, Belich wrote:

> Generally speaking, the constabulary were very good soldiers. They included men from disbanded colonial units such as the Forest Rangers, discharged Imperial regulars, and miscellaneous but tough recruits, among them British and American goldminers, sailors, and

> adventurers, and the odd Greek, Gurkha, and Frenchman. Organised in small units ('divisions') capable of acting independently, they were equipped for bush-fighting with revolvers and breech-loading carbines. (Belich, 1986, p. 238)

However, by the mid-1870s, following instances of significant fighting, the need for a militarised policing model had receded, and colonial administrators turned to thinking about how to police the new colony rather than tame it (Hill, 1989). In January 1877, the premier of the colony took the decision that the Armed Constabulary would absorb "the provincial police forces and was divided into distinct policing and military wings, with almost all the Māori AC … placed in the latter, the 'field force'" (Hill, 1986b, p. 85). This merging of civil and military policing being a "common phenomenon in the Empire" (ibid., p. 284). Subsequently, in February, the same year, following an officers' conference, it was decided that the AC would take on more of an Irish Constabulary flavour and move away from draconian policing to a more efficient bureaucratic model of social control under the new title of "New Zealand Constabulary Force" (NZCF) (ibid., p. 288).

By 1878, Hill reports that as the Police Branch of the NZCF "progressively became less overtly coercive", the decision was taken to stop issuing guns to police on foot patrols (ibid., p. 364). Policing in Aotearoa New Zealand had progressed to a point where police on the beat were no longer seen carrying a firearm.

The next major milestone occurred in 1886, when policing took a significant turn with the *Police Act* being passed (Hill, 1989, p. 365). This Act established the country's "… first national, civil, police force". The organisation created was to be an unarmed policing body (ibid., p. 365). It was at this point that the view, which New Zealand Police still adheres to, of Police being "a generally unarmed" service came into vogue.

The author regards that policy shift as the first of the five strategic policy changes in the development of the New Zealand Police firearms and lethal force-related policy from the 1880s through to the modern day.

The 1886 legislative move was part of a centralisation of many things in Aotearoa New Zealand as the frontier faded and a more established and stable colony emerged. The legislation created two separate entities out of the NZCF – the "New Zealand Police Force and the standing army" (Hill, 1986b). It also saw, in Hill's view, a further strategic shift from the "overtly coercive state policing strategy" to one which, in the final analysis, rested on the concept of order maintenance (ibid.).

"Generally unarmed", however, did not and does not mean unarmed. Reporting indicates that in 1889 all policemen (there were no female police) were to continue to have revolvers issued and that these would be of a standardised type (Shortt, 2000, p. 101). Osborne mentions 0.32 Smith and Wesson, and Colt, 6-shot, "pocket revolvers" being on issue around 1896–1905 (Osborne, 1990a, p. 17). While in 1905, an announcement was made that in the future police officers would not have revolvers issued on enrolment. Instead, senior ranking officers (ranks not specified) and detectives would routinely be issued with new 0.32 Smith and Wesson handguns, while in emergencies firearms could be obtained from Police armouries (ibid.).

The next significant change appears to have taken place in the early 1950s when personal issue firearms were withdrawn and station-based weapons became the approved practice (ibid., p. 102).

That change was the second strategic policy change regarding firearms and lethal force, in the author's view.

However, as the following anecdote from 1916 shows, police still had access to and resorted to using firearms, in a manner not dissimilar to the expeditions undertaken during the New Zealand Wars between colonists and Māori.

In that year, while World War I raged in far-off lands, an expedition of armed police was mounted to arrest the Māori prophet Rua Kenana, of the Tūhoe Iwi (tribe), who had established a religious community in an area of remote Iwi land. Kenana had become troublesome over his views on alcohol laws and the war currently being fought. Warrants were issued for his arrest, and the Police – at the behest of their commissioner – were galvanised into action. The enterprise had all the hallmarks of a military campaign with the commissioner of police as its leader, a commissariat attached and an Army Medical Corps officer assisting (Rattenbury, 2020).

The commissioner had assembled what he considered to be "… some strong athletic constables … suitable men to use the carbines who have served in the Army or the Royal Irish Constabulary" (ibid., p.39). In April of 1916, the party approached the site of the religious community. Two groups arrived before the main party and were met with peaceful behaviours including the provision of a welcome feast by the local adherents of the prophet (ibid., p. 40). The third group, including the commissioner, arrived the next day and insisted upon immediately arresting the prophet (whom it appears had intentions of surrendering on any account once niceties had been observed).

During the attempted arrest, a shot was fired by one of the police party. People scattered, some armed Māori fired back, and the scene degenerated into what police described as a "shoot-out", allegedly just as desired by the commissioner (ibid., p.40). While many police present later gave evidence that Kenana and most of his people were unarmed, at least two Māori were shot and killed in disturbing circumstances – one in the back while fleeing unarmed and another after having been overpowered and disarmed (ibid., p.41).

Police involved in the expedition were mentioned to have "a 0.303 carbine" and "revolvers", and images from the time show police officers carrying weapons (Rorke, 1993, pp. 356–360). John Osborne's work identified the weapons in Police hands as being 0.450 Webley revolvers and 0.303 Lee-Enfield, 6-shot, box magazine carbines (Osborne, 1990a, 1990b).

Perhaps, the events of the "battle" are best described, from the Police perspective, in the account of one of the police involved, Constable Bill Neil of Rotorua:

> I was the only one [in the contingent that travelled with the commissioner] without a rifle when we marched into Maungapohatu. I went ahead with an axe and cleared a path through the bush for my comrades, their horses and equipment. When we reached Rua's stronghold there was a gun battle. Four policemen were shot and wounded (including myself) and two of Rua's tribe. I saw Rua, and threw away my axe. I tackled him in a ditch and we fought

> there. Bullets were whistling over us. I had him in a stranglehold when he said, 'You can kill me now!' He was overpowered and taken into police custody. (Rorke, 1993, p. 57)

As mentioned, 2 Māori men were killed, 4 police were wounded, and 31 Māori were arrested during and after the melee. The subsequent court cases were turgid affairs with at least one constable refusing to give the evidence crafted for him stating to do so would have been to commit perjury (Rattenbury, 2020, p.42).

As the history detailed above shows, New Zealand Police continued to be confronted with situations involving firearms and which challenged their generally unarmed style of policing. Sadly, the events above were not an end to such challenges, and more would unfold which dramatically changed the way police organised and responded to events involving firearms.

However, as Swinton details in his working regarding firearms regulation in Aotearoa New Zealand, in general terms:

> The next 50 years [1930s to 1980s] were marked by a small number of firearms-related trends. First, there was a growing movement for the relaxation of certain regulation requirements … Second, guns continued to be a common presence in New Zealander's lives. Hunting, fishing, and other recreational uses of guns grew in popularity … Third, New Zealand enjoyed a period of 'peaceful enjoyment', one relatively devoid of firearms related crimes that gave little reason to expend political capital on gun regulations. (Swinton, 2019, p. 4)

Sadly, "peaceful enjoyment" did not mean no deaths. In one particularly poignant event, in 1941, four police officers were shot dead or mortally wounded on the West Coast of Te Waipounamu (South Island) (Ministry for Culture and Heritage, 2021). The shooter fled into the countryside, and a manhunt involving police, military and Home Guard personnel unfolded. Before it was over, two more men were shot and killed by the wanted man. The wanted man was subsequently ambushed by a Police party and mortally wounded by a rifle shot fired by a police officer (ibid.).

While arguably one of Aotearoa New Zealand's first mass shootings, the West Coast deaths were rare, and the period from 1941 through to 1963 reverted to Swinton's "peaceful enjoyment" and was a relatively quiet – but not silent – period with respect to deadly force used against police or other law enforcement officers.

Three officers were killed over those years as the result of criminal acts (New Zealand Police, 2021c). Two died as the result of firearms use (Kehoe, 1949; Hughes, 1951), while one officer died from a brain injury after being struck while intervening in a fight (Bidois, 1955; New Zealand Police, 2021c). The death of Traffic Inspector John Kehoe in late January 1949 is worthy of commentary as it highlights a number of firearms-related issues confronting New Zealand Police in the years following World War II.

Kehoe was on duty in the small provincial town of Whakatane, on Te Ika-a-Māui (North Island), when he gave chase to a speeding motorcyclist at about 8:30 pm one evening. The rider finally stopped but, upon being approached by Kehoe, drew a 0.38 revolver and shot the officer multiple times (Rorke, 1993, p. 241). As Kehoe lay dying, a concerned citizen approached the two men only to be shot and wounded himself. The wounded witness fled and alerted authorities to the shootings (ibid., pp. 241–242).

On finding the dead Kehoe and wounded witness, Police launched a major manhunt for the man believed responsible. Officers were brought into the area from various locations around Te Ika-a-Māui (North Island), including several from Auckland. One of those officers, Constable Allen Cross, wrote during his retirement some years later that after driving several senior officers to Whakatane:

> … We had a quick briefing, and were shown a photograph of McGill [the wanted-man]. I don't think any of us were in uniform. All of us had brought semi-automatic .32 Browning pistols with us and about five rounds of ammunition each. We had no holsters – it seems the police had none. … At the briefing it was thought McGill had one .38 revolver, and we had planned among ourselves that if we did encounter him we might have an opportunity to return the fire, as after emptying the chamber of the five or six shot revolver there would be a delay when he would have to reload. What a shock we got when we saw his weaponry after his body was found some five days later [McGill had killed himself]. He was armed with two .38 Smith and Wesson revolvers and in his holsters he had a fully-loaded .45 semi-automatic U.S. Colt, which was capable of about ten shots. McGill was in a position to have got away about 25 rounds before needing to reload. … [before discovery of McGill's body Cross went on to write] … At the briefing we had expressed concern about the inadequacy of the small .32 pistols we had, and asked if we could get some rifles. It was suggested to us that we might be able to borrow some from deer hunters or farmers in the area. The police had nothing in the way of rifles available. (ibid., p. 244)

Cross's description of how "out-gunned" the police were was a theme that would come back into focus some 41 years later when police faced off with a mass murderer in the sleepy village of Aramoana. But more of that tragic day later in this chapter. At the time of Kehoe's shooting, Osborne identified New Zealand Police as being armed with 0.32 handguns, probably the FN- or Colt-made Browning semi-automatics, or the Webley and Scott model 1911, automatic "pocket pistols" – as they were termed – introduced in the early to mid-1900s (Osborne, 1990a).

While deaths of law enforcement officers got recorded in the historic record, near death experiences such as wounding and near-miss shootings gained much less historical coverage or notoriety.

What follows are a series of examples chosen to give a flavour of what Police encountered during those otherwise tranquil years.

One such example was related in the 1960s, when a retiring constable told the story of how, after just 7 months in the Police (back in the late 1930s or early 1940s), he was confronted by a "mentally deranged man" who aimed and fired a loaded 0.303 rifle at him. Fortunately, the weapon misfired, and the constable was able to overpower the man and take him into custody (Rorke, 1993, p. 159). A tragedy avoided, but only just.

A similar misfire was also to save another police officer in the 1960s. In that incident, a man was being spoken to about a stolen yacht when he suddenly reached into his knapsack, removed two parts of a semi-automatic 0.22 rifle, assembled it and tried to shoot the police sergeant speaking to him. The rifle misfired, and after a violent struggle, he was overpowered and taken into custody without anyone being seriously injured. It was later discovered a flake of rust had jammed the mechanism of the rifle (ibid., p. 229).

But not all firearm events ended without injury or loss of life, as the following recollections reveal.

In December 1949, a depressed member of the Royal New Zealand Airforce began a shooting spree while holed up in a building on an Airforce base at Weedons near Christchurch. While no one was killed in the gunfire except the shooter, so many shots were fired by both police and Airforce responders that it was impossible to tell whether it was a police or Airforce bullet that killed the man involved (Rattenbury, 2020, p. 50; NZPA, 2008).

Four years later, in 1953, a police detective – B.D. Christofferson – was awarded the George Medal (civilian award for acts of great bravery) after being wounded arresting an armed youth. The shooting unfolded while the detective was searching a house occupied by a young man he had arrested for burglary. During the search, the arrested boy fled. He returned shortly thereafter with a friend. Both were armed with rifles. The detective and the boy's father were then held at gunpoint by the two; however, one left and went elsewhere on the property. A short time later, Christofferson heard a woman calling for help, and he broke away and rushed to her aid. In doing so, he was shot by both boys and received grave wounds, from which he eventually recovered (Rattenbury, 2020, pp. 51–52).

Sometime later, New Zealand Police again narrowly avoided tragedy in December 1960, when a man absconded from the Papakura Courthouse (just south of Auckland). He armed himself with a rifle and took up a position atop a sawdust extractor tower in a timber yard where he worked. From his vantage point, the man "shot at everything that moved in the near vicinity" (Rattenbury, 2020, p. 49). Rattenbury reports that armed police officers were present at the scene – members of Auckland's CIB Consorting Squad (a unit dedicated to preventing known criminals from meeting and working with each other on criminal enterprises) – however, they were restrained from returning fire while the officer in charge attempted to have the gunman dislodged through use of firehoses (ibid., p.50). It is most likely the CIB officers were only armed with the 0.32 calibre semi-automatic pistols still on issue to police at that time.

Unfortunately, the fire hose tactic further enraged the man who proceeded to shoot and wound five police officers and a firefighter. The matter was only resolved after 2 hours when the shooter took his own life using his rifle. On that occasion, five further near-miss events were added to the Police organisation's tally – although it does not appear a tally of such near misses was actually kept.

Not all firearms tragedies affecting New Zealand Police over the years were from external events. In 1958, tragedy was to strike from within. In March of that year, a detective inspector living in Lower Hutt, just north of Wellington, used a police-issue 0.32 semi-automatic pistol to kill his teenaged son, his father-in-law and himself. He also tried to kill his wife, but by sheer luck, she survived being shot in the face and raised the alarm. Apparently, personal worries, health issues and career disappointment led the senior CIB officer to undertake this horrific murder-suicide (Rattenbury, 2020, pp. 55–56). The apparent effectiveness of the police-issue 0.32

pistol is evidenced by the survival of the officer's wife who, despite being shot in the head at relatively close range, lived to recount the events that had unfolded.

The next major firearms-related events that substantially impacted New Zealand Police occurred in the months of January and February, 1963, and resulted in the third strategic policy change to the way Police armed and responded to the unlawful use of firearms.

On 6 January 1963, two Auckland CIB officers were shot and killed at an incident involving an armed and mentally unbalanced man in the Waitakere Ranges (New Zealand Police, 2021c). Four weeks later, on 3 February, two young uniformed constables were shot and killed – while still sitting in their patrol car – in Lower Hutt, attending an incident of what is now known as family violence, but which in those days was known as a domestic (ibid.).

Because of the four killings, the commissioner of the time was forced to act and to reconsider the "routinely unarmed" style of policing. He was also, as Rattenbury describes, forced to address the "untrained, lightly armed" nature of New Zealand Police when responding to armed incidents (Rattenbury, 2020, p. 53). A review of how police responded to armed people and incidents was quickly initiated with the result being a substantive change in the approach taken by New Zealand Police with agreement given to form Armed Offenders Squad (AOS).

By August 1964, a "hand-picked" group of police officers had gathered at Papakura military camp, south of Auckland, to begin training for the new entity (New Zealand Police, 2021a). In those early years, AOS was staffed by senior – through length of service – police officers from both the Uniform Branch and the CIB who often had military backgrounds and/or involvement in shooting sports and clubs (Rorke, 1993, p. 378) (Author's personal knowledge).

The squads were exclusively male (that finally changed, and since the mid-1990s, female officers have become members), and to gain entry, a police officer needed to be well thought of by all of the current members of the squad concerned. Training courses were organised when needed, particularly to stand-up new squads in places that previously did not have a dedicated unit (Rorke, 1993, p. 378).

At squad level, once "approved" by the current squad members and the appropriate senior officer approvals were signed off, an officer was inducted into the unit and trained by those already serving in it (Author's personal knowledge). There were also "Annual Camps" where two or three squads from adjoining districts would spend a week together undertaking arms-handling refreshers, shooting practice and tactics application, on either Army bases or suitable rural locations around the country (Rorke, 1993, p. 381) (Author's personal knowledge).

The AOS was, and remains, a part-time affair with the members carrying out "normal" police duties until a need for their services arises. When it does, the officers change into their AOS uniform, arm themselves and respond (Rorke, 1993, p. 378; New Zealand Police, 2021a).

The early squads[2] were armed with 0.38 Smith and Wesson, 6-shot revolvers obtained from the New Zealand Air Force's ex-WW2 stock and attached to the officer by a military-style lanyard (Osborne, 1990a, pp. 21–22). They also had 0.303 Lee-Enfield, bolt-action rifles – again ex-military stock. In later years, the handgun issued changed to the 0.357 Magnum Smith and Wesson, 6-shot revolver, and the rifle moved to be the standard Police-issue 0.222 Sako Vixen, 5-shot, bolt-action weapon (Rorke, 1993, p. 382).

The AOS still exists within New Zealand Police having withstood the tests of time and surviving 56 years of organisational change. More is written about the modern AOS later in this chapter.

The next major change to the New Zealand Police's armed response model came in the late 1970s. That was a time of international terrorism, bombings, aircraft hijackings, kidnappings, politically motivated murders and siege-hostage events (Battersby, 2019, pp. 36–37). Aotearoa New Zealand was not immune to those developments as the failed Ananda Marga plot of 1975 showed (Battersby, 2019).

The Police responded to the development of organised violence on the part of "terror groups" with the creation of the Anti-Terrorist Squad (ATS). The ATS (three sub-units were created, based in Auckland, Wellington and Christchurch) were also part-time in the same manner as the AOS and were made up of already serving AOS officers. The ATS received a higher level of specialist training and a wider range of equipment, as detailed later in this chapter. For example, they were issued with 0.22 American 180 carbines with modern Laser Lok sights and a 177-round magazine (Osborne, 1990b, p. 20), ex-Army 9 mm Stirling sub-machine guns and 0.357 Magnum, Smith and Wesson, 6-shot revolvers (Osborne, 1990a, p. 22). In 1991, due to the broader range of duties the ATS members were being tasked with, and the lack of terrorism incidents in Aotearoa New Zealand, the ATS was renamed the Special Tactics Group (STG) (Tso, 2018; New Zealand Police, 2016).

By 1977, when the author joined the New Zealand Police, the organisation relied on two weapons to arm its frontline staff when such a need arose. They were the 0.38 Smith and Wesson, 6-shot revolver (Osborne, 1990a, pp. 22–23) and the 0.222 Sako Vixen, 5-shot, bolt-action[3] rifle.

---

[2] While referred to nationally as the Armed Offenders Squad, the organisation was in fact made up of multiple squads that were based in various cities and towns around the country. This work will adhere to the Police tradition of referring to AOS in the singular, despite it comprising sub-elements.

[3] For those unfamiliar with the term "bolt-action", there are four predominant forms of rifle in use today. They are bolt-action, pump-action, lever-action and automatic (either semi or fully). The first uses a manual hand-operated "bolt" to feed a round of ammunition (which includes a brass casing holding the "gunpowder" with a bullet secured at the top) from the magazine into the firing chamber. Once the round has been fired and the bullet sent towards the target, the now empty casing is ejected through working the bolt, and a fresh live round is fed into the chamber. Pump-action rifles use a sliding manual "pump" action to do the same task, while a lever-action utilises a manual mechanism similar to a bolt to work a used casing out and replace it with a fresh round. Semi-automatic and fully automatic rifles use a mechanical process built into the rifle to complete the same process each time a bullet is fired. Semi-automatic means the trigger must be pulled each

Newly recruited trainees were introduced to these two weapons at the Police college and provided with range training to establish proficiency and ability to hit an unmoving paper target (Author's personal experience). Once graduated from the training college, freshly minted constables were posted to stations around the country to begin their careers, and there they also received at least 1, possibly 2, days of annual refresher training where they got to visit a shooting range, discharging 6–10 bullets from each weapon, again at static paper targets (ibid.). That "skill maintenance" training was overseen by training officers based in each of the districts and was known as district training.

In those days, to the best of the author's memory, there was no tactical training. The author defines tactical training as the discussion, practising and certification of the thinking and actions required to best equip and position one's self to undertake a safe and considered intervention against an armed subject. The author's memory is of often rushed returns to stations (where the firearms were kept), being issued with – mostly – a 0.38 Smith and Wesson revolver and a single chamber's worth of bullets (6) and then an equally rushed trip back to the scene of whatever it was that required the issue of the firearm(s) (ibid.).

Examples of how firearms were issued and carried in the early years of the author's service can be gleaned from two reminisces concerning guarding functions. In 1975, before the author joined police, three members of the Ananda Marga Hindu religious sect attempted to steal explosives from a rock quarry. Their intentions were to build a bomb and use it to attack the Indian High Commission in Wellington (Battersby, 2019). The plot was foiled, and no attack took place. But, as a result of the threat, an armed, uniformed, police presence was set up at the Indian High Commissioner's residence in Lower Hutt, a suburb of the capital Wellington.

The author, 3 years later on being posted to Lower Hutt, became one of the many police officers assigned to this duty randomly at the start of each rostered shift. The officer was based in a small room at the rear of the residence's garage. Inside were a table, a chair, a typewriter and little else. Each "guard" took over from the previous at the beginning of their shift and was handed the loaded 0.38 Smith and Wesson revolver on issue for the duty. The author cannot recall if this included a holster. It certainly only included six rounds of ammunition. If walking about during the shift, the revolver was often stuffed into the officer's trouser pocket.[4]

The second recollection regarding firearms, from around the same time, involved relieving another officer who was protecting a witness to a serious crime who had been admitted to hospital, for that officer's meal break. Again, the handover involved

time a bullet is to be fired, while automatic rifles require just one pull and hold of the trigger to continue firing until the trigger is released or the magazine is emptied.

[4] Rattenbury (Rattenbury, 2020, p. 215) makes a similar comment in his book of Police-related reminiscing where he recalls "No utility belts in those days, we carried everything in our pockets, including a revolver if need be. There was a cute little brown holster available but it was a pain to get on so most of us just grabbed the gun and six rounds and shot through".

the passing on of a loaded 0.38 Smith and Wesson revolver, and this time definitely no holster. At some point, the witness/patient needed to leave his bed and room to go to the toilet, and as the author rose from his chair to accompany him, there was a loud crash. The loaded gun had fallen from his trouser pocket and was now lying on the floor between the two. The witness/patient said "Well, it's lucky it's not loaded" to which the author replied, sheepishly, "Yes". Of course, it was. A heart-stopping and potentially career-limiting incident, but one which stayed out of official purview until written about here, for posterity.

The author was relieved to discover, while researching, that his anecdotal recollections were not unparalleled in Police history. For example, in the early 1920s, a Police escort was provided to a car carrying gold, from a bank in a town near the gold mine, to a nearby sea port. During one such journey, the driver asked the police officer if he was armed. The constable replied that he was and showed the driver an old service revolver he was carrying. The driver then asked "Is it loaded?" (sounds familiar). "He was met with a sheepish grin from the policeman, who produced six rounds of ammunition from the tin containing his sandwiches" (Rorke, 1993, p. 192).

A second tale, however, has added drama. Sometime in the 1950s to 1960s – history is vague on the date – an armed detective was provided to escort cash from bookmakers at a local horse race meeting to the nearby bank at the end of the day. The detective involved was issued with a pistol. On one occasion at the bank, after the detective had placed the weapon on a desk (history does not say why he did so; one may perhaps assume holsters were again missing in action), the question "Is that thing loaded?" was asked. "Sure is" was the reply, whereupon the detective picked up the gun and proceeded to shoot out two of the bank's ceiling lights. History does not record if the teller who asked the question was impressed, but neither the bank manager nor the detective's superintendent apparently was (Rorke, 1993, p. 97).

Upon reflection, there was a naivety and simplicity regarding firearms associated with the events described above. No pre-deployment briefings on intelligence or particular threats, no tactical training on static armed-guard duties, no holsters for the weapons, one load of ammunition – but no extra ammunition should it be needed, no protective clothing. It was almost as if the provision and presence of the firearm "ticked a box" and there was no – or little – expectation that the officer would ever have to use the weapon, well not against another person, lights perhaps.

All that was to dramatically change when on 13 November 1990, New Zealand Police were confronted with the most devastating mass murder since, 1941, in Aotearoa New Zealand. In the seaside suburb of Aramoana, just outside the city of Dunedin on Te Waipounamu (South Island), a man[5] went on a shooting rampage that left 13 people dead, including a police sergeant. The killings involved children, adults and senior citizens, all residents (with the exception of the sergeant) of the seaside community (Hunt, 2014).

[5] The author has determined not to name those responsible for the multiple killings detailed in this work. Commentary on those men's deeds is sufficient. It is felt their names add nothing of usefulness and may, unfortunately, add to their notoriety.

As the killings unfolded, police, alerted by an emergency phone call, dispatched armed officers to the scene to commence the first phase of the response – locate the shooter and cordon and contain him. Sadly, as the initial response officers moved into the village to locate the shooter, one of them, Sergeant Guthrie, was shot and killed when he encountered the man and called on him to surrender. At the time, Guthrie was armed with a standard issue 0.38 Smith and Wesson, 6-shot revolver. He was also a member of the Dunedin AOS, but at the time of the response, he was performing duty as a uniformed sergeant along with his colleagues from the Port Chalmers police station where he was based (Hunt, 2014; NZ History, 2020) (Author's personal knowledge). His opponent that day was armed with a 0.223 AK47 semi-automatic, military-style, assault rifle with a high-capacity magazine and a telescopic sight (now on display at the New Zealand Police Museum, Royal New Zealand Police College) (Swinton, 2019, p. 8).

By that evening, with AOS now performing cordon and containment of the village, Police commanders determined that a house-to-house search would be required to find the gunman and that due to his intimate knowledge of the area, the fact he had already killed a police officer and the fact he was armed with significant firepower, the ATS would be called in to conduct the search (ibid.).

The Wellington-based ATS unit was flown to Dunedin early the next day, where they joined the Christchurch unit, and with the assistance of the Royal New Zealand Airforce completed an aerial reconnaissance. Once briefed, the teams moved into the village and began their search. The gunman's house was entered using distraction devices (commonly referred to as stun grenades, a tool only available to ATS at the time) and teargas. He was not there. Further house searches were undertaken until finally the shooter was discovered in a building, resulting in him firing a volley of shots. As the man tried to leave his hiding place, challenging police to shoot him and firing randomly, he was shot and mortally wounded (NZ History, 2020). During this time, another police officer was hit and slightly wounded by the gunman's fire (ibid.) (Author's personal knowledge).

Police discovered the killer had seven rifles (including six semi-automatics) available to him (Swinton, 2019, p. 8). One had a silencer, another had a bayonet, and his most lethal – the 0.223 AK47, military-style, semi-automatic – had a telescopic sight and a high-capacity magazine fitted. He literally out-gunned the AOS weapons of the time and may well have matched the weapons being used by the ATS officers.

Aramoana was a water-shed moment for police and the country; it was the first time the ATS had shot a person. It was the first significant "active shooter"[6] situation encountered by Police since the 1940s; it was the first time since its formation that the AOS had been substantially "out-gunned" by an opponent who had a telescopically sighted, semi-automatic rifle with a large-capacity magazine, far more potent

[6] An active shooter is a person who is on the move and killing people as they go, rather than being static in one location. An active shooter requires a different tactical response to that used for a person holed up in a building or vehicle. Cordon, contain, appeal, for example (the standard Police response), becomes far less applicable in an active shooter situation.

than their own weapons (Author's personal knowledge). Interestingly, though, it was not the first time police in general were "out-gunned", as the Kehoe homicide in 1949 had already shown.

The massacre gave rise to debate on gun control and a 1992 amendment to the "regulations on military-style semi-automatic firearms" (NZ History, 2020). Unfortunately, it did not result in the banning of such firearms in Aotearoa New Zealand, just changes to the licencing regime (Swinton, 2019, pp. 8–9). Banning was not achieved until 2019 when a similar style rifle was used to kill 51 people in Christchurch "in a premeditated terrorist action" (ibid). More will be written about that event later in this chapter.

The tragic events at Aramoana were one of the reasons New Zealand Police reconsidered their choice of firearms and the practices they adopted in dealing with armed offenders. The result of that work was the introduction of the 9 mm Glock 17, semi-automatic, magazine-fed, 17-shot pistol, first to AOS and then to the wider police service. It also saw the AOS issued with second-hand 5.56 mm M16 rifles from the New Zealand Army. The rifles had had the automatic function on them disabled, but provided a 20-shot, semi-automatic capability for encounters with subjects who might be armed in the manner of the Aramoana shooter. Squads were also issued with telescopically sighted 7.62 mm rifles to enable at least one member of each section to have a longer range and more accurate weapon to engage a subject with (Author's personal knowledge and experience).

The Glock was not the first semi-automatic handgun used by New Zealand Police, as the history recounted here shows, but since 1964, the 0.38 revolver had been the general issue handgun for operational officers and AOS, with the exception of police officers stationed at international airports. Since 1989, they had been armed with the 9 mm GP Mark III, FN Browning, semi-automatic pistol (Osborne, 1990a, p. 20 & 24).

The years around that time, and when the author embarked upon the first tranche of his research – 1999 to 2000, were still ones where most officers had to return to a station and convince a sergeant or senior sergeant to allow them access to a police-issue firearm. A small number of police officers carried a firearm (almost always a handgun) when on duty. They included some detectives on what was known as "Crime Car" shifts, often during the night shift (23:00–07:00 hours); members of the Diplomatic Protection Squad, based in Wellington and responsible for patrols of embassy and High Commission premises and the homes of diplomats; personal protection officers on-duty to accompany VIPs; officers on-duty at international airports in accordance with international protocol; and occasionally senior staff (such as shift inspectors or senior sergeants) who were mobile in major cities (Author's personal knowledge and experience).

Police officers who staffed smaller rural stations or remote stations would, with or without authority, also carry the firearms issued to their station (a revolver and possibly a rifle) in their patrol vehicles. Due to their remoteness, "a quick trip back to the station" to get a firearm when needed was impracticable (ibid.).

One final anecdote encountered by the author during his research from around that time highlights the issue of whether the New Zealand Police were in fact an entirely "routinely unarmed service" or perhaps a blend of armed and unarmed police officers. On an Internet firearms discussion forum, an unnamed New Zealand Police officer recounted:

> In March 1993 ... At the time I was stationed in a rural town where, although an unarmed police force, we were authorised to carry firearms (S&W Model 10 .38 Special and Sako Vixen .222 rile) in the car at all times ... Every shift I would roll up, draw firearms and put the loaded M10 into my holster [the correspondent had purchased his/her own Sidekick duty holster rather than use the 'inferior' issued holster] before locking it away in the glove box of the car ... Truth to tell, most evenings after the bosses had gone home I pulled the holster and speed loaders [again a personal purchase] out of the glovebox and put them on my belt. Many the time I interviewed and arrested offenders who had no idea I was carrying under my duty jacket. One or two soon learned I had it when arrested at gunpoint. (Unknown, 2021)

In the author's experience of rural and remote policing at that time, the anecdote has a distinct ring of truth to it.

However, change was afoot, and during the decade of the 1990s, changes to the nature of the police firearms response and the types of firearms on issue to general police were taking place.

When the substantial change regarding ATS/STG occurred in 1991, the group was provided with an expanded mission beyond just responding to terrorism events (Tso, 2018; New Zealand Police, 2016). It was a move designed to take greater advantage of the specialist skills the STG provided to Police through their training with entities like the Aotearoa New Zealand and Australian army's Special Air Service troops (New Zealand Police, 2016). Those skills included bush-craft, long-term surveillance in a variety of settings including the ability to infiltrate and gather evidence in covert situations, such as Operation Eight which will be mentioned in greater detail below.

The refocusing of the STG also meant that they could be deployed more often to support the AOS and general policing, particularly in armed incidents where even the AOS felt their capabilities may be exceeded. The flip side of that greater use was the introduction of military-style tactics and shooting into incidents where previously they would not have, in the author's view, been countenanced. More about this later in the sections of this book dedicated to specialist groups and tactics.

By the early 2000s, following the global increase in newer forms of ideological and religious terrorism globally – in particular the 9/11 attacks in the USA – the STG was elevated from being an on-call unit, made up of specialised AOS members, to become a full-time specialised armed police unit. While that change did have its genesis in concerns over international developments, it was also partly driven by internal staffing issues within Police (New Zealand Police, 2016). The three districts which supported the STG (Greater Auckland, Wellington and Christchurch) were finding that the calls upon STG services were increasing and placing a strain on the "every-day" units that STG members were assigned to when not working in their highly specialised role that included their participation in the local AOS units that its members were drawn from (ibid.).

Therefore, to lessen the burden, and to respond to both domestic and global needs, the decision was taken to make the group a full-time national entity assigned to the operational oversight of Police National Headquarters in Wellington, but remaining based in the three major cities (New Zealand Police, 2016). The ability to deploy the STG also moved from being a decision by the commissioner to that of either the commissioner or a deputy commissioner if the commissioner was not available (Independent Police Conduct Authority, 2014). Ultimately, by 2014, that authority had been further expanded to include the Assistant Commissioner: Crime and Operations, if the other two commissioners were not available, but only for what was described as a "partial deployment as part of a Planned operation within New Zealand [emphasis in the original]" (ibid.).

It is the author's contention that the combined ATS renaming, expanded work refocus, permanent status and wider deployment authority, became the fourth strategic policy shift for New Zealand Police concerning lethal force and the deployment and use of firearms.

During the same period (the 1990s to mid-2000s), as already mentioned, the 9 mm Glock, semi-automatic pistol made an appearance in the hands of specialists like the AOS and STG, and then later the weapon was released to the wider organisation to replace the 0.38 Smith and Wesson revolver as the standard issue handgun. That change was subsequently followed in the mid-2000s by Police reviewing the suitability of the 0.223 Remington, bolt-action rifle and subsequently a decision to replace it with the more modern 5.56 mm XM15 M4A3, Bushmaster, semi-automatic rifle (New Zealand Police, 2005).

The primary differences were are that the handgun had gone from having a 6-shot capacity to a magazine-fed 17 shots and the rifle from a 5-shot bolt-action capacity to a semi-automatic 20-shot capacity weapon.[7] The rifle now also featured a sight enhancer to assist with aiming and a torch mounted on the weapon for night use (Buchanan, 2014). This modernisation of weaponry did not in and of itself change firearm deployment tactics, however, and, as will be discussed later, it took a specific review by senior officers in 2001 to identify the need to revisit the deployment practices of the past regarding individual firearms.

It was during that decade of weapon modernisation that in late April 2000, a police shooting took place in a small rural town in Taranaki on Te Ika-a-Māui (North Island). It was to have substantial ramifications for the officer who fired the fateful shots, but also for the wider police organisation, as it was the first time that a serving officer was charged with murder as a result of their on-duty actions.

The events concerned unfolded following an early-morning call about a man smashing property and resulted in a local constable and two police officers from a nearby larger town confronting a 23-year-old man named Steven Wallace

[7] In the IPCA reporting regarding the fatal shooting of Anthony Fane, on 13 February 2020, it is evident that AOS Bushmasters are equipped with a 30-round capacity magazine – see pages 4 and 6 (Independent Police Conduct Authority, 2021). In the Naitoko shooting report, the IPCA also refers to the magazines as holding either 20 or 30 rounds (Independent Police Conduct Authority, 2009a, 2009b, p. 41).

(Independent Police Conduct Authority, 2009b). Wallace, for reasons never disclosed (ibid., p.5), left his family home around 3:30 am in an "highly agitated state" (ibid.). He ultimately ended up in the main street of the small town of Waitara where he was seen breaking windows with a golf club. He also used a baseball bat to continue the destruction, while police were called by concerned bystanders. The first police to arrive at the town were a patrol from a nearby larger centre. Wallace attacked their car and broke the windscreen with his golf club (ibid., p. 7).

Witnessing the attack, the local constable decided to arm himself and one of the out-of-town officers, and so they obtained two Glock pistols from the local police station. Now armed, they returned to the main street of the town where they again encountered Wallace (Ibid., p. 8). Wallace menacingly advanced on the two now armed police officers, despite being called on by name and being told to drop his weapon (a golf club) (Ibid., p. 8). The golf club was then thrown at one of the officers, while the young man continued to advance on them, now with the baseball bat in hand (Ibid., pp. 8–9).

The local constable, upon whom Wallace was advancing, continued to back off and call out his warning that he was armed (Ibid., p. 9). A warning shot was then fired into the air, but it had no effect on the young man's advance. He was by now stating that he was going to kill the constable (Ibid., p. 9). The constable then fired four shots at Wallace, who fell to the ground. He had been hit four times and was mortally wounded (ibid., p. 12). He died at the scene a short time later (ibid.)

Wallace's shooting gave rise to widespread media coverage and debate. The coverage is summarised by the following quote from *The Press*, 2000 (p. 6), cited in Samkin et al.:

> Why was Mr Wallace shot dead when he was wielding only a baseball bat and a golf club? Why do the police shoot to kill and not to wound and disable? Why did the police not wait for a dog handler, or use pepper spray? Why did they not back off and seek to contain a man who, while acting threateningly and smashing windows, had not harmed anyone? (Samkin et al., 2010, p. 28)

Subsequently, the family of Steven Wallace launched a private prosecution of the constable alleging that he had murdered their son (ibid., pp. 15–16). In 2002, following a trial before a jury in the Wellington High Court, the constable was acquitted (ibid.). A coroner's inquest in 2007 issued conclusions that were critical of the way police handled the incident; however, these were dismissed by the police commissioner of the time who instead commended the three officers involved (ibid., pp. 16–17).

The events of that night in April, 2000, were profound. A young man's family was consumed by grief and anger and sought justice for their dead son. The police officer, called from his bed in the early hours of the morning, had to make the biggest decision of his life, one which ultimately contributed to him resigning from the police service a decade later (Rattenbury, 2020, pp. 69–72). Not only did the officer (and his family) have to grapple with the shooting; he was also publicly named (unusually for police involved shootings in Aotearoa New Zealand) – requiring him and his entire family to move to a different part of the country. He was subjected to a police criminal investigation (standard practice following a fatal shooting by Police), a charge of murder laid by the deceased's family, several court hearings, a coroner's inquest and then ultimately – 8 years later – after all the other proceedings had been completed, an Independent Police Conduct investigation and a public report.

In his own words, the police officer involved reflected "The cost to me and my family have been absolutely horrendous. I did what I was trained to do, I did what I was expected to do, I reacted in self-defence and I survived. Many police officers will face the same decision. My only words of advice to them is, think wisely, be so sure of your actions, get it right" (Rattenbury, 2020, p. 72).

The next series of high-profile events to impact New Zealand Police and its armed response model occurred before the Wallace shooting upheaval had settled. While many in Aotearoa New Zealand considered terrorism and the concept of armed resistance to legitimate government an issue for countries far away, Operation Eight and the events of 2005–2007 changed that.

As previously mentioned, Operation Eight involved Police surveillance of a group of people apparently engaged in military-style training camps in native forest on the land of the Tūhoe Iwi. After becoming aware of the group's activities, Police deployed elements of the STG into the forest to watch, record and monitor the activities. Officers recorded video of men and women conducting armed patrolling, throwing Molotov cocktails (petrol-filled incendiary devices) and conducting live fire target drills with a variety of rifles (Independent Police Conduct Authority, 2013).

Police did not just rely upon the surveillance being undertaken by the STG officers. They also applied for and were given permission to use technical surveillance of communications between the group's members. This part of the inquiry was handled by the Special Investigations Group (SIG) who had been formed to carry out investigations into matters deemed relevant to national security following the terrorist attacks in the USA, commonly referred to as 9/11, in 2001 (Author's personal knowledge).

As a result of both the physical and technical surveillance, Police formed a belief that the information gathered indicated a group of people – some with criminal and political activist backgrounds – were "training for potentially violent action in New Zealand. Police perceived the activities of the group as posing a very real threat to public safety" (Independent Police Conduct Authority, 2013, p. 17). In a final briefing to the police commissioner, the investigative team outlined six training camps, weapons use, explosives and Molotov cocktail use, ambush exercises, simulated vehicle ambushes, patrolling drills and engaging in interrogation techniques (ibid., p. 23).

During the preparation for the termination[8] of Operation Eight, in October 2007, New Zealand Police for the first time included references to the *Terrorism Suppression Act 2002* (NZL) in their search warrant applications alleging that they

[8] The term used by Police when they bring an operation to a conclusion. Termination refers to the day on which search warrants and other action by Police are taken to arrest or otherwise deal with the people who have been the "targets" of the operation.

believed evidence would be found to prove participation in a terrorist group (ibid., p. 20). Other alleged criminal acts were also included in the warrant applications including unlawful possession of firearms and unlawful possession of restricted weapons (ibid., p. 20).

Termination of the operation was authorised by the commissioner, and as a result, STG and AOS officers were used to enter and secure a number of "high-risk" addresses that were to be searched. Regrettably, the actual termination and the tactics employed – particularly with regard to the township of Ruatoki – became controversial and resulted in considerable media and public accusations of heavy handedness and unfair treatment of Māori who formed the nucleus of the people being sought and the majority of the population of Ruatoki. The spectre of the Rua Kenana police expedition of 1916 came back to haunt this more contemporary policing operation (Independent Police Conduct Authority, 2013, p. 26).

While Operation Eight's termination did not involve police firing any shots or anyone suffering any physical injuries, the police commissioner subsequently apologised for the tactics used and the psychological hurt inflicted. No charges under the *Terrorism Suppression Act 2002* (NZL) were laid (they required specific authority from the solicitor general), but other charges were, and they became the subject of protracted criminal proceedings going right up to Aotearoa New Zealand's highest court, the Supreme Court. Four people were subsequently convicted and sentenced for unlawful firearms possession offences (Independent Police Conduct Authority, 2013, pp. 14–15).

The nature of the activities undertaken by the people who were the subject of Operation Eight (as detailed in the Independent Police Conduct Authority's report), the fact that 26 firearms were recovered by police during search warrants and hours of both physical and technical surveillance identifying concerning behaviours and beliefs lead to a view – in the mind of the author – that Aotearoa New Zealand could no longer think of itself as a completely benign land far from the dangers and challenges faced by the wider world.

Three years after the conclusion of Operation Eight, New Zealand Police undertook yet another review of their "firearms training and accessibility" (New Zealand Police, 2010, p. 2). This one, instigated by the police commissioner, came about at the same time the New Zealand Police Association (the rank-and-file police officers' union) "called for the routine arming of police after nine officers were shot at – two fatally – in the preceding two-year period" (Hendy, 2012, p. 8). The deaths of the officers, and the killing of a police dog, gave rise to a "vigorous" public debate about whether police officers should have greater access to firearms and whether they should "more routinely and visibly carry firearms" (Independent Police Conduct Authority, 2010, p. 4). More details on the review and its outcomes are contained in Chap. 6.

Interestingly, around the time the review was taking place, the police commissioner was quoted as saying that armed response vehicles might be an option for Police to consider. In a magazine article quoting the commissioner, it was stated:

> In the June 2009 edition of online Police publication *Ten One*, Commissioner Howard Broad made reference to Armed Response Vehicles (ARVs) in the UK as a model that might work well in New Zealand. ARVs, he explained, are small teams of specially trained officers 'permanently on standby to respond to a serious threat'. 'They are not armed officers most of the time, and are able to carry out routine frontline duties, but they have immediate access to firearms from a small, secure armoury in their vehicles and are better trained than our current general staff to handle armed threats', he wrote. 'Some version of this could be useful in areas with a population base and number of incidents to justify it, such as Auckland. It is one option to consider for the future'. (Dynon, 2020)

The concept of ARVs, sadly, in the author's opinion, failed to gain traction at that time and was not taken any further until much later following a horrific set of events in 2019. The author's view was shaped by research he had completed earlier for his 2000 paper concerning the firearms deployment options for the New Zealand Police. That paper will be discussed in greater detail in Chap. 6.

Ultimately, the firearms training and accessibility review resulted in the decision that implementing the "Norwegian Police model" of carrying firearms in locked safes inside police patrol cars was appropriate for New Zealand Police (Perry, 2011, p. 2; New Zealand Police, 2012, p. 4). However, it would be the next commissioner and his executive team, entering office in 2011, who would drive the change (New Zealand Police, 2011, p. 8). That decision greatly expanded the deployment of police firearms into patrol vehicles and created a substantive change from a localised, district-by-district model to a countrywide one.

In his overview to the Police Annual Report, 2010–2011, (ibid.), the new commissioner, Peter Marshall (co-author of the much earlier "Use of Force Report", completed in 2001, with the assistance of Assistant Commissioner Ray Shuey of Victoria Police – discussed in greater detail later in this work), wrote:

> One of my first declared intentions was to improve access to firearms and Tasers for frontline staff. Work is under way to equip every response or road policing vehicle to hold a safe for the carriage of a Bushmaster rifle, Glock pistol, Taser, and two sets of ballistic armour. Such initiatives aim to increase the safety of our police and the public without recourse to routine arming. (ibid.)

The statement appears to have gone largely unchallenged by the public and politicians in Aotearoa New Zealand, as far as the author can determine. A quite extraordinary achievement for what was, in the author's view, the fifth strategic firearms policy change to affect the New Zealand Police since its early days as a newly created entity.[9]

It should be noted that by this time there had already been public debate as mentioned earlier and that at the time of the announcement, the country was focused (perhaps distracted) by 2 momentous events, one being a major earthquake that

---

[9] As will be recalled, from earlier sections, it is the author's view that the other four previous strategic firearms policy changes were as follows: 1) the partial disarming of the Armed Constabulary and creation of the New Zealand Police Force in 1886, 2) the further disarming of the New Zealand Police and storage of Police firearms in stations in the early 1950s, 3) the formation of the AOS and 4) the making of the STG a permanent full-time specialist firearms entity with a wider work remit during the late 1990s.

struck and devastated the city of Christchurch, on 22 February 2011, leaving 185 people dead and between 1500 and 2000 people injured (164 of them seriously) and an earlier coal mining disaster at Pike River that left 29 miners missing, presumed dead, after a series of 4 explosions rocked the mine on the 19, 24, 26 and 28 November 2010.

The commissioner's written comments in mid-2011, in a document few New Zealanders would read, may have, in the author's view, slipped under the radar while being fully welcomed with no great public fanfare by the police audience who would not have wished to provoke an outcry. Sometimes, timing is everything.

The strategic essence of the change was to place firearms within reach of police officers considered to be the Tier 1 responders.[10] Instead of the previous requirement of returning to a station to be issued with firearms on the approval of a sergeant or senior sergeant, officers could now do so of their own volition. Every operational patrol vehicle in Aotearoa New Zealand had effectively been turned into an ARV. Elsewhere in this work, the arming protocols related to this change are outlined more explicitly, but a requirement did exist for gaining approval – or at least advising the communications centre – that officers had armed themselves, however, in the heat of the moment, that requirement was not always adhered to as multiple IPCA reports confirmed (see commentary in Chap. 8).

It is the author's view that the fifth strategic policy shift outlined above meant it was no longer correct to refer to the New Zealand Police as a "routinely unarmed" police service (if in fact it ever was). From the time of that change, it was simply the *style* of arming that was up for debate, but to all intents and purposes, the New Zealand Police were now routinely well-armed. Reflecting on history, the New Zealand Police had in essence returned to its historical roots of the Armed Constabulary and New Zealand Police Force of the mid to late 1800s. Eight years later, history might also reflect that it was just in time.

On 15 March 2019, in Christchurch, the country's second largest city, situated on Te Waipounamu (South Island), an Australian citizen living in the country attacked 2 Islamic mosques, murdering 51 men, women and children and wounding a further 40 (Royal Commission of Inquiry, 2020, pp. Vol. 1, p. 10). The killer had a lawfully, but faultily, issued firearms licence (Royal Commission of Inquiry, 2020, pp. Vol. 1, p. 20). He had six firearms and other equipment with him during the attacks, including:

> … two semi-automatic rifles, two other rifles and two shotguns – along with loaded large capacity magazines (some of which had been coupled together to facilitate changing magazines rapidly) and rounds of ammunition … The individual had in his car four crude incendiary devices, two ballistic armour (bullet-proof) vests, military style camouflage clothing, a military style tactical vest, a GoPro camera, an audio speaker and a ballistic style tactical helmet. He also had a scabbard with a bayonet-style knife …. (Royal Commission of Inquiry, 2020, pp. Vol. 1, p. 40)

[10] Police now moved to Tier 1, 2 and 3 responder levels to differentiate the type of training being received.

In summary, the man was armed and prepared for battle – albeit a completely one-sided battle against unarmed worshippers. Shortly after leaving his second crime scene, and while en route to a third mosque to continue his violence, the man's car was intercepted by two police officers who were returning from routine firearms training. They were, therefore, equipped with Bushmaster rifles in their vehicle. The officer's rammed the man's car bringing it to a halt and arrested him at gunpoint without having to fire a shot. A third massacre was thus avoided. A fantastic achievement. The man subsequently pleaded guilty to multi-counts of murder and attempted murder and was sentenced to life in prison.

The Christchurch massacres gave rise to one further, but ultimately unsuccessful, attempt to change the way New Zealand Police deployed firearms. On 30 August 2019, 5 months after the horrors of 15 March, the then commissioner (who had been the Deputy Commissioner for Operations when firearms were deployed into patrol cars in 2010–2011) and police executive approved a trial of armed response teams (ARTs) in 3 of Aotearoa New Zealand's 12 Police districts – Manukau, Waikato and Canterbury. The concept, based on the successful armed response vehicles (ARVs) in the UK, was for small, highly trained teams of four AOS officers to be on patrol at all times with immediate access to their AOS weapons and equipment (New Zealand Police, n.d., p. 14). The trial became operational on 28 October 2019 (ibid.). The commissioner was quoted as stating:

> … Police must ensure our people are equipped and enabled to perform their roles safely and ensure our communities are, and feel, safe. This means having the right people with the right tools, skills and knowledge ready to respond at all times … They will be routinely armed, equipped, mobile and ready to support frontline police officers at incidents that require enhanced tactical capabilities …. (Reuters, 2019)

As previously noted, the deployment of ARVs in Aotearoa New Zealand had been raised as an option in both 2001 and 2009, but not acted upon. This trial, however, proposed a subtle but controversial difference to the earlier discussion of ARVs; the officers would be routinely armed with a pistol. Their rifles and other equipment would be carried in the vehicle with them. This appears to have been a step too far for the public, and the trial was beset with negative media and reporting almost from the start (New Zealand Police, n.d., p. 18; Reuters, 2019).

Compounding the negative perception of the trial, in the author's view, was the decision that the ART vehicles were to be large SUVs, painted black (as opposed to the standard white of other New Zealand Police vehicles) and fully decaled with Police livery with four officers inside each wearing a Glock pistol (TVNZ, 2020). In other jurisdictions using ARVs – for example, the Metropolitan Police Service in London, UK – the vehicles used resemble the standard police response vehicle, have between two and three officers and were only distinguishable from other police vehicles by a set of yellow dots and a unique roof marking (to aid aerial support identification) designed to help other police identify they are an armed response team (eliteukforces, 2021).

As criticism of the trial grew, including from ex-police officers, it seemed the concept was destined to fail (TVNZ, 2020; Bond, 2020; Mackenzie, 2020). Those against the trial suggested racial stereotyping, potential for an increase in police use of firearms, potential for negative changes in police behaviour towards citizens and "mission creep" with armed officers being used for response to non-firearms-related events (New Zealand Police, n.d., p. 18).

Unfortunately, much of the commentary, in the author's view, was ill-informed and failed to appreciate how responsible use of ARVs could quite probably reduce police use of firearms and lethal force, thus limiting tragic outcomes, and all the while supporting day-to-day policing so as not to be a drain on resources. The subsequent evaluation report of the trial supported these observations (New Zealand Police, n.d., pp. 15–18).

The ART trial left a distinct impression with the author of a concept that had been sitting on a Police administrator's "back-burner" for some time (perhaps years), and the terrible tragedy which unfolded in Christchurch gave rise to two opportunities regarding it. The first was for Police to be seen to be taking action and doing something in response to the massacres; the second was to test a concept that was worthy of consideration and which may have found its time in history to be trialled. The final impression was of an initiative implemented in haste and without consideration of the public – and surprisingly – police views. For example, the president of the Police Association was quoted as saying:

> If you don't build solid foundations on issues as potentially volatile as armed police, you can't possibly hope to take the community with you, and that is exactly what has happened in this case … [he went on to say in his remarks – pointing to mis-steps, including the appearance of the ART vehicles] … [they] looked pretty sinister in comparison to the police vehicles we are familiar with, despite the fact that those everyday police patrol cars have Glock pistols and Bushmaster rifles in them for officer to use when needed. (Dynon, 2020)

The trial's final evaluation report acknowledged that the trial had been initiated in a hurry and without the ability for evaluation criteria to be clearly set or for the evaluators to develop a methodology to monitor the trial (New Zealand Police, n.d., p. 15). Furthermore, the report highlighted there had been:

> … [a] lack of consultation, particularly with those Māori and Pasifika communities that felt they would be most impacted. It is clear from feedback received that many viewed the lack of early and meaningful consultation with the public, Iwi, and community groups as a significant issue, a threat to police legitimacy and a potential cause for future community tensions. (ibid., p. 18)

The ART trial was doomed, and, ultimately, the police commissioner called an end to it in April 2020, making it clear in nuanced language that due to community concerns, the vehicles were not going to make a return during his time at the helm (New Zealand Police, 2020). However, as late as July 2021, Aotearoa New Zealand's opposition party in parliament – the National Party – was publicly resurrecting discussion of ARTs by calling on the Minister of Police and the commissioner to "re-introduce armed response teams to address the rise in gun violence, in particular against frontline police officers" (Malpass, 2021). Perhaps the idea is not dead and buried after all.

The ARV/ART concept, however, may not have been completely removed from the New Zealand Police response options with regard to armed offenders. As reporting from the IPCA into the death of Anthony Fane (shot by police on 13 February 2020) shows, armed patrols have continued to be used under the label of "reassurance patrols" (Independent Police Conduct Authority, 2021, p. 1).

In the Fane case, four members of the Tauranga AOS were deployed in two marked police patrol cars following a double murder and before those responsible had been caught (ibid., pp. 2–3). The officers involved carried their AOS weapons, dressed in their black AOS uniform, but "… with caps instead of helmets and balaclavas" (ibid., p. 2).

While formalised and regular shift-based ARTs are seemingly off the agenda in Aotearoa New Zealand – at least for now – the same cannot be said with any certainty about the country experiencing a further terrorism-related event (or events). In a previously classified report, released to the "Stuff" news outlet, the government's own national security agencies were of the view that the chance of a "worst-case scenario attack occurring [was] 'very high' within the five years from June 2019" (Manch, 2021). The profile had been prepared in the months following the Christchurch attacks by the Police, Security Intelligence Service and the Department of the Prime Minister and Cabinet (ibid.). The two threat vectors for such an attack were identified as "right-wing extremism and Islamic extremism" (ibid.).

Before concluding this chapter, it is important to note that in 2021 the adjustment and development of policy, procedures and deployment with regard to lethal force and firearms continued to be addressed by the Police in response to what were described as "… high-risk situations" (New Zealand Police, 2021d). In a 2021 announcement, the commissioner detailed a number of new initiatives and funding to deliver yet further changes to the tactical response model. They included:

- Doubling the annual tactical training days for frontline staff, starting with Public Safety teams and Road Policing, with new scenario-based training focused on appropriate tactical response and de-escalation;
- Increasing the number of staff with Advanced Tactical Training (Armed Offender Squad qualified) to roster them on-shift across two areas:
  - As new positions to enable dog units to operate as a two-person dog team
  - As members of Tactical Prevention Teams, which will be part of existing investigative units that are primarily focused on planned operations …
- … having the right intelligence-led deployment framework to guide decision-making through comprehensive risk assessments and proactive offender management …. (New Zealand Police, 2021d)

The new work was described as a result of "… listening to more than 1250 staff around their concerns and ideas to improve staff safety", as well as doing something that seemed missing with the ART work, which was to "… [engage] with Maori, Pacific and Ethnic community leaders …" (ibid.).

The potted history of New Zealand Police presented above, with particular focus on its engagement with firearms and use of lethal force, has shown that while currently viewed by itself as a "routinely unarmed police service", the organisation is anything but. It has throughout its history been involved in one way or another with using, and having to respond to the use of, firearms. In point of fact, the New Zealand Police has gone, in the author's view, full-circle and arrived back at the point where policing started in Aotearoa New Zealand in the mid-late 1800s – namely, as a "heavily armed" agent of the state as reported by Hill (2021).

Many of the changes mentioned above did not happen in isolation. As with the formation of the AOS in the early 1960s, reviews and reports have helped shape the way Police equip, operate and think about armed response. Chapter 6 will provide commentary on four such undertakings from the late 1990s and into the first decade of the 2000s that provided input into those considerations and no doubt shaped the policy thinking and outcomes outlined above.

Bibliography

Battersby, J. (2019). The ghost of New Zealand's terrorism past and present. *National Security Journal, 1*(1), 35–47.

Belich, J. (1986). *The New Zealand wars and the victorian interpretation of racial conflict*. Penguin Books (NZ) Ltd.

Bond, J. (2020, June 5). Armed response teams trial: 'Bizarre' holes in callout data. In *RNZ News*.

Buchanan, K. (2014, September). *Police weapons: New Zealand*. Retrieved from loc.gov: https://www.loc.gov/law/help/police-weapons/new-zealand.php

Dynon, N. (2020). ARTs and the myth of the unarmed police officer. In *Line of defence magazine – Winter 2020*. Line of Defence Magazine.

eliteukforces. (2021, May 5). *Police firearms unit – SCO19*. Retrieved from eliteukforces.info: https://www.eliteukforces.info/police/CO19

Hendy, R. (2012). *The strategic impact of routine arming that New Zealand Police*. School of Government, Victoria University of Wellington.

Hill, R. S. (1986a). *Policing the colonial frontier – Part 1: The history of policing in New Zealand volume one*. V. R. Ward Government Printer.

Hill, R. S. (1986b). *Policing the colonial frontier – Part 2: The history of policing in New Zealand volume one*. GP Books.

Hill, R. S. (1989). *The colonial frontier tamed: New Zealand policing in transition, 1867–1886: The history of policing in New Zealand volume two*. GP Books.

Hill, R. S. (2021, February). *'Police', Te Ara – The encyclopedia of New Zealand*. Retrieved from www.TeAra.govt.nz: www.TeAra.govt.nz/en/police

Hunt, T. (2014, November 15). *Flashback: The Aramoana massacre*. Retrieved from Stuff.co.nz: www.stuff.co.nz/national/crime/Flashback:TheAramoanamassacre

Independent Police Conduct Authority. (2009a). *Police shooting of Halatau Naitoko*. Independent Police Conduct Authority.

Independent Police Conduct Authority. (2009b). *Report on the shooting of Steven Wallace*. Independent Police Conduct Authority.

Independent Police Conduct Authority. (2010). *Independent police conduct authority annual report 2009 – 2010*. : Independent Police Conduct Authority.

Independent Police Conduct Authority. (2013). *Operation eight: The report of the independent police conduct authority*. Independent Police Conduct Authority.

Independent Police Conduct Authority. (2014). *Fatal police shooting of Antony Ratahi*. Independent Police Conduct Authority.

Independent Police Conduct Authority. (2021). *Use of force during fatal shooting in Tauranga justified*. Independent Police Conduct Authority.

Mackenzie, S. (2020, April 17). Cops with guns will make us less safe. In *newsroom.co.nz*. newsroom.co.nz.

Malpass, L. (2021, July 21). *National Party calls on police to reinstate armed response teams*. Retrieved from stuff.co.nz: https://www.stuff.co.nz/national/politics/125813223/national-party-calls-on-police-to-reinstate-armed-response-teams?cid=app-

Manch, T. (2021, May 11). *Risk of worst-case terror attack 'very high' according to Government's Terrorism Risk Profile*. Retrieved from stuff.co.nz: https://www.stuff.co.nz/national/politics/125065298/risk-of-worstcase-terror-attack-very-high-according-to-governments-terrorism-risk-profile?cid=app

MinistryforCultureandHeritage. (2021, January 28). *nzhistory.govt.nz*. RetrievedfromStanGraham's killing spree on West Coast: https://nzhistory.govt.nz/stan-graham-killing-spree-on-west-coast

New Zealand Police. (n.d.). *Armed response team trial evaluation report*. New Zealand Police.

New Zealand Police. (2005, May 19). *Replacement due for police rifles*. Retrieved from police.govt.nz: https://www.police.govt.nz/news/release/1923

New Zealand Police. (2010, June 30). *New Zealand Police annual report for the year ended 30 June 2010*. New Zealand Government.

New Zealand Police. (2011, June 30). *New Zealand Police annual report for year ended 30 June 2011*. New Zealand Government.

New Zealand Police. (2012, June 30). *New Zealand Police annual report for the year ended 30 June 2012*. New Zealand Government.

New Zealand Police. (2016, December). *Inside the STG*. Retrieved from ten-one.police.govt.nz: http://www.ten-one.police.govt.nz/tenone/December2016National6.htm

New Zealand Police. (2019). *NZ Police tactical options research report 2018*. New Zealand Police.

New Zealand Police. (2020, April 24). *Armed Response Teams trial ends, evaluation underway*. Retrieved from police.govt.nz: https://www.police.govt.nz/news/release/armed-response-teams-trial-ends-evaluation-underway

New Zealand Police. (2021a, February 17). *Armed offenders squad*. Retrieved from police.govt.nz: https://www.police.govt.nz/about-us/structure/teams-units

New Zealand Police. (2021b, February 2021). *The establishment of New Zealand Police*. Retrieved from Police.govt.nz: https://www.police.govt.nz/about-us/history-and-museum

New Zealand Police. (2021c). *Officers killed by criminal acts*. Retrieved from police.govt.nz: https://www.police.govt.nz/aboutus/history-and-museum/memorial/officers-killed-criminal-acts

New Zealand Police. (2021d, September 22). *Improving the safety and capability of frontline Police*. Retrieved from police.govt.nz: https://www.police.govt.nz/news/release/improving-safety-and-capability-frontline-police

New Zealand Police Assurance Group. (2013). *Review of increased accessibility to firearms*. New Zealand Police.

NZ History. (2020, November 13). *Thirteen shot dead at Aramoana*. Retrieved from nzhistory.govt.nz: https://nzhistory.govt.nz/david-gray-kills-13-aramoana

NZPA. (2008, October 23). *Chronology of fatal shootings by NZ police*. Retrieved from nzherald.co.nz: https://www.nzherald.co.nz/nz/chronology-of-fatal-shootings-by-nzpolice/YKKKUQAUZCUPAGQLL4G4NSPNHE

Osborne, J. (1990a). *Handguns and police in New Zealand*. South Pacific Armoury.

Osborne, J. (1990b). *Carbines and police in New Zealand 1840 – 1990*. South Pacific Armoury.

Perry, N. (2011). *Firearms and Taser policy*. New Zealand Police.

Rattenbury, R. (2020). *A battered proud badge – Tales of policing a young country*. Rangitawa Publishing.

Reuters. (2019, October 18). New Zealand police to start armed patrols after Christchurch massacre. In *The Guardian world news*. The Guardian.

Rorke, J. (1993). *Policing two peoples: A history of police in the Bay of Plenty 1867–1992*. New Zealand Police.

Royal Commission of Inquiry. (2020). *Report of the Royal Commission of inquiry into the terrorist attack on Christchurch masjidain on 15 March 2019*. New Zealand Government.

Samkin, G., Allen, C., & Wallace, K. (2010). Repairing organisational legitimacy: The case of the New Zealand Police. *Australasian Accounting, Business and Finance Journal, 4*(3), 23–45.

Shortt, R. (1999). *Helensville shooting safety audit*. New Zealand Police.

Shortt, R. S. (2000). *Are the New Zealand Police on target? An investigation of alternative models of police response to dangerous and unlawful firearms incidents*. Victoria University.

Swinton, N. (2019, September). *A turning point for firearms regulation: Implications of legislative and operational reforms in the wake of the Christchurch shootings*. Retrieved from fullbright.org.nz: https://www.fulbright.org.nz/wp-content/uploads/2019/09/N-Swinton-AxfordFellow2019-Report-SEPT2019.pdf

Tso, M. (2018, December 23). *Crime – New Zealand Police anti-terrorist unit costs taxpayers $6.2 million*. Retrieved from Stuff.co.nz: https://www.stuff.co.nz/national/crime/109460758/new-zealand-police-antiterrorist-unit-costs-taxpayers-62-million

TVNZ. (2020, March 5). Armed response teams not being used for what police said they would. In *1 News*. TVNZ.

Unknown, O.-N. (2021, June 14). *Giving new life to a faithful old companion*. Retrieved from smith-wessonforum.com: http://smith-wessonforum.com/gun-leather-carry-gear/475155-giving-new-life-faithful-old-companion.html

Chapter 5
Policies, Procedures, Equipment, Training, Tactics and Specialist Groups

Policies and Procedures

In Aotearoa New Zealand firearm ownership, possession, use and sale are legislated for in the *Arms Act 1983* (NZL) (New Zealand Government, 1983). The Act, in section 3(2)(a)(ii) and (iii), specifically excludes the New Zealand Police from being governed by its requirements, alongside the New Zealand Defence Force, New Zealand Customs and various other government entities (ibid.). There is no legislation governing the deployment and use of firearms by New Zealand police officers. This is deemed a purely "operational decision" and left for the commissioner and Police executive to determine.

Possession, deployment and use of firearms by police are governed by internal policies and guidelines. Those various instruments include "General Instructions" with those relevant to firearms being found in the "F" (for Firearms) series, namely, F060, Carrying of Firearms by Police; F061, Use of Firearms by Police; F062, Fire Orders; F063, Police Firearms; and F066, Discharge of Firearms by Police (New Zealand Police, 2007) (New Zealand Police, 2009), and in a Police Manual with chapters on many topics which includes guidance and tools with regard to the use of force (New Zealand Police, 2017). Those two elements of the Police's use of force eco-system (General Instructions and the Police Manual) will be discussed below to help build a picture of how Police go about delivering responses that can include the use of lethal force.

The first element to be considered will be the Police Manual, and in particular the Use of Force chapter that is published and accessed, through the internal organisational Intranet (New Zealand Police, 2017). While the *Policing Act 2008* (NZL) does not mention this particular document (as opposed to its specific reference to General Instructions), it can be argued that it falls within the broader "… commissioner's circulars or applicable local orders …" that all Police employees (constabulary members) must obey and be guided by (New Zealand Government, 2008). The

R. S. Shortt, *Lethal Force and New Zealand Police*,
https://doi.org/10.1007/978-3-031-05269-9_5

manual will also be discussed first as it contains two specific decision-making tools designed to guide police officers in responding to incidents and in choosing which tactical options they should deploy at any given time, in any given circumstance. These decision-making tools are, in the author's view, most likely to be used before the guidance presented in the firearms-related General Instructions come "into play".

The section of the Use of Force chapter which discusses firearms revisits the law (both the *Policing Act 2008* and the *Crimes Act 1961* (NZL)) and provides organisational commentary on Police use of force (New Zealand Police, 2017). The chapter reminds officers that "One of the defining features of Police organisations, which captures their unique role in society, is their lawful authorisation to use force in certain circumstances" (note: reflect here on Seamus Miller's concept regarding "social institutions" and Police's "institutional justification" concerning the use of force) (ibid., p. 3).

In the subsection of the chapter titled "The strategic importance of use of force" (New Zealand Police, 2017, p. 3), officers are advised the use of force is a "key risk environment for constables and the public" going on to state that 1000 or more injuries occur each year through police use of force (ibid.). Later, the text refers to an important policy setting applying to the Police's use of force and the organisation's ability to learn from instances where force was used, namely, the "… strategic goals such as minimising risk and maximising safety" (ibid.).

The "minimising risk and maximising safety" goal is familiar to the author as it was introduced during the re-vamp of Police district training introduced after the Staff Safety Project in the late 1990s (New Zealand Police, 1998) (Author's personal knowledge as the primary architect of the Staff Safety Tactical Training (SSTT) programme).

The essence of the term was that police officers should always approach situations with the objective of minimising the risk to themselves, the public and the person(s) they are dealing with while also maximising the safety of themselves, their colleagues, the public and the person(s) being interacted with.

The rationale behind the statement was an attempt to have a high-level tactical aim for officers to consider when undertaking their duties at a time when the author was arguing through his research that there was a paucity of such clearly and concisely stated aims, at the strategic, operational and tactical levels, when it came to the use of force by New Zealand Police (Shortt, 2000, pp. 14–17).

An example of such a high-level statement was the one introduced by the Victoria Police, in Australia, as part of Project Beacon in the 1990s. There, Police determined that "the success of an operation will be primarily judged on the extent to which the use of force is avoided or minimised" (Office of Police Integrity Victoria, 2005). The statement and its application was subsequently further supported and reinforced by the Office of Police Integrity in its 2005 review recommendations regarding fatal police shootings in Victoria (ibid.).

The closest the New Zealand Police use of force chapter comes to defining such a position are the words under the heading "Factors to consider before using force" where it is stated:

> Police's preferred tactical option for resolving incidents where Police action is necessary in response to uncooperative subjects is tactical communication [in other words, talking the person into cooperation]. (New Zealand Police, 2017, p. 4)

The section involved goes on to state that while use of force should be avoided, if it cannot be, then the "constables must, according to law, use only reasonable force …" (ibid.).

In addition, the Police Manual's chapter equips officers with two decision-making tools to help them decide what to do in situations where force may be necessary. The first of those is the TENR operational threat assessment process (New Zealand Police, 2019). TENR is an acronym for Threat, Exposure, Necessity and Response. Police describe the process as:

> … not an end in itself – where appropriate, it guides:
>
> - effective training, specifically staff safety technical management
> - robust systems
> - operational preparedness
> - accurate and timely intelligence
> - effective communication
> - quality supervision and leadership
> - robust command and control framework
> - the Tactical Options Framework. (ibid.)

The TENR process is deemed to apply to "… all constables, authorised officers [personnel without a power of arrest, but who work with arrested persons and in custody areas and who wear a uniform that is different to that of constables], any other Police employees who from time to time may need to conduct a threat or risk assessment …" (ibid.).

TENR also applies additional administrative requirements on a police officer. It states:

> Employees **must** ensure [emphasis added]:
>
> - their training certifications in all required competencies are current [see references in the 'Training' section below to the introduction of SSTT training]
> - they carry their authorised equipment and appointments when they deploy on duty [see references in the 'Equipment' section below]
> - they are fit for duty
> - they understand and comply with legislation, policy and procedures
> - they follow lawful orders and instructions
> - they report identified training, knowledge and experience gaps to their supervisors and seek guidance when necessary. (ibid.)

With regard to firearms deployment and use, the above requirements mean an officer needs to have completed their mandated firearms refresher and skill maintenance training and been certified as competent to operate both the Glock pistol and the Bushmaster rifle.

Additionally, and importantly, as will be discussed later in this book, the TENR process also sets out the New Zealand Police's organisational responsibilities regarding the operational health and safety of police staff. It states that the organisation is responsible for:

- accurate policy and procedures;
- training;
- supervision, and
- suitable equipment. (New Zealand Police, 2019)

Furthermore, the TENR process details the organisation's responsibility for taking:

... reasonable steps to:

- acquire and keep up to date knowledge of work health and safety matters
- gain an understanding of the nature of the hazards and risks associated with
- operational policing
- use appropriate resources and processes to eliminate or minimise risk to health and safety from operational policing
- ensure appropriate processes for receiving and considering information regarding hazards and risks, and for responding in a timely way to that information. (ibid.)

Thus, the organisation establishes a direct link between its own policy and procedures and the wider national workplace health and safety regime applying in Aotearoa New Zealand under the *Health and Safety at Work Act 2015* (NZL) (Worksafe Mahi Haumaru Aotearoa, 2019). Unlike the Defence Force and the country's security and intelligence agencies, New Zealand Police are not exempted from the requirements of the Act (New Zealand Government, 2015).

Elsewhere in the TENR process, the question of "necessity for action" arises and is addressed. Here, the guidance is for officers to consider a delayed response if appropriate and to endeavour to, once again, "**maximise safety** and **minimise risk**" [emphasis in the original] (New Zealand Police, 2019).

TENR goes on to remind officers to act in accordance with their Police Integrated Tactical Training (PITT) (the next evolution of the SSTT programme mentioned above and below) and to consider the Tactical Options Framework (TOF).

The TOF was originally modelled on the Tactical Options tool instigated by the Victoria Police, Australia, following Task Force Victor and Project Beacon which examined the high number of people being shot by Victorian police in the 1990s and which brought about a change in operational philosophy, training and approach to volatile and dangerous incidents (Office of Police Integrity Victoria, 2005).

The framework is depicted as a multi-coloured circle with a single pivoting clock-style hand linking it to TENR commentary, and it guides a police officer through three "degrees" of engagement (New Zealand Police, 2019). The first and preferred is "Presence and tactical communication" (in essence talking with the person) and is used when a subject is deemed "cooperative" (ibid.).

The next segment is titled "Low degree of force" and is suggested for situations where the subject is displaying "Passive resistance" or verging into the "Active resistance" zone. The third and final segment is labelled "High degree of force" and is considered to apply when the subject is moving from "Active resistance" into "Assaultive" or at worst "GBH[1] or death". While "presence and tactical communication" is shown as continuing across all three "degrees", once an officer

[1] Grievous bodily harm – a serious assault covered in the *Crimes Act 1961* (NZL)

is assessing a subject as displaying "Active resistance" or worse, all the listed tactical options come into play (ibid.).

It is at this point that the use of lethal force is being considered, although those words are not used anywhere in either tool.

The framework lists the options and types of force as:

- officer presence and tactical communication
- mechanical restraints eg [sic] handcuffing
- empty hand techniques eg [sic] physical restraints and strikes
- OC spray
- baton – Taser – dogs – weapon(s) of opportunity
- Firearms and other force with serious implications. (ibid.)

The other guidance given to an officer considering using force is to "Prepare, show and use force" (ibid.). That is described in the framework as:

- 'Prepare' force means carriage of a tactical option.
- 'Show' force means presenting a tactical option at a subject.
- 'Use' force means the application of force on a subject. (ibid.)

The final important advice imparted by the framework states:

> The legal authority to use force is derived from the law, not the TOF. If you use force that is not authorised by law, or is excessive, the fact that you relied on the TOF will not justify or legitimise the use of that force. **Reasonable force** [emphasis in the original] includes force that is **necessary** and **proportionate**, given **all the circumstances known at the time**. (ibid.)

So, police officers planning on undertaking action against an armed, or potentially armed, subject must apply the TENR threat assessment tool, while also taking consideration of the TOF, all the while appreciating that the law will be used to judge the appropriateness of their decisions and actions, before then embarking on consideration of the next element of the Police use of force eco-system, General Instructions.

General Instructions are legislated for in the *Policing Act 2008* (NZL) under sections 28–30.

They are deemed lawful instructions (see s. 30 of the Act) along with any commissioner's circulars or "applicable local orders" that all Police employees (constabulary members) must obey and be guided by (New Zealand Government, 2008).

The instructions, with regard to firearms, remind officers of their use of force obligations as set out in the *Crimes Act 1961* (NZL) and describe when an officer can resort to using a firearm.

The F060 General Instruction, in essence New Zealand Police's overarching policy statement on firearms, says:

> (1) The New Zealand Police is generally an unarmed service. It is recognised however that firearms need to be available quickly, easily, and safely. The principle of minimum personal carriage and minimum visibility of firearms and related equipment is to be applied at all times.
>
> (2) Firearms are not to be carried on the person as a matter of general practice, but may be carried in authorised police vehicles to ensure they are available if needed. (New Zealand Police, 2007)

Following those "context setting" statements, the F060 instruction goes on to set out quite a broad range of instances when firearms can be carried on the authorisation of district commanders (officers holding the rank of superintendent and in charge of the 12 Police districts in Aotearoa New Zealand). The instruction states:

> (3) District Commanders may authorise the carriage of police approved firearms in police vehicles, as necessary to ensure members have ready access to firearms should the circumstances dictate. NCO patrols [Non-commissioned Officers of the rank of sergeant and senior sergeant], first response units [patrol cars], CIB patrols [Criminal Investigation Branch detectives], dog patrols, and single crewed patrols are examples where such authorisation should be considered. (ibid.)

The instruction goes on to say that the firearm(s) must be carried in approved security cabinets and that the security of the firearm(s) and cabinet keys are of high importance. Alarms can also be considered for vehicles that carry firearms, but the decisions around that issue and any other security measures are delegated to relevant district commanders. Carriage of any firearm on the person by an officer is described in the following manner:

> (6) Members may carry police issue firearms on the person when there is clear and specific evidence that a risk of encountering any of the circumstance referred to in General Instruction F61 exists. Carriage is to be authorised by a District Commissioned Officer or NCO or Police Communications Centre Commissioned Officer or NCO when practical to do so. If an authorising officer is not available members may exercise their own discretion, but shall advise their supervisor at the first reasonable opportunity. (ibid.)

An exception to the above is provided for commissioned officers and NCOs who are authorised to carry a police firearm in circumstances as outline above, but without the need to seek specific authority. They are simply required to advise the nearest communication centre officer or NCO about what they are doing (ibid.).

Furthermore, F060 (8) goes on to describe six other instances when a police officer may carry a firearm on their person when on duty:

- at 'security designated' airports [note: the author's understands this to mean international airports];
- on Diplomatic Protection Squad duties;
- performing duties described in F063;
- pursuant to a written operation instruction, and
- when specifically authorised by a District commander. (ibid.)

The above clearly outlines quite an extensive array of situations and instances where firearms can be carried in vehicles or by an officer when working on specific duties.

One of the most often quoted General Instructions related to firearms within New Zealand Police, and in PCA/IPCA reporting on police shootings, is F061 Use of Firearms by Police (New Zealand Police, 2007). While F060 sets out what the Police policy is on firearms and when they should be deployed or carried, F061 deals specifically with their use. It is, again in the author's 34-year experience in New Zealand Police, the instruction that is most often referred to in regard to firearms. For example, budding AOS members had to know the instruction verbatim when attending the AOS Induction and Qualifying course at the RNZPC while the author was involved with it. For that reason, F061 is reproduced in full below:

F061 – Use of Firearms by Police

(1) Members must always be aware of their personal responsibilities in the use of firearms. Under Section 62 of the Crimes Act 1961 a member is criminally liable for any excess force used. An overriding requirement in law is that the minimum force must bc applied to effect the purpose. Where practical Police should not use a firearm unless it can be done without endangering other persons.

(2) Police member shall not use a firearm except in the following circumstances:

(a) to DEFEND THEMSELVES OR OTHERS (Section 48 Crimes Act 1961) if they fear death or grievous bodily harm to themselves or others, and they cannot reasonably protect themselves, or others, in a less violent manner [emphasis in the original];

(b) to ARREST an offender (Section 39 Crimes Act 1961) if they believe on reasonable grounds that the offender poses a threat of death or grievous bodily harm in resisting his or her arrest;

AND the arrest cannot be reasonably effected in a less violent manner
AND the arrest cannot be delayed without danger to other persons;

(c) to PREVENT THE ESCAPE of an offender (Section 40 of the Crimes Act 1961) if

(d) it is believed on reasonable grounds that the offender poses a threat of death or grievous bodily harm to any person (whether an identified individual or members of the public at large)
AND he or she takes flight to avoid arrest, OR he or she escapes after his or her arrest
AND such flight cannot reasonably be prevented in a less violent manner.

(3) In any case an offender is not to be shot:

(a) until he or she has first been called upon to surrender unless in the circumstances it is impracticable and unsafe to do so
AND

(b) it is clear that he or she cannot be disarmed or arrested without first being shot
AND

(c) in the circumstances further delay in apprehending him or her would be dangerous or impracticable. (New Zealand Police, 2007)

The instruction is deemed so integral to Police that it is printed in an "aide memoire" format on the inside covers of all Police-issue notebooks as stated in F062 – Fire Orders (3) (ibid.). Furthermore, "Pocket-sized laminated cards bearing the same information shall be stored with all Police firearms, including firearms safes in police stations and in vehicle firearm security cabinets, to be available for members to uplift and carry with them should they deem it necessary" (Ibid.), and during formal firearms training, police officers are also expected to satisfy the instructor(s) that they have "thorough knowledge and understanding of F061" (ibid.).

These various efforts to communicate F061 to staff are entirely consistent with section 29 of the *Policing Act 2008* (NZL) which requires the commissioner to "… take reasonable steps to ensure that all general instructions are communicated to all Police employees" (New Zealand Government, 2008). Given the relevance of F061 to the use of lethal force, the multiple channels used to disseminate it is both understandable and to be applauded.

For anyone who has read the reporting of the PCA/IPCA concerning use of lethal force by Police, F061 and references to it will be familiar. However, in a number of the cases reviewed for this book, it is clear that a number of shootings unfolded rapidly and with high tension, and it is doubtful, in the author's view, that F061 was in fact re-read in any of the forms provided.

Instead, the author surmises, the familiar words from his days in policing were probably spoken or borne in mind – "Remember, F61 applies".

As can be seen from the layout of F061, it closely follows the wording of the *Crimes Act 1961* (NZL) and the use of force provisions discussed earlier in Chap. 2. Section (3)(a) of the instruction, the "called upon to surrender" requirement, gives rise to the words used in the title of Chap. 1 – "Armed police, drop your weapon" – the standard words imbedded in police officers' minds as the appropriate way a) to clearly identify yourself and the fact you are armed and b) to seek an unmistakable gesture of surrender.

Interestingly, it is Police who impose the call to surrender requirement on officers, while the *Crimes Act 1961* (NZL) is silent on the issue, other than to say "… [can you do this] in a less violent manner" in ss. 39 and 40. It can be reasonably concluded that Police added the call to surrender to the instruction to provide an opportunity for a "less violent" approach to materialise should the armed person hear the challenge and discard whatever weapon they may have.

However, as we read in F061 (3)(a), the call to surrender is conditional. The instruction removes the absolute need for it to be given by stating "… unless in the circumstances it is impracticable and unsafe to do so" (New Zealand Police, 2007). Sergeant Guthrie, the officer killed at Aramoana, called on the gunman he was confronting to surrender and was immediately shot dead (see Chap. 3, p. 41). So, returning to the opening paragraph in the introduction to this book, we now understand why the call to surrender may not have been issued to some of the people shot between 2000 and 2019, but more on that later in Chap. 8.

In essence, F061 requires an armed police officer to ask themselves three questions, in an often compressed and turbulent timeframe, while under the effects of adrenaline:

1) Am I, or another, at risk of death or grievous bodily harm?
2) Can I deal with the person(s) in a less violent way, perhaps later?
3) Is it safe for me to call on them to surrender?

The order of the questions can be challenged. Potentially, Question 2 should be the first question asked. The author suggests, however, that for this to be the case, Question 2 needs to be asked well before an armed police officer is "eyeballing" an armed person over the sights of a Police Glock or Bushmaster. Once that point has been reached, the argument could well be made that Question 2 has become redundant by dint of time, place and actions.

There is also an argument, the author posits, for F061 to be dramatically shortened to include just those three simple questions, particularly now that an officer must also consider TENR and the TOF. F061 has, however, "stood the test of time" (New Zealand Police, 2001) and seems, given the PCA/IPCA has never queried its structure, likely to stay unchanged for some time yet. And, ultimately, as the instruction reminds every reader in its second sentence, "Under Section 62 of the Crimes

Act 1961 a member is criminally liable for any excess force used" (New Zealand Police, 2007). A point well and truly made in all of the use of force policy and procedures reviewed here.

Having discussed the above matters, it is almost time to move on to consider other aspects of a police officer's environment regarding use of force – things like equipment and training – but, before we do, one important aspect of Police firearms use should be included here given its direct relevance to the policy and procedure context. That aspect is the philosophy of the New Zealand Police concerning the outcome sought from using firearms as the selected tactical option. What does the police officer set out to achieve when they pull the trigger? Put another way, what is the police officer's intention when they decide to pull the trigger?

New Zealand Police emphasise that the use of a firearm against another person is to quickly neutralise or incapacitate that person (Independent Police Conduct Authority, 2019, p. 21). In pursuit of that outcome, Police training is to shoot at the largest target area available – the subject's torso. The intent or objective is never framed as being to kill the person. The IPCA also resorts to the use of the term "incapacitate" in its reports into Police shootings. The New Zealand Police position is similar to that of Police organisations in the UK where instant incapacitation is the desired objective of the use of a police firearm (e.g. see Squires & Kennison, 2010).

Incapacitation and neutralisation are words used by New Zealand Police to also avoid the less palatable concept of "shooting to kill", one might suggest.

That was certainly the experience of the author, who was trained in the use of Police firearms and who carried them as a uniformed constable, detective, personal protection officer for VIPs and member of an Armed Offenders Squad. In Aotearoa New Zealand police officers were trained to aim for the centre mass of the torso and to shoot until the threat was incapacitated, the training recommendation during that time being to use a "double tap" where two shots are fired in quick succession or simply to continue firing until incapacitation is achieved (Report on the Shooting of Stephen Jon Bellingham, IPCA, 2009, p. 28) (Independent Police Conduct Authority, 2019, p. 21) (Author's personal experience) (also see Invercargill Shooting, Police Complaints Authority, 2001, p. 15).

Interestingly, the IPCA has also concluded in three cases that the shooting of a subject in the head at close range, an action almost certain to result in death, was justifiable and lawful. The findings arose during the IPCA's investigations of the shootings of Haidar Mahdi, Antony Ratahi and an unnamed hostage-taker.

In the Ratahi case, for example, an STG officer stated that his training was to shoot individuals in the head to achieve instant incapacitation and that he felt the need to achieve this outcome with regard to Ratahi and the situation he (the officer) was in. The Authority accepted that decision and explanation (Independent Police Conduct Authority, 2014).

Furthermore, the Authority has also accepted the need for officers to fire multiple shots at a subject until "incapacitation" was observed; for example, in the IPCA reports into the shootings of Wallace, Mahdi, Kelly-Tumarae, "Mr X", Marshall, and Toms.

Perhaps the most notable occasion where the IPCA has deemed multiple shots justified was the fatal shooting of Anthony Fane by two AOS officers in February 2020. During that encounter, the officers fired 49 shots from their Bushmaster rifles at Fane who was seated in a car some 5–10 metres from them. The shots were fired from the moment Fane's vehicle and the Police vehicles came to a stop and continued – as one officer recounted – until he "… saw Mr Fane slump down in his seat towards the right pillar" (Independent Police Conduct Authority, 2021, p. 6). The officer admitted he did not know how many shots he had fired. He had fired 22 of his available 30 rounds. His fellow officer had fired 27 (ibid., p. 4).

In summary, New Zealand Police would prefer police officers talk their way out of potentially violent situations while constantly assessing and reassessing the need to use force and endeavouring to maximise safety while minimising risk to all involved. But, the organisation accepts that on occasion a firearm will be the most appropriate tactical option and that incapacitation and neutralisation of the threat posed in such situations are best achieved by shooting until that outcome has been visibly achieved. A call to surrender before doing so may or may not be given, and ultimately the law of the land will determine whether or not the shooting was reasonable and, therefore, justified.

Equipment

When the author joined Police in 1977, the standard items of equipment carried by an on-duty constable were a notebook, pen, set of handcuffs (in a belt pouch), short wooden baton (e.g. the author's was 37 cm long[2], with a leather hand thong, carried in a long trouser pocket), torch (if it was evening or night shift) and a two-way portable radio (of varying reliability). At the commencement of a shift, the sergeant would ask for the presentation of appointments, and each constable would hold the aforementioned items (excluding the radio) for inspection.

The firearms available to police officers at that time consisted of the .38 Smith and Wesson, 6-shot revolver and the .22 Sako Vixen, bolt-action, 5-shot, hunting-style rifle (replaced by the .223 Remington Model 7, 5-shot, bolt-action rifle in 1993 – see New Zealand Police, 2005a). There was no body armour. The revolver had to be manually loaded, unloaded and reloaded as no mechanical means (such as a "speed loader") was provided. Small, belt-mounted, single restraining-dome, leather holsters were available. However, often – as previously commented upon in this work – they were shunned for the simplicity of stuffing the revolver into a trouser pocket. Perhaps, reflecting back to the early 1900s, when Police-issue pistols

[2] The author's baton was slightly longer (approx. 3–4 cm) and heavier than the baton issued to him by New Zealand Police during initial training. This was because he was given an older and much longer Mounted Police baton made of very hard wood and approx. 50–60 cm long. The baton was cut down to an acceptable length to fit in his baton pocket and was carried by him throughout his uniformed policing career.

were marketed and known as "pocket pistols" (Osborne, Handguns and Police in New Zealand, 1990a, pp. 10, 17–18, 20), an organisational habit had formed, ultimately, only history knows for sure.

That method of carriage also helped address another issue peculiar to the time, the reluctance of the New Zealand Police to have armed officers (with the exception of the AOS) seen on the streets or in media reporting. If a holstered revolver was worn, the expectation was that it would be covered from sight by a tunic, duty jacket or suit jacket if in plain clothes. This "firearms shyness" may also have contributed to the over-reliance by Police on issuing the revolver. The author cannot recall ever being issued with a rifle when called upon to attend an incident that required him to be armed until the late 1980s when he was a sergeant (Author's personal experience). Readers will no doubt recall that General Instruction F060 (1) still continues to seek " … minimum visibility of firearms and related equipment …" (refer above).

Times have changed.

Today, a uniformed police officer, in Aotearoa New Zealand, going out on duty will be equipped with an individually fitted stab-resistant vest (known by the acronym SRBA and capable of being made bullet-resistant through the addition of hardened plates); attached to it or on the duty belt will be a taser (see below), a canister of OC spray (pepper spray), an extendable metal baton (approx. 41 cm long when extended and 16 cm when closed and holstered) and handcuffs. This will be supplemented by a personal radio, police-issue iPhone, personal protective equipment pouch (containing surgical gloves and a CPR face-shield) and a high-powered – but compact – LED torch (Author's personal knowledge and experience).

With regard to firearms, and as previously mentioned, the modern police officer has access to a Glock model 17, semi-automatic pistol which fires a 9 × 9 mm bullet and has a magazine capacity of 17 rounds (the officer will also have a "quick fix" clip already on their duty belt to enable the rapid attachment of the Glock's holster and Glock when needed). The rifle is now the 5.56 mm Bushmaster XM 15 M4A3, Patrolman, semi-automatic weapon with a 20- or 30-round capacity magazine (New Zealand Police, 2005a) (Buchanan, 2014) (New Zealand Police, 2005b, p. 6) (Independent Police Conduct Authority, 2021).

Change was not limited to operational staff, however. By the mid-1980s, AOS officers, who originally just wore a different style shirt and trousers to their colleagues, or black one-piece overalls and a beret when the author joined their ranks, now also had access to personally fitted bullet-resistant vests and ballistic helmets to provide additional protection during callouts (Rorke, 1993, p. 382), "distraction device" grenades (commonly called "stun grenades") and a wider range of firearms than their uniformed colleagues, such as the 7.62 mm Ruger Marksman, "sniper-style" rifle; the 870 Remington, pump-action shotgun; and the 37 mm federal, tear gas canister launcher (Buchanan, 2014) (Author's personal knowledge).

These new additions to police officers' equipment inventory came over time and did not all arrive all at once. The first shifts in equipment and training occurred towards the end of the 1990s when the commissioner initiated a review of staff safety including equipment and training following a series of incidents in which police officers were seriously assaulted. The assaults had caused public concern and angst for the Police Association, the union representing rank-and-file officers (Author's personal knowledge as a member of the Staff Safety Review).

Later, in 2006, another significant development was the trialling and later introduction (in 2011) of the taser – initially selectively to specific officers and then later to all operational officers. The model chosen was the TASER X26, a conducted energy "less-than-lethal" weapon (Buchanan, 2014). It can be used by firing prongs (connected to the device by wires) which lodge in the subject's clothing or skin and deliver an incapacitating jolt of electrical energy or by having its prongs pressed against a subject and then activated. The taser comes with an attached recording capability that activates when the weapon is brought to the ready state and is presented (aimed at a person with the red dot aiming mark illuminated). It captures both sound and video footage of any presentation. Taser was viewed as a tactical option that would bridge the gap between equipment already on issue (baton, handcuffs, OC spray) and firearms.

As already mentioned, the equipment-related changes arose as the result of reviews and reports completed over the years. Some of those reviews and reports will be outlined and commented upon in Chap. 6.

In summary, the New Zealand Police now fields officers whose equipment is world-class and exceeds, in a number of ways, the equipment available to their nearest counterparts in various Australian police jurisdictions.

Training

New Zealand Police recruits the majority of its staff directly from the country's civilian population. Occasionally, forays are made into jurisdictions with similar legal and policing frameworks in an effort to recruit already serving police officers, such as the efforts made in the early 2000s to recruit police from the UK, when there was a pressing need to accelerate the process of recruitment and training. Those selected for training are known as recruits, and it is while they are at the Royal New Zealand Police College in Porirua (or at another temporary training site) that most new staff encounter firearms and are trained in their use.

The college-based 16 weeks of general training includes 9 days of specific training " … how to use Glock and Bushmaster M4 firearms, and the theory behind Police response, survival strategies, searching, high risk arrests, family harm interactions, high risk vehicle stops, and shooting in reduced light conditions" (New Zealand Police, 2021b, p. 26) and range work where proficiency in firing is developed (Newman, 2020). Some new officers may have experience with firearms from their civilian life (e.g. sports or hunting), and some may have previous military or police service which also brings with it familiarity in the use of weapons (New Zealand Police, 2021c) (Author's personal knowledge).

The fundamental difference, however, in the training police officers receive concerning firearms is that they are taught to use them to shoot people and to do so in the community which they police as part of the lethal force option with which Police are empowered. That, as Miller described, gives police officers a special role and power within a liberal, democratic society. A licence to kill, if you will. Once a recruit has successfully completed their training across all aspects of being a police officer, including use of weapons, they graduate and are posted to an operational district, of which there are 12 covering Aotearoa New Zealand.

Once in a district, the new officers join their colleagues in continuing to maintain their knowledge and skills in the use of firearms through what is known as "district training". That process is delivered by trainers who seek to ensure that all operational officers, irrespective of where they may be based across the country or their length of service, receive a standardised programme of refresher and skill maintenance training in all of the weapons on issue or available to them (New Zealand Police, 2021b, p. 26).

In the late 1990s, the Staff Safety Review (see additional commentary in Chap. 6), as well as recommending equipment changes such as the introduction of the extendable baton and OC spray, also recommended the redesign of district training to ensure dedicated time was allocated to tactics and the safe and effective use of equipment. That included the use of the standard police firearms. The training became known as Staff Safety Tactical Training (SSTT) (New Zealand Police, 1998, pp. 48–58).

Before the SSTT programme's introduction, district trainers would receive a list of topics to be covered by them during allocated training time and worked to fit in as much of the list as possible in the time they knew was available in their particular locations. While some targets were set for aspects of the training, such as refresher range practice with firearms and remedial training if needed, no formal accreditation process was applied to what was being delivered (New Zealand Police, 1998, p. 48) (Author's personal knowledge as the primary architect of the SSTT programme).

District training time was (and in all probability still is) a precious commodity in policing (New Zealand Police, 1998, p. 48). It comes at the end of a long list of duties that had first call on a police officer's time, for example, comments on that very issue were publicly aired in news reporting following the Christchurch massacres in 2019 when forest fires in the Tasman district meant firearms refresher training was disrupted (Newman, 2020). That was not by any means a new nor uniquely Aotearoa New Zealand phenomena, as was evidenced by Her Majesty's Inspectorate of Constabulary in the UK commenting in 1997 that "… refresher training deadlines are not being met; this exposes the police service and staff to increased risk and criticism …" (New Zealand Police, 1998, p. 17).

The "constant pressures" on refresher training, as referenced in the Staff Safety Project's report (New Zealand Police, 1998, p. 48), came from four primary areas.

Firstly, rostered shifts had to be staffed and covered, and so the re-rostering of officers from "less important" work to cover absences (both planned and unplanned) was paramount to maintaining 24/7 coverage. Secondly, officers were required to attend court to give evidence in their own or other officers' cases. Attending court was (and probably still is) taken very seriously, and nothing, not even night shift

(2300 hrs–0700 hrs), was allowed to interfere (Author's personal knowledge as the reviewer of district training for the Staff Safety Project).

Next came the need to cover extra duties that might arise from time to time in the form of "special operations" – for example, helping the CIB execute search warrants, staffing a visit by a VIP or policing a major sporting event. Then came leave, including accumulated time-off gained by doing the duties just mentioned that may have also led to rostered days off being missed. Leave balances are always an issue for Police management, and the reduction of leave and time-off owed was a high priority (ibid.).

Finally, at the end of the line, came district training. The training included the opportunity to have new, changed or recent case law explained, district orders or procedures updated or reinforced and – if you were lucky – some time spent in refresher training with batons and firearms (ibid.). As late as 2013, a district commander was still raising within the Police executive the "difficulty" of releasing staff to attend training (New Zealand Police, 2013a, p. 6).

SSTT, therefore, aimed to introduce three new concepts to tackle the issue of time and competency. The first was dedicated – "ring-fenced" – time in the district training roster for the delivery of integrated hands-on refresher and skill maintenance training with equipment such as batons, handcuffs, OC spray and firearms (and, ultimately, taser was added to that list). The second concept was competency and certification. Officers needed to demonstrate they could meet the standards required to be deemed safe and proficient in the use of the weapons they carried or accessed and be signed off by an approved and trained instructor – as they did when undergoing RNZPC training as recruits (New Zealand Police, 1998, pp. 48–58) (Author's personal knowledge as the primary architect of the SSTT programme).

The concept of the SSTT programme came about after reviewing the Victoria Police training introduced as the result of Project Beacon (New Zealand Police, 1998). That project arose out of a recognition by Victoria Police that officers were often resorting to the use of firearms to resolve situations and that despite firing less bullets than other police jurisdictions in Australia, they were killing more people. In other words, they were well trained in shooting and often chose it as an option (Office of Police Integrity Victoria, 2005, pp. 2–3) (Author's personal knowledge from speaking with Project Beacon staff).

The new-style training also set out to bring into New Zealand Police culture the concept of "maximising safety and minimising risk" also part of the Operational Safety Principles that Victoria Police had chosen to adopt into their operational culture (ibid.).

Since its beginnings in the late 1990s, SSTT and district training have continued to be reviewed and improved. One of the first reviews to include refresher training was a "Use of Force Report" initiated in 2001 by the deputy commissioner responsible for operations. The report, described as a "low-key, practical 'stocktake' of the current New Zealand Police use of force approaches and training" (New Zealand Police, 2001), presented a favourable analysis of use of force tactics, training and guidelines. It supported the SSTT programme and recommended some "fine-tuning" of it to reinforce the importance of staff doing the refresher training and any remedial training on a regular basis (ibid.).

The "Use of Force Report" will be commented upon in greater detail in Chap. 6. But, elements of it will also be covered in the Tactics section below where appropriate to that topic, for example, the choice of firearms issued to officers responding to a firearms incident.

Since its introduction, SSTT has matured into what is now known as "Police Integrated Tactical Training" (PITT). The new 3-day programme was introduced in July 2012 (New Zealand Police, 2013b, p. 7) (New Zealand Police, 2021b, p. 26) and was structured around a 3-year delivery programme (New Zealand Police, 2013b, p. 3). The change in the programme coincided with the substantive tactical shift to allow firearms to be carried in all operational patrol vehicles. The enhancements to training included well-received scenario and simulation training that attendees felt helped "[develop] decision making, especially when under pressure" (ibid., pp. 3 & 7).

The audiences for district training (either SSTT or the later PITT) have also been adjusted at various points, with one of the first adjustments being publicly signalled in 2009.

In September 2009, the Assistant Commissioner (Operations) announced refresher training at district level was to be moved away from a "one-size-fits-all approach" following a year-long project initiated in 2008 (New Zealand Police, 2020). The new model would see a tiered system of refresher training designed to deliver higher levels of skills to staff in specific roles (ibid.).

The three tiers were described thus:

- First responders and their immediate supervisors will have access to training for both the Glock pistol and Bushmaster rifle. If necessary they can take action to prevent casualties prior to the arrival of specialist staff such at [sic] the Armed Offenders Squad.
- Second responders would be given training in the Bushmaster rifle. Their role would be to cordon and contain.
- All other staff would receive training in defensive tactics such as baton and OC (pepper) spray but not firearms. (New Zealand Police, 2020)

The change was assessed to mean that 40% of police staff would fall into the first responder category and was marketed by Police as ensuring those officers were well trained and to a high level given their roles in responding to critical incidents involving firearms (New Zealand Police, 2020). The new system was also said to ensure "that NZ Police remain a routinely unarmed service", which was clearly an important notion for the organisation and in all probability – the author believes – the government of the day (ibid.).

However, there were those who did not approve of the new approach and who were already touting the changes as a cost-saving initiative that would result in under-trained staff potentially attending firearms incidents (ibid.). It is likely, the author suspects, one of those critics was the New Zealand Police Association. The other, it appears from New Zealand Police documentation, may have been members of the Criminal Investigation Branch (CIB) who – in many places, particularly metropolitan areas – did not necessarily fit into the first or even second responder categories (New Zealand Police, 2013a, p. 4).

Interestingly, from the author's personal perspective, one of the senior officers engaged in the 2008 review of refresher training raised with the author his university research paper from 2000 which had put forward as one of the options for New Zealand Police a move away from "... the 'one size fits all' model and adoption of different models, dependent upon geographic situation and risk management planning within districts" (Shortt, 2000). The officer advised the author that Police were now looking again at his paper and at implementing a different model of refresher training to respond to the pressures on it and the need to improve officer skills (Personal conversation with the author).

The author's 2000 paper will be discussed in greater detail in Chap. 6.

Following introduction of the three-tiered refresher training model, it appears pressure continued to be applied to the Police executive over a number of years for it to expand its scope and design because in early 2014 it was announced that additional changes were to be made to the programme. One of the "enhancements" was to expose more officers to refresher training in the use of the taser and firearms (New Zealand Police, 2014).

By that time, yet another police commissioner-initiated review into "... access and availability ... " of Police firearms had been commenced in 2010 and had delivered a substantive outcome impacting both training and operational deployment (Firearms Access and Availability team, 2010). The project, discussed in detail in Chap. 6, had led to all response police cars being equipped to carry pistols, rifles and ballistic armour from early 2011 onwards.

The pressure, and the increased access and availability project, led to yet further changes and a reshaping of the earlier three-tiered model into what was to be now known as "a three-tiered ***tactical response structure***" (emphasis added) (New Zealand Police, 2014). The structure would be used to determine what refresher training an officer received and balance this with the level of risk faced.

In announcing the changes, Police stated they were:

> ... introduc[ing] a three-tiered tactical response structure, with staff trained as Level 1, 2 or 3 responders, depending on their roles, responsibilities and level of risk. ... Level 1 responders represent those staff who will typically attend higher risk situations that may necessitate access to Taser or firearms, while Level 2 responders will receive Glock pistol training. Level 3 responders will be available to respond to all other incidents that are lower risk and make up the majority of Police interactions. 'All of our staff, regardless of responder level, will receive core tactical training in essential techniques, including defensive tactics, handcuff, pepper spray [sic] and baton, which are effective in resolving the vast majority of incidents we attend'. (ibid.)

To put the changes into context, the media release explained the numbers of staff across Police who would receive the various forms of refresher training. They were:

- 5,700 district staff to be refresher trained in the Glock pistol, Bushmaster M4 rifle and Taser (out of 8,100 district staff);
- 2,100 district staff will be refresher trained at Level 2 with Glock pistol training (ibid.)

Therefore, now 70.4% of district staff – as opposed to the earlier 40% – would be receiving refresher training via the PITT programme in the use of both the pistol and rifle, while 26% would only receive pistol refresher training. The remaining 3.6% of staff no doubt fell into the Level 3 bracket described above. In total, 96.4% of district-based police officers would be able to arm themselves if required. A significant change in the number of staff now receiving firearms refresher training.

An example of the pressure referred to earlier, which gave rise to these changes, can be seen in a New Zealand Police Association issued a press release declaring that "more than a third of constabulary police will not be trained in the use of firearms or Tasers" according to the Association's president (NZ Police Association, 2013). While the Association appreciated the increased amount of training that Level 1 responders were already getting, they were clearly disappointed that the Level 2 and 3 groups were as large as they were and would not be able to access either firearms or tasers as tactical options (ibid.).

It appears negotiations between the two parties resulted in the compromise announced in February 2014, whereby Level 2 responders would get both pistol and taser training.

Training – particularly district refresher training – was not, however, out of the woods as media reporting from 2019, following the deadly Christchurch mosques massacres showed. In that reporting, Police acknowledged they were again looking at their refresher training regime following complaints officers were not getting access to "… three days of weapons training annually, including tactical training and one day of live-fire using the police standard issue Glock pistol and M4 rifle" (Newman, 2020).

By 2021, Police were confirming that PITT training was a requirement for Level 1 responders and:

> … must be completed yearly by Level 1 responders and includes PITT certification, PITT tactics, and PITT live fire sessions. During this refresher programme, attendees also have to role play in realistic scenarios including, among others, high risk vehicle stops and burglary scenarios. During role-playing, instructors are directed to put cognitive pressure on trainees, such as including ongoing radio call signs as part of the scenario, so previous training is recalled more promptly. (New Zealand Police, 2021b, p. 26)

Furthermore, Police reporting also confirmed that formal training programmes were also able to be supplemented by "… informal training in tactical options use (outside PITT)…" and that that form of training was "… more common for firearms (both Glock and M4 Rifle) than other tactical options …" (ibid.). Unfortunately, no description was supplied of what this "informal training" may include or when it was undertaken, but, based on the author's own operational experience, it may include brief revision sessions by staff working together during pre-deployment briefings, on shifts where the section/team was more flexible in its deployment requirements (i.e. a system previously known as "swing shift") or at quiet times on night shifts (2300hrs–0700hrs).

However, despite those enhancements and informal opportunities, staff undergoing the training were reporting back to the organisation that they wanted more training and more "… scenario-based and high-pressure training", with one so-called popular suggestion being that the scenarios be "… as a section, so that staff who work together learn about each other's strengths and weaknesses and can better support one another" (ibid.).

The author makes a similar comment later in this book in Chap. 10 as a result of his research and analysis of Police use of lethal force and with regard to the use of lethal force used against Police.

As already mentioned, changes to training were continuing to be announced by Police as late as September 2021, when four additional days of training were announced under the title of the "Frontline Skills Enhancement Course" (New Zealand Police, 2021d). The programme, at the time of announcement, had already been undertaken by 780 officers, and it was envisaged that by July 2022, 2000 responders would have been through the process (ibid.).

In summary, training continues to be an important and controversial aspect of the Police use of lethal force. It continues to evolve as the environment being policed changes and through pressure being brought to bear by staff and their representatives. New Zealand Police officers clearly have an attachment to firearms and firearms training, as evidenced by the desire for the majority of them to have access to both, regardless of whether their role and its associated risks actually require it.

Tactics

It is the author's recollection that from the late 1970s through until the late 1990s, New Zealand Police firearms-related tactics essentially revolved around the "withdraw, cordon, contain, appeal" approach (Hendy, 2012, p. 12) coupled with police station-based firearms that were issued only when an event requiring armed officers occurred. The author's recollection also includes the fact that the handgun was issued far more often than the rifle.

That tactical approach arose in policing well before the author joined the ranks and no doubt had a significant history to it, much of which appears lost to the passage of time. The author recalls no training in how to apply the model during his operational career, beyond semi-regular attendances at the shooting range to show you could safely load, aim and fire the revolver and the rifle. That was until joining the AOS, when tactics became far more applicable and relevant.

The development of the Armed Offenders Squad (AOS) in the early 1960s was an important and much overdue tactical change and undoubtedly gave greater focus and standing to the "cordon, contain, appeal" approach, given there was now a more highly trained and better equipped specialist group available to help resolve situations. Important elements of the approach were the delivery of station-based firearms to the scene to arm the initial response officers and the activation of the nearest AOS team, who would assemble, dress, brief, arm and attend the scene of a firearms incident to take over the close-in cordon and containment role, while armed initial response officers would withdraw to an "outer-cordon" role focused on keeping the public away from danger. The AOS would also either appeal directly with the subject involved or use the services of trained negotiators known as the Police Negotiation Team (PNT) (Hendy, 2012, p. 12) (Author's personal knowledge and experience as a member of the AOS). That approach, as one can appreciate, was relied upon several variables including can the armed subject be safely located, can the subject be safely contained until police firearms arrive and will the subject stay in one place until AOS arrive and engage them.

Another important tactical change in New Zealand Police occurred in 1977 with the formation of the Anti-Terrorist Squad (ATS) (Shortt, 2000, pp. 94–95). That unit arrived at a time when terrorist events in places like the Middle East and Europe – especially the 1972 Munich Olympics massacre – had governments the world over working to bolster the capabilities of their police services to avoid another Munich-like debacle.

When the Staff Safety Tactical Training refresher programme was being designed in the late 1990s, a deliberate decision was taken to mirror the Victoria Police move to integrate tactics into a programme that had previously been essentially silent on the issue and focused principally on handling skills.

Therefore, the word "tactical" was incorporated into the programme's name along with words that focused of the programme being about enhancing staff safety. The programme, already outlined in some detail earlier, sought to provide trainers and police officers with an opportunity not just to refresh handling skills on the range but to also consider, discuss and practise the *tactics* associated with deploying police weapons.

That discussion may have also contributed, in the author's view, to an important tactical change that occurred around this time and which was reinforced in the "Use of Force Report" completed by Detective Superintendent (later Police Commissioner) Peter Marshall (New Zealand Police) and Assistant Commissioner Ray Shuey (Victoria Police) in 2000/2001 (Marshall & Shuey, 2021).

The change was to emphasise that rather than the habitual issuing of handguns to police officers responding to armed incidents, a rifle should also be deployed "in conjunction with and in support of Glocks" (ibid., pp. 31–32).

That was a major shift, not just regarding deployment tactics but also with respect to greater acceptance by New Zealand Police's hierarchy that armed officers would be more visible at incidents and could no longer be expected to keep their firearm(s) out of sight. The shift in thinking, acceptance and operational tactics has led to the far more visible presence of firearms at policing incidents in Aotearoa New Zealand as exhibited in media coverage of events such as the Christchurch massacre and other occasions such as those associated with gang activity.

While the report itself will be discussed in greater detail in Chap. 6, the shift in firearms deployment tactics by New Zealand Police is worthy of additional discussion here.

In regard to the "traditional" arming practice, Marshall and Shuey reported that there was a perception in police districts that the handgun was the "primary weapon" for officers to have when a firearm incident arose (ibid., p. 29–30). They put that view down to either "… a matter of convenience [or] the perceived lack of .223 Remington rifles or a lack of confidence with the rifle is not clear" (ibid., p. 30).

The above comment regarding "convenience" rings true with the experiences of the author and Rattenbury (Rattenbury, 2020) regarding their respective police service. It also aligns with a number of the earlier commentaries about firearm incidents involving police from the early 1900s through to more recent times. It is the author's view that the handgun was favoured (as previously stated) for both convenience and also the fact it could be concealed and not draw the public's attention to the arming of the what was the fondly viewed and guarded tradition of the "routinely unarmed" New Zealand Police.

Marshall and Shuey expanded on their view by advising that the Victoria Police Special Operations Group (the equivalent of a combined AOS and STG) had confirmed in 2000 "… the .223 Remington rifle as being highly recommended for operational deployment …" in that jurisdiction and that in Aotearoa New Zealand the AOS "… regarded the rifle as the primary weapon – the Glock being very much a secondary form of self defence …" (Marshall & Shuey, 2021, p. 31). They also commented that another issue with the handgun was, on occasions, that it was inherently "unsuitable to achieve the results required" (ibid., p. 30) – in other words, police had a handgun, while the subject of their attention was armed with a more powerful and longer-range rifle or shotgun giving them an advantage over police. In essence, as has been outlined in this work, Police were at risk of being out-gunned by their opponent.

While the Use of Force Report acknowledged the additional financial and human resource cost of increasing availability of the rifle and refresher training of a wider group of operational staff in its use, the reviewers recommended a "… strong message be sent to Districts reinforcing the need for the .223 Remington rifles to be deployed in conjunction with and in support of Glocks at the first available opportunity, whenever there is a need to respond to critical events …" (ibid. p. 31).

Interestingly, Marshall and Shuey also raised a concern with regard to the tactic of rifle deployment that spoke directly to one of the requirements of F061 – the immediacy of the threat being faced (ibid. p. 30). In their view, "the use of a rifle may bring into question the immediacy of a threat if a shot is fired from a distance and may commit a Police Officer to that course of action under circumstance when other options could have been deployed" (ibid. p. 30). History will show that this concern has not been borne out in practice when police shootings between 2000 and 2019 are examined in Chap. 8.

Another development, through the 1990s and into the 2000s, which impacted and called into question the traditional tactic of "cordon, contain and appeal" was the rise of a global phenomenon commonly referred to as the "active shooter". In earlier times, it was the expectation a person with a firearm would go to ground (or be forced to by the presence of police) in a building or vehicle or place where they could be contained by responding officers and inevitably be dealt with by AOS. The Aramoana shootings in 1990 and the 2019 Christchurch massacre were arguably Aotearoa New Zealand's worst mass murdering active shooter events.

For clarity, an "active shooter" has been defined by the Department of Homeland Security in the USA (the country with the most experience in dealing with this form of assailant[3]) as:

> ... an individual actively engaging in killing or attempting to kill people in a confined[4] and populated area; in most cases, active shooters use firearm(s) and there is no pattern or method to their selection of victims. (Department of Homeland Security, 2021)

The US Department of Homeland Security goes on to advise that such situations:

> ... are unpredictable and evolve quickly. Typically, the immediate deployment of law enforcement is required to stop the shooting and mitigate harm to victims ... active shooter situations are often over within 10 to 15 minutes .... (ibid.)

In 2011, in Aotearoa New Zealand, the term "active shooter" appeared in a draft Firearms and Taser Policy paper submitted to the New Zealand Police Executive for consideration (New Zealand Police, 2011, p. 16). The definition described such a person and situation as:

> In this chapter an active shooter is:
> 'An offender armed with a firearm who:
>
> - is either discharging shots with reckless disregard or purposeful intent, and
> - poses an immediate and serious threat to life within a defined area'. (ibid.)

Therefore, from the early 2010s, the concept of the "active shooter" was being considered and factored into Police response thinking, planning and training, even if such events were remarkably rare in Aotearoa New Zealand. References to an "active shooter" situation were found in five of the shooting reports reviewed for this work related to the shootings of Naitoko (2009), Morehu, Hall, Smiler, and a non-fatal Auckland Motorway shooting.

Active shooters do not allow time for returning to the police station to obtain weapons, a subsequent AOS activation and deployment or even a formal negotiation process. International and domestic experience establishes that such subjects are stopped only when they either take their own lives, are killed by police or are apprehended (Federal Bureau of Investigation, 2021). However, in the draft policy paper (New Zealand Police, 2011), the tactics for such an event were summarised as:

> When the actions of the suspect permit:
>
> - take time to cordon the area
> - contact specialist groups such as the Armed Offenders Squad or Special Tactics Group, and
> - adopt the wait and appeal role to negotiate a surrender. (ibid. p. 16)

The draft policy, however, did go on to state that:

---

[3] For example, the Federal Bureau of Investigation in the USA reports that in the years 2014 and 2015, there were 40 such instances in that country, with 231 casualties (92 dead and 139 wounded – including 4 dead and 10 wounded law enforcement officers) (Federal Bureau of Investigation, 2021).

[4] Following research in 2014, the Federal Bureau of Investigation no longer uses the word "confined" in its definition of an active shooter. https://www.fbi.gov/file-repository/as-study-quick-reference-guide-updated1.pdf.

> … the immediate danger of casualties may require action beyond the traditional cordon and contain response. Police must recognise that in many active shooter incidents, innocent lives are lost within the first few minutes of the incident. In some situations this dictates the need for Police to rapidly assess the situation and act quickly in order to save lives … Responses to an active shooter should be:
>
> - immediate
> - proactive
> - urgent. (ibid.)

It appears, to the author, that New Zealand Police were still endeavouring to adhere to their traditional tactics of "cordon, contain, appeal" while at the same time recognising that the new style of offender did not always allow for that approach. The two examples of an "active shooter" in Aotearoa New Zealand – Aramoana (1990) and Christchurch (2019) – show how the range of tactics may in fact be applied. In Aramoana, the active shooter had finally gone to ground after his rampage and the traditional tactics applied, whereas in Christchurch, the active shooter was en route to a third site where he was hoping to shoot more worshippers before he was stopped and arrested through "immediate, proactive and urgent" action.

The final, and perhaps most substantial, shift in New Zealand Police tactics was the adoption of the "Norwegian approach" of deploying Police firearms in all first response patrol cars as already described. The change meant that "cordon, contain and appeal" now no longer required a return to the station to obtain firearms, and it also meant that an almost immediate response could be initiated if an active shooter situation was encountered, as one was on 15 March 2019, in Christchurch.

One final, and quite recent tactical, change was announced in September 2021. This was the decision to make new positions available to transform dog handler units (who have traditionally worked alone with their canine companion) into two-person teams (New Zealand Police, 2021d). The change was described as ".. increase[ing] the day-to-day safety of handlers who will no longer respond to high-risk incidents alone. As a team they will provide additional specialist tactical support for frontline staff in responding to critical incidents" (ibid.).

While short on specifics, it appears the handlers will now have a "cover officer" with them who can, if the need was such, carry a firearm(s) when the handler and dog were being asked to engage with armed and/or dangerous persons. In the author's experience, dog handlers would often deploy armed with a pistol in high-risk situations in any case. It may be that given dog handlers are often more senior in service (years) than many Level 1 responders and are often a tactical option used at high-risk events, the second person and the handler now become a "de facto" and less obvious armed response team (ART). It will, however, take time for the policy and tactics change to work through the Police system, and it is definitely too early to make a definitive statement about the changes.

Unlike the previous attempt to launch ART's in Aotearoa New Zealand, the commissioner, when making the new announcement, was at pains to say "[f]or a member of the public, this won't look any different to what they see today" (New Zealand Police, 2021d). Again, time will tell.

In summary, tactics have changed, just as the environment has changed. Ultimately, the outcome sought has, hopefully, remained the same "maximising safety and minimising risk".

Specialist Units

Armed Offenders Squad (AOS)

Over and above the weapons detailed above, New Zealand Police (NZP) have access to two highly trained and better equipped specialist groups. The first is the Armed Offenders Squad (AOS) – mentioned earlier – which consists of officers who perform normal police duties until called upon to perform their specialist role. When that occurs, the officers change into tactical clothing, don bullet-resistant vests and avail themselves of the weapons described above but with additional access to shotguns, tear gas projectile launchers and 7.62 mm higher-powered, "sniper"-style rifles.

AOS units have been part of the police armed capability since their formation almost five decades ago and are maintained in all of the 12 Police districts. According to Police, there are nearly 300 members of the AOS. The squad's size and distribution within each district depend on the population being served and the area being covered. Many are based out of a headquarters station, for example, the Waikato District AOS was based at Hamilton station, while the Central District AOS had sections in Palmerston North, Whanganui and New Plymouth (Author's personal knowledge).

The squads are formed by two, three or four sections consisting of four to five constables with a sergeant-in-charge, and each has a leadership made up of an inspector who is in overall command and a second-in-command who assists the inspector and deputises as the "boss" if that officer is unavailable (Author's personal knowledge).

AOS members undertake a 3-day selection event, followed by a 3-week qualification course at the RNZPC where their capabilities for the work are assessed and refined. The course focuses on an individual's physical and mental fitness for the role and their ability to exercise good judgement when in stressful situations, such as extreme tiredness, for example.

When assigned to an AOS in a district, police officers receive regular refresher training which by 2010 had matured to be a "… minimum of 18 days per year" (Independent Police Conduct Authority, 2009, p. 81).

AOS tactics conform strongly to the New Zealand Police tactical approach of "cordon, contain, appeal" which, in the author's view, can be expanded to include "respond/arrest". The squads, in the author's experience with them, train and work very hard to ensure an armed person does not pose a threat to the wider community and that wherever possible the person(s) is taken into custody without the need to

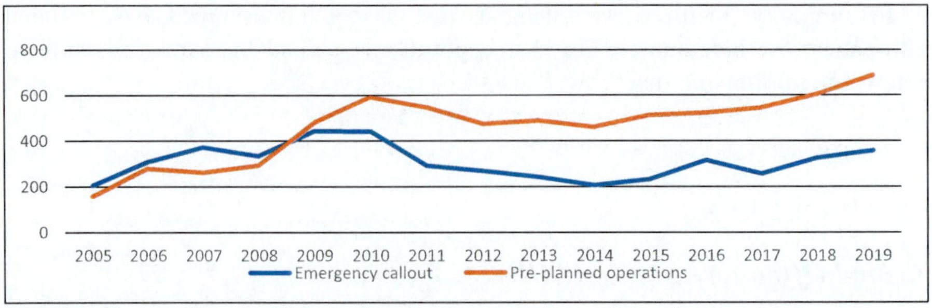

Fig. 5.1 Number of AOS deployments by type: 2005–2019. (New Zealand Police advised that "… data prior to 2005 is not held by Police, so is refused under section 18(g) of the Act (information not held)" (New Zealand Police, 2021a)). (Data supplied by New Zealand Police through an Official Information Act request)

resort to the use of lethal force. For the AOS, as for other police officers, the use of lethal force is a "last resort". It is acknowledged, however, that the phenomenon of the "active shooter" has altered the tactical approach, should one be encountered.

The nature of AOS work is split into two categories: emergency callouts and pre-planned operations. The first involves calls for specialist support when encountering an event involving firearms or dangerous weapons, and it is believed AOS can help resolve the matter. Pre-planned operations are situations where planning is underway to carry out a search of a place or to make an arrest, and it is believed specialist armed support is required to safely secure the premises prior to other officers conducting the search or to secure the person sought. Figure 5.1 shows the number of those tasks carried out nationally by AOS.

It is of interest that the prevalence of "emergency callouts" vs. "pre-planned operations" crossed in 2009 with "pre-planned operations" becoming the primary reason for squad deployments and "emergency callouts" becoming the secondary reason. During the 2008–2010 period (as depicted above), AOS emergency callouts did increase by over 100 additional callouts (2009 n=443, 2010 n=441) from the 2008 figure (n=334). That was the timeframe during which the Police executives were coming under pressure to consider greater firearms access and confronting the decision of how to respond (late 2010/early 2011). The data on emergency callouts then shows a gradual decline in numbers from 2010 until 2014 by which time the number had effectively halved, with 2014 recording 206 callouts, one more than the figure for 2005. The callout figures then began to slowly increase again, however, by that time "pre-planned operations" were effectively 2/3 of the national squad usage rate, with 1/3 being for emergency callouts. That shift, and in particular the decline from 2010 to 2014, may well be a reflection of the fact that firearms were then much more accessible to initial response staff following the Police decisions to place weapons in operational vehicles.

The continuing challenge surrounding the use of AOS for emergency callouts and pre-planned operations, however, continues to be a twofold one. Firstly, with respect to emergency callouts, there is the time delay experienced from the decision to activate AOS until they arrive on scene. For example, in the Naitoko shooting in Auckland, it took the AOS 28 minutes from activation to deployment (Independent Police Conduct Authority, 2009, p. 71), and in the Kelly-Tumarae shooting in the Hawke's Bay, the IPCA estimated the AOS were at least 30 minutes away from assisting (Independent Police Conduct Authority, 2013, p. 14). In the author's experience, in a Police district comprising a large provincial city and widespread surrounding rural areas, delays of between 15 and 60 minutes were the norm for the squad from activation until arrival "on scene" depending where in the district the incident was and how urgent the requirement was.

The second challenge is that AOS remains (with the exception of STG members) a part-time affair (Tso, 2018a, b). That effectively means the squad members have two jobs: their primary role as a day-to-day police officer, either on uniform or CIB duties, including as supervisors, and their secondary role as a specialist firearms response unit member. When the secondary role is activated, their primary role either is put on hold or prevents them from attending the emergency callout or preplanned operation (i.e. if the AOS member is in Court to give evidence or managing a case or is working on an important investigation – such as a homicide or serious crime case – they may not be able to respond). In most Police districts, the amount of time spent on AOS work does not justify a full-time squad arrangement. However, as will be discussed later in this book, there are locations that have a higher demand for use of firearms as a tactical option.

Special Tactics Group (STG)

The second specialist firearms response unit that Police can call upon is the Special Tactics Group (STG), which evolved from the Anti-Terrorist Squad (ATS) established in the late 1970s at a time when the world was experiencing aircraft hijackings and siege-hostage situations (e.g. the disastrous Munich Olympics in 1972). The squad was developed to intervene in terrorist situations and high-risk situations which were deemed to be beyond the standard AOS capabilities.

The ATS and subsequently the STG were armed with automatic and semiautomatic weapons including the .9 mm Heckler and Koch MP5, sub-machine gun (featuring a 3-round burst capability and also a silenced version) (Osborne, Carbines and Police in New Zealand 1840 – 1990, 1990b, p. 21) and, originally, a quite interesting .22 firearm known as the "American 180 Carbine" which came equipped with a 177-round drum magazine and one of the original Laser Lok laser sighting systems that put a glowing dot on the intended target (ibid., p. 20).

STG currently has a very modern arsenal of weapons including long-range, high-quality, sniper rifles of military grade, close quarter carbines and handguns and shotguns capable of deploying a variety of munitions, to name but some (New Zealand Police, 2016).

Originally, as mentioned, the STG was an on-call response unit like the AOS and staffed by police officers who were also already members of various major centre-based AOS units. By 2003, it was determined that the model was an unacceptable state of affairs placing too much strain on the districts hosting the group through STG officers being absent for long periods of time during training and deployments (New Zealand Police, 2016). The decision was taken, therefore, to make the group a full-time element of the Police.

The STG then became a more diversified unit developing a range of specialist functions and activities to supplement its primary task which was to undertake high-risk armed response in situations that the AOS felt they were not trained and/or equipped to do. The roles the unit now performs includes the ability to operate in "… many environments" such as:

- Members may deploy in GDB uniform if they need to appear non-tactical [standard Police uniform];
- 'grey role' for covert attire in city, town and suburbs;
- 'green role' for rural areas;
- 'blue role' for maritime;
- 'white role' for clandestine laboratories; and
- 'black role' for counter terrorism/hostage rescue work.

(New Zealand Police, 2016)

When it comes to training, the STG is described by its national commander as having:

> … a strong relationship with the Defence Force, including elements from the Special Air Service [SAS]. Operators [as STG officers are designated and referred to within Police] regularly attend tactical training courses in Australia. They may also train alongside other overseas tactical groups, Defence Force personnel and international experts in firearms, explosives and combat tactics … members are trained in rural manhunts, static siege events and mixed-mode attacks with active armed offenders. They train week-to-week when not deployed – and annually gather for a two-week, concentrated skills enhancement course culminating in prolonged reality-based scenarios. (New Zealand Police, 2021a)

The STG not only has a wide set of skills and capabilities; it also comes with a hefty price tag. In 2018, it was reported that the costs of the unit had "… increased nearly 30-fold since the World Trade Centre terrorist attacks in 2001, with Kiwi taxpayers now funding them to the tune of [NZ]$6.2 million" annually (Tso, 2018a, b). The funding for the unit, by comparison, was just NZ$226,000 in 1999–2000 (ibid.). That high cost was also likely a factor in the STG developing a wider array of skill-sets in an effort to be seen to deliver value-for-money back to taxpayers, rather than waiting constantly in reserve for a terrorist or serious hostage situation to arise, both, thankfully, still rare events in Aotearoa New Zealand.

In essence, and without being overly sensational, it is the author's opinion that the STG is the New Zealand Police equivalent of the New Zealand Defence Force's SAS. They train with the NZSAS, use the military-initiated title of "operator" for their personnel and are – by design – capable of delivering a military-grade armed response to situations that the part-time (but also highly capable) AOS cannot. The response includes military-grade weapons, tactics and mindsets, which include the ability to overwhelm an opponent by controlled use of explosive distraction and entry devices, firepower and shooting abilities that make "critical shots" (head shots) a routine element of training.

For example, in the words of an STG operator during an IPCA interview, describing why he used a "critical shot" (head shot) to kill a man holding his ex-partner hostage, the officer said:

> … we are an elite squad which trains full time for hostage rescue situations and other high risk jobs and our training tells that the best way to stop a goal driven and motivated offender is a shot to the head. Our training also tells us that a shot to his centre of mass [the target for all other Police firearms training], if an offender is goal driven and motivated will not necessarily stop him from following through with his actions …. (Independent Police Conduct Authority, 2014, p. 42)

Given the nature of the STG and its training, weaponry and mindsets (shaped by military tactics such as surprise, overwhelming force and shot placement), it has always required a high level of authority from within Police for the unit to deploy. The IPCA, for example, in the Ratahi report (Independent Police Conduct Authority, 2014, pp. 51–52), confirmed – with reference to the Police Manual – that:

> 230. The STG may be called in to assist the AOS and PNT [Police Negotiating Team] with armed incidents that are prolonged or require the STG's specialist skills and equipment. In July 2011 the Police Manual stated:
>
> '**Approving STG deployment**
>
> *This table details who can approve deploying the STG.*

Deployment size & situation	Approval must be given by
Full deployment in all situations *Partial deployment:* *In an emergency situation* *If STG deployment is overseas.*	*Commissioner or a deputy commissioner if the commissioner is not available*
Partial deployment as part of a Planned operation within New Zealand.	*Commissioner, Deputy Commissioner or Assistant Commissioner: Crime and Operations*

> ***Requests for STG deployment***
>
> *Requests for STG deployment must be in writing for emailing to required parties. They **must** include:*
>
> - *Risk Assessment*
>
> *And should include*
>
> - *a detailed Intel package (maps, photographs etc.) relating to the location of the operation, outline of the operation and/or persons(s) of interest*
> - *In emergency situations there may be insufficient time for the above requirements and verbal briefings may be substituted (see Deploying STG in emergencies)'.*
>
> 231. Examples of emergency situations requiring the deployment of the STG included '*escalating AOS call outs needing greater tactical resources*' and '*hostage rescues involving armed offenders*'. (Independent Police Conduct Authority, 2014) (Italics and bold text in original)

Examples of the international deployments included sending members to assist Australian authorities with the hosting of an APEC and subsequent G20 conference (Tso, 2018a, b).

However, it appears that following the 2003 decision to make the STG full-time, occasions have arisen where their continued "embeddedness" with their parent AOS (Auckland, Wellington and Christchurch) may have resulted in STG operators deploying under the banner of "AOS" and not having to go through the deployment criteria outlined above.

One such event, for example, was a police pursuit of armed and wanted men in Auckland, where three "operators" on duty at the time elected to participate in the pursuit and shootings that took place during it, as "AOS" members (Independent Police Conduct Authority, 2021). More is written about that event in later chapters.

Unlike earlier times, when the ATS and subsequently the STG were intermingled with other part-time officers and attended general policing callouts with them as a "mixed" grouping of responding specialists, it is now – it appears – possible for STG operators to be the "Johnnies-on-the-spot" due to their full-time role. Thus, it seems quite probable that entire AOS responses in Auckland, Wellington or Christchurch are – in the initial stages at least – made up of STG operators. That may appear, at first blush to be appropriate, a prudent use of expertise and money spent, one might suggest. However, the author is not convinced that the New Zealand Police executive conceived of a time when their specialist counter-terrorism unit (with its militarised training, weapons and mindset) were going to have such a role in day-to-day policing.

Undoubtedly, the Police executive is very aware of the high price it pays to maintain a unit like the STG and the fact that costs for it have risen rapidly since it was made a full-time entity (Tso, 2018a, b).

When it comes to the use being made of STG, and its specialist roles, outlined earlier, Figure 5.2 shows the deployment data supplied by New Zealand Police[5].

In terms of staffing, the only record on how many STG members exist – which the author could locate – came from a response to a 2008 question in the Aotearoa New Zealand parliament seeking exactly that information. In reply, the Minister of Police reported that there were "… a total of three tactical commanders, six team leaders and 30 operators" (New Zealand Parliament, 2008). Given the group is based in Auckland, Wellington and Christchurch, it can be assumed there are 3 equally staffed units of 18 staff in each location. Furthermore, in 2016, it was confirmed that an "… STG National Commander …" (New Zealand Police, 2016) was in place, which would round out the number of STG staff to 40. Given the passage of time between 2008, 2016 and now, that number may have risen (most likely, in the author's view) or decreased (less likely, again, in the author's view).

In summary, New Zealand Police have two specialist firearms support units available to respond to dangerous and unlawful uses of firearms or activities that

[5] Data prior to 2003 "… is not available … STG deployment is not categorised as Emergency or Pre-planned deployment" (New Zealand Police, 2021a).

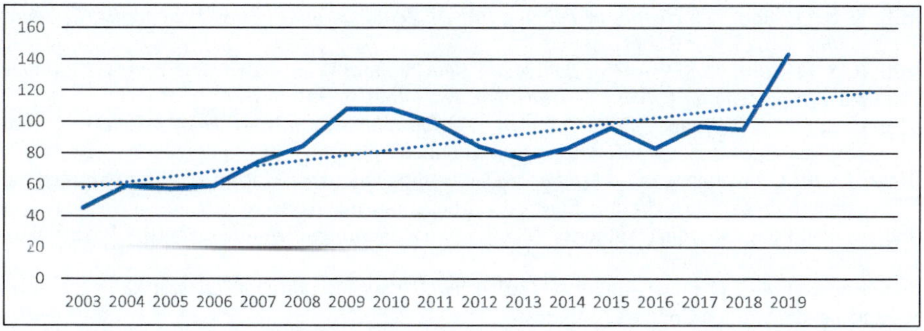

Fig. 5.2 Number of STG deployments (2003–2019) (plus trendline). (Data supplied by New Zealand Police through an Official Information Act request)

may involve firearms. Both are well trained, with one having access to military-grade equipment, skills and tactics. Over time, the main response specialists, AOS, appear to have shifted to a more "planned operation"-style unit, while the counter-terrorism specialists, STG, appear to be making greater inroads into "every-day" policing activities. Whether these shifts are appreciated or approved of by the public of Aotearoa New Zealand, or even the Police executive, is an interesting question to ponder.

Bibliography

Battersby, J. (2019). The Ghost of New Zealand's Terrorism Past and Present. *National Security Journal, 1(1)*, 35–47.

Belich, J. (1986). *The New Zealand Wars and the Victorian Interpretation of Racial Conflict*. Penguin Books (NZ) Ltd..

Bond, J. (2020, June 5). *Armed Response Teams trial: 'Bizarre' holes in callout data*. RNZ News.

Buchanan, K. (2014, September). *Police Weapons: New Zealand.* Retrieved from loc.gov: https://www.loc.gov/law/help/police-weapons/new-zealand.php

Department of Homeland Security. (2021, April 19). *Active Shooter How To Respond.* Retrieved from dhs.gov: https://dhs.gov/active_shooter_booklet

Dynon, N. (2020). *ARTs and the myth of the unarmed police officer. Line of Defence Magazine – Winter 2020*. Line of Defence Magazine.

eliteukforces. (2021, May 5). *Police Firearms Unit - SCO19.* Retrieved from eliteukforces.info: https://www.eliteukforces.info/police/CO19

Federal Bureau of Investigation. (2021, April 20). *Active Shooter Incidents in the United States 2014 and 2015.* Retrieved from fbi.gov: https://www.fbi.gov/file-repository/activeshooterincidentsus_2014-2015.pdf/view

Firearms Access and Availability team. (2010, November 24). *Review of the Access and Availability of Firearms – PEC presentation*. New Zealand: New Zealand Police.

Hendy, R. (2012). *The Strategic Impact of routine arming that New Zealand Police*. School of Government, Victoria University of Wellington.

Hill, R. S. (1986). *The History of Policing in New Zealand Volume One: Policing the Colonial Frontier - Part 1*. V. R. Ward Government Printer.

Hill, R. S. (1989a). *The History of Policing in New Zealand Volume One: Policing the Colonial Frontier - Part 2*. GP Books.

Hill, R. S. (1989b). *The History of Policing in New Zealand Volume Two: The Colonial Frontier Tamed: New Zealand Policing in Transition, 1867-1886*. GP Books.

Hill, R. S. (2021, February). *'Police', Te Ara - the Encyclopedia of New Zealand*. Retrieved from www.TeAra.govt.nz: www.TeAra.govt.nz/en/police

Hunt, T. (2014, November 15). *Flashback: The Aramoana massacre*. Retrieved from Stuff.co.nz: www.stuff.co.nz/national/crime/Flashback: The Aramoana massacre

Independent Police Conduct Authority. (2009). *Police Shooting of Halatau Naitoko*. Independent Police Conduct Authority.

Independent Police Conduct Authority. (2013). *Fatal Police Shooting of Lachan Kelly-Tumarae*. Independent Police Conduct Authority.

Independent Police Conduct Authority. (2014). *Fatal Police shooting of Antony Ratahi*. Independent Police Conduct Authority.

Independent Police Conduct Authority. (2019). *Fatal shooting of Jerrim Toms*. Independent Police Conduct Authority.

Independent Police Conduct Authority. (2021). *Use of force during fatal shooting in Tauranga justified*. Independent Police Conduct Authority.

Mackenzie, S. (2020, April 17). Cops with guns will make us less safe. *newsroom.co.nz*. New Zealand: newsroom.co.nz.

Manch, T. (2021, May 11). *Risk of worst-case terror attack 'very high' according to Government's Terrorism Risk Profile*. Retrieved from stuff.co.nz: https://www.stuff.co.nz/national/politics/125065298/risk-of-worstcase-terror-attack-very-high-according-to-governments-terrorism-risk-profile?cid=app

Marshall, P., & Shuey, R. N. (2021, March 12). *A strategic evaluation of the New Zealand Police position concerning the use of force when responding to potentially violent situations: a review of best practice, policy and training*. Retrieved from natlib.govt.nz: https://ndhadeliver.natlib.govt.nz/delivery/DeliveryManagerServlet?dps_pid=IE4285780

Ministry for Culture and Heritage. (2021, January 28). *nzhistory.govt.nz*. Retrieved from Stan Graham's killing spree on West Coast: https://nzhistory.govt.nz/stan-graham-killing-spree-on-west-coast

New Zealand Government. (1983, June 1). *Arms Act 1983*. Wellington, New Zealand: New Zealand Government.

New Zealand Government. (2008). Policing Act 2008. *Policing Act 2008*. Wellington, New Zealand: New Zealand Government.

New Zealand Government. (2015, September 4). *Health and Safety at Work Act 2015*. Wellington, New Zealand: New Zealand Government.

New Zealand Parliament. (2008, June 19). *5950 (2008). Ron Mark to the Minister of Police*. Retrieved from parliament.nz: https://www.parliament.nz/en/pb/order-paper-questions/written-questions/document/QWA_05950_2008/5950-2008-ron-mark-to-the-minister-of-police

New Zealand Police. (1998). *Improving Safety in the New Zealand Police - Report of the Staff Safety Project*. New Zealand Police.

New Zealand Police. (2001, December 14). *Use of Force Report explores options*. Retrieved from police.govt.nz: https://www.police.govt.nz/news/Use of Force Report explores options

New Zealand Police. (2005a, May 19). *Replacement due for police rifles*. Retrieved from police.govt.nz: https://www.police.govt.nz/news/Replacement due for police rifles

New Zealand Police. (2005b, June 30). *Annual Report for the year ended 30 June 2005*. Wellington, New Zealand: New Zealand Police.

New Zealand Police. (2007, September 27). *Use of Firearms by Police*. Retrieved from police.govt.nz: https//www.police.govt.nz/Home/News/Use of Firearms by Police

New Zealand Police. (2009, January 31). *the press - Police instructions concerning the use of firearms*. Retrieved from Stuff.co.nz: https//:www.Stuff.co.nz/the press/Police instructions concerning the use of firearms

New Zealand Police. (2010, June 30). *New Zealand Police Annual Report for the Year Ended 30 June 2010.* : New Zealand Government.

New Zealand Police. (2011). *Firearms and Taser Policy (draft).* New Zealand Police.

New Zealand Police. (2012, June 30). *New Zealand Police Annual Report for the Year Ended 30 June 2012.* New Zealand Government.

New Zealand Police. (2013a). *Assurance Group Report: Review of increased accessibility to firearms.* New Zealand Police.

New Zealand Police. (2013b). *Review of increased accessibility to firearms.* New Zealand Police.

New Zealand Police. (2014, February 17). *Further enhancements to Police Integrated Tactical Training.* Retrieved from police.govt.nz: https://www.police.govt.nz/news/Further enhancements to Police Integrated Tactical Training

New Zealand Police. (2016, December). *Inside the STG.* Retrieved from police.govt.nz: http://www.ten-one.police.govt.nz/tenone/December2016National6.htm

New Zealand Police. (2017, June 10). *Police Manual - Use of Force Laura Drew made this Official Information request to New Zealand Police.* Retrieved from fyi.org.nz: hptts//www.fyi.org.nz/request/5993/20241/attach/html/4/drew%20laaura%2017%

New Zealand Police. (2019, February 28). *Police Armament - TENR & Tactical Options Framework - Emmy Rākete.* Retrieved from fyi.org.nz: https//www.fyi.org.nz/Police Armament Emmy Rākete

New Zealand Police. (2020, April 4). *Review of police firearms training.* Retrieved from police.govt.nz: Https://police.govt.nz/news/Review of police firearms training

New Zealand Police. (2021a, September 15). Reference: IR-01-21-23592 Armed Offenders Squad Deployment Statistics 2000-2014. Wellington, New Zealand: New Zealand Police.

New Zealand Police. (2021b, August). *Appropriate Tactical Settings.* Retrieved from police.govt.nz: https://www.police.govt.nz/sites/default/files/publications/evidence-brief-appropriate-tactical-settings.pdf

New Zealand Police. (2021c, April 19). *Recruitment Process.* Retrieved from newcops.govt.nz: https://www.newcops.govt.nz/Can I Be a Cop/Recruitment Process

New Zealand Police. (2021d, September 22). *Improving the safety and capability of frontline Police.* Retrieved from police.govt.nz: https://www.police.govt.nz/home/news/Improving the safety and capability of frontline Police

Newman, T. (2020, April 8). *Police firearms training questioned after Christchurch mosque attacks.* Retrieved from stuff.co.nz: https://www.stuff.co.nz/national/christchurch shooting/ Police firearms training questioned after Christchurch mosque attacks

NZ History. (2020, November 13). *Thirteen shot dead at Aramoana.* Retrieved from nzhistory.govt.nz: www.nzhistory.govt.nz/Home/Events/13 November/Thirteen shot dead at Aramoana

NZ Police Association. (2013, March 26). *PITT training changes a necessary evil.* Retrieved from scoop.co.nz: https://www.scoop.co.nz/stories/PO1303/S00316/pitt-training-changes-a-necessary-evil.htm

NZPA. (2008, October 23). *Chronology of fatal shootings by NZ police.* Retrieved from nzherald.co.nz: https://www.nzhearld.co.nz/new zealand/crime/ Chronology of fatal shootings by NZ police

Office of Police Integrity Victoria. (2005, November). *Review of fatal shootings by Victoria Police.* Retrieved from www.ibac.vic.gov.au: https://www.ibac.vic.gov.au/docs/default-source/review-of-fatal-shootings-by-victoria-police---nov-2005.pdf?sfvrsn=da586175_8

Osborne, J. (1990a). *Handguns and Police in New Zealand.* South Pacific Armoury.

Osborne, J. (1990b). *Carbines and Police in New Zealand 1840 - 1990.* South Pacific Armoury.

Rattenbury, R. (2020). *A Battered Proud Badge - Tales of Policing a Young Country.* Rangitawa Publishing.

Reuters. (2018, October 18). New Zealand police to start armed patrols after Christchurch massacre. *The Guardian World News.* New Zealand: The Guardian.

Rorke, J. (1993). *Policing Two Peoples: A history of police in the Bay of Plenty 1867-1992.* New Zealand Police.

Royal Commission of Inquiry. (2020). *Report of the Royal Commission of Inquiry into the terrorist attack on Christchurch masjidain on 15 March 2019*. New Zealand Government.

Samkin, G., Allen, C., & Wallace, K. (2010). Repairing Organisational Legitimacy : the Case of the New Zealand Police. *Australasian Accounting, Business and Finance Journal, 4(3)*, 23–45.

Shortt, R. (1999). *Helensville Shooting Safety Audit*. New Zealand Police.

Shortt, R. S. (2000). *Are the New Zealand Police on Target? An Investigation of Alternative Models of Police Response to Dangerous and Unlawful Firearms Incidents*. Victoria University.

Squires, P., & Kennison, P. (2010). *Shooting to Kill? Policing, Firearms and Armed Response*. Chichester: John Wiley & Sons.

Tso, M. (2018a, December 23). *Crime - New Zealand Police anti-terrorist unit costs taxpayers $6.2 million*. Retrieved from Stuff.co.nz: www.stuff.co.nz/national/crime/New Zealand Police anti-terrorist unit costs taxpayers $6.2 million

Tso, M. (2018b, December 23). *New Zealand Police anti-terrorist unit costs taxpayers $6.2 million*. Retrieved from stuff.co.nz: https://www.stuff.co.nz/national/crime/109460758/new-zealand-police-antiterrorist-unit-costs-taxpayers-62-million

TVNZ. (2020, March 5). Armed Response Teams not being used for what Police said they would. *1 News*. New Zealand: TVNZ.

Unknown, O. -N. (2021, June 14). *Giving new life to a faithful old companion*. Retrieved from smith-wessonforum.com: http://smith-wessonforum.com/gun-leather-carry-gear/475155-giving-new-life-faithful-old-companion.html

Worksafe Mahi Haumaru Aotearoa. (2019, July 18). *Safety at Work Act 2015 – special guide*. Retrieved from worksafe.govt.nz: https://www.worksafe.govt.nz/managing-health-and-safety/getting-started/introduction-hswa-special-guide/

Chapter 6
Use of Force: Reviews, Reports and Changes

The five strategic policy shifts mentioned in the previous chapter did not happen in isolation or on the whim of some important or well-placed person. They grew out of a combination of factors. Those include recognition of changing societal needs and changing threats and are the result of reviews or reports undertaken to examine particular events or concerns. For example, the first strategic change was the passing of the *Police Act 1886* (NZL) creating the new-style New Zealand Police Force as a generally unarmed service. That was in recognition of the fact that the need for a mobile and armed force had diminished as a more stable society grew out of the tumultuous 1860s and 1870s. Alternatively, the third strategic change – formation of the Armed Offenders Squad – was directly linked to a review instigated by a police commissioner into two specific and tragic events in 1963.

This chapter will present overviews of four substantial pieces of work that, the author contends, had substantive impacts on the way New Zealand Police developed firearms strategy and policy between the late 1990s and 2010. That decade would see the most recent strategic policy change for the organisation that took, in the author's opinion, New Zealand Police from a "routinely unarmed" police service to what it is today, a well-armed, well-trained police service.

The first piece of work to be considered will be the 1998 Staff Safety Project initiated by the police commissioner after a series of serious assaults created concerns within police ranks and also the public. The second is a master's thesis completed by the author into the model of armed policing used in Aotearoa New Zealand in 2000 and what alternative options the organisation could consider. That research grew from his involvement with the Staff Safety Project, his later study of risk management and his recognition that the way firearms were being deployed was outdated and overdue for reconsideration. The third piece of work was conducted in 2001, by Marshall and Shuey, and titled "A Strategic Evaluation of the New Zealand Police Position Concerning the Use of Force When Responding to Potentially Violent Situations: A Review of Best Practice, Policy and Training" (commonly referred to in this work as the "Use of Force Report") (Marshall & Shuey, 2001). That review examined how New Zealand Police used force, including firearms, and was directly linked to the author's master's thesis. Finally, this chapter will consider the review described by the commissioner of police, in 2010, as "An extensive review of firearms training and accessibility of firearms to police …" in the New Zealand Police Annual Report in September 2010 (New Zealand Police, 2010, p. 2).

R. S. Shortt, *Lethal Force and New Zealand Police*,
https://doi.org/10.1007/978-3-031-05269-9_6

That work, in effect, formalised the shift of Police firearms from station-based armouries into operational police vehicles and completely changed the style of arming for the organisation.

Staff Safety Project (1998)

In May 1997, the police commissioner initiated the Staff Safety Project following concerns being raised about deployment practices and assaults on police officers. Particular concerns were raised by the New Zealand Police Association over an apparent increase in serious assaults and about deployment practices and equipment available to officers. Those concerns initially arose 2 years earlier in late 1995 and ultimately reached a level where the commissioner felt he needed to act. One of the issues raised was that there appeared to be a lack of data internally within police about the number and severity of assaults (Keay et al., 1998, p. 7).

During those years (between 1995 and 1997), despite anxiety over the number of assaults, history records just one Police fatality, Constable Glenn McKibbin who was shot to death on 21 April 1996. It occurred on a Sunday morning when McKibbin had stopped a motorist in suburban Flaxmere, near the provincial city of Hastings. While standing next to his police car, the constable was shot by the occupant of a passing car with whom McKibbin had had no interaction (New Zealand Police, 2021a). The killer – a former soldier – was eventually cornered after a 9-week manhunt and shot and killed by Police during a standoff (ibid.). McKibbin's death came after a period of 5 years in which there had been no killings of police officers, the last having been the 1990 deaths of Sergeant Guthrie at Aramoana (shot) and Senior Constable Umbers at Ranfurly (fatally assaulted) (Ibid.).

The Staff Safety Project also occurred at a time when the *Health and Safety in Employment Act 1992* (NZL) was gaining traction in workplaces across Aotearoa New Zealand and being picked up upon by those representing police officers' interests, particularly the New Zealand Police Association (Author's personal knowledge). The Act required employers to "take all practical steps to eliminate hazards" in the workplace if at all possible and, if not, then to isolate or minimise them (New Zealand Police, 1998, p. 3).

The commissioner set the project the task of focusing on matters related to operational policing and to determine how Police could go about "minimising risk and maximising safety" a phrase picked up from the Victoria Police, Australia, and their recently undertaken Project Beacon which had mirrored some of the Staff Safety Project work about to be embarked upon (Author's personal knowledge). The Aotearoa New Zealand project also arose 1 year after the 1996 Australasian Commissioners' Conference[1] had agreed that "law enforcers should not conduct

[1] The conference involved all the commissioners of the Australian police services and the Aotearoa New Zealand commissioner, as well as others from the region.

firearms and weapons practice without combining it with training in communication skills, conflict resolution, risk assessment and incident management" again strongly driven by the outcomes of Project Beacon (ibid., p. 10). This was a substantive shift away from the traditional style of training whereby firearms were treated as a topic of their own and involved a focus on weapon handling and shooting skills.

The project team – of which the author was a member – focused on three broad inter-related intervention areas "safety and tactics, training, and management systems" (New Zealand Police, 1998, p. 4). Those interventions saw the project examine a variety of areas including safety and operational equipment, deployment practice, how data was gathered and used, international developments, "best practice" and training (ibid., pp. 5–8).

From a firearms deployment and use perspective, two of the most relevant outcomes from the project were the recommendations for an integrated risk management/use of force model and the development and delivery of an integrated and certification-based training regime for both recruit and district refresher training (ibid., pp. 50–58). Those two outcomes continue to be reflected in the way New Zealand Police delivers its use of force training and in the variety of risk assessment and use of force tools available to police officers.

For example, the project ultimately gave birth to a newly styled and integrated recruit and district training programme. In districts, it was known as "Staff Safety Tactical Training" (SSTT). That programme took the older National Training Programme which structured district training and ring-fenced half of the time available to deliver an integrated use of force approach covering all weapons on issue, including firearms, and communication skills, to try and de-escalate conflict situations (New Zealand Police, 1998, pp. 48–58).

The programme was based around the model used in Victoria Police which was known as "Operational Safety and Tactical Training" (OSTT) (ibid. p. 14), following a visit to Victoria to review that programme by project members, including the author. The SSTT programme also went on to require participants to be certified by their trainers as being competent in the use of all the skills taught. That was deemed necessary to help reduce organisational risk regarding health and safety compliance by confirming staff were trained and refreshed in the skills needed to eliminate, isolate and minimise risk to them and others in the operational policing workplace (ibid., pp. 52–55).

The training introduced the concept of risk management into handling critical incidents and broadened the inclusion across all aspects of use of force training of the Use of Force model (commented upon under the title Tactical Options Framework (TOF)), already in use for the recently introduced less-than-lethal weapon, OC spray (ibid.).

The initial analysis in preparation for the new training regime indicated it may need to be delivered to around 80% of police officers in districts – based on the then accepted "one-size-fits-all" training requirement, which assumed that all operational officers, irrespective of where they worked, would require certification in all weapons on issue to Police. That requirement did not take account of localised risk assessments or the potential to use already available Police resources differently (e.g. the AOS). However, the new-style training did start conversations in policing about risk management, maximising safety and minimising risk and the need for certification on a regular basis to ensure skills were not lost or degraded over time (Author's personal knowledge).

The new programme was roundly welcomed by practitioners in Police, including management, trainers and operational officers (New Zealand Police, 1998, p. 56); in fact, some districts wanted to move ahead immediately with implementing the programme rather than waiting for a nationally developed syllabus to be rolled out (ibid.).

The Staff Safety Project, therefore, can be seen to have laid the foundations for several of the features of the current Police approach to the use of force. Those included the Police Integrated Tactical Training programme and the TENR and TOF assessment tools outlined in the Police Manual and previously discussed in this work.

The recommendations of the Staff Safety Project on training – the aspect of the project considered most relevant to deployment of firearms – are worthy, in the author's view, of inclusion here. They were:

> - A mandated training and certification system is introduced for staff deployed operationally to regularly qualify in operational tactics and the use of mandated equipment;
> - Designers of training programmes and authors of manual are to recognise the importance and relevance of safety principles being included;
> - All components of the recruit training programme are integrated, using the unified training principle, to ensure all instructors deliver a common safety message based on Police operation safety principles;
> - The Training Director ensures that operational safety skills are evaluated as a formal component of all recruit assessment processes and the linking of all aspects of operational safety training in the programme under one assessment band;
> - The Training Director ensures that operational safety is included in the occupational safety and health segments presented to NCO and Officer qualifying course (and non-sworn equivalent training) to highlight the issue and focus supervisors / managers on their role in implementing Police safety principles; and.
> - Issues relating to safety are included within internal promotion examinations / testing mechanisms (e.g., Practical Duties papers in the promotional examination syllabus) further focus attention on safety management. (New Zealand Police, 1998, pp. 57–58).

It is, therefore, contended that it is no exaggeration to say the project had a profound and lasting impact upon the way operational policing was approached in Aotearoa New Zealand, including with regard to use of Police firearms.

"Are the New Zealand Police on Target?": An Investigation of Alternative Models of Police Response to Dangerous and Unlawful Firearms Incidents (2000)

In 2000, as part of a Master of Public Management degree at Victoria University of Wellington, the author undertook research concerning the model of response used by New Zealand Police to "dangerous and unlawful firearms" incidents. A "dangerous" incident did not necessarily need to involve a firearm; it could, for example, involve a person armed with a bladed weapon who was posing a danger to themselves and/or others. The author's involvement on the Staff Safety Project 2 years earlier, and his time spent as an AOS member, sparked his interest in the subject, as did his recognition that the last major review of firearms deployment practice had happened in 1963, almost 40 years earlier. The research was not crisis driven and sought instead to apply various managerial techniques to the subject.

The work used a combination of strategic management techniques, risk management theory and case study comparisons to review the New Zealand Police firearms deployment model. The case studies compared Aotearoa New Zealand – where the majority of firearms were station-based and not carried by officers – to Australia, where police officers carried a sidearm at all times, and the UK (excluding Northern Ireland), where the majority of police officers were never trained to use or handle a firearm as part of their duties, instead relying on specially trained and deployed authorised firearms officers (Shortt, Are the New Zealand Police on Target - An investigation of Alternative Models of Police Response to Dangerous and Unlawful Firearms Incidents, 2000).

The research identified – unsurprisingly – that a threat from unlawful firearms use did exist in Aotearoa New Zealand and that New Zealand Police were duty bound to respond to that threat in support of the organisation's mission of enhancing community safety (ibid.) (note: this research occurred before the passage of the *Police Act 2008* (NZL) which established the legislated functions of the Police). At the time, the research characterised the threat as " small in number, and show[ing] no obvious sign of significant growth, at least over the years reviewed" (i.e. 1990–1999) (Shortt, Are the New Zealand Police on Target - An investigation of Alternative Models of Police Response to Dangerous and Unlawful Firearms Incidents, 2000).

In seeking to quantify the threat from firearms, recourse was had to the Thorp Report (1997) produced by retired judge Sir Thomas Thorp who enquired into the firearms licencing regime in Aotearoa New Zealand (ibid. p. 38). Thorp outlined that Aotearoa New Zealand "had traditionally been a rural-based society with a strong alignment to outdoor activities which include[d] hunting ... [and that] firearms (in particular rifles and shotguns) were relatively common items in many New Zealand homes in the first half of the century. With increased urbanisation and changes in lifestyles, firearms are less common in homes than they once were, but they still have a significant place in our communities" (citing Thorp, ibid., p. 38). In the report, Thorp estimated the number of firearms in Aotearoa New Zealand at between 700,000 and 1,000,000 (ibid.).

When considering the threat of "dangerous and unlawful" firearms use from a purely Police perspective, the research determined that between 1940 and 1999, 18 police officers had been killed on duty while intervening in the commission of a crime or breach of the peace (ibid., p. 45). Fourteen of those deaths were a result of illegal firearms use (ibid. pp. 44–45).

By way of contrast, the rate of fatal shootings by New Zealand Police for the period 1940–1999 (no data was kept for non-fatal shootings for the time span) showed 18 people had been shot and killed (ibid., p. 46), while during the decade immediately before the research (1990–1999), 18 people had been shot by Police, 8 fatally and 10 non-fatally (note: the 8 fatal shootings are included in the earlier 1940–1999 total) (ibid., p. 47).

In applying risk management theory to the issue, the author looked to the requirements of the *Health and Safety in Employment Act 1992* (NZL), as had the Staff Safety Project (ibid., p. 50), as well as applying the framework of the Australia New Zealand Standard for Risk Management (AS/NZS 4360 – as it was then titled) (Shortt, Are the New Zealand Police on Target - An investigation of Alternative Models of Police Response to Dangerous and Unlawful Firearms Incidents, 2000).

The practice of risk management through effective risk-based planning was described around that time by Eres Cole, in the UK, as being not only a "moral obligation" for government but also cost-effective (ibid., p. 52). At the same time, in Aotearoa New Zealand, the State Services Commission, while commenting on public service management (including policing), stated it consisted of:

> ... [risk management included] displaying a high level of knowledge and competence; delivering services and achieving results through organisational efficiency and fiscal responsibility and preparing advice, delivering services, and making decisions reached by using analytically sound, well-rounded, informed and inclusive approaches. (ibid., p. 52)

The commentary supported and underlined what the Staff Safety Project had set out to deliver through its focus on management systems, risk management and operational delivery in support of the *Health and Safety in Employment Act* and was deemed equally applicable to the research being undertaken into "dangerous and unlawful" firearms incidents.

In the comparative component of the research, the author reviewed the three Police firearms deployment models of Australia, the UK and Aotearoa New Zealand and measured them against six "key strategic factors" associated with any police firearms response model. Those factors were:

- The need to provide a 24-hour, nation-wide, response capability.
- The need to have public acceptance of the armed response model.
- The need to have police staff acceptance of the armed response model.
- The need for the model to be cost effective in its training, equipment and maintenance requirements.
- The need for the model to meet health and safety responsibilities, and.
- The need to have a tactical option to deal with events beyond the capability of the immediate response staff. (Shortt, Are the New Zealand Police on Target - An investigation of Alternative Models of Police Response to Dangerous and Unlawful Firearms Incidents, 2000, p. 70).

The research led to five potential models of firearms deployment, based on those used in the countries studied, that could be rated against the factors listed above. Those five models were:

1. Continue as per the current New Zealand Police model (no change).
2. General arming of staff – disband the AOS, but retain the STG (Aust. model).
3. General arming of staff – retain both AOS and STG (variant of Aust. model).

4. Adopt the UK model[2] – retaining AOS/STG.
5. Move from a 'on-size-fits-all' model and adopt different models dependent upon the geographic situation and risk management planning within individual Police districts. (ibid., p. 71).

From that work, it was determined that Models 1 and 5 offered the best fit when considered against the key strategic factors and, subsequently, when assessed against alignment with the views and expectations of key stakeholders (ibid., pp. 72–76).

Ultimately, following further analysis of the models and consideration of Aotearoa New Zealand's geography, distribution of population and threat environment, the research suggested that the Police should consider Model 5 further in a "blended" form using elements of Models 1 and 4 (Shortt, Are the New Zealand Police on Target - An investigation of Alternative Models of Police Response to Dangerous and Unlawful Firearms Incidents, 2000, p. 77).

The blended outcome could have, for example, allowed major urban centres (Auckland, Wellington, Christchurch and possibly Hamilton and Dunedin) to adopt the successful UK armed response vehicle (ARV)[3] approach – introduced there in 1991 – whereby AOS officers (or specially trained crews) would staff a number of armed response vehicles. They would be deployed on every operational shift to provide a highly trained and well-equipped armed response to dangerous events including those involving firearms. Meanwhile, districts with dispersed populations, smaller centres and large expansive rural areas – covered from single-officer or two-officer stations – could continue to train and equip all operational officers, or those determined to face particular risk, to provide the same initial response services. It would also have enabled districts with no rostered ARV deployment to respond to particular developments in their area of responsibility – even if for only a short timeframe – by allowing for ARVs to be "stood up" to meet a current threat such as increased gang violence or an armed and dangerous person on the loose.

The advantages of the blended model were identified as:

- Reduced refresher training audience and burden.
- Opportunity to reinvest funds saved from training into improved training programmes.
- Increased time for operational work or other training activities.
- Use of firearms being limited to a specific subset of staff who can be better controlled, monitored, and evaluated in the use of the firearms tactical option.
- Better quality and quantity of training leading to better tactical use of the firearms response option – this would result in better outcomes for the public and police in operations where it is deployed. (Shortt, Are the New Zealand Police on Target - An investigation of Alternative Models of Police Response to Dangerous and Unlawful Firearms Incidents, 2000, pp. 78–79).

Interestingly, despite this research taking place 2 years after the delivery of the Staff Safety Project's findings, the author discovered that New Zealand Police could

[2] Resulting in a significant reduction in the number of police officers who would be trained and authorised to use firearms within NZP (to levels somewhere between 10 and 25% to allow for NZ geographical issues) (ibid., 71).

[3] A more detailed description of the UK armed response vehicle concept is provided in Chap. 10.

still not answer four quite fundamental questions concerning its view of itself as a "routinely unarmed" police service. They were:

- How many police officers on duty at any given time in Aotearoa New Zealand are carrying firearms on their person or have them immediately available in their vehicles?
- How many hours of policing activity are undertaken while officers are armed in comparison to that undertaken while unarmed?
- How many shots were fired by New Zealand Police (outside of training and destruction of dangerous or injured animals)? And,
- How many people are shot and wounded by police officers annually? (ibid., pp. 81–82).

There were no databases or central points of information collection where answers to those four questions could be readily found. Quite an extraordinary lack of information to support the contention that the New Zealand Police were a "routinely unarmed" police service (ibid., pp. 82–83). The author was saddened to discover the situation had not improved 20 years later when an Evidenced-Based Policing Centre report stated:

> One difficulty in drawing any conclusions about the likely outcomes of routine arming is that we do not have good information about how often Police are currently armed with firearms, and therefore if Police are arming more frequently than in previous years. (New Zealand Police, 2021b, p. 22)

When completed, in 2000, the research paper was presented to the Deputy Commissioner for Operations and the Superintendent in charge of the Operations Group at New Zealand Police's national headquarters. The next time it was raised with the author was when he was interviewed as one of the contributors to the review being undertaken by Marshall and Shuey, in 2001. The author's research paper was noted in the bibliography of the subsequent report. It is the author's view that the Marshall and Shuey report was prompted, at least in part, by the work he had submitted.

Several years later, the author had his research raised with him when an inspector working on the final review to be covered in this chapter commented that the research report was part of the material being considered. Clearly, it had not sunk completely from sight and was, again in some small way, continuing to contribute to the thinking and conversations happening regarding use of force and firearms within New Zealand Police.

A Strategic Evaluation of the New Zealand Police Position Concerning the Use of Force When Responding to Potentially Violent Situations: A Review of Best Practice, Policy and Training (2001)

In mid-2000, the Deputy Commissioner for Operations (who had earlier received the author's thesis detailed above) determined that it was "timely for the New Zealand Police to consider training, policy and practice issues surrounding the question of lethal force and Police response to critical incidents" (Marshall & Sheuy, 2001). Two reviewers were selected, one being a New Zealand Police detective superintendent (Peter Marshall) and the other an assistant commissioner from the Victoria Police, Australia, (Ray Shuey). Shuey had recently visited Canada, the USA and Europe looking at "best practice" matters and was described as being "responsible for the implementation of Project Beacon which dealt with staff safety issues in Victoria … Beacon acted as the catalyst and formed the basis of New Zealand's SSTT programme" (ibid., 7).

The reviewers set out to not "… 're-invent the wheel' concerning areas referred to in the terms of reference. Rather it was a practical approach to scrutinise current training, policy and practices, compare those to international developments and to highlight specific areas where changes or improvements could be considered" (ibid.).

In the environmental scan section of the review, the author's described Aotearoa New Zealand as:

> … a rather unique environment in terms of international policing policy and practice when it comes to the armed response of its members in responding to critical incidents … New Zealand Police are not armed in the normal course of their duties … the New Zealand Government, the New Zealand Police executive, members of the New Zealand Police and the public at large overwhelmingly support this stance … New Zealand practice is a rather unusual 'one size fits all' approach, with the Armed Offenders Squad providing the backstop in terms of formal expertise. (Marshall & Sheuy, 2001)

The review authors went on to describe the New Zealand Police policy position, linking it to the previously summarised report by the author, as:

> … a measured and considered one, which is adhered to on a national basis … there is an increasing prevalence of firearms being seen and used in law enforcement situations. This raises the possibility of 'organisational creep' resulting in the New Zealand Police suddenly waking up to the fact that it is essentially armed in the practical sense. This concern was addressed in some detail by Inspector Richard Shortt in preparation for this Master's thesis. (ibid., pp. 9–10).

One of the matters touched upon by the reviewers as being imperative was a national staff safety database that could bring together information from across the police organisation on the use of force and all other aspects of staff safety (ibid. pp. 12–13). They were impressed by work underway to deliver such a system and were expecting it to be delivered in the first 6 months of 2002. The proposed register was envisaged to also capture data on the use of firearms and even situations where firearms were present, but not used (ibid., p. 12). It was hoped that this new national system would also be used to inform and, if needed, modify the training being delivered via the SSTT programme (ibid., p. 13).

The Armed Offenders Squad also came within the purview of the review, with a suggestion being made that the name and role definition might be changed to better reflect the use being made of such teams (ibid., pp. 13–14). The suggested changes went on to include training the members in the use of a wider variety of less-than-lethal options and weapons so they could be used in a wider range of potential or actual critical incidents (ibid., p. 14). It was hoped the shift would also encourage operational supervisors to be less reluctant in calling out the squad, which was reflected in the reviewers discovering that there had been a decrease in the number of squad callouts in recent years (Marshall & Sheuy, 2001, p. 14).

Separately, the reviewers noted that the AOS commander in Auckland had been tasked, by the Superintendent in overall charge of AOS nationally (Superintendent in charge of the Police National Headquarters-based Operations Group), to consider "the merits or otherwise, of full time deployment by AOS members in the pan-Auckland environment", being directly linked to the current author's suggestion in his research paper (ibid., p. 14). The author heard no more regarding that tasking and was not contacted for any comment or input so is unable to say how the matter was finalised, other than to note that ARVs did not eventuate in "pan-Auckland".

One final set of observations the reviewers made concerning AOS and its availability were regarding speed of response and the psychological aspect of having them close at hand. On speed of response, the reviewers acknowledged the inherent time delay in having AOS on scene with their requirement to first travel to a base location to dress, arm and brief, before departing to where they were required. That was at odds with the Victorian model where their equivalent staff have their uniform and weapons at home (protected by security paid for by the Victoria Police) and they are uplifted and deploy straight to the scene. The reviewers also noted with regard to how initial response staff may be influenced by AOS speed of deployment that "… know[ing] that a team of higher skilled operatives is available for deployment, [response officers] will be less likely to engage in a confrontational situation, as opposed to maintaining a containment function" (ibid., p. 15).

In their consideration of the SSTT programme, the reviewers determined that the Tactical Options Model in use by Aotearoa New Zealand, in fact at the heart of the model, benefited from its simplicity and was consistent with international best practice. They did recognise, however, that "marketing of this model and associated philosophy over the ensuing years will need constant reinforcement" (ibid., pp. 18–19).

When it came to delivery of the SSTT programme, the authors felt the need to highlight a risk to Police that the 100% attendance schedule was in danger of not being met (Marshall & Sheuy, 2001, pp. 18–19). That risk eventuated out of the New Zealand Police decision to make the 4-day programme a necessity for 100% of sworn employees (constabulary staff with the power of arrest) (ibid., p. 19). The reviewers instead suggested that while "all identified sworn employees need to undertake Days 1 and 3 (conflict resolution etc.) … the District Commanders should decide which members should have the full firearms training" (ibid., pp. 19–20). The review also noted that less than the optimal number of trainers was employed and that this also exacerbated the risk Police faced (ibid., p. 20). Harking back to earlier commentary in this book regarding the pressures on district training and attendance at it, the reviewers noted that they attended 1 SSTT session where the expectation was that 20 staff would be present; there were instead only 6 (ibid.).

Further adding to the reviewers' concerns regarding SSTT was disquiet expressed to them about the number of staff who "… have not received training and who accordingly are not certified to carry such equipment as OC Spray, PR 24 batons,

ASP batons and firearms" (ibid., pp. 21–22). The issue, they felt, left the New Zealand Police exposed to criticism and to provisions of the *Health and Safety in Employment Act 1992*.

On the matter of "less-than-lethal" weapons and alternatives, the review noted that the evolving nature of those items internationally should always be taken into account by New Zealand Police. Several promising options were arriving, such as 12-gauge shotgun baton rounds, tasers and a pepper ball system filled with OC powder for use over distance of up to 30 feet (or 9 meters). Victoria Police were also using a "fire extinguisher" form of OC spray and a foam form of OC spray for inside use where air conditioning might unhelpfully spread a spray (ibid., p. 23).

When it came to reviewing policies, procedures and guidelines, Assistant Commissioner Shuey found that while training material "embraced" the "maximise safety-minimise risk" mantra, other documentation in the structure of policy and procedure needed to "promote a consistency in message" (Marshall & Sheuy, 2001, p. 24). Furthermore, he offered the view that "operational safety policy statements and General Instructions must be concise and simple" (ibid.). The review suggested a simplification of policy for the use of firearms to "defence of life" and "only as a last resort" (ibid.). The reviewers also suggested an overarching critical incident management statement similar to:

> In dealing with armed or potentially dangerous situations, the primary consideration must be the safety of yourself, the public and the offender or suspect. In all instances, the minimum use of force is to be applied for resolution of any incident. The ultimate assessment of any actions undertaken will be 'were the actions taken reasonable considering all the circumstance which existed at the time 'MAXIMISE SAFETY, MINIMISE RISK. [emphasis in the original] (ibid.)

In their summary for the policy, procedure and guidelines section of their work, the reviewers reiterated that the "maxim" for use of firearms should be simply "*Defence of Life – Last Resort*" [italics in the original] (ibid., p. 25) and that international best practice advocates that policies "should be clear and simple, with detail, explanation or micro management being placed in training manuals" (ibid.).

Before moving on to consider some tactical aspects of firearms deployments, the reviewers touched on a series of other topics which will not be covered here in detail. Those topics included first aid kit access (recommending operational officers have access to well-stocked kits); breath/blood testing for officers involved in lethal or potentially lethal force incidents, recommending that it be investigated; PR 24 and ASP batons (recommending adding PR 24 training to SSTT certification process if that baton was to stay in service[4]); and carotid hold (attempts to withdraw use of this hold in New Zealand Police would attract great resistance, despite its

[4] The PR 24 baton was withdrawn from general operational use in 1999/2000 following a review sparked by the Staff Safety Project and replaced with the ASP extendable baton. Despite this, some units insisted on still carrying the PR 24 – but no certified training was provided, given the earlier removal. This issue sheds some light on the powerful interests that can operate within what is supposed to be a hierarchically directed police service and which can challenge the directions of the executive.

potential – if not used correctly – to cause death. A further review of its use was recommended) (Marshall & Sheuy, 2001, pp. 25–29).

The final section of the report was titled "14. Glock Pistols" (ibid., pp. 29–31). In it, the reviewers drew attention to the tactical approach in districts which was to see the pistol as "the primary weapon when critical incidents arise" (ibid., p. 30). It was not clear to the reviewers whether this was due to a lack of 0.223 rifles or whether there was a lack of confidence in using the rifle.

In essence, the reviewers sought a change in that tactical approach and for police officers to consider the rifle as the primary weapon, and the pistol as a secondary form of self-defence, much as the AOS did (ibid., pp. 30–31). The review recommended a national audit of firearms to see if indeed there were an inconsistent number of rifles to pistols and to send a "strong message to Districts reinforcing the need for the .223 Remington rifles to be deployed in conjunction with and in support of Glocks at the first available opportunity, whenever there is a need to respond to critical events" (ibid., p. 31).

This, as had been stated earlier in this book, was a substantial shift in tactical approach for New Zealand Police given the general instruction edict to avoid unnecessary display of firearms and the traditional approach dating back to the late 1940s and 1950s – and experienced by the author – of stuffing a revolver or other handgun into one's pocket when required to attend an armed incident.

The review, while suggesting some immediate changes, for the most part outlined areas where New Zealand Police could undertake further research or continue work already in train. In a press release about the review's findings, the deputy commissioner who had commissioned it hailed it as a "positive … analysis of our use of force operational approach, training and guidelines" promising yet more analysis and consultation around the recommendations (New Zealand Police, 2001).

Coincidentally, almost a decade later, at the time the next piece of work to be commented upon came into focus, Detective Superintendent Peter Marshall was finishing a term of secondment to the Solomon Islands Police Force as its commissioner and would shortly return to Aotearoa New Zealand to assume the commissionership of the New Zealand Police.

Review of Access and Availability of Firearms for New Zealand Police (2010)

Initiated by the commissioner of New Zealand Police, this review was commenced during the 2009–2010 financial year with a requirement for those responsible to report back recommendations by "…the end of 2010" (New Zealand Police, 2010, p. 2). The work would have a profound outcome for New Zealand Police, which – in the author's opinion – was to usher in the fifth strategic policy shift for the organisation regarding firearms.

As detailed in Chap. 4, the decade 2001–2010 had been a most notable one for New Zealand Police. Three officers were shot and killed, eight shot and wounded, and a number of others shot at but suffering no physical injury. The nature of the review that will now be discussed was, in the author's mind, not surprising; however, some of what it revealed was.

The first public acknowledgement of the work, which the author could find, was a five-paragraph section in the "Commissioner's Overview" contained in the New Zealand Police Annual Report for 2009–2010 (ibid.). Given the importance of the work's outcome, the segment is presented in its entirety below:

> **Staff safety.**
> While our staff strive to reduce violence in the community, they risk becoming targets themselves. This threat was highlighted in February 2010, when three officers were viciously attacked in separate incidents. The safety of our staff remains a high priority and we are constantly assessing policies, procedures and the equipment needed to keep officers from harm. We welcome the rollout of Taser throughout all districts. It is notable that in 90 percent of cases where Taser was presented, the situation was successfully de-escalated without the Taser being discharged. An extensive review of firearms training and accessibility of firearms to police was commenced. Recommendations are due by the end of 2010.
> (New Zealand Police, 2010, p. 2)

The statement was released in the Police Annual Report at the end of September 2010 (ibid, p. 3). By 15 November, a small team of five was updating the Police executive meeting with a slide-based presentation under the agenda heading "Item 2: Access and Availability of Firearms" (Ross, 2021, p. 2). The "action points" from the meeting identified that there were seven "key points covered": they were:

> Needing to put emphasis on national consistency.
> Need to consider safety in broader terms i.e. not just physical safety but emotional safety as well.
> Need to identify groups to have greater access to firearms – subset identified as at higher risk.
> 99% of time officers don't face significant risk. Need a consistent level of firearms access for remaining 1%.
> Risk assessments are key in every case responded to.
> Greater training on assessing risk and decision making is also key. (ibid.)

The presentation team were clearly well into their work and moving at pace. The meeting's minutes went on to note that the team would deliver another presentation "... next week prior to PEC" (Ross, 2021, p. 2).

The next mention of the team's work was a short extract from a document titled "Police Executive Meeting Action Points – 22 November 2010", some 7 days later. The extremely brief extract noted:

> Item 2: Access and Availability of Firearms (presentation).
> Presentation notes.
> Presentation to be given to PEC this week.
> For noting. (ibid.)

On 24 November 2010, a second presentation was made to the Police Executive Committee (PEC). Again, the presentation consisted of a series of slides, 30 in total

(Firearms Access and Availability Team, 2010). The slides were released by New Zealand Police following Official Information Act requests by the author.

The introductory slide contained a statement which, in the author's view, was likely to be a summary of the terms of reference for the project (note: New Zealand Police did not release any Terms of Reference for the work in response to the author's Official Information Act requests):

> Undertake a national review of the access and availability of firearms for Police District staff, and if required, options for increasing the access and availability of firearms for operational staff. (Firearms Access and Availability Team, 2010, p. 1)

Despite the commissioner's Annual Report statement referring to training, the training element of the project was not covered – in any detail – in the slides released by New Zealand Police. It, therefore, appeared that either that aspect of the work was given to a separate project team to run in tandem or it was undertaken after the accessibility and availability issues were resolved. As mentioned earlier, in Chap. 5 regarding training, considerable work and change did occur within the New Zealand Police tactical training regime during the period 2012 to 2014. It can be realistically inferred, in the author's view, that those changes quite likely had links to the accessibility and availability team's undertakings and the outcomes it achieved.

The second observation the author would make, based on the review's title, and the nature of the presentation referenced above, was that the commissioner had already turned his mind to the possibility of increasing access to firearms and that this had occurred sometime before the public announcement via the Annual Report in September 2010.

Returning to the contents of the presentation, a number of the slides are summarised below (note: the author elected to focus on the slides he believed were of greatest relevance, with two (slides 6 and 7) being reproduced in full after release under the Official Information Act), given the presentation set the stage for what came next in December 2010:

> (Slide 1) "Presentation will focus on two questions:
> What is the need for greater access?
> What are the options?"
>
> (Slides 2 and 3) "International Evidence … Conclusion.
>
> evidence is inconclusive: we have not been able to locate any research that has systematically tested the assumption that regular firearm carriage by Police makes Police or communities safer".

(Slide 4) "Police's current firearms policy

'... generally an unarmed service ... firearms need to be available easily and safely. ... principle of minimum carriage and minimum visibility of firearms ... must be applied at all times'".

Carrying firearms in vehicles: Policy is permissive – "District Commanders may authorise the carriage of firearms in Police vehicles to ensure ready access to them if needed".

(Slide 5) "Environmental Risk Factors

Illegal use of firearms:

Overall firearms specific violence ... trended only slightly up between 2004–09. 1.6 to 1.7 offences per 10,000 population;

Some serious offences involving firearms have increased: threatens to kill [up] 36% and aggravated robbery [up] 50% between 2004 and 2009;

Police intelligence on organised crime groups shows there had been an increase in the number of firearms found at drug operations;

Number of firearms seized as a result of a search has risen from 555 in 2005 to 805 in 2009, but so had the number of search warrants executed. Firearms are found at 19% of searches".

(Slide 6) "Assaults on Police":

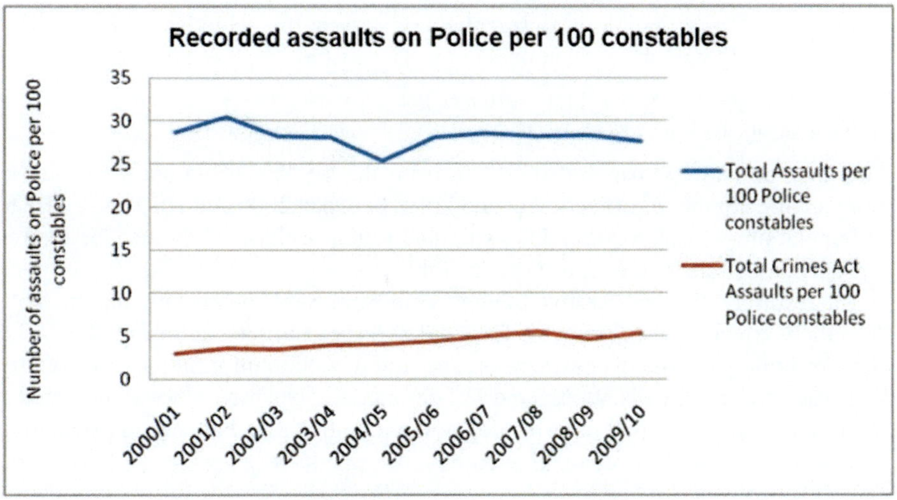

(Firearms Access and Availability Team, 2010)

(Slide 7) "Assaults on Police":

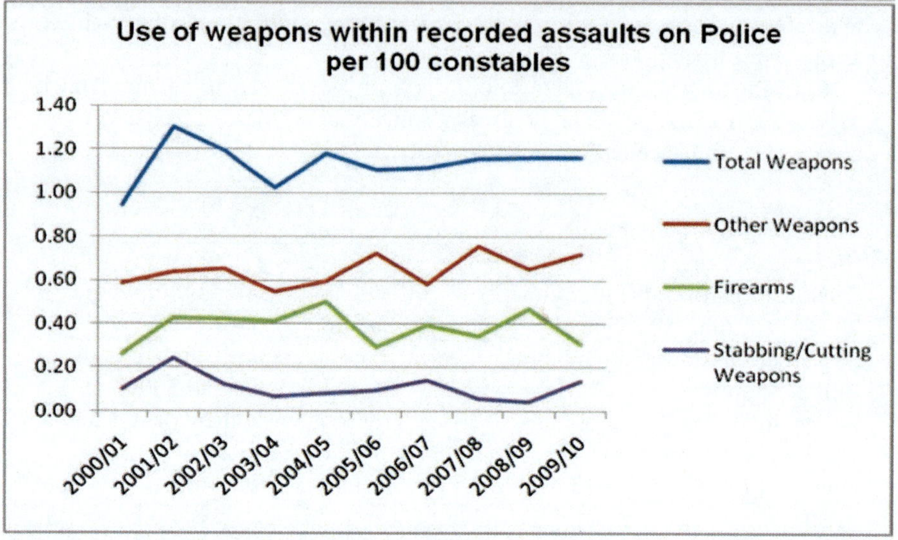

(Firearms Access and Availability Team, 2010)

In summary, the assault data showed a slight upward trend (from approx. 2.5 to 5.5/5.6 assaults per 100 constables) for Crimes Act assaults, but no trend increases were discernible for use of weapons against officers – except perhaps for "other weapons", in any of the three categories, across the decade presented.

Further on, information was presented concerning the "Number of Police officers shot" along with an international comparison (ibid., p. 9). That revealed:

> Between September 2008 and July 2010 nine Police constables have been shot, and there has been another five incidents where Police constables have been fired at.

The international comparison used data from the USA, Canada and Australia to compare the number of officers shot and killed between 2000 and 2009 and a "Head of population per Police office [sic] shot and killed (millions)" figure. The figures presented as "slide 9" are reproduced in Table 6.1.

Interestingly, the comparative figures came from English-speaking nations with "routinely armed" police services. They did not, for example, include the UK, who were "routinely unarmed". Furthermore, nor did it contain information on a country that was of interest to New Zealand Police, namely, Norway. Norway operated a model of "vehicle-based" firearms deployment, and it also had a total population similar to Aotearoa New Zealand (Hendy, 2012, pp. 46–47).

Table 6.1 International comparison of police officers shot (2000–2009)

Country	# police officers shot and killed: 2000–2009	Head of population per police officer shot and killed (millions)
NZ	3	1.4
Australia	5	4.5
Canada	17	2.0
USA	481	0.6

(Data obtained from New Zealand Police)

However, returning to the presentation, it went on to continue the analysis of the environment facing New Zealand Police and among other information stated:

> In 2009 4.1% of all Tactical Options used by officers (not including specialist squads) were with [sic] firearms – will be an over-representation as many low level tactical options are likely to be highly under reported. (Firearms Access and Availability Team, 2010, p. 11)

Later, additional context was supplied using two district-by-district aspects of the police environment. Firstly, information pertaining to the percentage of police vehicles in each district with firearms safes installed. Those were between 10% (lowest – Counties Manukau district) and 34% (highest – AMCOS[5]). Secondly, sets of data outlining population density, firearms violence per 10,000 people and total assaults per 100 constables. The data are reproduced below by the author in Table 6.2:

To help provide further context to readers unfamiliar with New Zealand Police's coverage, there are 12 operational Police districts (excluding AMCOS) that can, in the author's experience, be *roughly* classified – using population of significant urban centres and the overall geography of the district – as either *major urban centres* (population: 200 k–1.5 m), *medium urban centres* (population: 55 K to 200 K) and associated rural areas and *small urban centres* (population: 35 K to 54 K), with substantive associated rural areas. Given Aotearoa New Zealand's geography, even "major urban centres" have some rural locations associated with them. The Police district divisions, therefore, based on the author's view, are:

- **Major urban centres**: Waitemata, Auckland, Counties Manukau, Wellington (including Lower Hutt and Porirua cities) and Canterbury.
- **Medium urban centres and associated rural areas**: Waikato, Bay of Plenty, Eastern, Central and Southern.
- **Small urban centres, with substantive rural areas**: Northland and Tasman.

Halfway through the presentation, reference was made to health and safety obligations on employers in Aotearoa New Zealand. It was confirmed that employers were expected to use a "… systematic process to identify hazards, and use a

---

[5] AMCOS stands for Auckland Metro-Crime and Operations Support. A "pseudo-district" created by the three districts that make up the greater Auckland metropolitan area – Aotearoa New Zealand's largest city – to support various Auckland-wide policing activities (Author's personal knowledge)

Table 6.2 Police district comparison of population, firearms access, violence and assaults

District	Pop density (people per sq./km)	Vehicles with gun safes [best estimate based on bar chart]	Vehicles carrying firearms	Firearms violence offences (per 10,000 pop)	Total assaults per 100 constables
Northland	13	26%	8%	1.7	44
Waitemata	200	25%	9%	1.4	29
Auckland	758	12.5%	4%	1.7	31
Counties Manukau	192	10%	7%	3.3	24
AMCOS	383*	34%	14%	2.1*	28*
Waikato	24	14%	5%	1.7	27
Bay of Plenty	12	24%	12%	2	44
Central	12	22%	6%	1.9	29
Eastern	10	27%	22%	1.7	39
Wellington	68	15%	4%	1.3	38
Tasman	4	22%	16%	1.7	39
Canterbury	16	26%	13%	0.9	27
Southern	5	27%	24%	1.3	26

aGreater Auckland average [in original] (Data obtained from New Zealand Police)

hierarchy of controls to address and manage …" them. Furthermore, the presentation confirmed the hierarchy should aim to either "… eliminate, isolate or minimise [hazards], using all practicable steps". In concluding, the slide identified that "there is also the requirement that employees are adequately trained in the safe use of equipment that they may handle; and measures that are put in place are monitored for their effectiveness" (Firearms Access and Availability Team, 2010, p. 18).

The presentation then moved to present arguments for and against the question "Is there a need to increase access and availability of firearms?" (Firearms Access and Availability Team, 2010, pp. 19–21). In summary, the three slides stated:

Arguments for:

- Policing continues to be … challenging …unpredictable…9 officers shot;
- … another 5 shootings … in a two year period;
- Greater access to firearms will give officers the full range of tactical.

options (offensive and defensive);

- There is a need to increase the speed at which officers can access firearms for those unplanned incidents. … links with … underlying principles of … policy … that 'firearms need to be available quickly, easily and safely'.
- Police has Health and Safety Obligations to minimise hazards/risks for its employees.
- Evidence of some increasing risk - … serious assaults on Police, … greater presence of firearms at drug operations, increase in some serious firearms specific violence offences;
- There is District inconsistency. For reasons, not seem [sic] to be based on risk, staff in different Districts undertaking the same role have different levels of access to firearms;

- Increased availability will make Police and communities safer (no conclusive evidence). (Firearms Access and Availability Team, 2010, pp. 19–20).

Arguments against:

- Greater access will actually make Police Officers and the community less safe (no conclusive evidence);
- Encourages criminals to further arm themselves (no conclusive evidence);
- More people will be shot by Police;
- Officers will start using firearms more regularly, ahead of other tactical options;
- Greater visibility of weapons will affect the relationship between the Police and the law abiding community (no conclusive evidence). (ibid., p. 21).

This part of the presentation ended with a set of four bullet points that set out what was called the "Case for change"; it stated:

Case for change: There is evidence that

- Police officers could be presented with more firearms then [sic] we have in the past;
- Changes in the drug world – more arming within drug operations.
- Increase in 'risk' to Police at the serious end of criminal offending and more serious assaults of Police;
- Police has a permissive delegated policy which has been inconsistently implemented across Districts in regards to the availability of firearms.

Any changes in the access to firearms must be part of a wider system/approach – including policies, training, supervision, risk assessment, command etc..

(Firearms Access and Availability Team, 2010, p. 22)

The presentation then continued with some final slides that were fully redacted by Police when sent to the author. These were each imprinted with the reason for redaction being "section 6(c) of the Official Information Act 1982" (Firearms Access and Availability Team, 2010). The *Official Information Act 1982* (NZL) identified that content may be withheld if its release would "… prejudice the maintenance of the law, including the prevention, investigation, and detection of offences, and the right to a fair trial …" (New Zealand Government, 1982). The headings of each slide were visible, however, and consisted of two titled "Options being considered" (ibid., pp. 23 & 24), one titled "Options" (ibid., p. 25) and a final one titled "Immediate options" (ibid., p. 26). The redactions were referred back to New Zealand Police for reconsideration; however, no result had been received by the time this book was published.

The presentation then moved on to identify "Required future work" which also included an "indicative" implementation plan which required further work to develop definitive timelines, costings, configurations for safes, procurement plans, monitoring arrangements and an evaluation framework (ibid., pp. 28–29).

The presentation ended with the heading "Next Steps" with just one bullet point "Report to the Commissioner in the next week" (ibid., p. 30).

In essence, the Police Executive Committee (PEC) was "under the pump" to consider the presentation and to decide on a way forward (if in fact the redacted sections did not already make that clear) so that the commissioner could have his report in December 2010, as outlined in his September 2010 Annual Report overview.

In response to the author's Official Information Act requests, a draft memorandum from the PEC to the commissioner, dated 3 December 2010, was released to him. The three-page document was also redacted in part, again using the s. 6(c) grounds. The draft memorandum reminded the commissioner that the presentation team had delivered its overview to PEC, 11 days earlier, and outlined the options proposed, which were once again redacted. The memorandum, which is reproduced here in detail due to its substantive impact on the outcome of the project and New Zealand Police, stated:

Comment

PEC had a robust debate on this presentation with the presenters. Following the presentation, the presenters were asked to leave so that PEC could discuss the matter ' in committee'. Each PEC member was asked by the Acting Chair, Assistant Commissioner Jon White to express their views on the issue.

A number of themes were evident from the discussion relating to the need for national consistency in approach and the need for clarity for staff as to what they can and cannot do. The decisions should not turn on funding considerations and is not one that will be able to be decided on an evidential research base alone.

Nevertheless, there was a view that some of the analysis undertaken to date could be shored up e.g. it would be useful to understand what is done in different jurisdictions which would help build a case for change.

On balance, PEC members broadly agreed:

- notwithstanding that the number of recorded assaults on Police per one hundred constables is stable, and the evidence that carrying firearms makes Police of [sic] communities safer is inconclusive, there remains a case for change based on the fact that nine officers have been shot in two years (with three killed), and five other officers have been involved in shooting incidents where they have been shot at;
- the case for change should not be premised on an argument that greater access to firearms will *of itself* make Police officers or members of the public safer, but on a systems approach that suggests that [Italics in original]: increased access and availability + increased consistency in approach + refined risk assessment + consistent application of risk assessment + increased training and supervision = decrease in operational risk,
- by lifting each of these variables we will likely see an overall change in risk;
- increased access and availability in firearms will result, but not need to be defended [sic] as the only contributing factor – it is not a panacea in its own right (the question was asked whether in recent cases would better access compared to better situation planning and assessment have made a difference?);
- a systems approach will also see Police maximise the resources we currently have (rather than them being locked up in stations);
- there is a need for national consistency across districts – while the graphs presented at first blush may indicate that the practice across districts is variable, there may be good reason for this e.g. the higher percentages may relate to districts with more one-person stations in rural communities or to other rural/urban differences – the team should be tasked with interrogating the data a bit further;
- minimum standards of consistency need to define availability as well as accessibility – what do we mean by these?
- Language is important – are we talking *enhanced* availability v *increased* availability v *improved* availability? [Italics in the original].
- [redacted].

(Police Executive Committee, 2010, pp. 2–3)

The memorandum concluded by saying that "on balance there was agreement that there needs to be a change …" and that there was a need to "… define minimum standards of availability and accessibility …" given the discretion of each district commander to address district needs (Police Executive Committee, 2010, p. 3).

The author cannot confirm that this draft memorandum was the same as the one ultimately sent to the commissioner by the committee. However, it is clear that the committee was on side for a change in policy, wanted national consistency and believed that by providing greater access and availability of firearms, that risk to operational officers could be lessened.

Interestingly, nowhere in the documents was there any indication that the public had been spoken with or consulted by Police about their views on providing greater access and availability to Police firearms. Perhaps that was done, but it was not reflected in any the papers released by Police or in their commentary in annual reports where this issue received coverage, scant as that was.

In one of the slides from 24 November, it was evident from a New Zealand Police Association survey of their members (police constables, sergeants and senior sergeants, based on author's experience), "95% of members supported availability of firearms in every frontline police vehicle" (Firearms Access and Availability Team, 2010, p. 10). The slide went on to say that the "district consultation" with "… 365 staff in 5 Districts and at the RNZPC courses … mirrored NZPA consultation. Staff considered the major gap was in unplanned situations and that access to firearms is not timely as it could be" (ibid.).

Clearly, there was a groundswell of feeling among "rank-and-file" officers that they wanted greater access to firearms.

That situation aligned with commentary from Australia in the mid-1990s concerning the same issue. Professor Rick Sarre, in his work on the arming of Australian police, noted that it occurred through:

> … a process of incremental accretion with tacit yet popular public acquiescence, rather than as a result of a careful series of decisions following public debate. (Sarre, 1996)

Sarre went on to identify that the process described above was driven by:

> … the greater acceptance in most jurisdictions of allowing officers themselves to gauge their own levels of vulnerability and to request the carriage of a firearm as a means of addressing that. (Sarre, cited in Shortt, 2000, p. 33)

The next documented commentary regarding the proposal regarding increased accessibility and availability was in an "out of session" Police Executive Meeting (PEM)[6] report on the topic of "Firearms and Taser Policy" (Perry, 2011, p. 2). In the report, it was noted by way of background that:

> In April 2011 Police initiated the Firearms and Taser Project. The objective of the project is to increase the access and availability of firearms and Tasers for General Duty [uniformed

[6]PEM, as opposed to PEC, is a lower-level executive meeting within New Zealand Police. PEC occurs monthly, while PEM takes place weekly (State Services Commission; Treasury; Department of the Prime Minister and Cabinet, 2012).

> response officers] and Road Policing [uniformed officers responsible for the majority of traffic enforcement duty] as a means to maximise safety and minimise risk of harm for its employees and members of the public. (ibid.)

The report went on to confirm that a "key aspect of the project" was provision of a "range of tactical equipment" in the patrol vehicles used by the above two groups of Police staff (ibid.). That equipment was described as "... include[ing] Glocks, Bushmasters (or M4's), Ballistic Armour (Hard Armour Plate; HAP), Tasers and any related security arrangements for carriage of firearms and Tasers including safes and holsters" (ibid.).

Clearly, from what the document contained, the New Zealand Police commissioner had agreed with the proposal to take firearms out of police stations and to put them into a large number of police vehicles. In all likelihood, that was the recommended option from the redacted set of options presented in the previously discussed PEC presentation slides and memorandum to the commissioner.

Further confirmation of the substantial change came in the 2011–2012 Police Annual Report, where the newly appointed commissioner, Peter Marshall, confirmed that:

> Front-line vehicles are being fitted with safes for firearms and ballistic armour.
>
> Improved firearm and Taser accessibility is part of a coordinated approach to increase Police and public safety, including improved policies, procedures and training. The prime objective of Police's tactical response remains to cordon, contain, and communicate.

In the author's opinion, that was confirmation of the biggest strategic change to New Zealand Police's position on firearms access and use and, therefore, ability to use lethal force, since the creation of the Armed Offenders Squad almost 50 years earlier.

It was, again in the author's view, a return to the very origins of the New Zealand Police and the times when Armed Constabulary, and then New Zealand Police Force, officers carried pistols and carbines with them during their frontier duties in the mid- to late 1800s. True, the style was different, the weapons were in containers in vehicles, but the tactical outcome was the same; they were immediately to hand and no longer stored predominantly in stations.

The New Zealand Police was once again a routinely well-armed police organisation.

Bibliography

Firearms Access and Availability Team. (2010, November 24). *Review of the access and availability of Firearms - PEC presentation, 24 November 2010*. New Zealand Police.

Hendy, R. (2012). *The strategic impact of routine arming the New Zealand police*. Victoria University of Wellington.

Keay, D., Russell, N., & den Heyer, G. (1998). *The assault review - a study of assaults on New Zealand police officers*. New Zealand Police.

Marshall, P., & Sheuy, R. (2001). *A strategic evaluation of the New Zealand police position concerning the use of force when responding to potentially violent situations: A review of best practice, policy and training*. New Zealand Police.

New Zealand Government. (1982, December). *Official information act 1982*. New Zealand Government.

New Zealand Police. (1998). *Improving safety in the New Zealand police - report of the staff safety project*. New Zealand Police.

New Zealand Police. (2001, December 14). *Use of Force Report explores options*. Retrieved from police.govt.nz: https:/police.govt.nz/Home/News/Use of Force Report explores options.

New Zealand Police. (2010). *New Zealand police 2009/10 annual report*. New Zealand Police.

New Zealand Police. (2021a, September 30). *Officers killed by criminal acts*. Retrieved from police.govt.nz: https://www.police.govt.nz/about-us/history-and-museum/memorial/officers-killed-criminal-acts.

New Zealand Police. (2021b, August). *Appropriate tactical settings - Insights and evidence brief*. Retrieved from police.govt.nz: https://www.police.govt.nz/sites/default/files/publications/evidence-brief-appropriate-tactical-settings.pdf.

Perry, N. (2011). *Firearms and Taser policy - PEM/11/131*. New Zealand Police.

Police Executive Committee. (2010, December 3). *Review of access and availability of firearms*. New Zealand Police.

Ross, J. (2021, August 19). *Reference: IR-01-21-22061: Official information act request response*. New Zealand Police.

Sarre, R. (1996). *Firearms carriage by police in Australia*. University of South Australia.

Shortt, R. (2000). *Are the New Zealand police on target - an investigation of alternative models of police response to dangerous and unlawful firearms incidents*. Victoria University of Wellington.

State Services Commission; Treasury; Department of the Prime Minister and Cabinet. (2012). *Formal review of the New Zealand police (police)*. State Services Commission; Treasury; Department of the Prime Minister and Cabinet.

Part II
Reality of Lethal Force Use – 2000–2019

Chapter 7
Use of Lethal Force Against New Zealand Police and the Risks Faced

The importance of discussing use of force, including lethal force, against police lies in the fact that all 43 PCA/IPCA reports reviewed justified police use of lethal force under the self-defence provisions of section 48 of the *Crimes Act 1961* (NZL), with 35 of those cases using section 48 exclusively, while 8 included section 48 in combination with either section 39 or sections 39 and 40 in 1 instance. Self-defence requires the police officer, or another person, to be under a substantial threat before it can be claimed.

In the author's review of the PCA/IPCA publicly released reports spanning the period 2000–2019, six instances were found where there was a danger evident to people other than responding police officers (i.e. four involved a hostage or hostages; two involved armed men firing random shots either in or into public places); the rest of the cases primarily involved direct risk to responding police officers.

When considering the risks faced by police officers, it is useful to have both a context and a framework to help appreciate the environment and to quantify the level of risk being faced. The first part of this chapter will address the environmental context, while the second will use the Australia New Zealand Standard on Risk Management (Standards New Zealand, 2020) to analyse the level of risk police officers face.

With regard to the general historical perspective, there are some key points that need to be commented upon to understand the risks to police officers.

As was outlined in Chap. 4, firearms had become prevalent in Aotearoa New Zealand for a range of legitimate reasons, stemming from their introduction during the country's earliest colonial times. Despite the presence and prevalence of firearms, the numbers of shootings detailed above do not, in the author's view, reveal a country with an out-of-control firearms culture.

For example, as Swinton described (Swinton, 2019), the country was reasonably relaxed about the presence, ownership and use of firearms. In his work on the regulation of firearms, for example, he noted:

> The next 50 years [1930s to 1980s] were marked by a small number of firearms-related trends. First, there was a growing movement for the relaxation of certain registration requirements, both from Police, whose resources were strained by the paper-based registration system, and from gun owners … Second, guns continued to be a common presence in New Zealander's lives. Hunting, fishing, and other recreational uses of guns grew in popularity, aided by the Government's establishing the New Zealand Mountain Safety Council

R. S. Shortt, *Lethal Force and New Zealand Police*,
https://doi.org/10.1007/978-3-031-05269-9_7

> in 1965 to promote the safe use of firearms. Military interests in maintaining accurate sharpshooters during the two world wars and the return of soldiers from World War II with arms in tow further added to the presence of guns in daily life. Third, New Zealand enjoyed a period of 'peaceful enjoyment', one relatively devoid of firearms related crime that gave little reason to expend political capital on gun registration. (ibid., p. 4)

However, crime trends were shifting in the country, and Police – despite their views on the registration burden – were concerned enough by the changes to introduce one major policy shift in the 1960s regarding their own handling of firearms-related events, as detailed earlier.

From the context perspective, the author believes a major environmental milestone regarding risk occurred in the early 1990s and involved both the Aramoana mass murders and the subsequent political failure to address the issue of military-style semi-automatic rifles (MSSAs).

Following the use of an MSSA in the Aramoana mass murders, estimates suggested there were 60,000 of that type of firearm in Aotearoa New Zealand (Swinton, 2019, p. 9). The threat they posed was, according to Swinton, known by politicians of the time, with the then Police minister, for example, quoted, in 1992, as saying there was a "… flooding of the world market with AK47 look-alikes in semi-automatics … [m]any of the world's shootings have been committed with this type of weapon … the United States, England, and Australia had all banned importation of such 'tools of mass destruction'" (ibid.).

Sadly, the opportunity for substantial changes to the legislation surrounding the importation, ownership and use of MSSAs was missed (such as the outright banning of such weapons). However, some improvements such as licence endorsements and importation controls did get passed (ibid.). Giving rise to the lost opportunity was a belief that MSSAs could be used for "legitimate purposes, such as hunting" and that the bans introduced by other countries simply pushed the banned firearms underground (ibid.).

Some "tinkering" with the rules and regulations around MSSAs, firearm licencing and ownership did occur through passage of the *Arms Amendment Act 1992* (NZL), as mentioned above (ibid.), but the estimated 60,000 MSSAs remained in circulation, allowing a person access to a highly accurate, large-magazine capacity, imitation or real version of an essentially military weapon designed to kill an "enemy" quickly and in large numbers.

By 1996, the Thorp report[1] into firearm regulation "… estimated that there existed between 700,000 and 1 million firearms and approximately 205,000 licenced firearms users, down from the 327,000 that were estimated to exist six years earlier" in Aotearoa New Zealand (Swinton, p. 12). Those numbers included all the previously mentioned MSSAs. Furthermore, Thorp, as cited in Shortt (2000), went on to report that there continued to be "unreliable information" on the question of

[1] Report arising from the independent review initiated by the Minister of Police in 1996 and "led by a High Court judge named Sir Thomas Thorp". Thorp's report "[t]otalling more than 250 pages" was "widely regarded as the most extensive examination of New Zealand gun laws to date" (Swinton, 2019, p. 11).

the number of stolen firearms and the number and nature of crimes committed with firearms (Shortt, 2000, p. 38). Thorp's report, cited by Swinton, pointed out, troublingly:

> … Police lacked information about how many guns were in the country or how many were in the possession of any given licensee, had no control over sales or transfers of firearms, was unable to trace guns to their owners, and lacked information that would be helpful to inform and develop firearms policy … basic information about firearms, firearms-related crime, firearms suicides, and firearms accidents was necessary to enable meaningful reform. (Swinton, 2019)

Despite Thorp's warnings, it seems the country was lulled into a sense of security as very little substantive change resulted from his work. Society, and Police, moved on into what was the most notable and dangerous decade for Police in over 100 years.

Before moving on from the issue of firearms ownership and numbers, it is useful to include a more contemporary assessment of the environment which came from the Royal Commission of Inquiry into the Terrorist Attack on Christchurch Mosques, on 15 March, 2019, yet another massacre committed using an MSSA (Royal Commission of Inquiry into the Terrorist Attack on Christchurch Mosques on 15 March 2019, 2021). In the commission's evaluation of the firearm licensing system, it was noted that:

- "As at 31 October 2018, there were 248,764 current firearms licences, including standard, dealer and visitor licences";
- "In 2014, New Zealand Police estimated the total number of civilian-owned firearms to be around 1.2 million";
- "A 2018 report estimated that there were 1.212 million civilian owned firearms … [of which] … 65,837 were military style semi-automatic firearms, pistols and restricted weapons … Around two thirds of the 65,837 were pistols". (Royal Commission of Inquiry, 2021, Chapter 4, Section 4.3, paras. 8 and 10)

With regard to the impact of those firearms on Aotearoa New Zealand, the report noted:

> There were 2,181 hospitalisations due to firearms-related injuries between 2000 and 2017, an average of 121 per year. There were 867 firearms deaths from 2000 to 2015, an average of 54 a year. The most common cause of death by firearm was suicide, accounting for around 40 deaths a year. Between 2010 and 2017 there were around seven homicides a year caused by firearms … That said, these are comparatively low figures, particularly allowing for the number of firearms in circulation, the availability of semi-automatic firearms and easily evadable controls in relation to military style semi-automatic firearms. (Royal Commission of Inquiry, 2021, Chapter 4, Section 4.4, para. 13)

In respect of the earlier comments regarding the outcome of Thorp's report and Aramoana, to say no change happened is not completely accurate, for as discussed elsewhere in this work, Police did initiate changes to its armaments, principally, in the author's opinion, due to officers being "out-gunned" by the killer at Aramoana. The Glock pistol came into Police hands replacing the venerable 0.38 revolver that had been the standard handgun since the early 1960s (Osborne, 1990), and also, in the mid-2000s, semi-automatic rifles began to be introduced to replace the bolt-action standard issue rifles (New Zealand Police, 2005a).

Furthermore, by late 2006, tasers were also being trialled and considered for general rollout to operational staff (New Zealand Police, 2013). Subsequently, following a year-long trial, and evaluation of the usage data, tasers were set to be rolled out operationally from March 2009 to March 2010 (ibid.). The rollout occurred, and, ultimately, in 2015, Police went further to confirm that "[w]ithin 'weeks or months' all 5500 frontline police staff would carry the weapon … [t]his would include road police staff, beat cops, and any other frontline staff" as part of their standard tactical options equipment (Stuff.co.nz, 2015).

From the Police-specific perspective, when it came to considering the actual threat faced by police officers, some general historical Police data did exist from the 1980s to 1990s; the data also provided a "detailed snapshot" of the wider risks faced by police officers regarding assaults during the period 1994–1997. The data was available from The Assault Review (Keay et al., 1998), completed as a sub-project of the wider Staff Safety work in the 1998. These were useful in helping determining if the risk of assault being faced was increasing, decreasing or staying relatively the same over time.

The material found related to a set of high-level data regarding assaults on police officers between 1987 and 1998 and will be considered first. That data – found in Appendix A of The Assault Review (Keay et al., 1998, p. 41) – revealed that *Crimes Act* assaults on Police[2] presented as "… per 1,000 Sworn staff for the years ended 30 June" tracked gradually upwards from 22.87 in 1987 through to 36.97 in 1997 (ibid.). The data confirmed that, in 1987, when there were 5291 sworn police officers, 121 were subject to a *Crimes Act* assault, while by 1997, when there were 6492 sworn officers, 240 were subject to a *Crimes Act* assault per year (ibid.).

The "detailed snapshot" of data mentioned earlier was obtained from the same assault review work and resulted from a closer examination of "assault on Police" files ($n = 3757$) for the period 1 January 1994 to 30 June 1997 (Keay et al., 1998, p. 10). It was a more granular examination and provided data on weapons faced by Police during assault-related events.

The sample of files identified that Police faced "weapon involvement" (of any kind) during an assault on just 5% of occasions (ibid., p. 23), and firearms were present in just 5% of all the "weapon-involved" assaults mentioned (i.e. 5% of the 5%) (as cited in Shortt (2000), p. 48).

The Assault Review report confirmed that "weapons" of various descriptions were involved in 178 of the assaults reviewed, including 9 involving firearms and 19 a bladed weapon (16 knives, 2 machetes and 1 tomahawk axe) (Keay et al., 1998, p. 54).

When it came to injuries suffered by police officers, the files reviewed showed 2 officers received a "firearm injury" or "0.1%" of cases and 6 received "multiple injuries" or "0.2%" of cases, while "concussion/trauma … [&] … fractures/stiches"

[2]Serious assaults punishable by imprisonment, as opposed to *Summary Offences Act* assaults which could entail a monetary fine or lesser sentences of imprisonment

described the injuries to 37 (1.0%) of the 3757 officers assaulted. By contrast, "No injuries" were received as a result of 2325 of the assaults reviewed (ibid., p. 49).

It must be noted, with regard to The Assault Review's final report, that a separate Police digital record listing files related to assaults on police officers recorded 7459 assault-related events for the 1994–1997 period, but Police districts were only able to locate and provide a 3757 sample of the files to the reviewers (ibid., pp. 10–11).

The Staff Safety Project's final report (of which The Assault Review was a sub-project) commented that:

> The more serious assaults may be under-represented in the survey sample. Files relating to most grievous assaults, manslaughter, murder and attempted murder have generic (rather than police specific) code numbers and are not so easily identified. Some could have been missed in the data collection process. (New Zealand Police, 1998, p. 28)

Therefore, once again, the lack of accurate, easily accessed data was not helpful when considering the risk faced by police officers. More will be said about this in Chap. 12.

Having dealt with the environmental context, it is time to turn to the means of assessing the risk to police officers. For that, as mentioned, the Australia New Zealand Standard on Risk Management (Standards New Zealand, 2020) will be used.

In applying the standard, reference will be made to the risk matrix, which is a two-variable tool that aids risk practitioners to assess the *likelihood* of an event occurring and the *consequence* of that event occurring (Shortt, 2000, p. 62). Risk management is a process practiced within the New Zealand Police for some time, as is the use of the Australia New Zealand standard (e.g. see New Zealand Police, 2005b, p. 38; 2019, p. 160).

In the risk matrix, the two variables are further divided into five descriptors which often appear as *Likelihood* Rare, Unlikely, Possible, Likely and Almost certain, and *Consequences* Insignificant, Minor, Moderate, Major and Catastrophic (Shortt, 2000, p. 62).

In some instances, likelihood is also represented as a percentage. In such instances, risk managers add a percentage "chance" indication to the descriptors, for example, Rare (less than 1% chance of happening), Unlikely (1–20% chance of happening), Possible (21–50% chance of happening), Likely (51–90% chance of happening) and Almost certain (greater than 90% chance of happening).

The final part of the risk matrix process is determining the "level of risk" outcome from determining the intersection of the likelihood and consequence variables. Again, the intersection values are graduated, this time into four:

- Extreme risk (immediate action required);
- High risk (Senior management attention required);
- Moderate risk (management responsibility specified), and
- Low risk (manage by routine procedures). (Shortt, 2000, p. 63)

A fundamental start point for considering the risk of Police work is to understand that it requires police officers to confront dynamic and volatile situations. It requires police officers to deal with people who are in crisis, who are possibly having psychotic episodes that place themselves and others at risk of harm, or enraged, or under the influence of some form of licit or illicit substance(s), or suicidal. It requires police to respond to armed individuals who may be dealing with any of the situations described above, or who are intent on committing crimes, or who have already done so. Police officers, while using tactics to minimise the risks associated with their interventions, cannot fail to intervene, particularly when there is an associated risk of harm to the public. Thus, eliminating risk from policing is virtually impossible.

In accepting the above reality, Police have instituted a range of "risk treatments" (Standards New Zealand, 2020, p. vi) to help minimise the risks that officers, the public and the person being dealt with face.

In regard to the treatments, it is the author's view – based upon his experience and research – that Police have delivered to officers the opportunity for tactical superiority over the people they are dealing with in the majority of armed and unarmed encounters. The treatments all seek to safeguard everyone involved or affected by the situation. The author's view is supported by the data retrieved from examination of the 43 PCA/IPCA reports into situations where police officers have resorted to use of lethal force and, surprisingly, from the data about police officers who have been tragically killed or wounded through lethal force being used against them.

Those treatments are:

- *Superior numbers* – the data shows that police in the majority of instances outnumber the person(s) they are dealing with (e.g. out of 43 lethal force events, only twice was it "one on one" between Police and the other party, or when police officers were killed or seriously wounded).
- *Superior weaponry* – the Police Glock pistols and Bushmaster rifles are highly engineered, well-made and well-maintained firearms. They use the most appropriate ammunition for the weapon type. They exceed the range, firepower and capacity of the majority of weapons officers come up against or – at worst – equal their opponents' capabilities. For example, offenders are regularly found in possession of replica, bladed or modified weapons (e.g. cut-down firearms) that limit the range and reliability of their actions.
- *Superior equipment and protection* – Police have access to radio communication to coordinate action; they wear protective ballistic armour plates and stab-resistant vests and have other tactical weapons such as extendable batons, OC spray and tasers available.
- *Superior specialist support* – police officers have well-trained police dogs and handlers to assist them in finding and disarming people who have weapons, AOS and STG are available for support in firearms-related interventions, and during serious events, helicopters are available, particularly in the Metro-Auckland region and locations within flight range of where Police helicopters are based.
- *Superior preparation and training* – police officers are prepared through their RNZPC initial training course to interact with violent people and to use tactics effectively and are provided weapons (both lethal and non-lethal) and training in

them; they receive regular refresher training in districts to maintain their skills (i.e. the PITT programme). The people Police deal with may have previous hunting or sporting experience with firearms or have had military training; however, the data indicates that most do not.

Police tactical superiority does not, however, equate to risk elimination. Police officers are still killed and injured in the line of duty. When such events happen, it is apparent from the research that the officers are:

- Taken by surprise (i.e. ambushed)
- Failing to maximise their advantages (i.e. not taken advantage of the effective range of their firearms)
- Failing to work as a coordinated team (i.e. they have not involved all police present in a coordinated response)
- Allowing their advantage (in regard to either equipment, tactics, numbers or all three) to be negated by the actions of those they are dealing with (i.e. not worn protective equipment or have failed to contain and control a suspect to prevent them from accessing a weapon)

When it comes to who in New Zealand Police actually face the risks to be discussed, it is useful to examine the organisation's structure and deployment practices.

New Zealand Police is currently divided into two categories of staff: "constabulary" (those who have sworn the Police oath and who have the powers of a constable) and "employees" (staff who do not have the powers of a constable). Prior to the enactment of the *Policing Act 2008* (NZL), the categories were termed "sworn" and "non-sworn". It is constabulary staff who will be the focus of this chapter. Undoubtedly, some Police employees also face risk through their employment, but this work will not focus on them.

Within the constabulary ranks, it is police officers at constable and sergeant ranks who deliver the majority of "24/7" policing in Aotearoa New Zealand, including the initial response to reported crimes happening at any given time. Specialist officers, such as dog handlers, AOS members and detectives, are also – for the most part – drawn from within those two ranks. New Zealand Police spokespeople often use the term "frontline staff" when referring to that body of staff and the roles they perform (e.g. see (Stuff.co.nz, 2015)).

Police officers with the rank of senior sergeant, or above (e.g. inspectors, superintendents, etc.), tend to deliver supporting administrative roles within the organisation. However, a number of those higher-ranked police officers do spend time supporting the 24/7 response as shift supervisors or commanders. For example, in the Bellingham fatal shooting, the officer who fired was a senior sergeant fulfilling the role of a "senior field supervisor" that night (Independent Police Conduct Authority, 2009, p. 6).

The exact number of those higher-ranked police officers who would be exposed to the risks being considered is difficult to determine, but – based on the author's knowledge and experience – they are most likely to number in the tens, rather than hundreds, at any given time across the country. Therefore, a percentage allowance was made by the author to account for those staff in the following discussion.[3]

Of all the 33 law enforcement officers killed in Aotearoa New Zealand over the past 130 years, only 1 was an officer (Detective Inspector W. Chalmers, killed in 1963). The rest comprised 8 sergeants (including 1 detective sergeant) and 24 constables or traffic officers (including 2 senior constables and 2 detective constables) (New Zealand Police, 2021a). That equates, in percentage terms, to 73% of those killed being constables, 24% being sergeants and 3% being a person of higher rank. Therefore, 97% of those killed were constables or sergeants.

A separate data source, The Assault Review (mentioned earlier), identified that 82.5% of assaults were on officers engaged in either "Patrol … Traffic … Beat/Foot patrol … [or] Dog" duties. Furthermore, when it came to ranks, the review confirmed that where such information existed ($n = 1854$ out of 3757 files), 88% were constables, 8% were sergeants or senior sergeants and "… less than 3% were Detective Constables, Detectives or Detective Sergeants"[4]) (Keay et al., 1998, p. 12). Therefore, 96% of the assaults in the sample, where rank was confirmed, were committed on constables or sergeants. The review confirmed the findings were also consistent with international comparisons (ibid.).

To provide additional perspective and context regarding the number of constables and sergeants in New Zealand Police, the total number of constabulary police officers (of all ranks) for the years 2001–2020 was charted against the number holding the ranks of constable (Consts) and sergeant (Sgts). That data is presented in Fig. 7.1. Add to that data was the number of constables and sergeants (and others) likely to be employed in initial response – as Level 1 responders – therefore requiring them to receive refresher training in use of firearms.[5]

[3] For example, in 2014, New Zealand Police advised that 5700 constabulary staff would be trained to Level 1 responder level, involving refresher training in use of lethal force options. The author estimates 1%–2% ($n = 57$–114) of the total potentially includes senior sergeants and officers required to regularly undertake 24/7 policing supervisory or command roles or to staff AOS. Therefore, an additional 1% has been added to all discussions of constabulary staff numbers when considering those facing lethal force risks.

[4] Detective is a *designation* within New Zealand Police, not a *rank*. Thus, a detective holds the rank of constable but is referred to as a detective. This applies to all levels within the Criminal Investigation Branch (CIB) where detectives are employed (detective constable (still training to achieve full designation), detective, detective sergeant, detective senior sergeant, detective inspector, detective superintendent) (New Zealand Police, 2020a, 2020b).

[5] To determine the Level 1 responder figures, the author noted that in 2014, New Zealand Police confirmed Level 1 responder refresher training (including refresher training on the Glock pistol and the Bushmaster rifle) was to be given to 5700 officers countrywide (New Zealand Police, 2014). The author, using an assumption based on the discussion earlier about constables and sergeants, calculated that those 5700 officers reflected 71% of the constable and sergeant ranks for the 2014 year. The author, therefore, took the 71% and added 1% to make allowance for police officers of higher ranks who may also be exposed the Level 1 response risks (see discussion above). The rate of 72% – considered a conservative percentage – was then calculated across all 20-year displayed Chart 5.1, resulting in the grey line. This included setting the year 2014 at 72%.

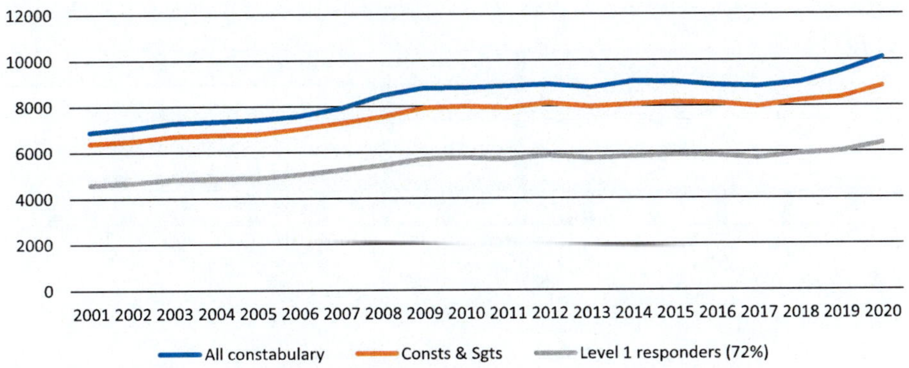

Fig. 7.1 Numbers of constabulary staff: constables and sergeants – Level 1 responders (2001–2020). (Data from New Zealand Police Annual Reports for the years ending at 30 June, found at www.police.govt.nz, and using the calculation explained in Footnote 3)

Having described the context within which Police work and identified the probable number of constabulary officers exposed to risk, it is appropriate to shift to consideration of the type of risks faced.

With respect to illegal firearms use, the two worst outcomes for police officers are death or being shot and seriously wounded which could bring medical complications and life-changing outcomes, both physically and psychologically. In the world of risk management, those two outcomes squarely fit the definitions of "Catastrophic" or "Major" consequences, defined as "Death results from the event" or "Admission to and treatment in a hospital is required as a result of the event – involves recovery time / time off work", respectively (Shortt, 2000, p. 62). Even if a police officer were not killed or seriously wounded, a less severe gunshot wound would still fit the "Major" consequence category (ibid.).

Having set the parameters for risk consideration, the commentary will now seek to determine, from the available data, where on the likelihood scale deaths and serious injury of police officers sit when it comes to the illegal use of firearms.

Fatal and Non-fatal Shootings of Law Enforcement Officers

Since the late 1800s, 33 police and traffic officers have been killed by criminal acts in Aotearoa New Zealand (New Zealand Police, 2021a). Some have been mentioned in earlier chapters; most have not. New Zealand Police maintain a memorial page on their website detailing each death and the circumstances (ibid.). Twenty-three of the officers killed were shot, eight lost their lives as the result of a violent assault, and two were lost through the criminal use of motor vehicles. Figure 7.2 displays when each of those deaths occurred, by decade.

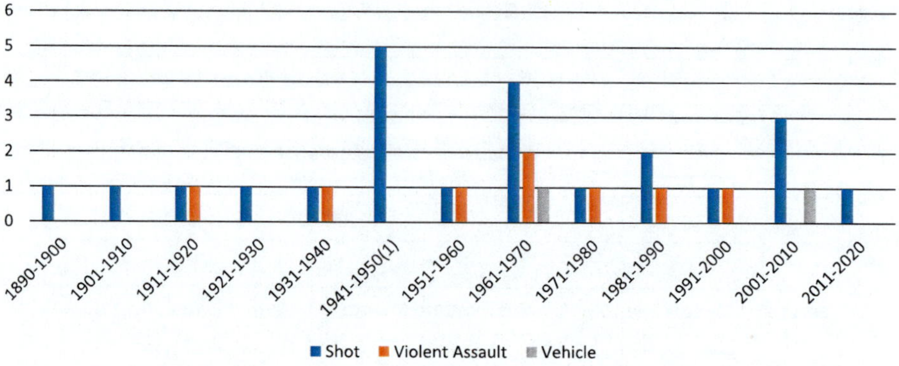

Fig. 7.2 Number of police and traffic officers killed by criminal acts (1890–2020). (Data obtained from New Zealand Police)

With specific regard to those who were shot, four decades standout – 1941–1950, 1961–1970, 1981–1990 and 2001–2010. The deaths included the fatal shooting of four officers in one incident on the West Coast of Te Waipounamu (South Island) in 1941; two separate incidents in the early 1960s with two officers shot to death at each; the shooting death of a traffic officer in 1986, followed by the 1990 death of a police sergeant as part of the Aramoana mass murders; and then, finally, the 2001–2010 decade with the deaths of three officers – shot in 2002, 2008 and 2009 – with four other police officers shot and injured during those same events and an additional four police officers shot and wounded in a series of three unrelated events, giving rise to that decade, in all likelihood, being the most notorious and dangerous for Police.[6]

Three of the decades with multiple shootings of law enforcement officers (1961–1970, 1981–1990 and 2001–2010) gave rise to strategically important shifts in New Zealand Police lethal force policy and firearms deployment practices as discussed in Chap. 4.

When looked at statistically, the 23 firearms-related deaths across the 130 years in Chart 5.2 equated to 1 death – on average – every 5.7 years. When specifically considering the two most recent decades (2001–2010 and 2011–2020), in the first, there was a fatal shooting of an officer – on average – every 3.3 years, while in the second, it was a fatal shooting of an officer, on average, once every 10 years.

However, if we include the available near-miss data about non-fatal shootings of police officers during those same years, as displayed in Fig. 7.3, the rate of shootings changes quite considerably. In the 2001–2010 decade, it shifts from one shooting every 3.3 years to one every year, while in the 2011–2020 decade, the rate of shootings becomes one every 1.4 years. Again, it is clear that the 2001–2010 decade

[6] Data on the wounding of police or traffic officers is lacking for the first 110 years covered in the chart. Therefore, the author is not able to definitively state that the 2001–2010 decade was the most dangerous. However, it is his view that that is highly likely.

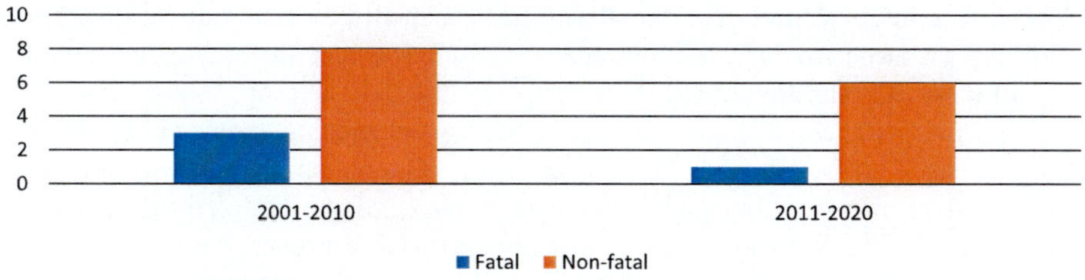

Fig. 7.3 Number of shootings of police officers in the decades (2001–2010 and 2011–2020). (Source: Independent Police Conduct Authority; New Zealand Police)

presented a very serious challenge to Police leadership when it came to the issue of managing risk.

However, it must be noted that the view presented may not be entirely accurate. In attempting to gather near-miss data, it became evident that such specific data is not recorded in easily accessible public records and attempts to locate such data for this publication from the New Zealand Police and the New Zealand Police Association were also unsuccessful (Aitken, 2021) (Cahill, 2021). Furthermore, the author cannot be certain that the near-miss data displayed is entirely accurate; at worst, it may be an under-reporting that under-represents the actual situation. Not a new issue, unfortunately, as The Assault Review authors highlighted the same gap as far back as 1998 (Keay et al., 1998, p. 14).

From the likelihood perspective in risk management, clearly, in the statistical permutations presented above, the likelihood of a police officer being fatally shot fits best with the descriptors "Possible" or "Likely" for any given year. One hundred and thirty years of data reveals it is an ongoing aspect of the work Police are tasked to do.

Therefore, given a fatal shooting was "Possible" or "Likely", and the consequence would be "Catastrophic", the risk matrix delivered a risk level rating of "Extreme", a level requiring attention and action from the very highest echelons of the New Zealand Police organisation (Shortt, 2000, pp. 62–63).

Clearly, in the decade 2001–2010, that was the situation facing Police leadership, and, as confirmed by information released for this book and presented in Chap. 6, it drove the consideration of greater access and availability to Police firearms.

Before moving on from the fatal consequences of the use of firearms against Police and considering less tragic risks, it was considered appropriate to briefly detail here the circumstances involved in each of the fatal shootings of police officers between 2001 and 2020 to provide insight into the ways in which Police have been exposed to lethal force in recent times. Four police officers were shot and killed during that period, and they were involved in different policing roles, but the roles and duties being undertaken were every-day ones.

The first officer to be killed during the period was Detective Constable Duncan Taylor – a plain-clothed and unarmed officer – working in the Criminal Investigation Branch of New Zealand Police. He was shot during an incident in 2002, aged 39. At the same time, a female police officer working alongside him was also shot, receiving a thigh wound. The female officer escaped the scene and survived and ultimately returned to duty. A young man, aged 17, was responsible for shooting the two officers (NZ Herald, 2002).

The circumstances were that the two officers were making enquiries regarding a failed teenage relationship and the actions of the young man involved. A protection order had been taken out against the young man after he had arrived at his ex-girlfriend's home and threatened to kill himself with a firearm he had with him. During the subsequent enquiries by the two officers, they encountered the young man in his Land Rover and followed him until he again drove into the driveway of his ex-girlfriend's home (New Zealand Herald, 2002). There, the unarmed detective constable got out of the police vehicle and approached the man's car and was confronted by him armed with "a stolen, high-powered rifle". The young man shot the officer point-blank, hitting him in the chest, and killed him (ibid.). The second officer, also unarmed, attempted to run to cover and while doing so was shot at three times by the man. She was hit in the thigh, but – despite her significant injury – managed to escape from the scene (ibid.).

The killer then took refuge in the house, and a 4-hour siege occurred during which more shots were fired but no one was injured (New Zealand Herald, 2002). Police AOS staff finally ended the siege with tear gas, and the young man was taken into custody (Ibid.). He was subsequently sentenced to life imprisonment for the murder and 10 years imprisonment for the attempted murder of the female officer.[7] He was also sentenced on four other matters related to the events of the day.

The second officer to be shot and killed was Sergeant Don Wilkinson, aged 46, in 2008. He was unarmed and engaged in specialist undercover duties with the Police Technical Support Unit. The sergeant was not dressed in police uniform at the time of his death. A second officer was also shot during the incident; however, he fortunately survived (Francis, 2010).

The circumstances reveal that a late-night/early-morning undercover operation was underway into people believed to be involved in the manufacture of the drug methylamphetamine (commonly referred to as "P") (Francis, 2010). The two shot officers worked for a part of New Zealand Police responsible for installing technical equipment to assist investigators in listening to, or tracking, people of interest. On the night concerned, they were attempting to affix a tracking device to a car parked at the suspect's home address.

Unfortunately, the officers were observed by the suspect on an undetected CCTV camera and – according to defence evidence at the subsequent trial – were mistaken for burglars. Two of the occupants of the house armed themselves with high-powered air rifles and ran outside, chasing the two officers – who attempted to

---

[7] For those unfamiliar with Aotearoa New Zealand law on the issue of homicide (the killing of a human by another, directly or indirectly, by any means whatsoever), the *Crimes Act 1961* (NZL) has two graduations of homicide: murder and manslaughter. Very briefly, for a death to be murder, the person causing it must have meant to cause death or known that death may occur and were reckless about whether it did (ss. 167 & 168); manslaughter is any homicide not amounting to murder (s. 171).

escape – "more than 100 metres" down the suburban street (Francis, 2010). A confrontation then took place in a dark driveway resulting in both officers being shot with one of the air rifles. One was shot four times but survived because he was wearing a protective vest. Sergeant Wilkinson was shot three times and was, sadly, not wearing a protective vest. He suffered fatal injures (ibid.).

The man who shot both officers was aged 37; he was convicted of murder and attempted murder for which he received sentences of life imprisonment and 10 years imprisonment, respectively. A second man, aged 33, was also convicted of manslaughter and attempted murder (Francis, 2010).

The third officer to die from gunfire was Senior Constable Len Snee, aged 53, in 2009. He was a uniformed officer. Senior Constable Snee was shot along with two uniformed colleagues who were both seriously wounded, as was a civilian who came to their aid. The killer was a 51-year-old man.

The events surrounding the death and injuries started one morning when the three unarmed police officers went to their killer's home to execute a search warrant related to a cannabis investigation (Smith, 2019). The killer was not at home, but the officers encountered the man's female partner at the house and entered to commence their search. A neighbour happened to visit and go inside around the same time that was happening (Smith, 2019).

The killer returned home from walking his dog to discover the police searching the house and having already discovered a sawn-off shotgun and cannabis plants. He immediately went to another part of the house and returned armed with a rifle. He ordered the police and neighbour out of the house. As Senior Constable Snee reached the roadside and turned to face the killer, he was shot by the man. A second constable was then shot in the back, while the third was shot in the arm and stomach (both injuries caused by the same bullet) (ibid.).

The neighbour tried to grapple with the killer and took hold of the rifle as it was being swung towards the wounded officers (ibid.). This allowed two of the wounded constables to flee. The neighbour was then also shot, and he fell to the ground (ibid.). The killer returned inside the house, and the neighbour used his cellular phone to call for assistance with the seriously wounded Snee lying metres from him, appearing to have been shot at least twice (Smith, 2019). While the neighbour waited for assistance to arrive, Senior Constable Snee died of his injuries. A prolonged 51-hour siege of the house, with the gunman inside, then unfolded (ibid.).

The siege ended after failed negotiations with the killer and the man fatally shooting himself with one of his own firearms (ibid.). The man – who had been a licenced firearms owner – had 17 firearms at his home (Newton & Hunt, 2010), which apparently included "… six pump-action or semi-automatic shotguns adapted to be held in one hand, three Ruger mini-14 semi-automatic rifles, and eight other guns" (ibid.).

The final police officer to be shot and killed was Constable Matthew Hunt, aged 28, in June 2020. Constable Hunt and a fellow officer were on traffic patrol duties when they encountered a vehicle they decided to stop due to the manner in which it was being driven (New Zealand Police, 2021a).

After making it clear to the occupants of the vehicle that the Police wanted it to stop, however, it sped away and tried to evade the two officers. When it did finally stop, following a crash into parked vehicles, Hunt's partner alighted from the Police vehicle. He was unarmed. He then realised that the passenger from the crashed car was also out of the vehicle and was armed with a rifle. As the constable fled, the armed man rapidly fired ten shots towards him, hitting the officer four times, fortunately only wounding him. By this time, Constable Hunt – also unarmed – had exited the Police car, and he was hit by four further shots and killed. Hunt was also trying to flee, and the shots that killed him came from behind (Kapitan, 2021; New Zealand Police, 2021a).

The 14 shots happened in a space of between 10 and 30 s according to evidence at the trial of the 25-year-old shooter. The gunman and his female companion then fled the scene taking with them two rifles that were in the possession of the armed man (Kapitan, 2021). The shooter had used a military-style, semi-automatic rifle to commit his crimes. The killer was found guilty of the murder and attempted murder of the two police officers (James, 2021).

Each of the shootings detailed above could have had even more tragic consequences had any (or all) of the wounded officers been fatally shot.

It is now appropriate to give wider consideration to the risks faced and to move on to non-fatal shootings of Police.

As discussed earlier in this work, Police do not shoot to wound; they shoot to incapacitate and do so aiming at the centre mass of a person in order to achieve that outcome, knowing there is a high likelihood of causing death. It is the author's contention that those who shoot at Police also do so to incapacitate the officer or officers concerned and also know (or can be expected to know) that there is a high likelihood of causing death. Those subsequently arrested for shooting at police officers are most often convicted of murder or attempted murder, a clear indication of an intent to kill being either admitted or evidenced.

However, from the PCA/IPCA cases reviewed during the research for this work, the author also formed the view that some of those who shoot *towards* Police may simply have been seeking to escape from them while hoping the gunfire would cause Police to stop pursuing.

As mentioned earlier in this chapter, data regarding lethal force near misses was difficult to find. Police confirmed that data about such events only started to be collected centrally from March 2019 (New Zealand Police, 2021b, p. 12). Fortuitously, in 2015, Police also instigated a more robust reporting system titled the "Tactical Options Report" and began gathering detailed data. Furthermore, in August 2021, Police published the "Appropriate Tactical Settings Insights and Evidence Brief" (New Zealand Police, 2021b), and this also provided additional useful data for the period 2010–2021. In the absence of any available historical Police data, the author focused on what could be found in other publicly available sources and other official non-Police sources. Through those sources, it was possible to identify least ten non-fatal shootings of police officers between 2000 and 2020, not linked to the fatal shootings of police officers as already mentioned above. Table 7.1 presents a brief summary of each of those non-fatal shootings.

Table 7.1 Wounding of police officers by firearms (2009–2016)

Year	Who was shot?	What were the circumstances?
2009	1 × unarmed uniformed constable	An unarmed constable was shot three times while making enquiries into a person seen acting suspiciously around vehicles in a driveway at 4 am. The officer received three wounds – one to each leg and one to his elbow – with one leg wound being very serious as the bullet struck an artery. A man was arrested, and three firearms (a shotgun, a high calibre pistol and a rifle) were seized (The Age, 2009)
2009	1 × armed AOS officer	During an AOS operation to arrest a man who was firing gun shots around his neighbourhood, an AOS officer received shotgun pellet wounds to his face when the man fired at a window of a room that the officer was in. The man responsible was subsequently shot and killed by other AOS officers (Independent Police Conduct Authority, 2010)
2010	2 × unarmed uniformed constables	Two constables (one with a police dog) were investigating the smell of cannabis from a house when an armed man confronted them. One officer was shot in the face and jaw, while the second was shot in the thigh. Both officers survived; however, the police dog was shot and killed. A 34-year-old man was arrested and charged (New Zealand Police, 2010)
2012	1 × unarmed uniformed constable	The constable stopped a car at 1 am in inner-city Auckland. As the officer attempted to remove the keys from the ignition, the passenger produced a hand gun and fired a shot which scrapped across the officer's arm and left a burn mark. The officer had just moved his head from the line of fire when the shot was fired (Steward, 2012)
2014	1 × unarmed uniformed constables	Two constables intercepted a man in a stolen van and forced him to stop. He emerged from the van with a sawn-off shotgun and was tackled by an officer who grappled with him. During the fight, a second officer arrived and joined the melee. Both barrels of the shotgun were fired, and one of the constables received wounds to his foot and leg (New Zealand Police, 2016)
2016	4 × armed AOS officers	During an operation to capture a man who had fired shots at a police cannabis recovery operation, three AOS officers received gunshot injuries – one to the head – when he fired on them after they entered the man's home. A fourth officer was injured during the subsequent siege. All survived, but one suffered a serious head wound. The man subsequently surrendered to police the next day (Stuff.co.nz, 2016)

The events in the table revealed that four of the shootings involved five unarmed, uniformed, police officers undertaking what can be considered standard policing duties, while the other five officers shot were members of specialist Armed Offender Squads (AOS) and were undertaking AOS duties at the time. At least three of the shot officers received what were described as serious injuries (e.g. an artery severed or shots to the head), while the others received less severe, but no less traumatic, injuries.

All the injuries described fit the risk management consequence descriptors of "Moderate" ("Medical treatment from a doctor … may involve admission to and treatment in hospital … may involve time off work for recovery" (Shortt, 2000, p. 62)) or "Major" ("Admission to and treatment in a hospital is required … involves recovery time / time off work" (ibid.)), in the risk management matrix.

The above commentary regarding non-fatal and fatal shootings could have been longer. A number of incidents occurred during the timeframe reviewed where shots were fired at Police but missed. One graphic example, recounted below, was an incident in 2005, when two unarmed constables chased a vehicle into a shopping centre carpark.

When the chased vehicle finally stopped, the driver alighted from it with "… a cut-down AK47 style assault rifle …" which he used to try and hijack two other vehicles. Upon seeing the police closing in, he pointed the firearm at one of the two officers seated in the police car and pulled the trigger. The weapon failed to fire. The constables then got out of the car and hid behind it; the man – having rectified the fault with his weapon – then fired a number of shots through the car's body towards them, one bullet passing close to a constable's head (Department of the Prime Minister and Cabinet, 2008). Later in the incident, one of the two constables deliberately showed himself to the armed man to draw fire when the constable felt members of the public were in danger (ibid.).

However, returning to the data regarding injuries to police officers, the structured and centralised monitoring system of the Tactical Options Reporting (TOR) regime, from 2015, provided the most reliable record of contemporary events, as presented in Fig. 7.4.

When the injury data in Fig. 7.4 was converted into percentages for comparison with the Assault Review snapshot,[8] it revealed:

- Between 66% and 78% of injuries resulted in 'self or no treatment' (The Assault Review revealed: 'Not treated' 88.4%);
- Between 19% and 29% of injuries resulted in 'medical treatment – no hospitalisation' (The Assault Review revealed: 'Doctor' 3.4%), and

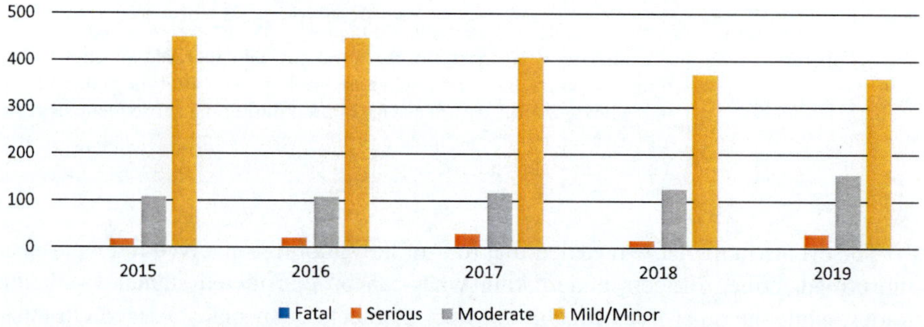

Fig. 7.4 Number of police officers injured at TOR events (2015–2019). TOR events per year: 2015 ($n = 4914$), 2016 ($n = 5055$), 2017 ($n = 4536$), 2018 ($n = 4398$) and 2019 ($n = 4860$). (Data obtained from New Zealand Police Tactical Options Reporting)

[8]The way both sets of data were recorded does not provide for an exact comparison, and The Assault Review data does not determine if, for example, hospitalisation occurred for the same reasons detailed in the TOR data. The alignment shown above is, therefore, an inexact comparison.

- Between 3% and 5% resulted in 'hospitalisation' (The Assault Review revealed: 'Hospital' 0.9%).

(New Zealand Police, 2020a; Keay et al., 1998, p. 17)

The final set of data to be considered, which provides the most contemporary context to the risk faced from illegal firearms use, comes from a relatively new centralised Police database known as "Gun Safe" (New Zealand Police, 2021b, p. 6). The database came into operation on 1 March 2019 and was designed to collect data regarding "... the frequency and risk of firearms encountered by Police" (ibid., p. 12).

Since inception in 2019, and up until 29 July 2021, the database recorded "... 21 verified events involving *discharges* [of firearms] by offenders at Police, (including discharges at Police Officers, Police dogs, Police vehicles and Police premises)" (bold highlight added) (ibid.). Of those 21 events, 3 resulted in an injury to police officers. Two of those were the fatal shooting of a police officer and the wounding of his colleague (the death of Constable Hunt). The third was the wounding of a uniformed police officer who was shot in the arm during a traffic stop (ibid.).

Beyond the 21 *discharges* at Police, Gun Safe recorded a further 25 incidents where firearms were *presented* at Police, but not fired (ibid.). The report determines that Gun Safe data reveals "... 46 events, or about 1.5 events each month in which firearms were presented at Police" (New Zealand Police, 2021b, p. 12).

In risk management terms, when taking into account the wounding of police officers (whether as part of a fatal shooting of a police officer or as individual events – Table 7.1), and considering the serious injuries to police officers from assaults, it is clear that the likelihood of such events is again "Possible" to "Likely" in any given year and the consequences of such events are either "Moderate" or "Major", which again result in overall risk levels ratings of "High" to "Extreme", once again requiring senior Police to actively monitor and action risk treatments to protect police officers (Shortt, 2000, pp. 62–63).

Perception of Risk

Beyond the physical manifestations of risk, such as death or serious injury, one further aspect will be considered in this chapter, namely, the perception of risk. Perception of risk, in the author's opinion, is separate to actual risk. That view is reinforced by research from scholars such as Itiel Dror who has written about the perception of risk and the decision to use force in a policing context (Dror, 2007).

New Zealand Police have also considered the perception of risk in their analysis of the risk environment when dealing with the vexed issue of firearms carriage by officers which continues to undergo internal consideration and research (New Zealand Police, 2021b). Police refer to the issue as "Perceived Cumulative Assessment" (PCA) and base their analysis around data accumulated through the TOR process and the use of the TENR assessment tool discussed elsewhere in this work (ibid.).

The author's view on the perception issue is very similar to that of the Police. In his view, perception of risk is the important step before lethal force is applied (or not), where a police officer infers from a range of inputs (e.g. information from the communications centre, or colleagues, and/or visually interpreting a scene upon arrival) that risk is present and that the lethal force tactical option is an appropriate one to "activate" by removing a firearm(s) from a vehicle-mounted gun safe and carrying it with them into the situation they are approaching.

Importantly, and a subject explored by scholarly research, is a phenomenon described as dispatch priming, researched, for example, by Paul Taylor and published in *Police Quarterly* (Taylor, 2020). The point Taylor's research makes, and which is supported by the author's own policing experience, was that an officer approaches a situation primed with information provided by the dispatch centre and, therefore, already has biases activated in their decision-making process.

Despite the events of the 2001–2010, decade, accurate measurement of "perception of risk" was still a further 5 years away. It was the introduction of the TOR regime – closely linked to the rollout of tasers – that enabled the capture of perception-related data. The data existed through the recording of the number of times tactical options were deployed by police officers (New Zealand Police, 2020a, 2020b), and – of principal interest to this work – the number of times officers resorted to arming themselves with firearms, irrespective of whether or not they fired them.

That reporting (see Fig. 7.5) determined that Police responded to a total of 28,727 events during the years 2014–2019, where a tactical option of any kind was required/used by responding officers (i.e. empty-hand techniques, handcuffs, baton, OC spray, taser, firearms). Out of those events, 2076, or 7.2%, resulted in police officers resorting to arming themselves with a firearm.

The arming events are likely to have been where police officers feared facing a person(s) with a weapon(s), which may have included a firearm. The TOR data, for example, identified that, in 2015, 45% of TOR events involved facing a "cutting/stabbing" weapon, while 18% of events involved a "air/BB/pellet [or] firearms", while, by 2019, reporting identified 48% of events involving "cutting/stabbing" weapons and 17% "air/BB/pellet [or] firearms".

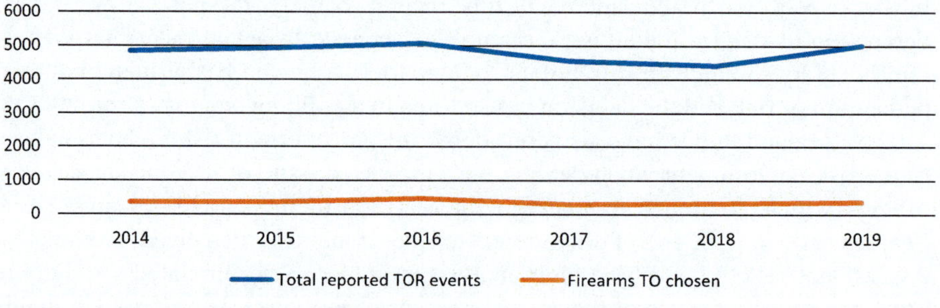

Fig. 7.5 Number of TOR events and events where a firearm was chosen (2014–2015). (Data obtained from New Zealand Police (2020a, 2020b))

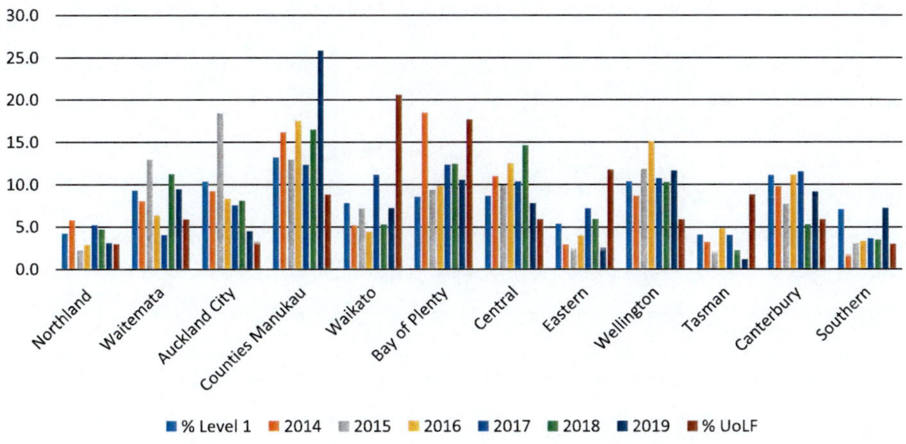

Fig. 7.6 District: % of Level 1 responders: % of events when firearms chosen (2014–2019): % of uses of lethal force (miss/kill/wound) (2014–2019). (Data obtained from New Zealand Police, Tactical Options Reports for 2014–2019, 2014–2019 (Tactical Options Reporting was only available for the years from 2014. Use of Lethal Force data was available until 27 May 2019 only. Two cases where the cause of death was unable to be confirmed as Police shooting not included. Seventy-two percent of staff in a district deemed to be Level 1 responders))

Using the national TOR data and supplementing it with the percentage number of Level 1 responders in a district, compared with the percentage number of arming events (by year) by district, and then adding the district's percentage of the national total of uses of lethal force, Fig. 7.6 resulted.[9]

In considering the picture painted by Fig. 7.6, one aspect stood out and related to the percentage of lethal force uses, between 2014 and 2019 (n = 34). The data included all shots by Police that either missed or caused a fatal or non-fatal injury. The districts with the highest percentage of lethal force uses, in comparison to the percentage of Level 1 responders and the number of arming reports recorded for the district, were Waikato, Bay of Plenty, Eastern and Tasman. The statistics are worthy of further analysis, if in fact that has not already been undertaken.

The final method of considering the perception of risk in the New Zealand Police context was to consider the deployment of the AOS based in each district and the STG.

Data obtained from Police for the years 2005–2019 (Fig. 7.7) revealed that nationally "emergency callouts" of the AOS (i.e. when Level 1 responders encountered a dangerous person/situation) rose steadily from 2005 until plateauing in the years 2009/2010.

Then demand for AOS then declined from 2011 until 2014 (reaching the previous 2005 level of demand) before again rising through to 2019. STG also experienced a gentle rise in its deployment demand until 2009/2010 and showed a similar,

[9] There are 12 Police districts across Aotearoa New Zealand, 9 on Te Ike a Maui and 3 on Te Waipounamu.

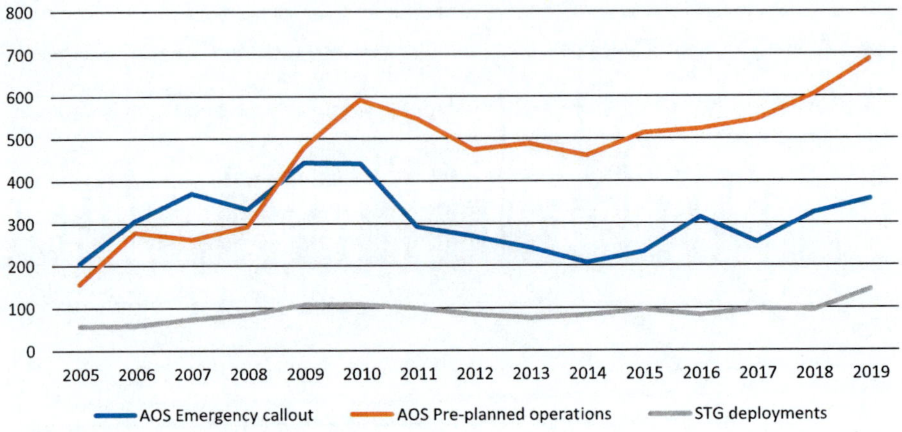

Fig. 7.7 Number of AOS and STG deployments by type (2005–2019). (Data obtained from New Zealand Police through an Official Information Act request)

but gentler, decline from 2011 through to 2013/2014, before showing a gradual increase to 2019.[10]

Interestingly, the 2010–2013/2014 decline in callouts and deployment demand aligned with the policy shift to more widely accessible and available firearms for Level 1 responders. The second interesting point was that in 2008/2009, the number of AOS "emergency callouts" and "pre-planned operations" reversed order with "pre-planned operations" use increasing to become, in effect, 68% of the AOS workload, while "emergency callout" demand dropped to represent 32% of the national workload.[11] That change has remained consistent from 2010 onwards. The overall impression left by viewing the national AOS and STG deployment data is that perceived risk was not driving a sustained and substantial growth in the "call-out" demand for the units. However, there was clearly an increased demand evident for "pre-planned" operational support for AOS.

To conclude the discussion on perception of risk, it is appropriate to consider how the perception played out with regard to the number of times a police officer, who had perceived risk, then made the fateful decision to fire their weapon at another person. Figure 7.8 presents the data on the number of times police officers used lethal force (it includes missed shots (n = 12)).

The steep rise in shootings in the 2011–2020 decade, evidenced in Fig. 7.8, clearly stands out, following two important aspects of the 2001–2010 decade. Both have been mentioned before, but as a reminder, that decade was the most dangerous

[10] STG deployments are not "… categorised as Emergency or Pre-planned deployments" (Ross, 2021).

[11] Pre-planned operations, 68.8% in 2015, 68% in 2017 and 65.8% in 2019; emergency callouts, 31.2% in 2015, 32% in 2017 and 34.2% in 2019.

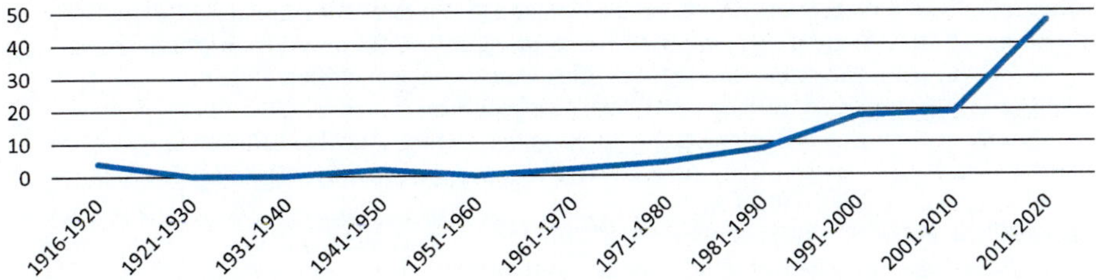

Fig. 7.8 Number of shootings by police: by decade (1916–2020). (Data obtained from New Zealand Police, 2021c)

for police officers with three fatally shot and eight wounded, and that resulted in Police making firearms much more accessible to responding officers.

More will be said about the shootings that made up that quite dramatic rise later in Chap. 8, where use of lethal force by Police will be discussed in greater detail.

To summarise the chapter, clearly the risks of death and serious injury exist for police officers in Aotearoa New Zealand, especially those arising from the illegal use of firearms. Those risks have been a part of policing since its earliest years, but in the most recent two decades, as data on non-fatal shootings have become more available, there does seem to have been an increase in the number of instances when officers will confront those risks.

In response to those risks, police officers resort to arming with lethal force capable tactical options in less than 10% of all instances.

Finally, it is evident that the perception of risk and the resort to lethal force use are not evenly experienced across the country. Some districts exhibited higher levels of perceived risk, but recorded a lower percentage of lethal force use, while others had lower perceived risk levels, but resorted to use of lethal force more often.

Bibliography

Aitken, M. (2021, August 21). Request IR-01-21-23389 (OIA request for information on injuries to police officers).

Alpers, P., & Morgan, B. (1995). Firearm homicide in New Zealand: Victims, perpetrators and their weapons 1992–94. In *National Conference of the Public Health Association of New Zealand*. National Conference of the Public Health Association of New Zealand.

Auckland Council. (2021). *Auckland's population*. Retrieved from aucklandcouncil.govt.nz: https://www.aucklandcouncil.govt.nz/plans-projects-policies-reports-bylaws/our-plans-strategies/auckland-plan/about-the-auckland-plan/Pages/aucklands-population.aspx

Cahill, C. (2021, September 27). E-mail response to request for information from New Zealand Police Association.

Crime.co.nz. (2021, August 2). *The murder of Detective Constable Duncan Taylor.* Retrieved from crime.co.nz: http://www.crime.co.nz/c-files.aspx?ID=24619

Department of the Prime Minister and Cabinet. (2008, May 3). *Special honours list 3 May 2008 (Bravery awards)*. Retrieved from dpmc.govt.nz: https://dpmc.govt.nz/publications/special-honours-list-3-may-2008-bravery-awards

Dror, I. E. (2007). Perception of risk and the decision to use fore. *Policing*, 265–272.

Francis, C. (2010, August). *Sgt Don Wilkinson's killers jailed.* Retrieved from stuff.co.nz: https://www.stuff.co.nz/national/crime/4074883/Sgt-Don-Wilkinsons-killers-jailed

Gardiner, J., Norton, R., & Alphers, P. (1995). *Firearms misuse: Licence status of perpetrators and legality of the firearms*. Injury Prevention Research Centre, Auckland University.

Independent Police Conduct Authority. (2009). *Report on the shooting of Stephen Jon Bellingham.* Independent Police Conduct Authority.

Independent Police Conduct Authority. (2010). *Public report into police shooting of Shayne Richard Sime*. Independent Police Conduct Authority.

James, L. (2021, July 27). *Matthew Hunt's killer guilty of attempting to murder Auckland policeman.* Retrieved from tvnz.co.nz: https://www.tvnz.co.nz/one-news/new-zealand/matthew-hunts-killer-guilty-attempting-murder-auckland-policeman

Kapitan, C. (2021, July 13). *Eli Epiha trial: Prosecutors play audio of moment constable Matthew Hunt was killed.* Retrieved from nzherald.co.nz: https://www.nzherald.co.nz/nz/eli-epiha-trial-prosecutors-play-audio-of-moment-constable-matthew-hunt-was-killed/XTHPTELYJTZIN55I35LNUMT4MM/

Keay, D., Russell, N., & den Heyer, G. (1998). *The assault review – A study of assaults on New Zealand police officers*. New Zealand Police.

New Zealand Herald. (2002, September 20). *Schoolboy killer's fatal attraction.* Retrieved from nzherald.co.nz: https://www.nzherald.co.nz/nz/schoolboy-killers-fatal-attraction/2QB55LIGOUZOFIWULEXCZIVGJY/

New Zealand Police. (1998). *Improving safety in the New Zealand Police – Report of the staff safety project*. New Zealand Police.

New Zealand Police. (2005a, May 19). *Replacement due for police rifles.* Retrieved from police.govt.nz: http://www.police.govt.nz/home/news/replacement due for police rifles

New Zealand Police. (2005b). *Annual report for the year ended 30 June 2005.* Retrieved from police.govt.nz: http://www.police.govt.nz/publications

New Zealand Police. (2010, July 15). *Courageous injured officers will soon be home.* Retrieved from police.govt.nz: https://www.police.govt.nz/news/courageous injured officers will soon be home

New Zealand Police. (2013, December). *New Zealand Police TASER reintroduction period research report 1 March 2009 to March 2010.* Retrieved from police.govt.nz: https.//www.police.govt.nz/publications/New Zealand Police TASER Reintroduction Period Research Report 1 March 2009 to March 2010

New Zealand Police. (2014, February 17). *Further enhancements to police integrated tactical training.* Retrieved from police.govt.nz: http://www.police.govt.nz/home/news/further enhancements to Police Integrated Tactical Training

New Zealand Police. (2016, August 1). *Police Commissioner pleased officers' bravery recognised by top honours.* Retrieved from police.govt.nz: https://www.police.govt.nz/news/Police Commissioner pleased officers' bravery recognised by top honours

New Zealand Police. (2019). *Annual report 2018/19.* Retrieved from police.govt.nz: http://www.polic.govt.nz/publications

New Zealand Police. (2020a, May 19). *Tactical options research reports.* Retrieved from police.govt.nz: https://www.police.govt.nz/home/aboutus/publicationsandstatistics/tactical options research reports

New Zealand Police. (2020b, September 18). *What's in a rank?* Retrieved from police.govt.nz: https://www.police.govt.nz/news/ten-one-magazine/whats-rank

New Zealand Police. (2021a, July 12). *Officers killed by criminal acts.* Retrieved from police.govt.nz: https://www.police.govt.nz/about-us/history-and-museum/memorial/officers-killed-criminal-acts

New Zealand Police. (2021b, August). *Appropriate Tactical Settings.* Retrieved from police.govt.nz: https://www.police.govt.nz/sites/default/files/publications/evidence-brief-appropriate-tactical-settings.pdf

New Zealand Police (2021c). https://www.police.govt.nz/sites/default/files/publications/tactical-options-supplement-shootings-by-police-august2021.pdf

Newton, K., & Hunt, T. (2010, September 4). *Gun laws under fire after siege*. Retrieved from stuff.co.nz: https://www.stuff.co.nz/national/crime/4094695/Gun-laws-under-fire-after-siege

NZ Herald. (2002, September 18). *17-year sentence for schoolboy who killed constable Taylor.* Retrieved from nzherald.co.nz: https://www.nzherald.co.nz/nz/17-year-sentence-for-schoolboy-who-killed-constable-taylor/DRLVRDMZJHL7Z7A3LRN65J5KH4/

Osborne, J. (1990). *Handguns and police in New Zealand 1840–1990*. South Pacific Armoury.

Ross, J. (2021, September 15). OIA request response: Reference IR-01-21-23592.

Royal Commission of Inquiry into the Terrorist Attack on Christchurch Mosques on 15 March 2019. (2021). *4. The firearms licencing system – an evaluation*. Retrieved from christchurchattack.royalcommission.nz: https://christchurchattack.royalcommission.nz/the-report/part-5-the-terrorist/the-firearms-licensing-system-an-evaluation/

Shortt, R. (2000). *"Are the New Zealand police on target": An investigation of alternative models of police response to dangerous and unlawful firearms incidents*. Victoria University of Wellington.

Smith, A. (2019, June 20). *Eyewitness: 10 year on from Napier Siege*. Retrieved from rnz.co.nz: https://www.rnz.co.nz/national/programmes/eyewitness/audio/2018699450/eyewitness-10-years-on-from-napier-siege

Standards New Zealand. (2020, December 20). *AS/NZS ISO 31000:2009*. Retrieved from standards.govt.nz: https://www.standards.govt.nz/shop/asnzs-iso-310002009/

Steward, I. (2012, November 16). *Police shooter jailed for eight years*. Retrieved from stuff.co.nz: https://www.stuff.co.nz/national/crime/7959651/Police-shooter-jailed-for-eight-years

Stuff.co.nz. (2015, July 31). *New Zealand police to routinely carry Tasers*. Retrieved from stuff.co.nz: https://www.stuff.co.nz/dominion-post/news/70711858/new-zealand-police-to-routinely-carry-tasers

Stuff.co.nz. (2016, July 29). *Kawerau siege officers' long road to recovery*. Retrieved from stuff.co.nz: https://www.stuff.co.nz/Kawerau siege officers' long road to recovery | Stuff.co.nz

Swinton, N. (2019, September). *A turning point for firearms regulation: Implications of legislative and operational reforms in the wake of the Christchurch shootings*. Retrieved from fullbright.org.nz: https://www.fulbright.org.nz/wp-content/uploads/2019/09/N-Swinton-AxfordFellow2019-Report-SEPT2019.pdf

Taylor, P. L. (2020). Dispatch priming and the police decision to use deadly force. *Police Quarterly*.

The Age. (2009, December 22). *Shot NZ officer 'lucky to be alive'*. Retrieved from theage.com.au: https://www.theage.com.au/world/shot-nz-officer-lucky-to-be-alive-20091222-lb8c.html

The University of Melbourne. (2018, May). *Risk assessment methodology*. Retrieved from safety.unimelb.edu.au: http://safety.unimelb.edu.au/__data/assets/pdf_file/0007/1716712/health-and-safety-risk-assessment-methodology.pdf

Chapter 8
Use of Lethal Force by New Zealand Police

Having considered the risks faced by Police, let's move on to the use of lethal force by Police. This chapter focuses on the years 2000–2019 and the shooting of people by police. The commentary will be based on available PCA/IPCA public reporting and will be presented as aggregated commentary, not as individual cases. Chapter 9 will contain a set of more detailed case studies to highlight various issues that the author believes contextualises the environment concerning lethal force use by New Zealand Police.

This chapter is not an attempt to reinvestigate or relitigate the individual events or actions of those involved. That has already been done by the Police and the PCA/IPCA, or in a court of law. This chapter merely aims to consolidate – as best it can – a series of otherwise unrelated shootings that involve the New Zealand Police and their use of firearms. It was hoped that by aggregating the data, common traits or issues could be identified that ultimately can be used to consider how such tragic outcomes can be avoided, if possible, in the future.

It should also be noted, that, for example, New Zealand Police data reveals that Police officers resorted to shooting someone on 30 occasions between 2012 and 2019, while during that same period, they armed themselves on 2710 occasions while attending some 38,558 events where officers resorted to use of a tactical option of any kind.

Clearly, this research does consider the "tip of a large iceberg", but that said, it is nonetheless an important and worthy tip to be so considered.

Shootings: 2000–2019

Between 2000 and 2019, New Zealand Police used lethal force on 61 occasions (using the author's expanded definition of lethal force which includes occasions where Police shots miss their intended target). As a result, 23 of the people being shot at received a fatal injury, and 22 received a non-fatal injury, and on 12 occasions the shots missed their intended target. Tragically, 2 of those 61 people were uninvolved bystanders, 1 was fatally shot, while the other received non-fatal injuries (New Zealand Police, 2020, p. 65).

R. S. Shortt, *Lethal Force and New Zealand Police*,
https://doi.org/10.1007/978-3-031-05269-9_8

The author's research located 43 publicly available reports by the PCA/IPCA published on the Independent Police Conduct Authority's website for fatal and non-fatal shootings by Police during the time under review. Those published reports form the basis of the analysis of shootings by police officers presented in this chapter, along with data located in Police public reporting that was also deemed relevant.

The 43 reports detailed the circumstances surrounding the shootings of 45 of the 61 people shot by Police (note: one report covers the shooting of three people – 2 bystanders and 1 armed man who was being chased by Police). It appears that 18 of the 61 uses of lethal force were either not independently investigated by the PCA/IPCA, or reports on them were not uploaded onto the organisation's website, or a combination of both situations.

Before moving on to the research, it was thought useful to situate the number of people shot by New Zealand Police with regard to those shot elsewhere. In this case it was done using Australia, Aotearoa New Zealand's nearest neighbouring country, and relied on *fatal* shooting data, as the Australian information did not contain details of non-fatal injuries or of shots that missed.

In Australia, Police *fatally* shot 154 people between mid-2000 and mid-2019 (Australian Institute of Criminology, 2021). At the midpoint of the 2000–2019 decade, Australia had a population of approximately 22.477 million people (Australian Bureau of Statistics, 2010), while Aotearoa New Zealand had just 4.351 million, according to the World Bank and the United Nations. Therefore, on a per capita basis, Australian Police fatally shot 0.68 people per 100,000 people, while New Zealand Police fatally shot 0.48 people per 100,000 people.

Alternatively, using the same data sources, and breaking the two decades into two blocks, 1 of 10 years and the other of 9, Table 8.1 presents the per capita results of the number of people fatally shot (using the population data for 2006 and 2015 for each country).

As the table reveals, in the first 10 years, Australian Police fatally shot more people per capita than the New Zealand Police. But, in the second sample of 9 years, that situation had reversed with New Zealand Police shooting more people per capita than their trans-Tasman colleagues.

Unfortunately, there was no comparable Australian data available for the number of times Police used lethal force and either missed or wounded the people they were shooting at. Therefore, we are unable to determine if the New Zealand Police were simply more accurate and deadly than their Australian counterparts during lethal force encounters.

What we do know is that Australian Police, in all of the country's eight police services, carried a pistol on their person when on operational duties during the entire two decades, whereas before 2010–2011, New Zealand Police very rarely did so and relied on station-based weapons. However, after 2010–2011, New Zealand Police moved their station-based firearms out into vehicle-mounted gun safes and made them more available and accessible to operational officers.

Now, moving back to Aotearoa New Zealand, let's consider who were some of those who were shot and the circumstances around those shootings.

Table 8.1 Per capita fatal shootings: aotearoa new zealand and australia, 2000–2010 and 2010–2019

Country	Years (mid-year to mid-year)	Population (year)	Fatal shootings	Per capita fatal shootings (per 100k people)
Aotearoa New Zealand	2000–2010	4,185,000 (as at 2006)	5	0.12
Australia	2000–2010	20,700,000 (as at 2006)	39	0.19
Aotearoa New Zealand	2010–2019	4,609,000 (as at 2015)	14	0.30
Australia	2010–2019	23,820,000 (as at 2015)	50	0.21

Data obtained from New Zealand Police (2021), Australian Institute of Criminology (AIC) (2021), World Bank and United Nations population data

Who Was Shot and Who Shot Them?

The PCA/IPCA reports confirm 44 men and 1 woman were shot by police between 2000 and 2019. The ages of those shot ranged from 19 through to 65. The median age was 33. When their ages are viewed in decades, 1 person was 19 when shot, those aged 20–29 accounted for 14 shootings, those aged 30–39 accounted for 15, those aged 40–49 accounted for 6, while 50–59 accounted for 5. One person was aged 65 when shot.

There were 57 police officers involved in the shootings. They came from various roles within New Zealand Police. Thirty-four of the officers were uniformed staff (i.e. Level 1 responders); 17 were members of the AOS; 4 were STG members; and 2 were CIB detectives.

Police data, presented in Fig. 8.1, reveals the ethnicity breakdown for those shot (or shot at) between 2000 and 2019:[1]

Why Were They Shot?

The shootings involved a variety of reasons for Police becoming involved with the people they shot, and in some instances, there were multiple reasons which overlapped. In summary: 14 of the shootings were preceded by activity now described

[1] The data includes two bystanders (one of Pasifika ethnicity and one of European ethnicity) who were unintentionally shot by police officers. It excludes two shootings where the cause of death could not be confirmed as Police shots (one case involving a person of European ethnicity and the second of a person for whom no ethnicity could be determined). It also excludes four shootings where ethnicity was listed as "unknown".

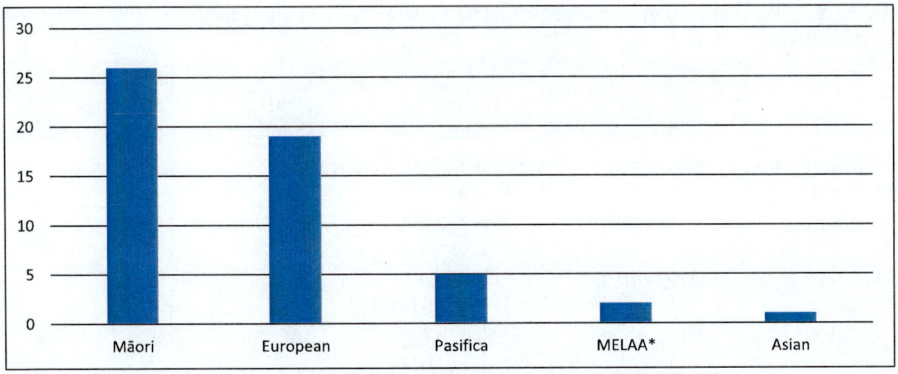

Fig. 8.1 Ethnicity of people shot (2000–2019) (includes miss, non-fatal and fatal outcomes). *Middle Eastern, Latin American and African – descriptor used by Police. (Data obtained from New Zealand Police documents. Note: the IPCA reporting does not include ethnicity)

as family harm incidents; 27 were preceded by various forms of criminal activity; while 18 showed evidence of mental health issues, including suicidal indications; 13 involved physical harm to another person (or persons) before Police became involved; 20 involved threats being made but no harm being inflicted. As mentioned above, in some instance there were multiple pre-shooting factors; they were 12 events which involved both criminal activity and mental health/suicidal indications before the shootings. Nine of the events were also preceded by references to drug use, and eight also had references to alcohol consumption.

In 19 of the cases reviewed,[2] the author was left with the impression that the person shot may well have decided to end their own life through what is commonly referred to as "suicide by cop".[3] In one instance, the shooting of a man named Williams, in 2001, the PCA made a similar observation. Examples of the behaviours leading to the author's impressions were that the individuals had either already made suicidal comments, or taken suicidal actions; they knew they were confronted by armed police officers, but chose to provocatively advance on the officers – despite being challenged, firearms were pointed at police officers, but not fired, and/or the individuals made no effort to escape from the Police. However, the author is not a

[2] See shootings of 26-year-old male (2000), Wallace (2000), Williams (2001), Bellingham (2007), Mettam (2008), Sime (2009), Hartley (2011), Ratahi (2011), Taite (2011), Unnamed car-hijacker (2012), Hall (2015), Hurinui (2015), Smiler (2015), Cerven (2015), Stephens (2016), Suos (2017), Mr. X – Nelson (2017), Toms (2018) and Hooper (2019).

[3] Suicide by cop (SbC) was described by Hendy – citing V.J Gerbeth, "Suicide by Cop" *Law and Order* (1993) – as the phenomenon where "... individuals, bent on self-destruction, engage in life-threatening and criminal behaviour in order to force the police to kill them" (Hendy, 2012, p. 80). He went on to cite Lord and Sloop who suggested that SbC "differs from self-inflicted suicides in that SbC incidents usually commence with the commission of an armed criminal act and culminate in the failure to surrender a weapon to police" (ibid.).

psychologist and will leave it to those more appropriately qualified to offer a definitive view on the actions of those people.

Examples of the types of behaviours occurring before shootings took place included damage to property, assaulting a person with a weapon (not a firearm), drug dealing, burglary, hostage-taking, dangerous driving, threatening with a weapon, shooting a person, being wanted on warrant, and presenting a firearm at police or other persons. In two cases the person shot had murdered another before Police were called to investigate their actions, and on several occasions, the person shot had taken partners, ex-partners or family members hostage. One shooting occurred after concerned family members asked Police to make a welfare check on their mentally unwell relative.

On six occasions there was no preceding criminal activities mentioned in the reports before Police came into contact with the person shot. Five of those situations involved clear indications of the person becoming suicidal because of events in their lives.

And, in one extremely unusual situation, when police officers responded to a noise complaint that resulted in a man being arrested, the arresting officers were rapidly approached by an aggressive and agitated relative of the arrested man. He was armed with a machete, which he refused to drop when called upon to do so, resulting in him being non-fatally shot.

Once Police became involved with the people they shot, and only three other people were shot or injured. Two were uninvolved bystanders hit by Police shots during the pursuit of an armed man, and one was a police officer slightly injured by shotgun pellets fired by the person Police were attempting to deal with. During the confrontations with Police, Police officers also tried to use other tactical options on 11 occasions. A TASER or a police dog was used on three separate occasions each, OC spray was used twice, a TASER and OC spray were used together during one incident, and on two occasions TASERs were fired almost simultaneously with police firearms being discharged.

All of the people shot knew they were being confronted by police officers. The majority knew that those police officers were armed. That knowledge was either conveyed by officer(s) calling out to the person that they were armed, or it was visually obvious to the person that the police officer(s) were holding firearms. In the majority of cases, the person shot was told to drop their weapon before being shot. However, on one occasion, a man may not have realised there was an armed police officer near him when he was confronted by police officers after committing a burglary while armed with a cut-down 0.22 rifle and firing a shot when confronting Police.

Forty-one of the people shot had some form of weapon – or what appeared to be a weapon – on them at the time of the shooting. Two pretended they had a weapon, but in reality they did not.

Mental Illness

This aspect of the use of lethal force by Police is worthy of a closer examination. As detailed above, 18 of the PCA/IPCA shooting reports (42%) had commentary – *before* a shooting took place – that the person subsequently shot had a mental illness history, or exhibited indicators of mental illness, or had expressed suicidal intentions, or a combination of all three. Report commentary covering the *actual* shooting events and subsequent findings included 13 instances (30%) where mental illness or suicide was mentioned.

An Australian study, cited in Hendy (2012, p. 79), detailed that in the state of Victoria, 53% of fatal shootings by Police "… during the period 1990-2004 involved individuals suffering from a mental illness or disorder." And, by way of further comparison, research from the USA identified that out of a sample of 812 fatalities resulting from the use of lethal force by law enforcement, 18% were suspected "…'suicide by cop incidents'" (DeGue et al., 2016).

Only one report (PCA, 2000) spoke of "suicide by cop" (SbC) as a probable explanation for the use of lethal force, although a second IPCA report regarding a 2009 shooting also raised the possibility that SbC was the deceased's desired outcome. However, the author is of the view that four of the cases reviewed (9%) displayed indications that the person shot used the Police to fulfill a suicidal desire.[4]

Since 2015, the New Zealand Police TOR regime has included mental illness and suicide as two matters about which data has been captured. That data, displayed in Figs. 8.2 and 8.3, is the subjective assessment of the reporting police officer and should not be mistaken for a clinical diagnosis.

The data in Fig. 8.2 indicates a growing number of events requiring the deployment of tactical options which involve an assessment that mental health matters are a relevant factor, while the number of events involving suicide and the need for tactical options deployment have stayed stable. With specific regard to the deployment of firearms (Fig. 8.3), the small sample of data available (note: just 2 years of TOR reports provided the data) makes it difficult to comment on trends, but the data does confirm that firearms are being deployed when attending mental health/suicide related calls for service.

The data in the two charts (Figs. 8.2 and 8.3), it is contended, supports the data regarding mental illness and SbC observations revealed by the review of the 43 PCA/IPCA shooting reports. Mental illness, suicide and SbC are clearly aspects of the New Zealand Police lethal force environment, and while the overall numbers are comparatively small, in comparison to the total number of TOR events attended, they do warrant careful consideration, particularly where an individual seeks to make a police officer the means by which they end their life.

[4]The author acknowledges, once again, that he is not a trained medical practitioner and is making these observations from a lay person's perspective.

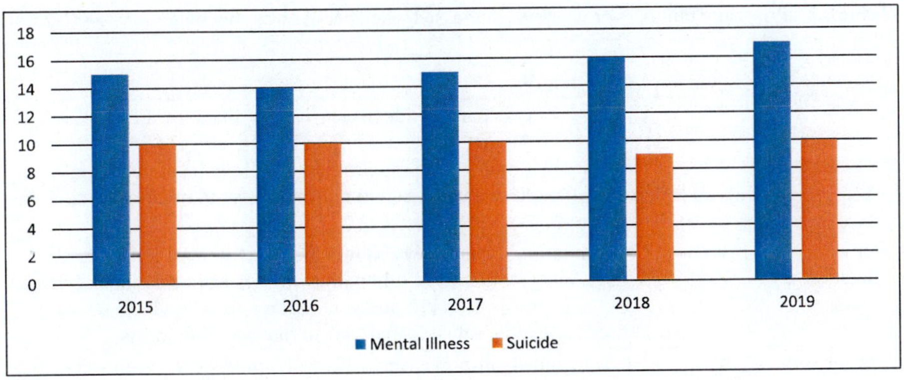

Fig. 8.2 Percentage of all TOR events where mental health/suicide reported as a relevant factor (2015–2019). (Data obtained from New Zealand Police Tactical Options Reporting for the years 2015–2019)

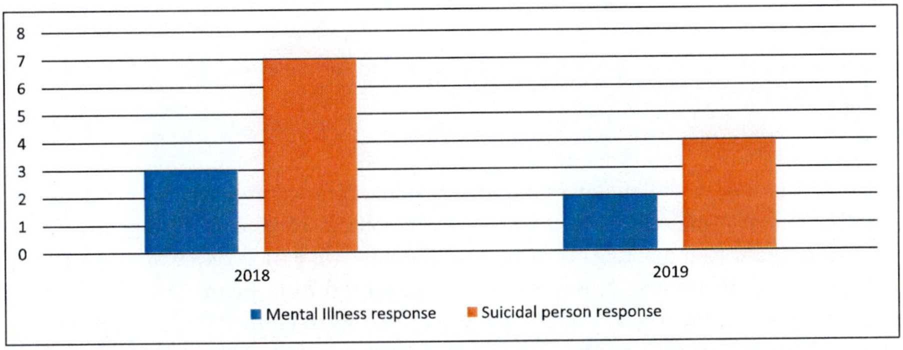

Fig. 8.3 Percentage of TOR involving mental health/suicide events where firearms were chosen as tactical option (2018 and 2019). (Data obtained from New Zealand Police Tactical Options Reporting for the years 2018 and 2019)

What Were the Weapons Involved on Both Sides?

The following is a list of weapons police were confronted with when they used lethal force (Table 8.2):

As noted above, on two occasions police officers were "tricked" into thinking the person they were confronting had a weapon and that they were at risk. Both men involved were shot, one fatally, while the other survived.

By way of interest and for context regarding the use of lethal force when confronting a person armed with a knife or other cutting weapon (i.e. knives, machetes, slashers), Norwegian naval special forces "consider a knife attack within a radius of 6–8 metres as deadly … [while] … [t]he Swedish police's dignitary protection [staff]

Table 8.2 Types and numbers of weapons possessed when person was shot by police (2000–2019)

Type of weapon	Number	Comments
None	2	One man had his hand inside his shirt and walked towards police stating he had a gun and was going to kill the officer (Taite, 2011), while another man rapidly presented his cell phone at police, in a darkened park, in a way that led police officers to believe it was a gun (Cerven, 2015)
Replica/ imitation or airgun	6	One 'imitation' weapon was in fact pieces of wood wrapped in a singlet. The man involved told police officers he had a gun and that he was "… coming out to kill police with the gun …" (Mr X, 2017). Others included air pistols that looked like actual firearms
Handgun	4	These included cut-down rifles – for example, two were cut-down 0.22 rifles
Rifle	6	Descriptions given, for example, included "0.308 rifle", "hunting rifle" and "0.308"
Shotgun	11	Including those that had been sawn-off but did not fit the pistol definition, and pump-action, multi-shot shotguns
Bladed or other types of weapons	14	These included machetes, slashers, knives, a spanner, a golf club and a baseball bat

Data obtained from 43 PCA/IPCA public reports released between 2000 and 2019, www.ipca.govt.nz

considers this distance to be 10 metres" (Hendriksen & Kruke, 2020). In essence, those services believe that a person armed with a knife – at the distances stated from another person – can kill that person before they themselves can be stopped.

With regard to the actual firearms encountered[5] ($n = 21$, or 48.8% of weapons), not only were they present, but shots were also fired from them. In total 133 shots were fired – at best count – by the people Police were confronting. Unfortunately, some of the PCA/IPCA reports did not give clear and definitive counts of the shots fired. It must also be noted, that in one incident alone, 110 shots were fired by the man Police were attempting to contain, leaving just 23 shots for all other events. He was one of the people the author suspected of committing "suicide by cop", and it was during this event that a police officer received shotgun pellet wounds to his face. Fortunately, that police officer and a neighbour (who also received shotgun pellet injuries before Police arrived) were the only people injured by the large number of shots fired.

Once Police engaged with the person they were responding to; no one else was recorded in any of the PCA/IPCA reports as receiving any injuries from any of the shots fired by those people.

From the Police perspective, the author established that 203 shots were fired by officers. The Police relied upon their Glock pistol and Bushmaster rifles mostly; however, on two occasions specialist rifles on issue to AOS and STG officers were

[5] In this instance the term "actual firearms" excludes replicas and airguns.

used. The type of weapon used and the result of the shots fired are displayed in Fig. 8.4.

By far the most Police shots fired came from Bushmaster rifles. There were 17 shootings involving the use of the Bushmaster, with 10 of those shootings being by AOS or STG officers. Seven were by uniformed or CIB officers. On three occasions both a Glock and Bushmaster were fired. On two occasions the rifles used were "specialist" weapons on issue to AOS and STG units. Glock handguns were primarily used by uniformed officers, with only three instances of AOS or STG officers firing them.

Of the shots fired by police officers, 74 hit the person being aimed at. By contrast, 107 shots missed the person, with 2 striking uninvolved bystanders.

Interestingly, when seven or more shots were fired from a Glock (or multiple Glocks) ($n = 4$),

the chance of a hit dropped to 50% or less with the more shots that were fired. For example, the most Glock shots fired in one encounter was 14, with only 4hits and 10 misses. In all cases where only one or two Glock shots were fired ($n = 8$), all hit the person aimed at.

With the Bushmaster, if nine or more shots were fired during an encounter, either by one or multiple rifles, ($n = 5$), the hit rate also fell to 50% or less the more shots that were fired. Two examples of this were as follows: 1 encounter in which 18 shots were fired, with 5 hitting and 13 missing; in a separate encounter 35 shots were fired with only 2hitting and 33 missing the person.

In summary, the chart below displays the number of shots fired by Police in the 43 encounters reviewed and compares the shots that hit the person aimed at with those that missed and displays the percentage that missed (Table 8.3).

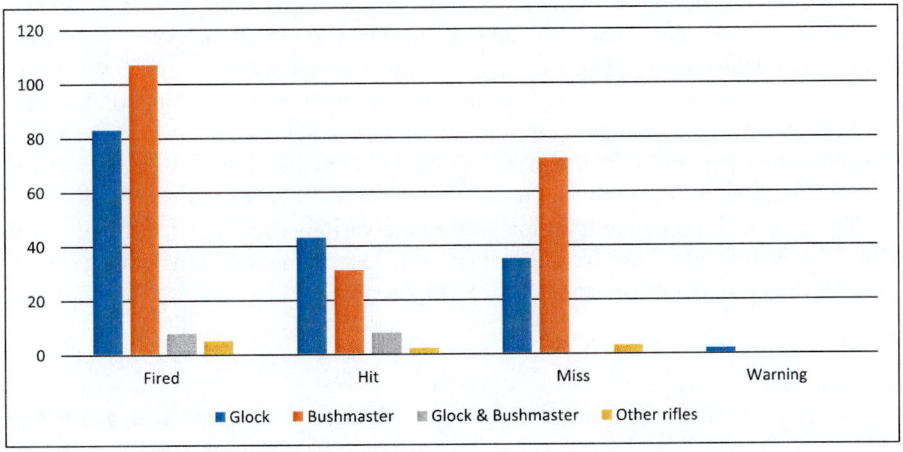

Fig. 8.4 Type of weapon and outcomes from shots fired by police (2000–2019). (Data from the 43 PCA/IPCA public reports into shootings released between 2000 and 2019, www.ipca.govt.nz)

Table 8.3 Outcome of shots fired by police firearms (2000–2019)

Weapon	Fired	Hit	%	Miss	%
Glock	83	48	57.8%	35	42.2%
Bushmaster	107	35	32.7%	72	67.3%

Data from 43 PCA/IPCA public reports released between 2000 and 2019, www.ipca.govt.nz

The above numbers are, it appears, by no means rare or unusual in Police use of force encounters where shots are fired. Michael White, for example, reports "… police officers who use deadly force *miss* their intended targets far more often than they hit them" (Italics in the original) (White, 2006, p. 304). He went on to state "Hit rates vary notably across police agencies but rarely exceed 50% …" (ibid.).

By way of comparison, in a British report, undertaken by Burrows in 1996,[6] it was identified that in 23 shootings "… of the shots fired by police at suspects, fully 56% missed their targets". While, in a Norwegian review of 24 instances where that country's Police shot at someone, 3 instances resulted in officers missing the person they shot at (Hendriksen & Kruke, 2020). The Norwegian study also revealed "[t]he average number of shots fired by police in 24 instances was approximately 3.5, with a median of 1" (ibid.); in comparison the New Zealand Police average number of shots fired was 5.1, with a median of 3 (based on combined Glock and Bushmaster shooting data).

Elsewhere, a 1994 New York City police department (USA), report into the transition from the 6-shot revolver to the Glock Model 19, semi-automatic pistol, revealed that the average number of shots now fired at incidents (involving the Glock) was 4.4 "… with relatively fewer hitting their intended targets". The average number of shots fired from the Glock in the Aotearoa New Zealand sample was 4.1, while the median was 3.

The author pondered whether the numbers may simply reflect the fact that officers now have at least 17 shots available in their Glock and 20 (or more) shots available in their Bushmaster. Historically, as already discussed, the revolver only offered six shots and the bolt-action rifles just five. However, one research study in the USA looking at the impact of moving to semi-automatic pistols from revolvers found "… the adoption of semi-automatic pistols did not lead to an increase in the number of rounds fired per incident, nor did it improve accuracy" (White, 2006, p. 308).

The origin of the police firearms used in the various shootings identified that in 26 of the events, they came from a "car cabinet", 5 were issued from a police station, and 14 were obtained from an AOS or STG armoury.

[6]Burrows, C. (1996). A review of the Discharge of Firearms by Police in England and Wales 1991–1993. Joint Standing Committee on the Police Use of Firearms in consultation with the PCA, unpublished

What Distances Were Involved?

Police shootings with a Glock pistol occurred over relatively short distances. Nineteen of the Glock-only shooting reports had information on distances, and that revealed the average distances being 4.3–6.6 m, while the median[7] distances were 2–5 m. The shortest Glock distances were 1–2 m. The longest distances were 21–30 m. The Glock pistol is reported to have an effective range[8] of 50 m.

Distance did not appear to impact accuracy in the use of the Glock, except for two instances where the distance between the police officers and the persons being shot at were the two longest in the data. One involved a distance of between 15 and 17 m. On that occasion 14 shots were fired with four hitting the person and 10 missing. In the second instance, a Glock was fired three times over a distance of between 21 and 30 m, with 1 shot hitting the person and two missing.

When it came to use of the Bushmaster rifle, the distances were calculated from the 14 reports that held such data. The average distances were 16.8–19.8 m, with the median distances being 15–16 m. The shortest Bushmaster distance was 2.5 m, while the longest distances were 21–30 m. The Bushmaster rifle is reported to have an effective range of 550 m.

Distance also appeared to impact accuracy at the high end of the distance spectrum for use of the Bushmaster. In four instances – the longest distances in the data – multiple shots were fired with 50% or less hitting the subject. For example, over 40–45 m, 18 shots were fired with 5hits and 13 misses; over 40 m 10 shots were fired with 1 hit and 9 misses; over 30 m 9 shots were fired with 5 hits and 4 misses; and over 25–30 m, 35 shots were fired with 2 hits and 33 misses. Two of these examples involved AOS officers, while the other two were uniformed officers. A summary of the minimum and maximum distances is presented in Table 8.4.

For comparative purposes, Hendriksen and Kruke's review of Norwegian Police shootings between 2005 and 2018 reported on 24 instances of Police firing at a person and confirmed "[t]he average distance between police and the subject (based on 21 of the 24 instances) was approx. 8.5m, the median distance was 5 m, with a range of approximately 1–60 m" (Hendriksen & Kruke, 2020). Norwegian Police, like the New Zealand Police, are equipped with a 9 mm pistol (Heckler & Koch P30), but instead of a rifle, they have access to the Heckler & Koch MP5 9 mm submachine gun, both of which are secured in the patrol vehicle until they are required (wikipedia.org, 2021). In data from Sweden, Hendy reported that 42% of shootings by Police occurred across a range of 0–3 m (Hendy, 2014).

The Norwegian and Swedish distances closely equate to those revealed in the Aotearoa New Zealand data for use of the Glock. However, when a Bushmaster was used, the average and median distances were longer (see Table 8.4). But, while the

[7] "The median is the middle value … the median is less susceptible to extremes at the edges of the distribution." (Prunckun, 2010, p. 113)

[8] The maximum distance at which a weapon may be expected to be accurate and achieve the desired effect.

Table 8.4 Distances (minimum and maximum) at which police weapons fired

Weapon type	Average minimum (m)	Average maximum (m)	Median minimum (m)	Median maximum (m)
Glock pistol	4.3	6.6	2	5
Bushmaster rifle	16.8	19.8	15	16

Data from 43 PCA/IPCA public reports released between 2000 and 2019, www.ipca.govt.nz
m metres

Norwegian study reported the maximum range for a shooting as being 60 m, in Aotearoa New Zealand the maximum was just 45 m, just less than a tenth of the effective range of the rifle.

When considering the two primary Police weapons, for example, the Bushmaster is effective out to 550 m, which is well beyond the effective range of handguns, sawn-off shotguns or edged weapons. However, the Bushmaster was never reported on as being used over such longer distances. The Glock, with an effective range of 50 m, was also mostly used over much shorter distances, right down to 1 m. Why were Police so close?

It was clear from the 43 instances reviewed that the distances between officers and the people they were responding to were the result of two distinct factors: firstly, where the encounter happened – most often dictated by the other person, and, secondly, the tactics chosen by the police officers concerned which put them into close proximity with the person being responded to. The geography and layout of the places where Police encountered people, and the ability of the responding officers to deploy the recommended Police tactic of cordon and containment, also played roles in bringing police officers and the person being policed into close contact.

While some police officers encounter armed people in open environments and away from other people and buildings, others do not and are faced with situations in populated and built-up areas. The greater the distance between police officers and the subjects of their interventions, the greater the potential for those people to evade the Police or to harm another person, particularly in dark environments, or in built-up areas. Police officers are faced with a dichotomy between the safety provided by the effective ranges of their firearms and the tactics they need to use to contain a subject and to prevent harm to others.

Given the challenge of "circumstances over capability" mentioned above, lets now review where the shootings happened.

Where and in What Circumstances Did the Shootings Occur?

The author approached the "where" aspect of the data by capturing it across three categories. They were "inside" for shootings occurring when the person shot was inside a building (i.e. a house, shop, hotel or factory), "outside" for shootings of people in open areas (i.e. driveways, footpaths, roadways or parks) and "vehicle" for

Table 8.5 Locations where shootings by police occurred (2000–2019)

Location	Number of shootings
Inside	8
Outside	26
Vehicle	9

Data obtained from 43 PCA/IPCA public reports in to shootings by Police

shootings that occurred when the person was inside a vehicle. If a person had been "inside" a building, or in a "vehicle", but had exited and was then shot, the data was captured under the "outside" category irrespective of how little time elapsed between being "inside" and then "outside". The location data is presented in Table 8.5.

The small number of shootings inside a building may, in the author's experience, reflect the heightened danger that exists for Police who enter a building looking for an armed offender. During the author's training, and subsequent work with the AOS, it was recognised that entry into a building should be a last resort. Every effort should be made to encourage the person to come outside, or to force them out using tear gas or a police dog, if necessary. The dangers of confronting an armed person inside a building were graphically realised in the earlier discussion of police shootings when three AOS officers were wounded when they entered a house searching for an armed man and – separately – when two uniformed constables were wounded and a police dog killed when they entered a house and were confronted and shot by an armed man.

Unfortunately, the development of the "active shooter" situation does limit the opportunity police officers have of avoiding building entry if lives are at stake and immediate action is called for. Fortunately, none of the PCA/IPCA shooting reports involved the need for Police to enter a building to search for an "active shooter".

Of interest were the nine events where the person was in a vehicle. Interacting with vehicles and their occupants is a very common aspect of Police work. Furthermore, vehicles are often used by people travelling to or from crimes, or seeking to avoid or evade Police. A number of the cases reviewed involved armed people travelling in vehicles and refusing requests from Police to stop. Such events create a heightened level of danger for all involved, including the public, as vehicle pursuits are dynamic and difficult to control and can result in serious injury or death, all without adding an armed person into the mix.

In a small number of the vehicle-related shooting events ($n = 3$) police officers shot at the person while the person's vehicle was in motion, in one instance Police were also firing from a moving vehicle. All the other vehicle-related shooting events ($n = 6$) occurred once the vehicles were stationary either through Police actions (i.e. use of road spikes to deflate tyres) or due to a decision made by the driver to stop but remain inside their vehicle.

Shooting at someone inside a vehicle presents additional challenges and risks for Police. Bullets can be deflected from their trajectory by the vehicle's glass, bodywork, or inside features such as seat-frames; meanwhile, the target area visible to the shooter is reduced due to the vehicle's structure and the person's sitting position.

The other challenge and risk presented to Police when engaging a person inside a vehicle is not knowing for certain that no one else is inside. For example, a restrained or unconscious person, a child or infant may not be visible to someone outside the vehicle without getting extremely close. One event occurring in 2020, and outside the timeframe of the PCA/IPCA reviews, graphically highlighted the issue.

A man, wanted by Police on suspicion of murder, was repeatedly shot by police officers after he stopped his car following a pursuit. He was killed by the gunfire. His car was examined the next morning in daylight and his dog was found alive inside next to his body. None of the police officers involved had seen the dog before firing or when shooting, nor afterwards when they briefly examined the car and confirmed the man was dead. This same man had 2 days earlier taken his two young children to a relative and left them there before later encountering Police (Independent Police Conduct Authority, 2021).

The next segment of this chapter uses two charts to present data obtained from one relatively recent Police source. That source was a list of all shootings by New Zealand Police – from 1916 to 2020 – contained in the 2019 New Zealand Police Tactical Options Report (New Zealand Police, 2020). The charts present the data for each of the 12 Police districts, whose geographic locations are depicted in the map of Aotearoa New Zealand on the next page (Fig. 8.5).

The timeframes in the charts have been constructed around four blocks of 5 years. As a point of interest, the two later blocks of time – starting from 2011 – representing the time when Police firearms began being placed in operational vehicles and were, therefore, far more available and accessible to officers responding to incidents.

The charts provide insight into the number of times police officers in districts shot at a person (i.e. used lethal force) and missed, killed or wounded them (Fig. 8.6) and the total number of uses of lethal force by Police across the four time periods, but not broken down by district (Fig. 8.6).

The black lines on Fig. 8.6 represent the lowest and highest median number of shootings by Police (Lowest n = 0.5, 2000–2004; Highest n = 2.5, 2016–2019) across the four blocks of time used.

As can be seen in Fig. 8.6, the highest median line for lethal force use was crossed eight times, with seven of those occurring since 2010, after Police moved firearms into operational vehicles. Furthermore, as depicted in Fig. 8.7, use of lethal force by Police use has increased each period since 2000–2004, with the number of uses in 2016–2019 being almost four times that of 2000–2004.

The final set of data captured for this segment came, once again, from the 43 PCA/IPCA public reports. It looked at whether the shootings occurred during a "planned police operation/response" (including where AOS and/or STG were deployed), or from an "unplanned dynamic incident" for which the Police had little or no warning.

Fig. 8.5 New Zealand police district boundaries. (Map obtained from https://www.police.govt.nz/about-us/structure/police-districts. Reproduced with the permission of New Zealand Police)

The data revealed 11 of the shootings fell into the "planned operation/response" category, while 32 were coded as "unplanned dynamic incident". That meant in 74% of the 43 shootings it was Level 1 responders dealing with an armed, or potentially armed, person, which corresponded with other data from the same reports that revealed 63% (n = 36) of the officers who fired shots were performing uniformed non-specialist roles, while 37% (n = 21) were AOS or STG officers operating in their specialist roles.

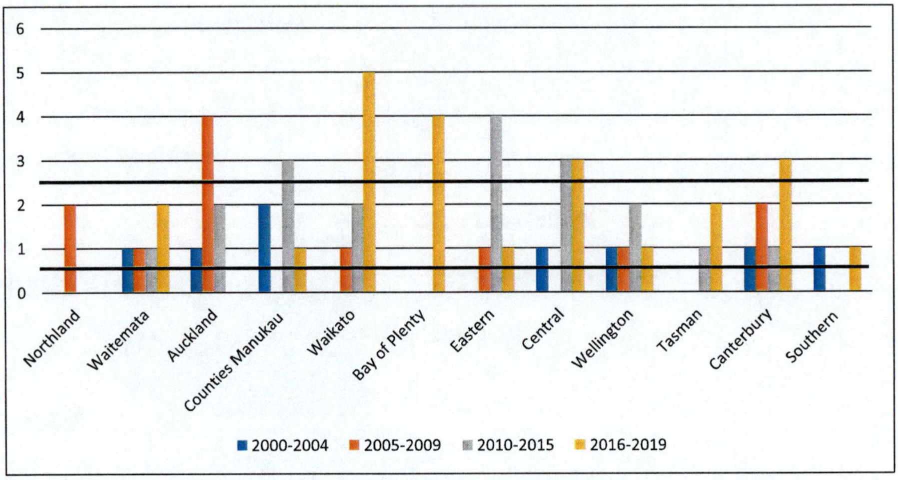

Fig. 8.6 Number of shootings by police: by district (2000–2019) (includes miss, non-fatal and fatal outcomes). (Data obtained from New Zealand Police, 2021)

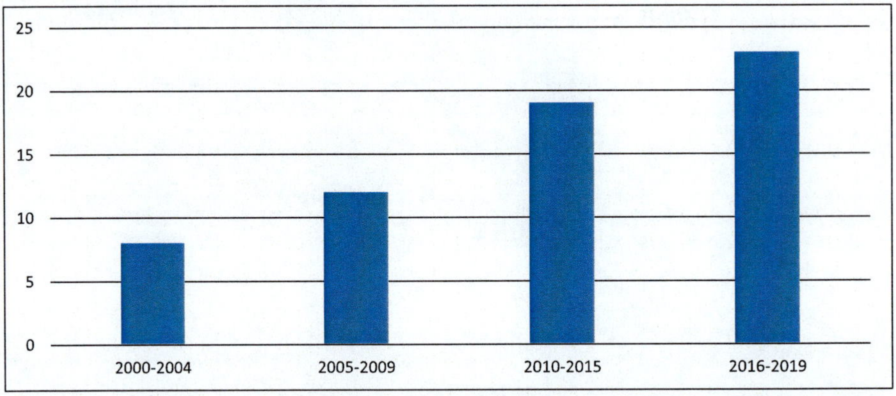

Fig. 8.7 Number of shootings by police (2000–2019) (includes miss, non-fatal and fatal outcomes). (New Zealand Police, 2020)

Were Any of the Shootings the Subject of Adverse Comment by the IPCA?

All of the shootings by police officers between 2000 and 2019 were found to be justified under the provisions of the *Crimes Act 1961* (NZL) regarding use of force; however, several were the subject of adverse commentary by the Authority, as commented upon earlier in this book.

Examples of the findings commentary included concerns about tactics chosen by police officers, failures to follow Police policy and procedure (e.g. failing to put on body armour, failures to notify others that officers had armed themselves), the failure of Police to test officers who had shot someone for drug and alcohol use after the event and in one – quite serious case – concerns over the number of shots fired and when they were fired.

One of the commonly raised concerns expressed by the Authority was with regard to communication. Under Police policy, officers who now arm themselves using weapons carried in operational vehicles are under a policy and procedural obligation to inform the centralised Communications Centre that oversees them. By not advising the Communications Centre, it also meant the district-based Command Centres were also likely to be unaware that they now had armed staff in the field. That lack of situational awareness meant there was a risk that insufficient senior oversight was applied to those situations and that alternative tactics and operational support (e.g. AOS or police dogs) was not activated and dispatched to help resolve the incident.

Another critique which appeared in PCA/IPCA reporting was regarding the testing of police officers for drugs and alcohol after they shot someone. That issue, as previously discussed, was – for a time – a regular concern to the Authority before it was resolved by Police through policy and procedure changes.

Any concerns that New Zealand Police had, internally, regarding any of the shootings carried out by their officers were not made publicly available, unless the organisation commented on the findings of the PCA/IPCA public reports when they were released. The same applies to any actions taken internally by Police, such as counselling of officers or additional training requirements.

An Official Information Act request lodged with the Police by the author sought information regarding any sackings, disciplinary actions, remedial training or counselling revealed that between 2000 and 2019:

- 70 police officers were involved in shooting incidents;
- 25 of those officers subsequently experienced "… some form of further action" related to the shootings, including:
  - "Four disciplinary actions" [no further details provided]
  - "10 remedial actions" [no further details provided]
  - "10 policy/procedure actions" [no further details]
  - "One criminal charge … [described as arising from a] … careless use of [a] firearm causing injury … [when] a slung firearm discharge[ed] 'hands free' during an arrest. The officer was acquitted." (Ross, 2021, p. 1)

Seven of the 43 reports contained specific commentary by the Authority, which help provide an overview of how the Authority viewed situations and commented upon them, including matters related to procedural issues arising in the heat of a volatile and dangerous situation (Bellingham 2007; Naitoka 2009; Kelly-Tumarae 2011; Morehu 2013; Cerven 2015; Toms 2018; Hooper 2019). These will be outlined in greater detail as case studies in Chap. 9.

Bibliography

Australian Bureau of Statistics. (2010, December). *3101.0 – Australian Demographic Statistics, Dec 2010.* Retrieved from abs.gov.au: https://www.abs.gov.au/mediareleasesbyCatalogue/3101.0 – Australian Demographic Statistics, Dec 2010

Australian Institute of Criminology. (2021, October 12). *datatablesdeathsinpolicecustody2019-20.xlsx.* Retrieved from aic.gov.au: https://www.aic.gov.au/sites/default/files/2021-10/datatables-deathsinpolicecustody2019-20.xlsx

Crime.co.nz. (2021, August 2). *The murder of detective constable Duncan Taylor.* Retrieved from crime.co.nz: http://www.crime.co.nz/c-files.aspx?ID=24619

DeGue, S., Folwer, K. A., & Calkins, C. (2016, November). Deaths due to use of lethal force by law enforcement. *HHS Public Access*, pp. 173–187.

Department of the Prime Minister and Cabinet. (2008, May 3). *Special honours list 3 May 2008 (Bravery Awards).* Retrieved from dpmc.govt.nz: https://dpmc.govt.nz/publications/special-honours-list-3-may-2008-bravery-awards.

Francis, C. (2009, May 20). *Napier gunman shot himself in head – Coroner.* Retrieved from stuff.co.nz: http://www.stuff.co.nz/national/2407196/Napier-gunman-shot-himself-in-head-coroner

Francis, C. (2010, August). *Sgt Don Wilkinson's killers jailed.* Retrieved from stuff.co.nz: https://www.stuff.co.nz/national/crime/4074883/Sgt-Don-Wilkinsons-killers-jailed

Greenwood, C. (1979). *Police tactics in armed operations*. Paladin Press.

Hendriksen, S. V., & Kruke, B. I. (2020). Norwegian police use of firearms: Critical decision-making in dynamic and stressful situations. *Nordic Journal of Studies in Policing, 7*, 99–120.

Hendy, R. (2012, January). *The strategic impact of routine arming the New Zealand Police.* Victoria University of Wellington.

Hendy, R. (2014). Routinely armed and unarmed police: What can the Scandinavian experience teach us? *Policing*, 1–10.

Independent Police Conduct Authority. (2010). *Public report into police shooting of Shayne Richard Sime*. Independent Police Conduct Authority.

Independent Police Conduct Authority. (2012). *Police shooting of Halatau Ki'anamanu Naitoko.* Independent Police Conduct Authority.

Independent Police Conduct Authority. (2021). *Use of force during fatal shooting in Tauranga justified*. Independent Police Conduct Authority.

Mitchell, J. (2020, July 24). *Steven Wallace's family's long search for justice.* Retrieved from rnz.co.nz: https://www.rnz.co.nz/news/national/421893/steven-wallace-s-family-s-long-search-for-justice

New Zealand Police. (2010, July 15). *Courageous injured officers will soon be home.* Retrieved from police.govt.nz: https://www.police.govt.nz/news/release/24716.

New Zealand Police. (2016, August 1). *Police commissioner pleased officers' bravery recognised by top honours.* Retrieved from police.govt.nz: https://www.police.govt.nz/news/release/police-commissioner-pleased-officers'-bravery-recognised-top-honours.

New Zealand Police. (2020). *Tactical options 2019 annual report*. New Zealand Police.

New Zealand Police. (2021, July 12). *Officers killed by criminal acts.* Retrieved from police.govt.nz: https://www.police.govt.nz/about-us/history-and-museum/memorial/officers-killed-criminal-acts

Newton, K., & Hunt, T. (2010, September 4). *Gun laws under fire after siege.* Retrieved from stuff.co.nz: https://www.stuff.co.nz/national/crime/4094695/Gun-laws-under-fire-after-siege

NZ Herald. (2002, September 18). *17-year sentence for schoolboy who killed constable Taylor.* Retrieved from nzherald.co.nz: https://www.nzherald.co.nz/nz/17-year-sentence-for-schoolboy-who-killed-constable-taylor/DRLVRDMZJHL7Z7A3LRN65J5KH4/

Prunckun, H. (2010). *Handbook of scientific methods of inquiry for intelligence analysis.* Scarecrow Press, Inc.

Ross, J. (2021, October 12). *OIA response reference: IR-01-21-25129*. New Zealand Police.

Smith, A. (2019, June 20). *Eyewitness: 10 year on from Napier Siege.* Retrieved from rnz.co.nz: https://www.rnz.co.nz/national/programmes/eyewitness/audio/2018699450/eyewitness-10-years-on-from-napier-siege

Squires, P., & Kennison, P. (2010). *Shooting to kill? Policing, firearms, and armed response.* John Wiley & Sons Ltd.

Steward, I. (2012, November 16). *Police shooter jailed for eight years.* Retrieved from stuff.co.nz: https://www.stuff.co.nz/national/crime/7959651/Police-shooter-jailed-for-eight-years

Stuff.co.nz. (2016, July 29). *Kawerau siege officers' long road to recovery.* Retrieved from stuff.co.nz: https://www.stuff.co.nz/national/crime/82610755/kawerau-siege-officers-long-road-to-recovery

The Age. (2009, December 22). *Shot NZ officer 'lucky to be alive'.* Retrieved from theage.com.au: https://www.theage.com.au/world/shot-nz-officer-lucky-to-be-alive-20091222-lb8c.html

White, M. D. (2006). Hitting the target (or not): Comparing characteristics of fatal, injurious, and noninjurious police shootings. *Police Quarterly, 9*, 303–330.

wikipedia.org. (2021, October 14). *Norwegian Police Service.* Retrieved from wikipedia.org: https://en.wikipedia.org/wiki/Norwegian_Police_Service

Chapter 9
Seven Case Studies

While the PCA/IPCA determined that all of the shootings it reviewed between 2000 and 2019 were justified under law, they also found areas for Police reflection on tactics, tactical options, policy and operating procedures regarding use of firearms and responding to potentially dangerous events.

While seven cases were chosen there were others that could have been used. All of the other PCA/IPCA reports are worthy of reading and reflection. The published reports are all on the IPCA website at www.ipca.govt.nz.

Each study is a summary of quite detailed reporting. The author has tried to capture salient and important elements from each case, but acknowledges that some – on all sides of the events that unfolded and with direct involvement – may feel that this was not adequately achieved. In reality, only by reading each of the IPCA reports can a detailed understanding be reached. The author has sought to use direct quotes where possible to ensure the narrative is as true to the reporting as possible, particularly when it came to criticism, findings or conclusions by the Authority.

The author drawers the reader's attention to the earlier mentioned and described tactical superiority "risk treatments" that New Zealand Police bring to the majority of lethal force encounters. Each case study reflects occasions where tactical superiority was not, in the author's opinion, leveraged to maximum advantage. The Authority makes similar commentary.

Stephen Bellingham: Fatally Shot 2007

On the evening of 26 September, 2007, in Christchurch, Stephen Bellingham was shot and killed by a police officer (Independent Police Conduct Authority, 2009). He was armed with a hammer. In the days prior to the shooting, Bellingham, "… was not sleeping or eating and was taking party pills. He was also, uncharacteristically, drinking heavily" (Independent Police Conduct Authority, 2009, p. 3). During the evening his flatmates reported him to be behaving strangely, being "… very weird …" and saying things like "I'm not of this world. I'm going to Jerusalem to kill some Muslims" (ibid.). He left the shared house that fateful evening and proceeded to smash up a van parked in the street with what was described as "… a golf club/crow bar, 'stick, baton thing'" (ibid.). Police were summoned, and one of the

R. S. Shortt, *Lethal Force and New Zealand Police*,
https://doi.org/10.1007/978-3-031-05269-9_9

officers who arrived first requested a police dog also attend, but was told it had been sent to a different event (Ibid., p. 7). However, 7 minutes later, the dog unit came free from that task and headed towards the Bellingham incident (ibid, pp. 16–17).

Following the arrival of police officers on the scene, one of the three police officers present reported that Bellingham made an aggressive movement and advanced on him with a raised hammer in his hand. The officer drew the Glock pistol he was wearing and challenged Bellingham to drop the hammer. After a brief pause in his advance, Bellingham ran at the officer with the hammer raised and when he was about 1–1.5 metres away, the police officer fired four shots at him, two of which hit and killed him (ibid., pp. 7–10). Despite the earlier commentary regarding drinking alcohol and use of pills, Bellingham's post-mortem toxicology report found no alcohol in his system, but did register a positive result for cannabis and "BZP – party pills" (ibid., p. 11).

In the IPCA report about the shooting, a number of adverse comments were levelled at Police. The first, a "post-shooting'-related comment" was that, "… contrary to best practice …" and "… a Commissioner's memorandum dated 24 November 2005 which emphasised the importance of 'the principles of independence' in investigations into serious complaints or allegations against Police", local Christchurch CIB officers had investigated the fatal shooting (Independent Police Conduct Authority, 2009, p. 9). However, the Authority did not feel this oversight prejudiced the outcome of the homicide investigation which was overseen by the IPCA (Ibid., p 9).

Later in the report, the Authority gave considerable attention to the question of which areas of the law regarding the use of force might apply in the situation leading up to Bellingham's death (ss. 39, 48 and 62 of the *Crimes Act 1961* (NZL)), what Police general instructions sought from officers and what witnesses had reported seeing that evening (ibid., pp. 20–27). The Authority concluded that the officer was both justified in law to shoot Bellingham and justified – due to his police training – to have shot at him multiple times (ibid., pp. 27–29).

However, in considering the tactics employed by the police officer involved, the Authority felt that a "cordon and containment" approach could have been considered and applied if the officer had not placed himself in "… close quarters without support …" and had better used the other two police officers at the scene (ibid., p. 30). Furthermore, the Authority went on to consider the use of other tactical options, such as retreat, verbal commands, a police dog, batons and OC spray, but ruled each of these out for a variety of reasons (Independent Police Conduct Authority, 2009, pp. 30–35).

Ultimately, in delivering a "justified shooting" report, the IPCA took the opportunity to comment upon several issues around the adherence to Police standard operating procedures and general instructions by the officer who shot Bellingham. These included:

- The officer should "… have briefed Officers B and C and advised South Comms [Southern Communications Centre] that he was on his way to the scene. [He] failed to take command and control of the available resources…". (ibid., p. 35).

- He had a Glock pistol in "… A locked glove compartment …" which "… is not an adequately secure place to store a gun, and storing a gun in the glove compartment is a breach of General Instructions … Not completing the Firearms Register was a technical breach of General Instructions". (ibid., p. 36).
- "The process used to secure Officer A's weapon [the officer who fired the shots] as an exhibit was not strictly in accordance with General Instructions, but this did not materially affect the investigation" – the officer had returned to the police station "… where he cleaned his weapon and handed the magazine and round from the chamber to an officer, along with the gloves he had been wearing". (ibid.)
- Officer A's failure to wear body armour was in breach of General Instructions but had no impact on the outcome of the incident. (ibid., p. 37)
- By wearing an empty holster, Officer A was in breach of General Instructions. However, this had no bearing on the outcome of the incident. (ibid.)
- Officer A breached General Instructions by not advising SouthComms that he was arming himself. (ibid., p. 38).

In an interesting commentary, the Authority also noted that: "Officer A has been the subject of previous complaints, and had also received a commendation for bravery … The Authority has considered the complaints in detail … and is of the view that the number of complaints against the officer A [sic] may reflect both his long service in front line duties, and be an indicator of a somewhat uncompromising style of policing. However, the Authority does not find those complaints of any direct relevance to the events of 26 September 2007" (Independent Police Conduct Authority, 2009, pp. 38–39).

The report went on to confirm that in 1999, Officer A, was "… involved in an incident in which he shot a person who was armed with a sawn-off shotgun (another officer shot and wounded the person)". The officer received the highest internal Police bravery award for that shooting (ibid., p. 39).

Of particular interest regarding the case study, in the author's opinion, were three factors. Firstly, the rank the shooting officer held he was a police senior sergeant, the highest non-commissioned officer rank in New Zealand Police. Secondly, on the night of the shooting "Officer A" (as he was referred to by the IPCA) was working as " … the Senior Field Supervisor on the shift … Officer A was responsible for supervising the greater Christchurch area, and in that capacity would be advised of any serious incident requiring him to take command and control, and to manage resources and equipment necessary for dealing with such incidents" (Independent Police Conduct Authority, 2009, p. 6). As the senior field supervisor that night, it is the author's view, that "Officer A" was also responsible for ensuring – whenever possible during the shift – that the correct Police policy, procedure, standards and tactics were applied by the officers working under his oversight, in effect that "best practice" was being followed. The third and final factor, perhaps the most critical, was the tactic chosen by "Officer A" in approaching an "aggressive" and armed Bellingham (ibid., p. 32).

Despite the responsibilities for command and control and 'best practice', at the beginning of his shift, "Officer A" had retrieved a Glock pistol from the gun safe in the boot of the patrol car he was using and placed it in the glove box of the car. When he heard the details of the event involving Bellingham over the radio he armed himself "… by taking the pistol from the glove box and putting it in his holster" which he was already wearing in apparent breach of Police general instructions (ibid., p. 6 and 37).

Upon arrival at the scene of the event, "Officer A":

> Having made a decision to approach Mr Bellingham at close quarters without support, [he] limited his options and effectively negated the opportunity to tactically deploy Officers B and C to contain the situation and await assistance. (ibid., p. 30).

As events then unfolded:

> Given the distance between him [Officer A] and Mr. Bellingham, and the speed with which the situation changed, there was no realistic opportunity for Officer A to meet the criteria of a warning shot … [Overall Finding] Officer A stated that he did consider less violent alternatives but, once he had confronted Mr. Bellingham, these alternatives were not viable. Given the circumstances and the speed at which the threat escalated, Officer A could effectively resort only to his firearm. (Ibid., p. 33–34).

Ultimately, the only tactical option left in play for "Officer A" was to resort to use of deadly force.

The IPCA report concluded by finding "The Authority supports the Police view that Officer A could benefit from further mentoring and training in command and control before he is approved for any return to front line duties" (ibid., p. 40). In her conclusions, reproduced here in their entirety, Justice Goddard stated:

> 217. In responding to the incident concerning Mr. Bellingham, Officer A should have communicated his intentions, and the fact that he was armed, to SouthComms, so that a decision could have been made on whether to formally transfer the incident control to him. He did not utilise available resources and failed to communicate any plan of action (such as containment) to Officers B and C, or to coordinate a response by them to the situation.
> 218. Instead, Officer A made a decision that placed him in a confrontational position with a man who was on a violent rampage and had damaged property with a weapon. In doing so he reduced the options available to him and found himself in a position of having to immediately protect himself and possibly members of the public.
> 219. Once confronted, Mr. Bellingham's action in aggressively approaching Officer A with a weapon after failing to respond to voice commands placed Officer A in the position of having to use his firearm.
> 220. In shooting Mr. Bellingham in self-defence, Officer A acted lawfully in the execution of his duty. The force he used was not excessive in the circumstances.
> 221. Although there were a number of breaches of best practice and General Instructions, these did not amount to misconduct or neglect of duty. They nonetheless do raise questions about Officer A's approach to frontline policing and support the view that he will benefit from mentoring and training in command and control before any return to front line duties.
> 222. The Authority expresses its deepest sympathy to the family and friends of Mr. Bellingham. (Independent Police Conduct Authority, 2009, p. 42).

In the author's opinion, a very nuanced and carefully worded rebuke of the police officer and the tactic he chose, and of the New Zealand Police regarding the general handling of the situation from which lessons needed to be learnt. The overriding lesson here, again in the author's view, is that tactical choices are incredibly important.

But, Stephen Bellingham's death was not the first time New Zealand Police officers had faced a man armed with a weapon other than a firearm and had used the tactic of lethal force to resolve the situation. The Bellingham shooting bore striking resemblances to the death of Steven Wallace in 2000, already detailed in this book in Chap. 3. In that instance there were also three police officers at the scene, although just two were actively engaged with Wallace.

Halatau Naitoko: Fatally Shot 2009

One of the most tragic shootings to occur during the review period was the fatal shooting of bystander, Halatau Naitoko, and the wounding of bystander Richard Neville, on 23 January 2009, in Auckland. The two men became unwitting bystanders to a Police pursuit of an armed and wanted criminal who was described by the IPCA as "… an extreme risk to police officers and members of the public" (Independent Police Conduct Authority, 2012).[1]

The events of that day unfolded when two plain-clothed officers saw a car they thought may be stolen and tried to stop it. The car failed to stop and drove off with two occupants, a female driver and a 50-year-old male passenger (ibid., p. 41). A car chase ensued. Just under 2 minutes later, the car stopped, and a police officer got out of his car to approach it. The male passenger of the chased car was seen to be holding a "short-barrelled gun, which he pointed at the two officers through the window" of the chased car (ibid., pp. 6–7). The weapon was later identified as a "… .22 calibre semi-automatic Ruger rifle, with the butt and barrel cut down to make it pistol size … the magazine was capable of holding 10 rounds" (ibid., p. 7). The gun was not fired and the Northern Communications Centre having been advised of its presence arranged for additional support to attend the incident. That included the Police helicopter and other police officers (ibid.).

The two people in the wanted car then ran off carrying bags. Members of the public who encountered them were also warned off by the man who brandished the firearm at them, but again it was not fired (bid., p. 8). Shortly after this a police officer encountered the two and also had the firearm brandished at him, causing him to back off. This behaviour continued over a number of minutes and involved other police officers (ibid., p. 9). A short time later, the man was seen by an officer to aim the cut-down gun at the Police helicopter and fire at it; fortunately the helicopter was not hit (ibid.). The Auckland AOS were then called out to assist. Over the following minutes, considerable confusion was recorded with no clarity on which officers were armed, who was in charge, and no one realising the helicopter had an unauthorised civilian "ride along" in it (ibid., pp. 10–12).

[1] The IPCA report is very detailed, consisting of 107 pages of information, excluding blank pages. What follows is a summary to the best of the author's ability.

Meanwhile, the armed man had been trying to get another vehicle and finally succeeded in commandeering a car from its occupants. At one point the man stopped and again waved his "pistol "at pursuing police officers (some of whom were armed) who were pursing him. Again, it was not fired. The officers retreated and the man drove off (ibid., p. 12). As the pursuit continued, a call made by the helicopter crew – and not reported by any ground officers – stated that the man was still armed and "… he had taken shots at the staff on Great North Road" (ibid., p. 13). By this time a considerable force of police officers was involved, including two senior sergeants and three dog units (ibid., p. 14).

Around this time, the armed man stopped at an address and demanded the keys to yet another vehicle which he was given. At one point during this action, two police officers confronted the man, and it resulted in him and an armed officer pointing their respective firearms at each other. Despite commands to stop, the man again ran off, presenting his gun at several more officers, but not firing (Independent Police Conduct Authority, 2012, pp. 14–15). The armed man then fled the area in his newly commandeered car (ibid.). A further pursuit unfolded with references to the armed man's car being "extremely dangerous" "fishtailing" and "losing control" (ibid., p. 16). Around this time the identity of the until then unknown man was confirmed. It was established that he had a long criminal history, including for "drug use, of carrying and using firearms and other weapons, and of assaulting police" (ibid.). At one point during this chase, the man braked his car and reversed at speed into the police dog van that was the first car in the pursuit which an onlooker had identified as being 19 police cars long (ibid., p. 17).

The Auckland AOS then joined the pursuit, with five officers deploying in two cars, and, not long after doing so, they caught up with the armed man's damaged car, which had entered the North Western Motorway. The man's car slowed and stopped against the median barrier (ibid., pp. 18–24). As he stopped the man held his gun up so it could be seen by the officers closest to him, and he then fled from the immobilised car (ibid.).

At around this point, witnesses reported the man pointing his firearm "… at on coming traffic, and three witnesses said he fired shots in the direction of on coming traffic or police, though no police staff saw or heard him fire these shots" (ibid., p. 24). As he fled an armed officer – with a Glock pistol – called on him to stop and warned him he was armed. The man again pointed his weapon towards the officer who responded by firing a shot at him (ibid., p. 24). It missed.

A short distance away, two AOS officers had alighted from their car and were now pursing the man on foot. They did not stop to discuss their tactics (ibid., p. 26). Fearing the armed man may again try to stop and commandeer a car, the two AOS officers individually determined that he could only be stopped by use of their firearms (ibid., p. 26).

As this happened, Mr. Neville, a civilian driving a truck, saw the armed man running onto the roadway and that he had a firearm. Neville decided to drive into the armed man and so continued forward but thinks he must have ducked and his foot came off the accelerator. His vehicle did not hit the man, and it came to a stop with what sounded like the armed man trying to force open the locked passenger's side door (ibid., pp. 26–27).

As the truck rolled to a stop, the two AOS officers fired four shots at the armed man. Both were armed with Bushmaster rifles. By this time the armed man was moving along the side of the truck and eventually climbing onto the tray (ibid., pp. 27–30). One of the shots fired missed the armed man and went into the cab of the truck causing fragments to strike Mr. Neville in the chest, arm and hand (ibid., pp. 27–30 and 40). Shrapnel from one of the other bullets that missed did strike the armed man causing slight injuries. Sadly, one of the shots that missed travelled past the armed man and struck the driver of a courier van which caught up in the chaos of the moment. That driver was 17-year-old Halatau Naitoko, and the bullet strike to his chest was fatal (Independent Police Conduct Authority, 2012, pp. 31–37). The armed man dropped to the deck of the truck's tray he was standing on and was taken into custody by police officers (ibid.).

It was later confirmed that the armed man had consumed two half-gram doses of methamphetamine, earlier that day (ibid., p. 38).

Subsequent to the shooting, the two AOS officers who fired their weapons took the firearms back to the AOS squad room where later the AOS commander "… cleared the weapons, and removed the magazine, sling, Aimpoint optical sight, pop sight and torch from both" (ibid., 39).

In its report the IPCA identified that a police investigation into the actions of the AOS commander had concluded:

> [The officer] has clearly breached General Instructions F066 and instructions relating to procedure to be followed when someone had been shot by police. He had interfered with the firearms exhibits when the instructions clearly prohibit him from doing so. (ibid., 47).

A Police Code of Conduct/employment investigation into the officer's actions resulted. No result is known.

The actions of the first officer to fire a shot that day as the man fled across the roadway (which missed and was found on a property that bordered the roadway), Officer W1, also came under scrutiny; however, it was concluded that no legal action was necessary. A subsequent internal Code of Conduct enquiry found "That whilst the actions of W1 do not constitute misconduct, they do warrant an informal intervention", and so the officer was counselled on "firearms strategy and was not to be issued with a firearm until he had successfully completed firearms training …" (ibid.).

When it came to the actions of the two AOS officers who fired the four shots, a coroner ruled that the death of Mr. Naitoko was "accidental" (Independent Police Conduct Authority, 2012, p. 48). In the coroner's findings, he felt the firing of the shots were justified. The coroner also expressed concern about the pairing of the two AOS officers together as they were the "least experienced" of the responding AOS (Independent Police Conduct Authority, 2012, p. 48). He was also concerned that the two officers had missed in the shots they took from reasonably close range (between 7 and 9 metres) along with the "… failure of [Officer 84] to appreciate what was within the line of fire …" recommending further training (ibid. 49).

In their report the IPCA detailed the training that the two AOS officers had undergone to become and remain as squad members. It confirmed both had attended a 3-day selection course which had assessed physical and personal attributes and traits, and they had then attended a 3-week qualification course. The course involved firing the Glock pistol but not the Bushmaster rifle. Course candidates underwent "… room clearing exercises, emergency action drills, a live firing exercise while wearing protective clothing, and an exercise using FX simunition [paintball-style ammunition]". At the end of the course, there were "drills and a qualification shoot to check the participant's competency" (ibid., p. 80). Following that course the two attended, in one case were 14 local training sessions with the squad – 2 of which included live firing and in the other case 8 training sessions – with one involving live firing. They also received "shoot, don't shoot" scenarios in their training but had "… limited experience of shooting at moving targets, or of shooting while on the move" (ibid.).

As a result of the investigation, the Authority made a number of findings concerning the events of the day. They included:

- That the first two officers who commenced pursing the man and woman did not "… have legal justification for commencing the first phase of the pursuit and did not initially comply with the pursuit policy; however they then complied with policy in relations to communication and risk assessment" (ibid., p. 65).
- NorthComms did not establish and maintain firm command and control over the pursuit (ibid.).
- AOS should have communicated information about their numbers and tactics to the NorthComms shift commander (ibid., p. 68).
- Police resources should have been controlled more effectively … (Independent Police Conduct Authority, 2012, p. 68).
- The AOS commander should have been notified as soon as the firearm sighting was reported; however the delay in the AOS response was not significant – the report noted that once activated the available AOS staff were mobile within 28 minutes (ibid., p. 71).
- The AOS tactical response was compromised by the limitations of their radio communications. It was a high risk assumption on the part of the AOS commander that his staff could hear his instructions on the AOS channel [once the limitation was identified when the two units were mobile and he could not hear radio calls from his two junior officers in the second car]. In the circumstances, the AOS should have communicated with NorthComm on the general channel (Independent Police Conduct Authority, 2012, p. 72).
- The inaccurate marksmanship occurred because the officers were operating in a highly stressful and challenging shooting environment for which their level of training and experience had not equipped them (ibid.).
- The standard of shooting and failure to see Mr. Naitoko's van in the line of fire has raised concerns about the depth and degree of AOS weapons training. Given the circumstances in which Officer 84's failure to accurately identify risks in the line of fire occurred, the defence of lawful justification necessarily arises and would undoubtedly negate the application of any of the legal provisions considered above (ibid., p. 84).
- The dismantling of Officer 81 and Officer 84's weapons by the AOS Commander was bad practice and contrary to policy. The post-incident process was not well managed or sufficiently robust. Officers 81 and 84 should not have been returned to active AOS duties without there having been a more comprehensive assessment of

their competency to do so – both officers had returned to AOS duties on 3 February 2009, just 11 days after the fatal shooting (ibid., p. 92).

In her conclusions, Justice Goddard, summed up the situation thus:

> Stephen McDonald [the armed man at the centre of events] created a situation on the North Western Motorway that was dangerous to all involved, and Officers 81 and 84 [the two AOS members] found themselves having to take immediate action. While the environment was challenging and the officers were under considerable stress, having never before been in such a situation, the shots fired by Officers 81 and 84 were not accurate or safe, as demonstrated by the outcomes. Their failure to shoot accurately and, in Officer 84's case to identify the risk beyond the target [Mr Naitoko sitting in his van], does raise concerns about the depth and degree of their weapons training, including experience in 'shoot, don't shoot' decision-making. The officers had a responsibility not only to hit the target but to ensure that the line of fire beyond the target was clear when their shots were fired. (Independent Police Conduct Authority, 2012, p. 94).

In the situation described, while armed with a cut-down rifle, McDonald had several opportunities during the hour he was being pursued to fire it at both the police officers and members of the public. The IPCA report identifies 11 specific occasions when the firearm was presented at individual police officers. Two officers each had the gun presented at them three times (ibid., p. 4).[2] McDonald did fire a shot towards the helicopter; another shot was fired inside one of the cars he used (for reasons, or in circumstances, not explained in the report) (ibid., pp. 43–44), and he was later said to have fired at police and vehicle traffic near the end of the pursuit (which was not verified by officers at the scene, or confirmed in the IPCA report), but he did not fire at officers or civilians during the unfolding event when he had opportunity.

Was that non-firing ever considered by anyone on the ground? Did anyone in a "command and control" role note that, or ask questions about the gun's use? Or, did that fact get lost in the confusion of the unfolding event? Perhaps, that fact reinforced Justice Goddard's concluding comment that "Stephen McDonald committed serious offences whilst armed and under the influence of drugs. *He had one objective, which was to evade arrest by any means* ..." (Italics added) (ibid., 93). Could acknowledgement of the fact the gun was not being fired, combined with awareness of the driving danger he presented, have led Police to conclude that to let him escape, especially once his identify was confirmed (by Officer E who had arrested McDonald's female companion), may have been the safer option?

Hindsight commentary by "armchair experts from the safety of their lounge", or in the author's case from the desk in his office, are bound to be robustly contested. And, as already stated, the author is not seeking to relitigate the case studies presented, but to try and use them as learning opportunities.

Therefore, the comment regarding the learning from Mr. Naitoko's death was, in the author's view, the importance of someone in a Police command role being able to think clearly and dispassionately about circumstance unfolding – no matter how

[2] A 12th occasion is mentioned in the report at page 24, when Officer W1 was chasing the armed man on foot across the motorway and said that he "... saw him point his firearm back in the direction of the police" (Independent Police Conduct Authority, 2012).

dramatic they are – and being organisationally empowered to say "Stop". That tactic was used, and is still used, by New Zealand Police to manage the dangers created by vehicle pursuits. It should also be an accepted tactic in managing events like this.

The second learning from the event and its outcome is that even specialists can get it wrong. If specialists, with their opportunities to train more and to a higher standard, can encounter situations that are beyond their training and capabilities, how are constables and sergeants on uniformed patrol duties expected to cope?

Perhaps the most fitting way to end the case study is to quote a man intimately involved in developing tactical guidance for Police in the UK when it came to armed offenders, who wrote:

> The object of the police is to eliminate the danger caused by an armed criminal and in doing so, they must not be permitted to cause more danger than was in fact being caused by the person whom they are attempting to neutralise. (Greenwood, 1979, p. 4).

Lachan Kelly-Tumarae: Fatally Shot 2011

19-year-old, Lachan Kelly-Tumarae, left his grandmother's house in the middle of the night on 27 March 2011, armed with his deceased grandfather's shotgun and ammunition for the weapon. He also took his grandmother's car without her permission. Earlier in the evening, he was reported to have consumed alcohol and cannabis (Independent Police Conduct Authority, 2013, p. 7 and 11). He had lived much of his life with his maternal grandparents and was described as "... very upset" when his grandfather died 16 months earlier (ibid., p. 16).

A short time later, two patrolling constables saw the young man crouched down beside a car and stopped to see what he was doing. Kelly-Tumarae pointed the shotgun at them – "... the gun would have only been five centimetres from my passenger's window ..." – causing the two officers to rapidly drive away from him. He then got back into his grandmother's car and drove off.

A vehicle pursuit then ensued with additional officers being directed to assist by the Central Communications Centre (ibid., pp. 7 and 12). One of those officers armed himself with a Glock pistol from the arms cabinet in his car (Independent Police Conduct Authority, 2013). A request was made to activate the AOS (ibid., p. 12). All of the officers on duty that night had access to Glock pistols and Bushmaster rifles in their patrol vehicles, along with ballistic armour vests (ibid. pp. 11–12).

Following a considerable pursuit, Kelly-Tumarae, stopped his car beside the cemetery of a local Māori marae (meeting place). The armed officer stopped his car some 14–15 metres behind him. The intention was to contain the armed man until AOS could attend. Unfortunately, two other officers parked their car directly opposite the armed man's car, and Kelly-Tumarae, "... grabbed the double barrel shotgun and before he got out of the car he discharged the shotgun once ... which appears to have been accidental ... through the front passenger floor" (ibid., p. 14);

he then got out and presented the shotgun at the two officers, before running off in the general direction of the armed officer who was using his car as cover (ibid.).

The armed officer then stepped out from cover and challenged the young man by stating "Armed Police" (ibid.). As he did so, Kelly-Tumarae turned to face him and lifted up the shotgun and pointed it at him. The officer "… fired a volley of shots …" and then seeing that Kelly-Tumarae was still standing, "… fired another volley" (ibid.). He stopped firing when the young man fell onto the ground. The officer fired a total of 14 pistol shots (ibid.). They proved fatal, and subsequent toxicology reports showed a high concentration of alcohol in Kelly-Tumarae's blood (between 169 and 205 milligrams per 100 millilitres) and the indication of recent cannabis use (ibid., p. 19).

The scene examination identified that there were two spent shotgun rounds in the car (including a hole in the passenger's side floor caused by a close-range discharge of a shotgun) (ibid., p. 18). The shotgun was discovered to have one live round and one spent round in it (ibid., p. 17).

The Authority reached the view that the officer was justified in shooting at Mr. Kelly-Tumarae and was justified in firing the number of shots that he did. However, the Authority had a number of concerns with the way the event unfolded (Independent Police Conduct Authority, 2013, p. 8). These included:

- … other aspects of the Police response … did not comply with relevant policies or meet the required standards of good practice.
- The [AOS] was not activated as quickly as it should have been.
- During the pursuit there was a lack of clarity about who was in charge, and about the tactics to be used.
- At times officers acted instinctively, in ways that were contrary to the disciplined and cautious approach advocated by Police policy, which seeks to cordon and contain armed offenders where possible rather than confronting them directly.
- There were also breaches of policy on the management and carriage of firearms.
- One of the officers responding also should not have been carrying firearms.
- Officer F [the officer who fired] did not put on body armour even though the policy required him to.
- The Authority's investigation also found deficiencies in the Eastern District's management and auditing of firearms and ammunition prior to the shooting. (Independent Police Conduct Authority, 2013, p. 8).

The Authority did, however, highlight that Mr. Kelly-Tumarae, bore "… the [principal] responsibility for the way events unfolded … He armed himself and deliberately engaged with and threatened Police before and after the pursuit … He initiated, and for the most part controlled, the sequence of events that were to end tragically with the loss of his life." (ibid.).

In the findings regarding this shooting, the Authority stated:

- The CentComms shift commander, as the incident controller, did not take command and exercise control according to policy. Field staff did not know who was in command, and once the pursuit got under way there was no clear tactical plan for safely containing Mr Kelly-Tumarae. (ibid. p. 35)
- Officer M should have responded more clearly and quickly when he was asked to activate the Armed Offenders Squad. (ibid.)

- Officers A, D, E, F, G, H, K were all justified in arming themselves or in being directed to arm themselves; however, "Officer L breached policy by arming when he was not certified to carry and use a Police firearm. He should have told Officer G that he was not certified, and Officer G as his supervisor should have known that". (ibid., p. 37).
- Officer F did not clearly inform CentComms that he was armed, and he breached policy by not putting on his ballistic body armour. (ibid.)
- Officer K (as driver) and Officer L (as the senior officer in the car) breached policy and good practice in the manner in which they stopped next to the Primera [the car used by the young-man]. This action was risky and ill-considered, and limited subsequent Police tactical options for responding to Mr. Kelly-Tumarae. (Independent Police Conduct Authority, 2013, p. 40)
- Officer F breached Police policy by stepping out from the cover provided by his Police vehicle. Although his reaction appears to have been instinctive and to have been motivated by a desire to prevent casualties, the appropriate action under the circumstances was to remain under cover and appeal to Mr Kelly-Tumarae from there ... The officer continued to fire only as long as he believed that his life was in immediate danger, and stopped firing when he saw that Mr Kelly-Tumarae had fallen to the ground and the danger had passed .... (ibid., p. 54)
- The appropriate tactical option as Police arrived at Taihape Road was to wait under cover and seek to safely contain Mr. Kelly-Tumarae ... Safe containment became much more difficult after Officers K and L arrived and stopped right next to Mr. Kelly-Tumarae's vehicle ... Officer F limited his tactical options by leaving the cover provided by his vehicle and confronting Mr. Kelly-Tumarae. (ibid.)
- In most respects the Police criminal investigation was thorough and professional. Although there were some omissions, these did not affect the overall conclusion that Officer F was justified in shooting Mr Kelly-Tumarae. (ibid., p. 60).

In his conclusions, Sir David Carruthers – the Authority, stated:

> ... Responding to armed offenders is one of the unavoidable hazards of Police work. The officers who were called on to respond to Mr Kelly-Tumarae were willing to put their lives in danger in order to carry out their duties. The Police response was in many respects exactly as it should have been. On the occasions in which officers sought to contain Mr Kelly-Tumarae in a limited area where they could appeal to him without endangering themselves or other, and where they sought to follow at a safe distance, they were acting exactly as they should under these difficult circumstances.
>
> There were also times when the Police response fell short of what was required. The AOS should have been activated more quickly ... At times it appeared that officers were acting instinctively, in a manner that was inconsistent with the disciplined and cautious 'cordon and contain' approach required under the circumstances ... in particular when ... Officers K and L pulled in close beside Mr. Kelly-Tumarae's car ... and when Officer F stepped out from cover. (ibid., p. 65).
>
> There were also several occasions in which officers failed to comply with policies on the carriage and use of firearms ... Officer L arming himself when he did not have the required certification, and Officer F choosing not to wear body armour ... Some of these failing limited the tactical options Police had available to them, and contributed to the circumstances that ultimately led to Officer F confronting an armed Mr Kelly-Tumarae. (ibid., p. 66).

The Authority made a recommendation that identified the most significant issues in this case being "incident control" and "compliance with policy" (ibid., p. 69). The Authority went on to state that the policies themselves were "sound"; however, it was incumbent on Police to ensure officers were familiar with them and comply with them (ibid.). His final recommendation to Police was that they: "Continue developing, as a matter of urgency, policy and procedures for compulsory drug and alcohol testing of officers involved in critical incidents" (ibid., p. 70).

Adam Morehu: Fatally Shot 2013

In June, 2013, 26 months on from the shooting of Lachan Kelly-Tumarae, another Police shooting drew the ire of the IPCA. On that occasion, Adam Morehu was fatally shot by police officers after being involved in the burglary of a New Plymouth golf club. In the early hours of a Saturday morning, alarms at the club activated and Police responded (Independent Police Conduct Authority, 2015, p. 5). Three units were sent, a dog handler and dog, a sergeant and two constables in three police vehicles. At the club the unarmed dog handler met a security officer who was opening the gate; the handler took his dog and entered the grounds. The other two units were deployed to help cordon the club site to prevent the escape of anyone on the premises (ibid., p 7). A short time later, the dog handler confirmed that the club had been broken into (ibid.).

The dog handler then began to use his dog to track whoever was involved. He encountered a motorcycle with two people on it and challenged them to stop (ibid.). The police dog was released, and it chased the motorcycle further into the grounds and then towards the gate. The dog was recalled, but sent into attack the two people again when the handler saw the motorcycle tip over on a mound (ibid., p. 8). The dog latched on to one of the persons, while the handler tackled the second, only to leave that person briefly to assist his dog which was having problems (ibid.). The handler then returned to grapple with the other man, and during this confrontation, he was told the man had a gun, a comment the handler dismissed. The handler then managed to use OC spray on the man, and a second threat about a gun was made (ibid., p. 9).

Unfortunately, due to the darkness, there was confusion as to where the dog handler was, and this was delaying his colleagues coming to his assistance (Independent Police Conduct Authority, 2015, p. 9). That was compounded when the dog handler's radio accidentally switched channels during the struggle that was taking place. Once again the handler left the man he was grappling with and went to aid his dog, and following that he turned to return to his man when he "… heard a firearm discharge and saw Mr Morehu [the man he had been struggling with] silhouetted in the muzzle flash" (ibid.). The handler retreated taking the second man and his dog with him (ibid.).

Earlier, when the dog handler alerted his colleagues that a break in had occurred, yet another police officer was dispatched to assist. That officer arrived, but failed to confirm this to the communications centre. The officer subsequently entered the golf club grounds and apparently encountered the armed Morehu and ran back to where the security officer was at the gate yelling "gun, gun, gun", and both the police officer and security officer both moved away from the scene in the security officer's vehicle (ibid., p. 10). About this time the dog handler managed to alert other staff by radio that there was an armed offender at the golf course (ibid.).

The officer who had backed off with the security officer, then armed himself with a Glock pistol from his car (ibid.). He did not "... take a ballistic vest or Bushmaster rifle, stored in the boot of the vehicle, as he considered that there was insufficient time to do so ..." (ibid., p. 11). As the armed officer positioned himself on the golf club grounds, and fearing the potential for other armed persons being present, he turned his portable radio off (ibid.). No one was aware he was on the scene, and he no longer had radio communication with the other police officers present, or CentComms (ibid.). The officer finally took up a position in bushes overlooking Morehu who was "... pacing and intermittently yelling in an agitated manner" near the motorcycle (ibid.).

Other officers were by now arriving at the scene. Some confusion reigned as various officers tried to arm themselves or were told to arm but did not. None donned ballistic vests. As these officers closed in on the dog handler, one saw Morehu and fearing for the handler tried to distract him by challenging him and presented her TASER at him (ibid., p. 12). Despite being called away by a sergeant who had arrived, the officer with the TASER approached Morehu and fired the weapon (ibid., p. 12). The TASER hit the man, but had no noticeable effect. She then ran back to join the dog handler who was still struggling on the ground with the second person (ibid.). At this point she believes another gunshot was fired (ibid.). This fact was not communicated to the Central Communications Centre.

Two further police officers arrived on the scene, only to discover the car they were in was not equipped with firearms. They also failed to arm themselves from one of the cars already at the golf club because it was locked. Neither had ballistic protection, but one did have a TASER he had brought with him from the Police station (ibid., p. 13). These two officers, plus the officer who had fired her TASER, and the sergeant, then moved together onto the golf course and towards Morehu (ibid.). None were aware that an armed officer was present (ibid.), until he was observed by them approaching the armed man from behind (ibid.).

After repeated challenges to Morehu, one of the approaching officers fired a second TASER at him, while the first TASER officer tried unsuccessfully to fire her now discharged one (ibid.). As she did so, the armed officer fired his Glock, and then the first officer refired his TASER at about the same time as the armed officer fired his Glock for a second time (ibid.). Morehu then fell to the ground where he continued to struggle as they attempted to restrain him with handcuff (ibid., p. 14). A short time later, Mr. Morehu began to show signs of acute distress, and first aid and CPR were attempted, and an ambulance was urgently requested (ibid.).

It was not until 24 minutes later, following the arrival of two ambulances at the scene, that one of the paramedics asked Police if the man had been shot (ibid. p. 15). It was confirmed that he may have been, as up to that point officers thought he was just displaying symptoms from having been tasered (ibid.).

Mr. Morehu died shortly thereafter as a result of the gunshot wounds he had indeed suffered (ibid., p. 15). It was late confirmed that the weapon Mr. Morehu had was a "... sawn-off .22 semi-automatic rifle ..." (ibid.). A scene examination found one fired 0.22 shell casing; two unfired cartridges were discovered jammed in his gun's mechanism, and three unfired cartridges were found on the ground in and around where the struggle and action had taken place (ibid., p. 16). Three TASER probes were located in Mr. Morehu's clothing, none of which had made contact with or penetrated his skin, a requirement for a successful TASER use (ibid.). Two empty Police 9 mm cartridges were also found at the scene (ibid.).

The Authority made a number of findings regarding the shooting, including that the officers who had armed themselves were justified in doing so (ibid., p. 21) and that the officer who shot Mr. Morehu was also justified in doing so (ibid., p. 32). However, the Authority also found:

- Officers G and H should have ensured that they were equipped with firearms and ballistic body armour before responding [from the police station] to this incident. Officers B, E, D, G, and H should have put on ballistic body armour. (ibid., p. 22)
- Officer B breached policy by failing to ensure that his firearms certification was current. (ibid.)
- Officer B should have provided CentComms with a situational report and warned his colleagues about the serious risk of harm posed by Mr Morehu. He was negligent in not doing so. (ibid., p. 24)
- Officer B should not have turned off his Police radio. (ibid.)
- The actions of Officer B and Officer E limited the tactical options available to other staff, and unnecessarily placed themselves and their colleagues at risk of harm. (ibid.)
- Police communication during this incident was poor. (ibid., p. 35)
- The CentComms shift commander, as the incident controller, did not take command and exercise control according to policy. (ibid.)
- Officer D did not use his initiative, as senior officer in the field, and take control of forward activities. His inaction can be attributed to deficiencies in his training for frontline duties. (ibid.)
- The absence of command and control resulted in field staff making decisions that put themselves and their colleagues at unnecessary risk of harm. (ibid.)

As with all fatal Police shootings as well as the homicide investigation, it was accompanied by a "... 'Practice, policy, and procedure' review ...", and the Authority was advised by Police that five of the officers involved were the subject of "... employment investigations ..." (ibid., p. 36).

In his conclusion, Sir David Carruthers, Chair of the Authority, went on to state "... that, even under optimal conditions, this would have been a highly volatile and stressful situation for any individual to have been involved in" (ibid., p. 37). However, he concluded the most significant issues arising were "... with regards to Police practice, concerning incident control and compliance with policy ..." (ibid.); he went on to conclude "... Police failed to comply with Police policy relating to the carriage of firearms, and responding to armed offenders and active shooters ..." (ibid.). He ended by voicing his opinion that various of the matters mentioned above were either "unjustified", "undesirable", "negligent and unreasonable" or just "unreasonable" (ibid., p. 38), strong words for a judge to use.

David Cerven: Fatally Shot 2015

David Cerven was a 21-year-old Slovakian national, who travelled to Aotearoa New Zealand with his partner in March 2015, for a working holiday. On 2 August, 2015, he was fatally shot by police officers in Myers Park, Auckland City. The Park is located a short walking distance from the Auckland Central Police Station (Independent Police Conduct Authority, 2016, p. 4).

Cerven had taken out two substantial bank loans before embarking on the joint working holiday, and these had been playing on his mind. Between April and July, Cerven's behaviours began to change, and people close to him noticed these changes and were concerned (Independent Police Conduct Authority, 2016, p. 6). The night before the fatal shooting, his partner described him as "… quiet and sad" (ibid., p. 7).

Unbeknownst to the young woman, Cerven had recently committed two robberies for cash at liquor outlets while armed with a knife and one unsuccessful attempted robbery of a dairy where the assistant fought back and Cerven was disarmed and left, leaving behind his backpack with his identification in it (ibid.). Police issued a wanted notice for him using his personal details and photograph on their website on 2 August 2015 (ibid.). That afternoon he confessed to his partner what he had done and that he was now being sought by the Police (ibid., p. 7).

The two then made contact with an Auckland couple who they had lived with for some weeks and sought their advice. Cerven was visibly upset and crying; he confessed his actions and made statements to the effect that he was going to give himself up to Police (ibid.). However, he ran off from the house in an upset state and subsequently turned his phone off after texting his partner to tell her he would surrender to Police the next day (ibid., p. 8).

The next sighting of Cerven was later that evening, when he was seen on CCTV footage walking in central Auckland and heading into Myers Park at about 7.17 pm (note – this footage came to light post the shooting) (ibid.). At 7:20 pm, Cerven called the Police via the 111 emergency call telephone system (ibid., p. 9). He told them where he was and that he was sought by Police with regard to a robbery (ibid.). He spoke with a strong accent, and his English was "… not particularly good", so his name was not recorded accurately by the person taking the call (ibid.). Due to the error and, therefore, Police finding no reason for them to be interested in the name written down, no one was immediately dispatched to see him, and the matter was actually downgraded in the calls for service management system (ibid.).

This was relayed back to Cerven by the person he was talking with on the 111 system (ibid.). He was asked to walk the short distance to the central police station, but he refused to do this (ibid.). Further conversations unfolded at the Police end culminating in Cerven being asked to respell his surname which he did (ibid., p. 10). It was then realised that he was of interest to Police and that there was believed to be sufficient evidence for him to be arrested (ibid.).

The call was then reprioritised to the highest dispatch level and relayed to patrolling officers who agreed to attend and locate him. A description of his clothing was asked for and given by Cerven, and the 111 call ended (ibid.). Two uniformed constables responded to the call in a patrol car from the nearby station (ibid., pp. 10–11). Attempts were also made to view the park using CCTV monitoring equipment at the police station but due to a technical issue Police were not able to see Cerven (ibid.). Two plain-clothed CIB officers were also detailed to attend the park, and they drove there also (ibid.). Meanwhile, two further CIB officers responded to the radio talk about the park and were directed to also attend (ibid., p. 12). At about the same time, a further two uniformed officers offered to assist, and they too were directed to attend. There were now eight police officers in four separate vehicles heading towards Cerven (ibid., p. 13).

The officers were all directed to cover different entrances to the park, with the first two arriving being the last two who had been told to attend. The two unarmed uniformed officers (with no firearm or TASER) got out of their car and walked into the park (ibid. 13). As they did so "…Mr. Cerven called out to them almost immediately, saying calmly, 'I'm over here guys'" (ibid.). Cerven was standing in an unlit area, and the two constables asked him to move from where he was to a lit area, but he did not (ibid.). He also refused requests to show his hands or to get onto the ground. These officers failed to advise the communications centre that they were in the park, or that they were in voice and visual contact with Mr. Cerven (ibid.).

Four of the other officers had now reached the park, and they coordinated with each other the timing of their entry, with one party discussing but dismissing the need to take a Glock pistol with them (ibid., p. 14). One of those officers was armed with a TASER (ibid.). At about this time, the first two officers broke their radio silence to announce they were with Cerven and that "… he's got a high vis on, saying he's got a gun now" (ibid.). The two officers then backed off (ibid.). As a result of the radio traffic, a ninth, and more senior, police officer also determined that he would attend the scene (Independent Police Conduct Authority, 2016, p. 16).

Two of the plain-clothed officers, upon hearing that the man claimed to have a gun, obtained firearms from their car (ibid., p 17). Both put on ballistic armour vests, while one officer armed himself with a Bushmaster rifle and the other with a Glock pistol (ibid.).

The armed officers then entered the park, and because of the darkness, they sought to get as close to Cerven as possible (ibid., p. 18). Shortly after they did so, one of the armed officers challenged Mr. Cerven shouting "…'armed Police, get down on the ground, get down on the ground now' … or words to that effect" (ibid.). Cerven then "… looked away for a split second and then he put his right hand into his right pocket and 'grasped something'. He drew the object and moved towards Officers E and F [the two-armed officers] 'as though he's pointing a gun'…" (ibid.). The officer again challenged Mr. Cerven to drop "… his weapon …" (ibid.). The other officer in the armed duo reported "… he heard a 'swooshing noise' that was made by Mr. Cerven's jacket. He then saw Mr. Cerven put a hand in and then out of his pocket and then 'punch it out towards me'" (ibid., pp. 18–19). The officer with the Glock pistol fired three shots at Mr. Cerven (ibid., p. 18). The second officer also fired "a number of rounds" at Cerven, the scene examination concluding five were fired from his rifle (ibid. P. 19).

Mr. Cerven had been shot twice, once in the jaw and once in the stomach (ibid.). An ambulance was immediately requested, and first aid was provided, but he was pronounced dead after the ambulance crew arrived (ibid.).

A search of the area around Mr. Cerven found no firearm, but did locate a black phone (ibid.).

The IPCA carried out its own investigation and made a number of findings. It found several aspects of the events around the shooting were handled appropriately, including the call handling and several of the decisions made by attending officers. However, the Authority also made findings that were critical of the response. They were:

> - Officers I and J [the first two to enter the park and speak to Cerven] did not provide sufficient information to NorthComms about their movements. They should have provided situational reports when the entered Myers Park, saw Mr. Cerven and approached and talked to him. (Independent Police Conduct Authority, 2016, p. 27)
> - Officers E and F [the two-armed CIB officers, one of whom shot Mr Cerven] should have radioed NorthComms and advised of their intention to approach and challenge Mr Cerven. (ibid., p. 33)
> - Officers E and F chose to immediately approach and challenge Mr Cerven. In terms of their TENR assessment, their focus was on the risk Mr Cerven posed to the unarmed officers at the scene and not on a complete assessment of the situation. In making their decision, they did not give sufficient weight to the risk members of the public in the park and in nearby buildings were exposed to or whether it was necessary to immediately engage Mr Cerven. [Myers Park has a number of apartment and other forms of accommodation buildings around its perimeter. It is centrally located in Auckland city] (Ibid.)
> - There were other options that Officers E and F should have considered and their actions precipitated Mr Cerven's response. (ibid.)

Despite those findings, the Authority found the shooting of Mr. Cerven to have been justified. Cerven was unarmed; he knew there were multiple police officers in close proximity, and he knew the police officers were armed, but elected to act in a manner that can only be described by the author as provocative.

Jerrim Toms: Fatally Shot 2018

> At 2.51am on Saturday 31 March 2018, Mr Toms' mother, Ms Y, called 111 to ask Police to carry out a welfare check on her son. She said Mr Toms was 'really agitated' and had made her leave her home. She told the 111-call taker she had called the mental health crisis team, who advised her to call Police. (Independent Police Conduct Authority, 2019, p. 4).

The mother went on to advise Police that her son had with him a "... large bayonet-like knife, about 10-11 inches in length, strapped to his hip" (ibid). She was also able to tell them that he had taken "P" (methylamphetamine) that day and had threatened to burn the house down (ibid.).

A single police officer was sent to carry out the check, and around 3:10 am he reported that the house was empty and that the son's car was not at the address (ibid.). When the attending officer cleared the call for service entry using the code

"K1", the details disappeared from the dispatcher's screen. No additional alert – via radio – was given about Mr. Toms to other police officers, nor was any information provided about the car he was probably in (ibid., p. 5).

At about the same time, a different police officer encountered a car parked on the side of a main highway with its hazard lights on. The unarmed uniformed officer stopped behind the car, and as he did so, it moved forward slightly. The officer then drove up beside the car with his flashing lights activated. He saw a man sitting in the car and described him as "wild-eyed" (ibid., p. 5). The man, later identified as Mr. Toms, demanded the officer's details and then got out of his car with a "… machete in his hand" (ibid.); he struck the roadway with the machete and then walked to the front of the patrol car. As Toms advanced on the car, the officer reversed back away from him. The officer also radioed for assistance, and four officers, including a dog handler, replied and were directed to assist (ibid., pp. 5–6). Subsequently the NorthComms shift commander also sent the Police helicopter to assist (ibid., p. 6).

Because of his concerns, the officer involved with Toms armed himself with a Glock pistol from the gun cabinet in the car. He did not don ballistic armour, nor did he tell the Northern Communications Centre that he was now armed (Independent Police Conduct Authority, 2019, p. 6).

After Toms tried to drive off, the officer also moved off in front of Toms' car and then u-turned to face back towards it. He saw that Toms was now standing in the roadway waving the machete. The officer, fearing for Toms' safety, repositioned his car to slow traffic. Toms then drove off and the officer followed (ibid., p. 7). As this happened other officers were moving to assist.

Two police officers, in two separate cars, confirmed they were en route, and one of them had armed himself with a Glock pistol from the car's gun safe. He did not don protective body armour (ibid.). Two other officers also en route decided to arm themselves and accessed the pistols in their patrol car's cabinet; they also failed to put on protective armour (ibid., p. 8).

As Toms' car continued to drive at speed with its headlights off, NorthComms then gave permission for road spikes to be used to try and deflate the tyres and bring the vehicle to a halt (ibid., p. 9). The first attempt to "spike" the tyres took place as the helicopter reached the area, and Toms drove over the spike strip at an estimated speed of 140 kmph (ibid.). A short time later, the spikes had an effect, and the car came to a stop. Toms jumped from it with the machete and ran up to the following police car and struck the passenger's side window with it. The car reversed away, and Toms got back in his car and drove off again (ibid., p. 10).

By now an armed dog handler had joined the slow moving "pursuit", and Toms' car was showing more signs of wheel distress and moving only 20–30 kmph (ibid., pp. 10–11). As it continued to drive, it was spiked a second and then a third time (ibid., pp. 10–11).

Toms' car finally stopped on the main road. A police car stopped behind it, and the other police vehicles involved stopped behind that car in a variety of positions. Toms got out of his car and again walked "purposefully" back towards the police car with the machete in his hand (ibid. p. 12). The two-armed constables positioned themselves behind the open doors of their car and challenged Toms to stop. He did not (Independent Police Conduct Authority, 2019, p. 12). Behind then, the dog handler was retrieving his dog from his van (ibid.). A fourth armed officer got out of his car and headed towards where Toms was, while his patrol partner aimed a rifle at Toms (ibid.).

As Toms continued to advance, ignoring challenges to stop, both the closest armed constables fired at him – one officer firing five shots and the second officer firing seven shots (ibid., p. 13). Four shots hit Toms. By that time Toms was about 1.5 metres from the officer (ibid., p. 14). Toms then turned and "… began running away immediately after shot 4 was fired …"; he still held the machete, and one of the two officers who had fired believed none of the shots had hit him (ibid.).

Both officers then advanced and fired at him again (ibid.). As they advanced the two officers fired six more times as Toms was moving away from them. The last of these shots appears to have struck his arm and caused him to drop the machete (ibid.). One officer then stopped firing, but his companion then fired two more shots at the retreating and now unarmed man (ibid., pp. 14–15). Toms ran a short distance and before collapsing to the ground (ibid.).

First aid was applied and an ambulance was called; however, after arrival of the ambulance, he was pronounced dead (ibid., p 15). All the officers were tested for alcohol and drugs, and the results were negative (ibid.).

Toms body had five bullet entry wounds, two to the front left chest, one to the side of the left hand, one to the lower left back and one to the right wrist. Two appeared to have been caused while Toms was facing those firing and three while he was facing away from the shooters (ibid., p. 16). One bullet appeared to have caused two wounds (one to a thumb and one to his chest). The two chest wounds caused his death and had entered from the front (ibid., p. 16).

The IPCA investigation into the shooting found all of the officer involved were justified in arming themselves. But it noted that seven of the officers failed to alert the communications centre to the fact that they had armed (ibid. p. 20). Five of the officers also breached policy by failing to wear protective ballistic body armour (ibid.).

The Authority went on to carefully and methodically consider the justification for all of the 12 shots fired at Mr. Toms (Independent Police Conduct Authority, 2019, pp. 20–26). Ultimately, the Authority found that all of them were justified (ibid., p. 27). However, the Authority did go on to find:

> Officers B and C [the two who fired] should have turned their minds to coordinating a response capable of bringing the incident to a safe conclusion rather than putting themselves into a position of immediate danger. (ibid., p. 27).

Furthermore, the Authority went on to deliver strong criticism of the most senior officer overseeing the events of that early morning when he found:

> The Shift Commander did not provide adequate communication, control and command of the incident. The Shift Commander should have ensured there was a clear, specific plan broadcast over the Police radio to all attending Police officers. The Shift Commander should have advised the officers pursuing Mr. Toms of the information from the earlier 111 call from Mr. Toms' mother as soon as he became aware of it". (ibid., pp. 36–37).

In his final conclusions the Authority stated:

> … The Authority had concluded that this incident was not well managed. There was no clear understanding of the roles and responsibilities of the different Police units, particularly where command and control lay between the Shift commander and Eagle.
>
> This led to poor communication and a lack of coordination and planning between Police staff. The Police field units were unaware of which officers were actively involved in the incident, which ultimately led of Officers B and C believing they were alone [six other officers were on the ground, four of whom were armed, and one also had a police dog with him (ibid., p. 25)]. This affected their risk assessments and led to the action that they took.
>
> The Shift Commander assumed Police field officers would act on the commentary by [the Police helicopter crew] and undertake a high-risk vehicle stop once Mr. Toms' car came to a halt. No overall structure for the implementation of the high-risk vehicle stop was articulated by Police field officers over the radio and the Shift Commander was not proactive in ensuring that there was a proper plan in place. In the absence of any communication between them, each unit operated independently, leading to an uncoordinated response that meant the potential range of tactical options available to Police was not known or used. (ibid., p. 38).

Astin Hooper: Fatally Shot 2019

Astin Hooper, aged 29, set in motion the events leading to his death by taking his father's utility vehicle without permission, along with his father's shotgun and ammunition and driving off from his parent's home. Before leaving he fired a shot from the gun – while everyone else was safely inside the house. Hooper's stepmother contacted Police via the 111 emergency call system, resulting in two police officers being dispatched to the house (Independent Police Conduct Authority, 2021, pp. 2–3).

A short time later, Hooper entered a local credit union (bank) carrying the shotgun and demanded money, which he was given (ibid., p. 3). The staff activated a silent duress alarm, resulting in a private security company ringing Police to advise of the alarm's alert (ibid.). Police responding to both calls arrived at Hooper's home and the credit union at about the same time. All involved were armed and wearing ballistic protection (ibid.). The staff at the bank identified the man as Hooper, as he was known to them and he had not attempted to disguise himself (ibid.).

As these events unfolded, the Northern Communications Centre (NorthComm) advised one of the local officers – a sergeant – that he was now to assume the role of "incident controller designate" (ibid.). This passed operational control of the search for Hooper to that officer. The officer concerned acknowledged his newly assigned role (ibid.). Because of Hooper's actions, history and apparent "… fatalistic approach to his offending that day", the incident controller requested AOS support (ibid.).

Five or so minutes later, a report was received that Hooper was at a location on a local road. Officers coordinated and organised themselves, in what was described as "… a very calm and organised way" and moved to put road blocks in place to stop

Hooper leaving and then tried to contact the man via his mobile phone. He did not answer (ibid., p. 4).

Unfortunately, one of the responding police vehicles, driven by the incident controller (the designate title having been removed by NorthComm), drove forward and into the parking bay where the armed man was parked, and following some to and fro driving between the police car and the utility, Hooper drove off from the parking area and out onto the road. No firearms were presented during this encounter by either of the parties involved (ibid.).

Police vehicles began to follow Hooper without their flashing lights or sirens on, but this ultimately became a pursuit with lights and sirens in use in an attempt to have Hooper stop, which he did not.

During this time a degree of confusion arose about the "command and control" of the event between the incident controller and the shift commander in NorthComms, due to the shift commander "assum[ing] the role of 'pursuit controller' in line with the Police 'Fleeing driver' policy". However, most officers involved still regarded the sergeant as the "incident controller" (Independent Police Conduct Authority, 2021, p. 5).

The pursuit carried on for 30 minutes (ibid.), with Hooper's driving described as "... safe, and his speed var[ing] from 60 to 80 kph on open roads with 100 kph speed limits" (ibid). During this time Hooper made a brief stop at a cousin's house where he threw the money he had taken from the bank onto the driveway. He then drove off again. Permission was given by the shift commander to deploy road spikes to try and deflate his tyres (ibid. p. 6).

An officer deployed the road spikes a short time later, and as Hooper approached, the officer presented his Glock pistol towards Hooper and demanded he stop; Hooper drove around the officer and kept on going. He did not present his shotgun, and the officer did not fire his weapon (ibid., p. 6).

While these actions were taking place, the AOS were travelling from their main centre base towards the rural location where the pursuit was taking place. Four AOS members deployed, with two in each of two police vehicles. One of those vehicles was several minutes ahead of the other in the journey and met up with the local officers just as Hooper brought his vehicle to a stop (ibid., pp. 6–7).

At this point further changes took place regarding who was in command. The senior AOS officer appointed himself the "forward commander" for the AOS during the event – in line with Police policy. That role was a task specific role, not an overall coordination and command role. The officer knew the sergeant had been assigned the incident controller role. Within 2–3 minutes of arriving on scene, the AOS forward commander then announced over the radio "we're getting behind this I'm gonna take incident control" (ibid., p. 7); this was an unclear announcement, and in his role of forward commander, he "... should have consulted the Incident Controller and obtained his approval for the AOS's plan to move forward towards Mr Hooper, rather than just telling him that it was going to happen" (Independent Police Conduct Authority, 2021, p. 7).

The incident controller did not challenge the commentary from the AOS member believing that such officers have the right training to make such decisions (ibid.,

p. 8). At the time the incident controller was thinking the AOS members would have attempted a "... high risk vehicle stop, rather than the 'cordon, contain and appeal' tactic" (ibid.). He was also concerned about what Hooper would do if given time to think (ibid.).

The AOS officers later told the authority that the closest police vehicle to Hooper was 80 metres from him and that they felt they needed to reduce the distance to more effectively contain Hooper should he try to drive or run from the location (ibid.). As a result, the AOS asked the sergeant to drive his vehicle closer the Hooper's utility; the sergeant did not hear that transmission and later told the IPCA investigators that if he had, he would have been reluctant to get closer to the armed man (ibid.).

The two AOS officers then arrived on the scene and, seeing where the other police vehicles were, they determined to drive past them to get closer to Hooper and his vehicle. As they did so, they noted movement in the utility vehicle and "... saw the person inside (Mr Hooper) was holding a firearm and pointing it towards them through the driver's window" (ibid. p. 10). The AOS stopped 30 metres from Hooper and his vehicle, and one officer got out and took cover behind the door of the Police car and aimed his Bushmaster rifle at Hooper, calling on him to get out of his vehicle. The second AOS officer took up a position behind the Police vehicle's boot (ibid.).

Hooper at that point picked up the shotgun, pointed it out the window of his car and fired a single shot that went over the heads of the AOS and landed 35 metre behind them (ibid., p. 12). Both AOS officers then returned fire with their Bushmaster rifles (ibid., p. 12). One officer fired six shots and the other three (ibid.).

They stopped firing when Hooper slumped forward in the vehicle. Hooper did not fire again (Independent Police Conduct Authority, 2021, p. 12). He had suffered five gunshot wounds to his head, neck, chest and shoulder (ibid.). His injuries were not survivable, and the ambulance crew who arrived to assist confirmed that he had died of his injuries (ibid., pp. 14–15).

In its findings the Authority stated:

- Police responded to the two initial incidents involving Mr Hooper in a timely and effective manner. Police managed the search for Mr Hooper, and the subsequent pursuit, appropriately and in line with Police policy. (Independent Police Conduct Authority, 2021, p. 6)
- AOS Officers A and B should have stopped at the cordon and sought to de-escalate the situation by communicating with Mr Hooper. The AOS officers also should have consulted the Incident Controller and obtained his approval for their arrest plan. (ibid., p. 12)
- Both AOS Officers A and B were legally justified in firing at Mr Hooper to defend themselves and each other in the immediate moments after he shot at them. (ibid., p. 14).

The most important finding, in the author's opinion, was the second.

Elsewhere in the IPCA report into the shooting, the Authority commented:

> ... AOS Officers A and B were committed to their initial plan of a non-compliant vehicle stop, and failed to adequately reassess the situation when they heard Mr Hooper had already stopped ... AOS Officer B drove forward nonetheless, breaking the cordon. Neither AOS

> Officers A nor B considered other options, one of which was to remain at the cordon and commence voice communications. While this would have likely meant a prolonged standoff, it may have prevented a fatal shooting.
>
> By immediately driving closer to Mr. Hooper, the AOS officers unnecessarily escalated the situation, put themselves within range of his shotgun and promoted his reaction. Mr. Hooper's decision to aim and fire his shotgun at the AOS officers was entirely his own responsibility, but the Police response should have afforded him a greater opportunity to reconsider his actions and surrender. While Mr. Hooper was stopped in a remote area, Police should have used the time to strengthen their cordons, get the Police Negotiation Team in place, and prepare to take action if Mr. Hooper moved towards Police and threaten them.
>
> For these reasons, we find AOS Officers A and B's actions in driving past the cordon to get closer to Mr Hooper were not justified. (Independent Police Conduct Authority, 2021, p. 11).

A strongly worded set of statements by the Authority.

Each of the case studies presented above has involved a person who – for a variety of reasons – has failed to comply with Police directions and who, through their own actions, have caused police officers to resort to the use of lethal force. In one instance, resulting in loss of an innocent life. However, as seen in the commentaries from the IPCA, Police have in some instances, in the Authority's view, contributed to those outcomes through the decisions they made and the actions they took. Furthermore, the Authority has highlighted issues with command and control and adherence to policy and procedure.

At the same time, the cases above resulted in 12 police officers having to make the decision to use lethal force. Those officers will carry those decisions and the outcomes from them for the rest of their service with Police and their lives. Some will carry an extra burden, that of adverse commentary by the IPCA. As stated earlier in this work, the impact of shooting a person (or at them) had serious implications for a police officer. For some it brings their career to a premature end.

As mentioned in the lead in to these case studies, each event reflected poorly, in the author's view, on the way Police leveraged (or did not) the tactical superiority they took into each situation, poor coordination, poor communication, failing to wear body armour, failure to alert the relevant authorities and comrades to the fact officers had armed and failure to use tactical options that were available, such as a police dog in one instance. These studies all presented opportunities for New Zealand Police to learn and to improve their practices when it comes to responding to armed or dangerous people.

The upcoming chapter will consider the outcomes mentioned above, and in other IPCA shooting reports, and discuss what they mean for New Zealand Police and its officers.

Bibliography

Greenwood, C. (1979). *Police tactics in armed operations*. Paladin Press.
Independent Police Conduct Authority. (2009). *Report on the shooting of Stephen Jon Bellingham*. Independent Police Conduct Authority.
Independent Police Conduct Authority. (2012). *Police shooting of Halatau Ki'anamanu Naitoko*. Independent Police Conduct Authority.
Independent Police Conduct Authority. (2013). *Fatal police shooting of Lachan Kelly-Tumarae*. Independent Police Conduct Authority.
Independent Police Conduct Authority. (2015). *Fatal police shooting of Adam Morehu*. Independent Police Conduct Authority.
Independent Police Conduct Authority. (2016). *Fatal police shooting of David Cerven*. Independent Police Conduct Authority.
Independent Police Conduct Authority. (2019). *Fatal shooting of Jerrim Toms*. Independent Police Conduct Authority.
Independent Police Conduct Authority. (2021). *Fatal shooting of Astin Hooper near Kawerau*. Independent Police Conduct Authority.

Part III
Observations and Suggestions Regarding the Future

Chapter 10
Observations Regarding the Use of Lethal Force

Firstly, it is the author's belief that the New Zealand Police are learning, modifying and adapting policies, processes, training and behaviours as a result of being at the heart of the matters written about in this book. For example, in 2019, the organisation confirmed that:

> A key role of New Zealand Police Response and Operations: Research and Evaluation (RORE) is research, analysis, monitoring and evaluation of Police use of force, to provide accountability and assist evidence-based decisions making, to improve police and public safety. (New Zealand Police, 2020)

Reporting from this source has formed the basis of elements of this book. The author is extremely grateful that New Zealand Police do such work and publicly release it.

In 2021, the Appropriate Tactical Settings Insights and Evidence Brief (New Zealand Police, 2021a) reinforced that belief and presented evidence that Police are committed to constantly reviewing and assessing how they operate, particularly when it comes to the use of lethal force. The final substantive addition to the learning arsenal came with the March 2019, introduction of "Operation Gun Safe" and the database associated with it, which aims to monitor firearms incidents and to reduce, if not eliminate, the poor records maintained regarding events involving firearms (New Zealand Police Association, 2019).

However, it cannot hurt for an outsider, albeit one who was once an insider, to offer observations and perspectives grounded in experience, research and a genuine desire to help lessen the number of times a citizen or police officer is shot. Because, while some may argue there are "winners and losers" in such events, the author is of the view that, sadly, there are only those that are impacted and the impacts extend far beyond those who are shot, or those who do the shooting.

The most important observation, in the author's view, was that New Zealand Police have firearms and the authority to use lethal force for very sound practical and moral reasons. The practical reasons are set out in various parts of this work, but in summary they include mass shootings when a person has embarked on a killing

R. S. Shortt, *Lethal Force and New Zealand Police*,
https://doi.org/10.1007/978-3-031-05269-9_10

spree and must be forcibly stopped, when a person is posing immediate and real danger to the lives of others (e.g. hostages) and has failed to respond to calls to surrender or to release them and when a police officer is confronted by a person who is armed with a weapon and then uses (or attempts to use) that weapon against another person or the police officer.

Coincidentally, as the author was drafting the above words (September, 2021), news reports came in from Aotearoa New Zealand to say that a man had been shot dead by police officers in a downtown Auckland supermarket after stabbing six people in what was described as a "terror attack" carried out by a "known extremist" according to the country's Prime Minister (Corlett, 2021), a further tragic example of why New Zealand Police have firearms and the legal authority to apply lethal force.

The reasons for having firearms and lethal force authority are also legislated for in the *Policing Act 2008* (NZL) under the functions of the New Zealand Police, in particular (and in summary): maintaining public safety and law enforcement. Those functions, as Miller discussed, also give rise to a moral obligation on a police officer to use lethal force in certain situations, as outlined and graphically emphasised in the paragraph above.

To help structure the commentary ahead, Professor Rick Sarre, based in Australia, and a long-time scholar with considerable knowledge about Police and policing, presented a useful framework arising from his research. He expounded that there are four important variables impacting the number of people shot by Police. They are:

- The extent of police militarisation;
- The rules that pertain to the use of lethal force;
- The standards of firearms training, and
- The gun culture in the society in which officers operate. (Sarre, 2019)

In considering Sarre's four points, the author concluded that the "rules pertaining to the use of lethal force" in Aotearoa New Zealand had not changed, despite their being substantial change regarding the process New Zealand Police used to deployed firearms. The General Instructions governing the use of firearms are, as best as the author can determine from the research are unchanged from the early years of his career, but the places where Police firearm can be obtained from have.

Therefore, putting aside the second of Sarre's points, the author will commence with the professor's last point, the gun culture in the society in which officers operate, which was believed to be the best starting point as it provides a context for what follows.

The Gun Culture of the Society

Four observations falling under this heading warrant presentation.

The first is in respect to the type of firearms Aotearoa New Zealand allows to be in the hands of citizens. In 1990, the country was shocked and appalled at the mass shooting of 13 children, women and men (including a police officer) by a man who had multiple firearms and in particular a military-style semi-automatic (MSSA) rifle. He outgunned responding police. The opportunity to begin ridding the country of MSSAs in civilian hands was not taken, and it required a further mass shooting of 51 people in 2019 before a political leader finally announced that MSSAs were to be banned (New Zealand Government, 2019). The author considers the move has taken a brave step due to the existence in Aotearoa New Zealand of a strong shooting culture that traces its roots back to the very early years of colonisation of the country, as discussed earlier in this work. Taking on that "lobby" risked political capital that other political leaders and Ministers of Police had not been willing to expend over the previous 30 years.

The government followed through on its stance, and legislation was enacted banning MSSAs and creating a "gun buy-back" scheme administered by the Police to help remove as many of them from circulation as possible, along with any other firearms owners wished to dispose of (stuff.co.nz, 2021).

Much has been said about the success or otherwise of the scheme and its costs; what cannot be disputed, however, is that it removed in excess of 60,000 firearms and prohibited firearms-related items from society. It did not eliminate all military-style semi-automatic firearms from the land, but it did put a stop to future importation and supply, and it did remove a considerable number from use. The full benefits of the legislation and buy-back(s) will be, in the author's view, felt and recognised only over time, maybe decades. Meanwhile, Aotearoa New Zealand continues to be a country with a vibrant, and legitimate, firearms community who lawfully own and use a variety of weapons for legitimate sporting, business (i.e. pest destruction), farming and recreational activities – for example, hunting.

Police have, since the legislation change and buy-back programme, launched Operation Tauwhiro, described by the commissioner as:

> … a long term, nationally coordinated operation focused on harm prevention and enforcement … A key focus of the operation will be investigating and disrupting the illegal supply of firearms to gangs and organised crime groups, which is enabling firearms violence. This includes the illegal manufacture, modification, and supply of firearms to gangs and organised crime groups. (New Zealand Police, 2021b)

That work, coupled with the earlier discussed changes, means Aotearoa New Zealand society has changed its relationship with firearms. Those moves, it is posited, bode well for the future and for the wider environment within which Police must operate and on occasion use lethal force.

However, Aotearoa New Zealand is not "out of the woods" as the old saying goes, with regard to unlawful firearms use. Media reporting in March 2021 revealed the number of firearms-related charges laid by New Zealand Police has increased since the Christchurch massacres (Strang, 2021), almost "…double that of a decade earlier" (ibid). Furthermore, the reporting confirmed that 1862 firearms had been seized by Police "… more than double the 860 that were seized a decade earlier" (ibid.).

The second important issue regarding society is the reality of situations in which Police need to consider and use lethal force. The 20 years of PCA/IPC data reveal that it is not just gangs and organised crime who present a risk to Police and society, but mostly the regular citizens spoken of earlier in this book. That is not to say that organised crime and gangs don't present a danger; they do, but as the Police themselves state, their research and intelligence identifies:

> … individuals within the organised crime environment are acquiring firearms as a form of protection, perceiving a heightened threat of violence by rival gangs and/or organised crime groups, as opposed to protecting themselves from Police. (New Zealand Police, 2021a, p. 13)

Police concede, that while the deportation of gang and crime figures from Australia to Aotearoa New Zealand has "… increased inter-gang tensions …" (ibid., p. 14), the more significant background factors impacting risk from shootings include "… mental health/suicide and drug use …" (ibid.).

Which leads us to the third observation regarding society and Police use of lethal force, namely, mental illness and associated issues such as drug addiction. From the author's research, it was revealed that 42% of shootings by Police were preceded by indicators of mental health issues concerning the person subsequently shot, and 30% had commentary regarding such indicators during or post the shootings in them. Furthermore, 9.3% of shootings left the author with a view that "suicide by cop" (SbC) was a likely contributor. Compounding the mental health issue was that alcohol use or traces thereof ($n = 11$), or drug use or traces thereof ($n = 14$), or both ($n = 11$), were identified in the PCA/IPCA reporting on the 43 events.

Unfortunately, when a society with a legitimate and vibrant firearms culture collides with mental illness and substance use and/or abuse, it is the Police who end up responding to and endeavouring to resolve the inevitable crises.

These are complex, "wicked" issues if you like that involve hard policy decisions, which may in turn – like banning certain forms of firearm or deinstitutionalising the mentally ill – result in unexpected and undesired consequences (such as underground firearms caches and suppliers and mentally ill people accessing firearms from within family homes) (Shortt, 2015).

Prevention, the author argues, remains the best tactic when it comes to avoiding mentally ill individuals with firearms creating unwinnable confrontations with armed police officers.

The final observation under this heading concerns the way Police have responded to illegal firearms use in Aotearoa New Zealand. The particular aspect to be commented on is the New Zealand Police policy regarding access to and availability of firearms, with the most substantial policy change regarding New Zealand Police firearms, over the last five decades, occurred in 2010–2011 when the police commissioner implemented a national policy to move firearms out of station-based armouries and to put them in vehicle-mounted cabinets.

What drove that change? Readers will note that this work has not delved into the crime statistics on illegal use of firearms in the country, other than by reference to those instances where firearms were used to kill, injure or deter Police. However, with regard to the focus of the book, statistics regarding the number of times Police felt the need to arm – which likely precede many instances of charges being laid for firearms crimes – have been presented and discussed. Furthermore, this work

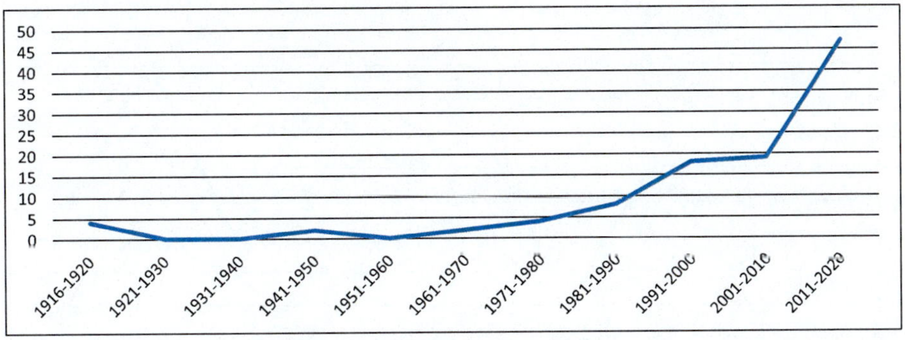

Fig. 10.1 Number of shootings by police: by decade (1916–2020). (Data obtained from New Zealand Police)

identified the 2001–2010 decade as being – potentially – the most dangerous for Police from the perspective of being shot or shot at, in the organisation's history.

What impacts did the dangerous decade and the move of firearms to vehicles have? One possible impact visible in the data was the fact that shootings by Police (including those involving misses, fatal and non-fatal outcomes)[1] rose substantially from 2001–2010 to 2011–2020[2], jumping from 19 events to 47. Refer to Fig. 10.1:

The rise in shooting cannot be attributed to just the change in Police policy on where firearms were placed. Clearly, additional research of crime statistics regarding the illegal use of firearms would be needed to draw any such inference. However, the data used to inform this book does indicate that there was an ongoing increase in the need for Police to arm and in some instance use lethal force, evident from the 1980s and culminating in the 2010s. The author, therefore, posits that the shift in Police use of lethal force does speak to shifts in society and its "gun culture" or at least to the use of guns within a society that has a well-founded gun culture. However, other forces may be in play, such as the easier access officers have to firearms, resulting – potentially – in them accessing them more and using them more often.

In exploring that contention further, the data for the most recent three decades was broken down into years to see what pattern of activity was discernible. The results of that breakdown are presented in Fig. 10.2.

As can be seen, in the two earlier decades, the number of years with four or more uses of lethal force amounted to just two (1996 and 2009), while during the most recent decade, 7 out of the 10 years reached or exceeded four (with 6 months of 2020 still unreported). Furthermore, in the two earlier decades, each contained 2

[1] Data regarding shots by Police that missed only began to appear in 2001. Prior to that time, Police do not appear to have kept records on such events, simply recording shots that killed or injured the person being shot at (New Zealand Police, 2020).

[2] The use of lethal force data for 2020 is incomplete. It only shows data from 01 January until 27 May 2020. New Zealand Police had not published the finalised use of lethal force data for the complete year at the time this work was being prepared.

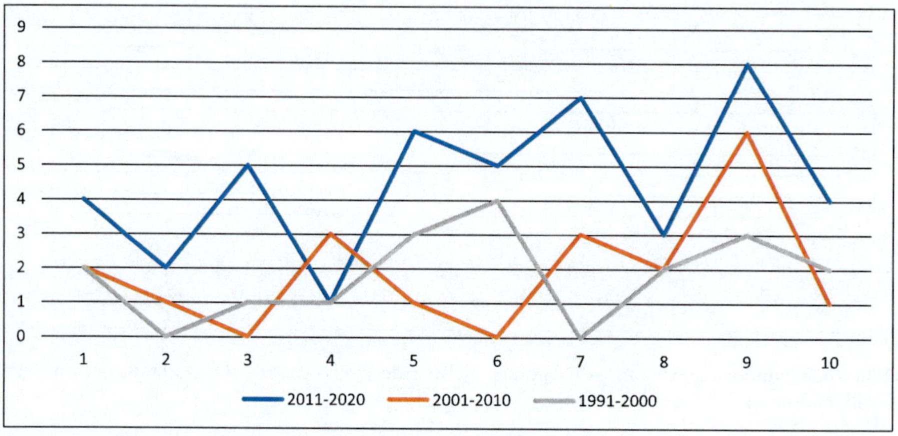

Fig. 10.2 Number of shootings by police: by year within decades – 1991–2000, 2001–2010 and 2011–2020 (including miss, non-fatal and fatal outcomes). (Data obtained from New Zealand Police)

years where Police did not record using lethal force at all (1992 and 1997; 2003 and 2006). There were no zero-use years for the most recent decade.

Finally, when the median number of shootings for each of the decades was calculated, it revealed the medians were 2.0 for 1991–2000, 1.5 for 2001–2010 and 4.5 for 2011–2020.

In examining who was using the lethal force detailed above, only the 2000–2010 and 2011–2020 decades could be resorted to as the author did not have data for the earlier decade. Furthermore, the data only related to fatal and non-fatal shootings investigated and reported on by the PCA/IPCA.

That examination revealed in the 2001–2010 decade. six uses of lethal force were by Level 1 responders and four by AOS. By 2011–2020, those numbers had risen to 22 uses by Level 1 responders, 8 by AOS and 4 by STG. The data clearly presents a substantial increase in Level 1 responder use of lethal force following their increased ready access to firearms in their vehicles.

Again, the above commentary cannot be used to draw conclusions between the policy shift and the increase in uses of lethal force. There remains a requirement for further investigation before such views can be expressed, but there exists a strong case, the author believes, to undertake that work to discover if the hypothesis that easier access and greater availability has in fact led to greater use of lethal force.

Having stated the above, the author observes that the rise in lethal force use does warrant carefully monitoring by the New Zealand Police and Independent Police Conduct Authority for other just as important reasons.

One of those reasons is what the author terms the "justification trap". The trap refers to the fact that just because a use of lethal force has been justified by those who investigated it, it does not mean it sits well, or is considered reasonable, within the "court of public opinion". That can become particularly problematic when the ethnicity of those being affected by Police use of lethal force is taken into account.

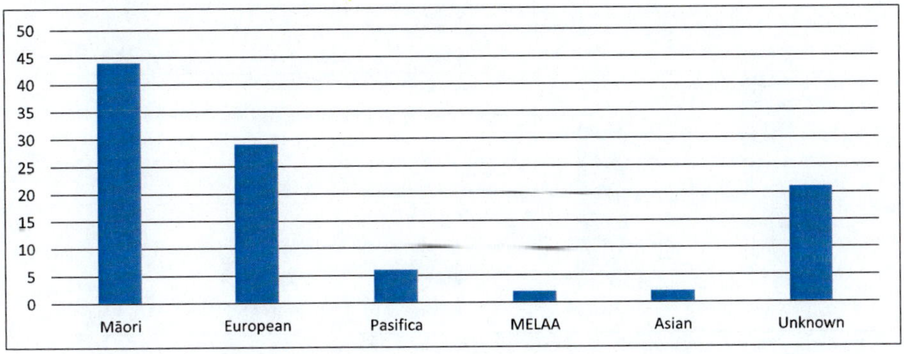

Fig 10.3 Number of people shot or shot at by police: by ethnicity (1916–2020) (note: shot at data available only from 2000 to 2020). (Data obtained from New Zealand Police)

By way of reminder regarding that point, the data revealed surprisingly high numbers of people identified as Māori being shot by Police based upon the proportion of the population that Maori comprised. For example, see Fig. 10.3. The chart revealed 42.3% of those shot by Police over the 100+ years, where records exist, were identified as Maori, despite the European population of the country very quickly overtaking the indigenous inhabitant's dominance in the early years of colonisation. For example, one historical resource suggested there were between 100,000 and 200,000 Maori at the beginning of the nineteenth century, in comparison to just 50 Europeans. By 2018, 16.5% of the population was Maori and 70.2% was European (Statistics New Zealand, 2019).

Meanwhile, the data for the period of the author's PCA/IPCA focused research, 2000–2019, revealed the picture presented in Fig. 10.4.

The chart shows 49% of those shot were identified as being Māori, while 36% were identified as being European. For context, Statistics New Zealand, 2018, census data reveals 16.5% of the population identified as Māori, while 70.2% identified as European. Using the same source, the situation for the other three ethnicities in the Police data was:

- 1916–2020:
  - Pasifika: 8.1% of population – 5.8% of people shot or shot at
  - MELAA: 1.5% of population – 1.9% of people shot or shot at
  - Asian: 15.1% of population – 1.9% of people shot or shot at
- 2000–2019:
  - Pasifika: 8.1% of population – 9.4% of people shot or shot at
  - MELAA: 1.5% of population – 3.8% of people shot or shot at
  - Asian: 15.1% of population – 1.9% of people shot (Statistics New Zealand)

For additional context, Fig. 10.5 shows the ethnicity of people involved in all TOR events between 2014 and 2019, again using Police supplied data.

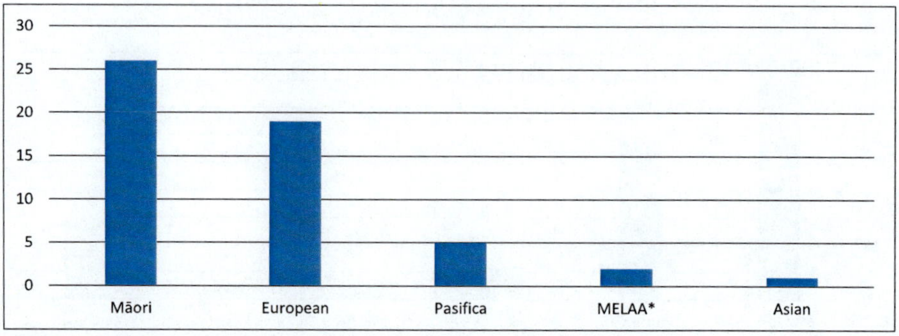

Fig. 10.4 Number of people shot or shot at by police: by ethnicity (2000–2019). (Data obtained from New Zealand Police)

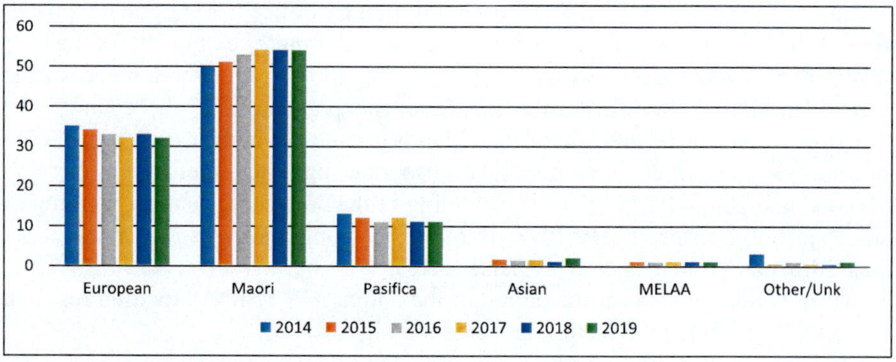

Fig. 10.5 Ethnicity (as a %) of those involved in all TOR events (2014–2019). (Data obtained from New Zealand Police Tactical Options Reporting)

The justification trap is not unique to Aotearoa New Zealand and has been observed for a number of years elsewhere. For example, Victoria Police (Australia) encountered the "justification trap" 30 years ago. Between 1985 and 1994, Victoria Police fatally shot 30 people, 9 in 1994 alone. All were justified, but following a public outcry, the organisation was forced to institute Project Beacon to review and revamp its entire organisational approach to the use of lethal force (Springvale Monash Legal Service Incorporated, 2005, p. 7). Some of their findings and approaches were subsequently adopted by New Zealand Police.

The USA continues to be battered by the justification trap when it comes to the deaths of Black and other non-White Americans at the hands of predominantly (but not exclusively) White law enforcement officers. For example, see the discussion regarding two police shootings in Hawaii (The Guardian, 2021c) and commentary about the Federal Bureau of Investigation's attempts to track deaths caused by law enforcement officers in that country (The Guardian, 2021d).

Nearer to home, as this was being written, two Australian police officers are on trial accused of murder regarding the deaths of two indigenous Australians, one in the Northern Territory and Western Australia, both as a result of the use of lethal force involving firearms (The Guardian, 2021a, b). The charges came following years of debate surrounding the deaths of indigenous Australians while in prison, or when encountering Police, despite the vast majority of the deaths being determined by investigators as justified. The speed with which the charges were laid in the respective jurisdictions lead the author to ponder whether the "justification trap" and public debate had finally led to a more rapid evidence collection, examination and decision-making process on the part of senior Australian police when an aboriginal person was killed.

For the sake of Aotearoa New Zealand, and its Police, the justification trap needs to be avoided, and there are already indications that it has the potential to be sprung. For example, see the "Ideasroom" adverse commentary from three Victoria University of Wellington commentators regarding the ART trial and its impact on Maori and Pasifika peoples (Mackenzie et al., 2019).

To avoid the trap, one of the things the author believes the organisation needs to do is closely monitor and report – with public transparency – on its use of lethal force. The relatively new Tactical Options Reporting regime is considered a good start, as is the Gun Safe data initiative. These reports should be easily located on the departmental website. They can provide a public window into a world that is otherwise left to journalists and academics, with one seeking sensation, while the other delivers slow, methodical and often obscure reporting. A public window – it is argued – will assist in framing and expanding the debate about lethal force use and its appropriateness.

Currently, within New Zealand Police policies, procedure or instructions, "… there is no definition of, or reference to, the terms 'use of lethal force' or 'lethal force'" (New Zealand Police, 2021c). The revelation was not surprising, given the historic reliance on wording such as "incapacitation" of people and "neutralising" of threats. The reality remains that they are both referring to lethal force and its use.

It is the author's view that the organisation should consider adjusting its doctrine to include a definition for use of lethal force, as the author has done in this work, which includes not just fatal and non-fatal shootings but is instead focused on an officer's intention regarding their use of a firearm or where another form of incapacitating force that may result in death is resorted to. Below is an example:

> Lethal force means every occasion a police officer intentionally uses force against another person (including for example, but not limited to, the presentation and firing of a Police firearm – except when loaded with 'non-lethal' ammunition – at another person, or strikes another person about the head with a baton, or deliberately drives into another person with a vehicle) with intent to incapacitate them knowing, that such use of force may result in death.

The suggestion above eliminates any confusion over whether use of Police firearms in training situations are captured by the definition or whether it applies to accidental discharges of weapons or their use in other settings such as destruction of animals. It also expands the use of lethal force definition to include other weapons such as batons, vehicles or restraint holds.

It does, however, deliberately exclude occasions when "non-lethal" ammunition – such as "beanbag", "sponge" or even "rubber" bullets – are used as it is accepted that such ammunition is not designed to kill, notwithstanding that they can still present a risk of death if they strike a person in the head or some other locations on the body. If a death did occur through use of such ammunition, or some other use of force, the lethal force definition becomes moot, replaced by the outcome.

Why have such a definition and expand its use to the times when the IPCA must be informed by the commissioner? Because the difference between an independent and transparent IPCA investigation could literally be 1 or 2 centimetres. In 1 or 2 centimetres in one direction, a fatal or non-fatal shooting results in an enquiry (s. 13 *Independent Police Conduct Authority Act, 1988* (NZL), but using the same measurement, in the other direction, a resulting miss creates no legislative requirement for the IPCA to intervene. The fundamental difference between the two situations? Nothing, as an officer intentionally aimed a firearm at a person and fired a live round(s) of ammunition at them, with the intention of incapacitating a person and knowing they may die. More on the issue in Chap. 11.

The second observation regarding the above is that the AOS and STG exemptions from full engagement with the TOR regime requirements needs to cease (for example, see (New Zealand Police, 2019)). The two specialist units are integral parts of the lethal force eco-system within New Zealand Police and the country and, therefore, should not sit outside any reporting and data capture structure associated with that use of force. The New Zealand Police even acknowledged the point being made above in their "Appropriate Tactical Settings" research where they stated "[t]he AOS/STG exemption from reporting firearm and TASER presentations adds a layer of complexity to developing robust inferences from the data" (New Zealand Police, 2021a, p. 19).

Even in 2021, New Zealand Police continue to lament a lack of data regarding how often its officers arm themselves and resort to use of lethal force (New Zealand Police, 2021a, p. 22). That is unacceptable. It was identified as an issue to the organisation as long ago as 2000 by the author, and yet it continues to be an issue. If the TOR regime needs to expand to capture all "arming decisions – irrespective of use", it should in the author's view be so expanded. And, if technology-based mechanisms for monitoring removal of Police firearms from vehicle-mounted gun cabinets are necessary to further support and validate the TOR data (assuming such technology does not currently operate), then that technology should be installed.

The IPCA regularly highlighted officers, in the heat of the moment (and sometimes not), failing to report the decision to arm as required by Police policy and procedure. As the most serious form of force, lethal force should be – common sense would suggest – the most rigorously monitored of all the tactical options. Currently, there are still obvious gaps.

While still on the subject of data and its use, the work in Chap. 7 suggested some further analysis by Police of the data they currently have could prove useful. That work may well be happening; the author hopes it is. If it is not, his suggestion is to consider closely those districts that have high perceptions of risk associated with staff resorting to arming themselves and districts where staff use lethal force at levels above what one might expect. Why do they stand out? What sits behind the decisions officers are making, and how best can those officers be supported by the organisation?

The Standards of Firearms Training

Another of Sarre's four key variables was firearms training. This next segment presents observations regarding that topic.

Associated with the rules and data related observations are the tactical superiority factors mentioned earlier in Chap. 7. How is it that despite tactical superiority, police officers still must resort to use of lethal force and still get killed or injured? It is, of course, unacceptable to say "Well, it's just a dangerous job" or "It goes with the territory". The laws on health and safety in the workplace have made such observations lawfully unacceptable, and thankfully the Police show signs of not accepting such statements either. Furthermore, the Bill of Rights and the abolition of the death penalty in Aotearoa New Zealand raises a very high bar for situations where agents of the state determine it is necessary to resort to lethal force.

A question arising from the research was: Does the PITT training programme empower officers to leverage those tactical superiority factors to their advantage? Does the training include team-based engagement where operational Level 1 responders work on "shoot-don't shoot" scenarios with their teammates and colleagues (particularly supervisors) so that they learn to work as a coordinated and collaborative team? Does the training provide tactical insight into how to avoid being surprised (ambushed) by an armed person, and if an officer is, how to use the items immediately available to them to best protect their life (e.g. their vehicle)?

AOS and STG train and work as teams, so should – in the author's view – Level 1 responders because, as the data has shown, the vast majority of uses of lethal force (against, or by, Police) happen when groups of officers are present, seldom, if ever, is it just one officer or even just two. For example, see the IPCA commentary in the Jerrim Toms fatal shooting case on this topic (Independent Police Conduct Authority, 2019, pp. 31–38).

The other important outcome of training is that it provides greater frequency of lethal force decision-making and tactics practice than the operational arena often does. It is through well-structured and safely repeated training that officers can hone their response skills so that when confronted with actual lethal force encounters, they have an "experiential" foundation upon which to base their perceptions of risk, their decision-making and their physical responses (for example, see Dror, 2007, pp. 270–271).

Ultimately, however, as the author believes from his own experiences, and as Dror comments on (Dror, 2007, p. 271), there is nothing like actual operational experience to prepare people for the roles they undertake. Given this, it was interesting to note that the evaluation of the Armed Response Team trial in Aotearoa New Zealand also drew attention to this factor when it stated "… the data [suggesting] that a primary factor driving increased perceptions of safety [on the part of operational response officers] was principally the availability of addition *skilled* frontline resources and *highly trained* personnel rather than just specific tactical options available through the ARTs" (Italics added) (New Zealand Police, 2021d, p. 16).

Being able to put more experienced and more highly trained officers into the operational environment is a challenge for New Zealand Police. The ART trial was one, ill-fated, attempt at doing so, and in 2021, the organisation announced it was again moving to "… improve the safety and capability of frontline staff" (New Zealand Police, 2021e), as detailed in Chap. 3.

A further training-related observation involves the number of shots fired by police officers and the number of shots that hit or miss the intended target. Police commented on this issue in their Appropriate Tactical Settings research brief (New Zealand Police, 2021a, pp. 28–29), where they also discussed training and shotfall. The data from the author's research was quite clear that when more than one or two shots were fired, the likelihood of a miss rose considerably and with that the likelihood that a bystander may be killed or injured (as was seen in the Naitoko shooting in 2009). Such outcomes need to be avoided, and trigger discipline would appear to be the simplest and easiest means of achieving that.

Training officers to fire a small number of aimed shots (two ideally), when under pressure, and to them pause and consider the impact of their rounds should be the approach taken. It would definitely avoid the multiple round shooting that caused the IPCA to carefully consider culpability concerning the 12 rounds fired in the Jerrim Toms shooting in 2018 (Independent Police Conduct Authority, 2019), or the 49-round fusillade of shots fired by two AOS officers in the 2020 shooting of Anthony Fane (Independent Police Conduct Authority, 2021b) which will be discussed further, later in this chapter.

Perhaps the most fitting closure to this aspect of the commentary is to repeat the words of Colin Greenwood who, in 1979, wrote in "Police Tactics in Armed Operations":

> The object of the police is to eliminate the danger caused by an armed criminal and in doing so, they must not be permitted to cause more danger than was in fact being caused by the person whom they are attempting to neutralise (cited in (Shortt, 2000, p. 83)).

Associated with the issue of missed shots and the number of shots fired are the weapon types and choices made by Police. Observations regarding this will be considered under the next of Sarre's headings and perhaps the most contentious, militarisation.

The Extent of Militarisation

Militarisation of policing has become a substantial topic of discussion, particularly in the USA, but also more widely in the past decade; for example see Nolan's commentary regarding protesters and police (2020) and commentary on the Australian experience from White (2019), which also discussed police weapon choices. Sarre identified it as one of the variables that impacts the number of people shot by Police (2019).

Delaforce, in her 2019 article citing McCulloch, also highlighted the "paramilitarisation of the police" which was viewed as being evident via "… joint police-military training, similarities in uniform, use of military weapons and equipment, application of "extremely high levels of force" and the movement of personnel from military to policing roles" (Delaforce, 2019, p. 23). She went on to note that scholars had identified the creation of "tactical response groups" as further example of the trend, particularly the fact that "… specialised paramilitary units in state and territory police forces now include counter-terrorism and hostage rescue capabilities" (Delaforce, 2019, p. 23).

In Aotearoa New Zealand, militarisation has also been raised as an issue, including with regard to the firearms that police officers have access too. For example, in 2020, the Aotearoa New Zealand defence minister was quoted as questioning why Police were armed with military-grade assault rifles, particularly now that the government had moved to outlaw military-style semi-automatic (MSSA) rifles (Dynon, 2020). New Zealand police even devoted commentary to militarisation in their 2021, Appropriate Tactical Settings paper (New Zealand Police, 2021a, pp. 33–34).

Therefore, the first issue to be considered, with observations from the research, is the use of the Bushmaster rifle by (non-specialist) Level 1 responders. The author draws a deliberate distinction here between Level 1 responders and members of the AOS and STG who provide the specialised armed support to more complex encounters.

When it comes to the number of times Police miss a person when using the Bushmaster rifle, the data revealed that out of 107 shots fired, 72 (67%) missed. Given the Bushmaster has an advertised effective range of 550 metres, that is a lot of bullets with plenty of carrying power behind them going somewhere other than where intended. Tragically, two bystanders have been the victims of two of those missed shots.

The Bushmaster is modelled on a military assault rifle. It looks like a military assault rifle and was introduced to the New Zealand Police in 2005 (New Zealand Police, 2005). The primary reasons given at the time, by the assistant commissioner responsible, who would later go one to become the Police commissioner and oversee moving firearms into operational vehicles, was that it:

> … would be more operationally compatible with the other police standard issue firearm, the semi-automatic Glock … [the rifle it was to replace] was introduced in 1993 and is a bolt action styled rifle, so each time a shot is fired, the operator has to take one hand off the rifle to action the bolt. Once the bolt is actioned, the operator has to reposition their hand as well

> as re-sight the weapon and this could be dangerous in certain situations. This is not the case with the new Bushmaster. (New Zealand Police, 2005)

However, the statistics on misses do not bear out the optimism regarding the greater accuracy a semi-automatic would deliver. The only other benefit mentioned in the press release was that the new rifle would be of a length that would suit "... some smaller-built staff ..." (ibid.). So, improved accuracy through semi-automatic capability and suitable for smaller-build police officers. What wasn't mentioned, but which has been elsewhere here, was that the Bushmaster also came with a 20- or 30-round magazine capacity. The bolt-action rifle had just five rounds available to the shooter.

There was also no mention of how the rifle would interface with the tactics of the New Zealand Police, namely, the "cordon, contain, appeal" approach as detailed in Chap. 5, which requires officers to be in relatively close proximity to the armed person, nor was there mention of the 550-metre effective range of the new rifle, important, no doubt on a battlefield, but less so in policing. As the data revealed, the longest distance over which a Bushmaster was used to shoot someone was 40–45 metres, with the median distance being 15–16 metres, from 20 years of actual shooting data.

The author, following the above revelations, considered that the defence minister may well have had a valid point when he questioned whether the Police were "... inappropriately armed against members of the public" (Dynon, 2020). That view was reinforced when considering the data on what weapons Police confronted in actual shootings. Only 6 out of 42 were rifles. The majority of weapons faced were bladed or clubbing weapons ($n = 14$), shotguns ($n = 11$) or replica/imitation/airguns ($n = 6$), with just four being handguns (note: one man presented a cellular phone).

Does that mean Police do not need a rifle? Is it sufficient for them to have just a Glock pistol? Again, referring back to the data on fatal and non-fatal shootings, and focusing on Level 1 responders, the author believes a Glock pistol (effective range 50 metres) is not, by itself, sufficient for all situations where an officer may be required to use lethal force.

The majority of Glock involved shootings ($n = 16$) happened between 1 and 7 metres. However, three Glock shootings happened over distances ranging from 10 to 30 metres. The data reveals Glock pistols proved themselves extremely effective over shorter ranges and when small numbers of bullets were fired. But, in the hands of a Level 1 response officer, with only the required district-based PITT and enhanced training under their belt, using a Glock pistol over ranges exceeding 7–10 metres creates risk. The data revealed that in four shootings involving the Glock, over distances ranging from 7 out to 30 metres, 35.5% of shots hit the intended target ($n = 11$), while 64.5% missed ($n = 20$).

Pistols have inherent limitations in accuracy over longer distances due to their short barrels. As Marshall and Shuey reported back in 2001 (see Chap. 6), the Glock pistol has its place in policing, but should be considered "... a secondary form of self defence ..." (Marshall & Shuey, 2001, p. 31).

Therefore, are there accurate, but potentially less risky, alternative longer-barrelled firearms that could suit a Police role? The author considered there are probably any number that could be considered and commented upon, but for this work, he has chosen to focus on one example, as – just that – an example and because it is already in the New Zealand Police inventory. It is a weapon favoured by a number of European police services, including the Norwegian Police whose vehicle-based deployment model New Zealand Police followed. The weapon is the 9 mm Heckler & Koch, MP5, sub-machine gun.

In his publication about the carbines and rifles used by the New Zealand Police, John Osborne (Osborne, 1990, p. 21), described the MP5 as "… very accurate" and in service with the (West) German police since 1966. He noted the MP5 was selected for use by the New Zealand Police ATS in 1983, and updated versions were later introduced in 1989.

On the Heckler-Koch website, in the military and law enforcement category, the MP5 is marketed as "[t]remendously reliable, with maximum safety for the user, easy to handle, modular, extremely accurate and extraordinarily easy to control when firing – HK features that are particularly appreciated by security forces and military users worldwide" (Heckler-Koch, 2021), marketing "hype" perhaps. Commentary from users of the MP5, in various internet videos, confirmed the gun was an easy-to-use and accurate weapon.

The technical data for the weapon, from a weapons-focused website, (Weaponsystems.net, 2021), and supported by other Internet commentary from users of the MP5 reviewed by the author, identified the maximum effective range for the gun is at between 150–200 metres, with users/commentators firming on 100 metres as the "accurate/effective distance" for use. Well within the needed range (based on the empirical data) for a Police, longer-barrelled, Level 1 responder weapon[3]. The gun can use a 15-, 20- or 30-round capacity magazine. It is compact, light and suitable, it would seem, for "smaller-built" officers. While also marketed for military use, the author contends that the weapon does not look like a traditional military assault rifle, in the way the Bushmaster does.

The MP5 does not completely address the issue of misses and the travel of a bullet that has missed. But, it is known to be an accurate, easily used and compact longer-barrelled weapon that could fulfill the requirements of a police service wishing to provide a longer-range weapon to compliment the pistol, effectively doubling or tripling the range over which a Level 1 responder could engage an armed person.

Given the MP5's relative compactness (delivered through a telescoping stock), consideration could even be given to securely mounting the weapon inside the passenger compartment of operational Police vehicles, in order to overcome the current inability of officers to access the Bushmaster without first accessing the luggage compartment of their vehicles.

[3] To help the reader envisage what 150–200 m looks like, a rugby field has a playing area that is 100 m long and 70 m wide. So, the marketed effective range is between 1 1/2 and 2 rugby fields in length.

But, this was just an example, and it is not intended to turn the section into a weapons forum, simply to confirm that missed shots are an issue, so is the actual distance people are engaged over, and finally, the appearance of a rifle that is based, almost without distinction, on a military firearm.

Did any other "militarisation" matters come to light during the research? Two that did are worthy of mention. Within the data, they were not issues that led directly to any increase in shootings by Police, but they have, in the author's opinion, potential to, or to at least impact in the area of the "justification trap" mentioned earlier.

First is the use of the STG as first-line responders to situations that would have previously attracted AOS personnel and associated with it the use of the "militarised" STG (weapons, titles and tactics).

STG was formed to combat organised terrorism at a time when that phenomenon was quite foreign and abstract to the people of Aotearoa New Zealand. Over time they morphed into a more specialised "all-rounder" capability to respond to a variety of challenging situations. However, the underlying firearms training and tactics did not change. They were there for the "heavy" jobs, those beyond even AOS skill sets. Such events happen very rarely, even today, in Aotearoa New Zealand, thankfully.

The vast majority of uses of lethal force by New Zealand Police involve "traditional" situations and people with crises in their lives, with mental health issues, with addictions, with crimes gone wrong or with a combination of all of those situations. None of the 43 shootings reviewed in the data – from over 20 years – involved extremists focused on doing the maximum amoun of harm to society before they could escape or give their life in the cause of their fanaticism.[4] They were really somewhat ordinary people for the most part, who had for the reasons stated step over an invisible line into the extraordinary.

Undoubtedly, terrorism and extremism and major acts of harm are a reality of the world we live in. Aotearoa New Zealand has seen two cases in the past 3 years of such people, its authorities have thwarted or deterred others (see (Police intervened in two potential mass shootings within weeks of March 15, counter-terrorism hui hears, 2021). Aramoana and Napier also witnessed extreme events linked to firearms use. There is a place for the STG, their weapons, their skills and their tactics; the question is about whether that is in responding to every-day situations where constabulary powers and tactics are needed as opposed to militarily-trained and equipped "operators"?

The "mission creep" (for want of a more appropriate term) of STG from a highly trained in-reserve capability into an everyday response element of New Zealand Police has happened over 40 years, accelerating from 2003 onwards when the group was made a full-time entity within New Zealand Police (New Zealand Police, 2016). That same timeframe saw the cost of maintaining the group increase "thirty-fold" by 2018, costing the taxpayer NZ$6.2 million annually (Tso, 2018). It is perhaps

[4] It is acknowledged that in 2021, a man was shot and killed by STG when he went on a stabbing rampage in an Auckland supermarket. Early reporting of that event did characterise it as a terrorist activity. No IPCA reporting has yet been released to enable further consideration of the motivation(s) that underpinned the action.

understandable that Police would want to maximise the return on such an investment; however, the author thinks the greater use of the STG and its weapons and tactics may have come about much more subtly than via an informed policy decision on how lethal force capability should be deployed day-by-day.

Such an incremental "mission creep" may well have arisen, in the author's view, from the administrative situation that sees the STG members in the three cities that host the group still being considered members of the wider local AOS teams. Thus, if AOS is activated, the STG members also respond, and – since 2003 – if the STG members happen to be working a rostered-on duty, they will inevitably arrive more quickly at an emergency call out than their part-time AOS colleagues.

While it takes a Police executive-level authority for STG "operators" to deploy as the STG, it just requires a standard AOS activation for STG "operators" to be on the streets, armed with STG weapons, and all the while trained in military style tactics, responding to what may be a mental health crisis or an armed criminal who's been intercepted by other police staff. The author is not convinced, as earlier stated, that that scenario is a policy decision.

As is often the case with any issue, none of this is a problem, until it is. To highlight this issue and how military training and attitudes towards overwhelming firepower and aggression may permeate into civilian policing, an anecdote from the author's time as an armed officer comes to mind to help illustrate the point and provide a foundation for the commentary to follow.

It arose in the mid-1980s when he worked as an armed Personal Protection Officer guarding, amongst others, the country's prime minister and visiting VIPs. The unit he worked with contacted the NZ Special Air Service (NZSAS) squadron and asked for advice on how to best respond to an armed attack on a VIP vehicle convoy. A short while later, the NZSAS invited the Police unit, including the author, to a demonstration at one of their purpose-built shooting ranges.

The demonstration involved a car with four NZSAS troopers driving onto the range to simulate the lead protection car in a VIP convoy. As it approached "hostile" targets set up in front of it, live gunfire erupted from inside the vehicle as the front-seat passenger and one of the rear-seat passengers began firing through the windscreen at the targets. The troopers then all exited the vehicle while continuing to put down heavy live-fire onto the targets – with precision magazine changes when necessary – using the car body as cover. They then re-entered the car, still firing, and reversed out of the "ambush" – still firing from within the car – and drove off the range having, no doubt, allowed the rest of the imaginary VIP convoy to safely depart under the cover of their hailstorm of gunfire.

The senior NZSAS trooper who had organised the display then turned to the group of stunned police officers and simply said "That's how we'd do it." The watching police officers were silent and very impressed with the skills on display. However, they acknowledged to each other later that they would never be permitted to train with live ammunition in the manner shown, nor to promote such aggressive tactics, irrespective of them being what was in fact needed in an aggressive armed ambush scenario (Author's personal knowledge and experience).

The NZSAS demonstration to Police, described above, was neither new nor rare. The NZSAS were actively involved in helping NZP establish the ATS in the late 1970s and in training them on through until the present day when it is known as the STG, particularly with close quarter battle (CQB) inside buildings and aircraft and with sniper training to specialist officers. The training may also extend to surveillance and observation skills which are also a speciality of the STG (Author' knowledge) (New Zealand Police, 2016).

Very similar aggressive, some might posit militarised, tactics have now been on display on the streets of Aotearoa New Zealand, for example, when three STG "operators" entered into a pursuit of two armed criminals on a busy Auckland motorway and proceeded to fire on the criminals from a moving police vehicle, once by firing directly through the windscreen of the police vehicle (see the IPCA report (2021) for the Non-fatal Police shooting on motorway north of Auckland). Furthermore, in two separate incidents (one in Taranaki and the other in Tauranga, on Te Ika-a-Māui), STG officers used the "head shot" (instant incapacitation shot) technique to kill two men who had been holding hostages (one his ex-partner, the other his own children) (Independent Police Conduct Authority, 2014) (Independent Police Conduct Authority, 2020). The technique, as discussed elsewhere in this work, was developed to instantly incapacitate suicide bombers, active terrorists or those protected by body armour and running amok.

As with all the other shootings, these were all determined by the Authority as justified, but the author does ponder what might have been the outcome, if, for example, in the pursuit shooting, the Police shots had resulted in a dead bystander or in an uncontrolled crash of the criminal's fast-moving getaway car on a busy motorway. In the author's policing experience, the tactics used in all of those incidents were not typically those of the AOS or of Level 1 responders.

To close out the observations regarding the STG, the final remarks regarding their militarisation concerns the use of the term "operator" to describe police officers performing policing tasks in a country that prides itself on having a community-focused police service.

The term "operator" was, in the author's understanding, first coined by military units operating under the "special forces" banner, around the world. It was then picked up by policing agencies as a way of distinguishing their own "special forces" officers and, in the New Zealand Police case, to provide a designation level that could attract additional remuneration/allowances for skills and risk. It is not used, as far as the author knows, by the AOS. Their members still hold the ranks of sergeant and constable (or more senior ranks).

In the UK, for example, it appears the term is not used by Police. There, for example, the Metropolitan Police Service (MPS) in London, use terms like:

- … Counter Terrorism Specialist Firearms Officers each team consists of Inspectors, Sergeants and Constables
- Firearms Training Team each team consists of Inspectors, Sergeants, Constables and Band P police Staff
- Specialist Firearms Commanders – Superintendent rank

- Tactical Firearms Commanders – Inspector rank … (Metropolitan Police Service, 2021)

The New Zealand Police "Appropriate Tactical Settings" briefing (New Zealand Police, 2021a, pp. 39–40) also confirmed the Police in England, Wales and Scotland also use the term "Authorised Firearms Officer" (AFO) as the technical skill title for a police officer trained and authorised to use firearms.

The term "operator" does not appear within the MPS or wider UK policing lexicon. They apply a technical skill label and beyond that continue to refer to members of those units using standard Police ranks (i.e. constable and sergeant).

It is the author's view that its usefulness in the New Zealand Police specialist ecosystem is questionable, particularly if the organisation wishes to avoid "militarisation" and its potential impact when it comes to Police shootings and the 'justification trap' that could ensnare the service. Specialist role titles, such as those used by the MPS, aligned with the standard Police ranks, would – it is argued – help to demilitarise the STG and, hopefully, help ground the police officers involved in their organisation and its civilian ethos avoiding the potential for an elitist mindset developing. For example, see the IPCA report into the shooting by STG of Antony Ratahi, where the STG officer who fired the fatal shot stated "… we are an *elite squad* which trains full time for hostage rescues situations and other high risk jobs …" (Italics added) (Independent Police Conduct Authority, 2014, p. 42).

The second issue is the aggressiveness of police tactics. Coupled with the aggressiveness already recounted above is a second incident that occurred in the city of Tauranga.

An armed man was being sought in relation to the murder of two people. Two marked Police patrol cars, each containing two uniformed AOS officers, were deployed in a "reassurance" capacity during the hunt (but giving the author the distinct impression of them being Armed Response Vehicles). On the evening on which the shooting occurred, the AOS officers located the wanted man driving a car and gave chase. The man, by the name of Anthony Fane, was armed, and he used his weapon(s) to "… fire shots at them [Police] on numerous occasions while driving …"; furthermore, on one occasion he stopped his car "… got out … and fired directly at the officers (who were still in their cars)" (Independent Police Conduct Authority, 2021b, p. 1); however, the police officers did not return fire (and were not injured), and the pursuit continued (ibid.).

Finally, as the IPCA report records, on a section of state highway, the armed man stopped his car and remained sitting inside it. The following commentary is taken directly from the IPCA public report:

> … Officer B stopped the lead Police car approximately ten metres behind the [armed man's car], and slightly to the right. The second Police car stopped directly behind the [armed man's car], five to ten metres to its rear. Officer F stopped a distance back from the AOS officers' Police cars and parked across the lanes to block the road from incoming traffic.
>
> Officer C, the passenger of the lead car, fired one round at Mr Fane (who was in the driver's seat) through the windscreen of the Police car with his rifle, then leaned out of his window and fired more rounds in Mr Fane's direction. Officer D, the passenger in the second Police car, got out of the car. He positioned himself between the tow ball and left edge of the [armed man's car], and fired rounds with his rifle, at Mr Fane, through the

> back windscreen. When Officer C saw Officer D shooting, he stopped, as he considered Officer D had a better angle to shoot at Mr Fane.
>
> Officer D stopped firing when he saw Mr Fane slump to the side, which signalled to him that Mr Fane was incapacitated. Officer C also saw this. Neither of them were aware of how many rounds they had fired, or how long they were firing for. An examination of Officers C and D's magazines after the fact showed that Officer C discharged 27 rounds and Officer D discharged 22. (ibid., p. 4)

No information was contained in the IPCA report to indicate how many of the 49 bullets fired hit Fane. He was, however, killed by the gunfire. The Authority went on to comment that the firing of a shot through the windscreen of the Police car was not done in accordance with any policy, as there was no policy covering that tactic nor was the tactic one that was the subject of training by Police (Independent Police Conduct Authority, 2021b, p. 7).

The Authority ruled the shooting was justified. The Authority made no comment about the number of shots Police fired, other than to confirm the police officers had been fired at on five different occasions (ibid., p. 5). The 9-page long report did not provide details on what sort of firearm Fane was armed with and using; however, a Stuff news report regarding the earlier homicides stated Fane and his accomplice, his brother, had a "… shotgun and a sawn-off .22" when they committed the double murder Fane was being sought for (Bathgate, 2021); it may be that one or both of those weapons were in his possession when he was shot. Fane was also implicated in the killing of his partner 2 days before the double homicide, believing she was having an affair with one of the men killed. On that occasion Fane used a crossbow to commit his crime (Bathgate, 2021).

The author was stunned to read that 49 shots had been fired by the two officers. The AOS rifle is a semi-automatic weapon and so requires a deliberate trigger-pull each time an officer wishes to fire. That's 49 separate trigger-pulls in total and over 20 for each officer. He was also surprised to read that one shot had been fired through the windscreen of the Police vehicle and that no attempt had been made to position the Police vehicles further back, given all the AOS were armed with Bushmaster rifles with an effective range of at least 500 metres.

The author was further surprised to learn that no effort had been made to communicate with Fane before the salvo of shots had been fired at him.

Fane was clearly a violent, armed and dangerous man with, what some may describe, as little to lose. He had already killed three people (although at that time Police only suspected him of being responsible for two deaths), and no doubt appreciated he faced a lifetime in prison if convicted of the crimes he was responsible for, and – it must be remembered – he had fired shots at Police on at least five occasions during the pursuit. But, when he stopped, finally, Police officers closed to within, in the author's opinion, a surprisingly close range, and then delivered a staggering salvo of rounds at him inside the car.

Did Police know for certain that there was no one else in the car with Fane – willingly or unwillingly –when they shot him? They didn't know a dog was. Fane's dog was discovered, unharmed, in the car the next day when Police were examining the scene in daylight. Unfortunately, the IPCA report is silent on this question, if it was in fact asked.

It is the author's opinion that the event displayed a military-style "overwhelming firepower" tactic in bringing to an end Fane's actions, not a traditional Police "cordon, contain, appeal, arrest or respond" approach.

The Authority determined the shooting to be justified. That is the end of the matter. The author does not seek to challenge the Authority's finding. But, once again, the author does refer to the "justification trap" and acknowledge Fane was a man who may have engendered no public sympathy.

That concludes the observations the author felt compelled to make regarding the research and his views arising from it, with the exception of three elements that will be incorporated into the next chapter of this work. Those matters concern the IPCA, Police policy, practice and governance and use of force legal requirements.

Bibliography

Bathgate, B. (2021, July 30). *'Coward' double murderer sentenced to minimum of 17 years imprisonment.* Retrieved from stuff.co.nz: https://www.stuff.co.nz/national/125914732/coward-double-murderer-sentenced-to-minimum-of-17-years-imprisonment

College of Policing. (2021, March 25). *Armed policing discharge of firearms.* Retrieved from app.college.police.uk: https://www.app.college.police.uk/app-content/armed-policing/armed-deployment/discharge-of-firearms/#critical-shot

Corlett, E. (2021, September 3). *Man Shot dead in New Zealand after 'terrorist attack' in Auckland that injured five.* Retrieved from theguardian.com.au: https://www.theguardian.com.au/Man Shot dead in New Zealand after 'terrorist attack' in Auckland that injured five

Delaforce, R. (2019). The Expanding Security Gap: Australian Gendarmes and Policing. *Salus Journal*, 20–41.

Dror, I. E. (2007, September 24). Perception of risk and the decision to use force. *Policing*, 265–272.

Dynon, N. (2020). *ARTs and the myth of the unarmed police officer.* Retrieved from defsecmedia.co.nz: http://defsecmedia.co.nz

Elliott, J. K. (2019, March 15). *New Zealand shooter covered weapons with names of Canada's Alexandre Bissonnette, other killers.* Retrieved from globalnews.ca: https://globalnews.ca/news/5059136/christchurch-shooter-guns-names-new-zealand/

en.wikipedia.org. (2021, October 19). *Special Tactics Group.* Retrieved from en.wikipedia.org: https://en.wikipedia.org/wiki/Special_Tactics_Group

Funnell, A. (2019, September 20). *Why the creeping militarisation of our police has experts worreid.* Retrieved from abc.net.au: https://www.abc.net.au/news/2019-09-20/creeping-militarisation-of-police-why-experts-are-concerned/11517266

Heckler-Koch. (2021, October 19). *MP5 The most popular submachine gun.* Retrieved from heckler-koch.com: https://www.heckler-koch.com/en/products/military/submachine-guns/mp5/mp5/overview.html

Home Office. (2020, March). *Police use of firearms statistics England and Wales: April 2019 to March 2020.* Retrieved from assets.publishing.service.gov.uk: https://assets.publishing.service.gov.uk/government/uploads/system/uploads/attachment_data/file/907015/police-use-firearms-statistics-england-and-wales-april-2019-to-march-2020-hosb2120.pdf

Independent Police Conduct Authority. (2012). *Police shooting of Halatau Ki'anamanu Naitoko.* Independent Police Conduct Authority.

Independent Police Conduct Authority. (2014). *Fatal Police shooting of Antony Ratahi*. Independent Police Conduct Authority.

Independent Police Conduct Authority. (2016). *Fatal Police shooting of Pera Smiler in Upper Hutt*. Independent Police Conduct Authority.

Independent Police Conduct Authority. (2017). *Fatal Police shooting of Shargin Stephens in Rotorua*. Independent Police Conduct Authority.

Independent Police Conduct Authority. (2019). *Fatal shooting of Jerrim Toms*. Independent Police Conduct Authority.

Independent Police Conduct Authority. (2020). *Tauranga shooting of a man in defence of hostages justified*. Independent Police Conduct Authority.

Independent Police Conduct Authority. (2021a). *Non-fatal Police shooting on motorway north of Auckland justified*. Independent Police Conduct Authority.

Independent Police Conduct Authority. (2021b). *Use of force during fatal shooting in Tauranga justified*. Independent Police Conduct Authority.

Lohr, S. (1988, September 18). *British Commandos Testify on Gibraltar.* Retrieved from nytimes.com: https://www.nytimes.com/1988/09/18/world/british-commandos-testify-on-gibraltar.html

Mackenzie, S., Bradley, T., & Lindsay, A. (2019, October 24). *Cops with guns will make us less safe.*. Retrieved from newsroom.co.nz: https://www.newsroom.co.nz/ideasroom/cops-with-guns-will-make-us-less-safe

Marshall, P. B., & Shuey, R. N. (2001). *A strategic evaluation of the New Zealand police position concerning the use of force when responding to potentially violent situations – A review of best practice, policy and training*. New Zealand Police.

Metropolitan Police Service. (2021, October 19). *Freedom of Information Request Reference No: 01.FOI.19.012737.* Retrieved from met.police.uk: https://www.met.police.uk/SysSiteAssets/foi-media/metropolitan-police/disclosure_2020/february_2020/information-rights-unit%2D%2D-organisational-structure-mo19?__cf_chl_captcha_tk__=pmd_H0nOGXUKVFfx82A50vn77FgO_KksfY8Gapssc8DRsGY-1634621228-0-gqNtZGzNA7ujcnBs

New Zealand Government. (2019, March 21). *New Zealand bans military style semi-automatics and assault rifles.* Retrieved from beehive.govt.nz: https://www.beehive.govt.nz/release/new-zealand-bans-military-style-semi-automatics-and-assault-rifles

New Zealand Police. (2005, May 19). *Replacement due for police rifles.* Retrieved from police.govt.nz: https://www.police.govt.nz/home/news/replacementdueforpolicerifles

New Zealand Police. (2016, December). *Inside the STG.* Retrieved from ten.one.police.govt.nz: http://www.ten-one.police.govt.nz/tenone/December2016National6.htm

New Zealand Police. (2019). *NZ Police tactical options research report 2018 #7.* Retrieved from police.govt.nz: https://www.police.govt.nz/home/aboutus/publicationsandstatistics/tacticaloptionsreports

New Zealand Police. (2020, May 19). *Tactical options research reports.* Retrieved from police.govt.nz: https://www.police.govt.nz/home/aboutus/publicationsandstatistics/tacticaloptionsresearchreports

New Zealand Police. (2021a). *Appropriate tactical settings insights and evidence brief.* New Zealand Police.

New Zealand Police. (2021b, February 19). *Police Operation to prevent firearms-related violence.* Retrieved from police.govt.nz: https://www.police.govt.nz/news/release/police-operation-prevent-firearms-related-violence

New Zealand Police. (2021c, November 9). Reference: IR-01-21-30907. *Written response to Official Information Act Request*. New Zealand Police.

New Zealand Police. (2021d). *Armed response team trial evaluation report*. New Zealand Police Evidenced Based Policing Centre.

New Zealand Police. (2021e, September 22). *Improving the safety and capability of frontline Police.* Retrieved from police.govt.nz: https://www.polic.govt.nz/home/new/improvingthesafetyandcapabilityoffrontlinePolice

New Zealand Police. ((unknown)). *TENR-Operational threat assessment.* New Zealand Police.

New Zealand Police Association. (2019, June 7). *Aiming for accurate gun data.* Retrieved from nzpa.org.nz: https://www.policeassn.org.nz/news/aiming-for-accurate-gun-data

Nolan, T. (2020, June 2). *Militarization has forstered a policing culture that sets up protestors as 'the enemy'.* Retrieved from theconversation.com: https://theconversation.com/militarization-has-fostered-a-policing-culture-that-sets-up-protesters-as-the-enemy-139727

Office of Police Integrity. (2021, September 5). *Review of the use of force by and against Victorian police.* Retrieved from ibac.vic.gov.au: https://www.ibac.vic.gov.au/docs/default-source/reviews/opi/review-of-the-use-of-force-by-and-against-victorian-police%2D%2D-july-2009.pdf?sfvrsn=c4586175_8

Osborne, J. (1990). *Carbines and Police in New Zealand 1840–1990.* South Pacific Armoury.

Police Complaints Authority. (2006). *Report of the police complaints authority into the fatal shooting of Haidar Ebbadi Mahdi at Auckland on 14 August 2004.* Police Complaints Authority.

Police intervened in two potential mass shootings within weeks of March 15, counter-terrorism hui hears. (2021, June 15). Retrieved from stuff.co.nz: https://www.stuff.co.nz/national/politics/125443202/police-intervened-in-two-potential-mass-shootings-within-weeks-of-march-15-counterterrorism-hui-hears

Sarre, R. (2019, November 13). If Australian police officers are allowed to shoot to kill, the should be better trained. *The Conversation.* Australia: The Conversation.

Shortt, R. (2000). *"Are the New Zealand police on target?" An investigation of alternative models of police response to dangerous and unlawful firearms incidents.* Victoria University of Wellington.

Shortt, R. S. (2015). *Intelligence meets enforcement: Policy and practice benchmarks from a comparison of approaches in Denmark, Finland and New Zealand.* Charles Sturt University, Australia.

Springvale Monash Legal Service Incorporated. (2005). *Police training and mental Illness – A time for change.* Springvale Monash Legal Service Incorporated.

Squires, P. (2015, July 22). *The catalogue of errors that killed Jean Charles de Menezes.* Retrieved from theconversation.com: https://theconversation.com/the-catalogue-of-errors-that-killed-jean-charles-de-menezes-45011

Squires, P., & Kennison, P. (2010). *Shooting to kill? Policing, firearms and armed response.* John Wiley & Sons.

Statistics New Zealand. (2019, September 23). *New Zealand's population reflects growing diversity..* Retrieved from stats.govt.nz: https://www.stats.govt.nz/news/new-zealands-population-reflects-growing-diversity

Strang, B. (2021, March 15). *Rise in gun crime despite government clampdown after terror attack.* Retrieved from rnz.co.nz: https://www.rnz.co.nz/news/national/438377/rise-in-gun-crime-despite-government-clampdown-after-terror-attack

Stuff.co.nz. (2020, February 17). *Police name man shot dead after firing at officers during Tauranga pursuit.* Retrieved from stuff.co.nz: https://www.stuff.co.nz/national/119591867/police-name-man-shot-dead-in-tauranga-pursuit

stuff.co.nz. (2021, January 22). *Government set to roll out fresh firearms buy-back scheme.* Retrieved from stuff.co.nz: https://www.stuff.co.nz/national/124028255/government-set-to-roll-out-fresh-firearms-buyback-scheme

TeAo–MaoriNews.(2021,March23).*FatalpoliceshootingofTaurangaman 'justified'.*Retrievedfrom teaomaori.news: https://www.teaomaori.news/fatal-police-shooting-tauranga-man-justified

The Guardian. (2021a, October 9). *I was trying to talk to her police officer tells court of moments before indigenous woman was shot dead.* Retrieved from theguardian.com: https://www.theguardian.com/australia-news/2021/oct/08/i-was-trying-to-talk-to-her-police-officer-tells-court-of-moments-before-indigenous-woman-was-shot-dead?CMP=Share_iOSApp_Other

The Guardian. (2021b, September 11). *Zachary Rolfe case further delay to NT police officers trial.* Retrieved from theguardian.com: https://www.theguardian.com/australia-news/2021/sep/10/zachary-rolfe-case-further-delay-to-nt-police-officers-trial?CMP=Share_iOSApp_Other

The Guardian. (2021c, July 6). *'We say it's a racial paradise': How two police killings are dividing Hawaii.* Retrieved from thguardian.com: https://www.theguardian.com/us-news/2021/jul/05/honolulu-police-killings-hawaii?CMP=Share_iOSApp_Other

The Guardian. (2021d, May 18). *The FBI is supposed to track how police use force – Years later, it falling well short.* Retrieved from theguardian.com: https://www.theguardian.com/us-news/2021/may/17/fbi-police-use-of-force-data-records?CMP=Share_iOSApp_Other

Tso, M. (2018, December 23). *New Zealand Police anti-terrorist unit costs taxpayers $6.2 million.* Retrieved from stuff.co.nz.

Weaponsystems.net. (2021, October 19). *Heckler & Koch MP%.* Retrieved from Weaponsystems.net: https://weaponsystems.net/system/227-Heckler+%26+Koch+MP5

White, V. (2019, November 4). *The 'militarisation' of Australia's police: Another view.* Retrieved from www.aspistrategist.org.au: https://www.aspistrategist.org.au/The'militarisation'ofAustralia'spolice:anotherview

Chapter 11
Use of Lethal Force Law, Governance, Policy and Procedure

As mentioned in the previous chapter, some of the observations from the research relate to the IPCA, Police and the legal aspects of using lethal force, and, while Chap. 10 dealt with what might be considered the "hard" side of lethal force observations, this chapter will focus on the "soft" side, in three specific areas:

- Independent Police Conduct Authority
- Police policy, practice and governance
- Use of lethal force legal matter

Independent Police Conduct Authority

The legislated functions of the IPCA, under its Act (New Zealand Government, 2021), when it comes to the use of lethal force, state:

> **12 Functions of Authority** …
>
> (1) (b) to investigate of its own motion, where it is satisfied that there are reasonable grounds to carry out an investigation in the public interest, any incident involving death or serious bodily harm notified to the Authority by the Commissioner under section 13. (bidi.)

And, to refresh the readers mind regarding Chapter 3, section 13 of the IPCA Act requires:

> **13 Duty of Commissioner to notify Authority of certain incidents involving death or serious bodily harm**
>
> Where a Police employee acting in the execution of his or her duty causes, or appears to have caused, death or serious bodily harm to any person, the Commissioner shall as soon as practicable give to the Authority a written notice setting out particulars of the incident in which the death or serious bodily harm was caused. (New Zealand Government, 2021)

It is the author's view that there is one substantial fact and two steps that must exist for s. 12 of the Act to be activated and for an independent investigation to be undertaken. The substantial fact is that *death or serious bodily injury* must have occurred. The first of the two steps is the commissioner of police *notifying the Authority*, while the second step is the Authority being *satisfied there are reasonable grounds* to carry out an investigation in the public interest.

R. S. Shortt, *Lethal Force and New Zealand Police*,
https://doi.org/10.1007/978-3-031-05269-9_11

When it comes to the view the IPCA has of itself, and the role it plays in society, the organisation describes itself on its website as an integral part of the Aotearoa New Zealand justice sector with the important role of contributing to the "protect[ion] of citizens against … excessive force, improving Police practice and policy … enhance[ing] public trust and confidence in the justice system and contribut[ing] towards the justice sector outcomes of a safe and just society" (Independent Police Conduct Authority, 2021).

To achieve the legislated functions and role outcome stated above, the IPCA must be seen by the public to be both independent and capable of carrying out thorough investigations. It must also, the author posits, be seen to be involved on every occasion a police officer uses lethal force against, or takes the life of, or seriously injures, a citizen. To not be involved in all three of those circumstances leaves a gap that is troubling and difficult to explain.

Why, therefore, is the *taking* of a life, or the *causing* of a serious injury, more important than either the *trying* to take a life or *trying* to cause serious injury? Imagine if you can, for example, the Police only agreeing to investigate successful homicides, but leaving attempted homicides, where no death or injuries results, outside their purview. Such a situation would simply defy explanation.

To be clear, the author does not doubt that every death or instance of serious bodily harm is communicated to the Authority; however, the Authority is then permitted by law to determine that reasonable grounds do not exist for an independent investigation. That does not sit well with the author either, given the country does not have a death penalty, and enshrines the right to life in its Bill of Rights legislation. In theory, at least, some deaths or serious injuries may not pass the test the Authority is obliged to apply. Therefore, some deaths by "an instrument of the Crown" (Police) may not be subjected to independent investigation and consideration. For example, between 2000 and 2019, Police used lethal force on 61 occasions (using the author's definition that includes missed shots), but only 43 PCA/IPCA reports could be located. Potentially, 18 uses of lethal force were either not investigated independently or the author failed to find those reports.

Furthermore, as previously discussed in this work, the likelihood of an independent investigation into the use of lethal force is premised solidly on the laws of physics regarding gunfire and not on the *intent* of a police officer who deliberately points a loaded firearm at another person and fires it.

Notification of missed shots may indeed still happen under the Memorandum of Understanding existing between the Police and the Authority, if there was "reputational risk" or "corruption" involved (refer to Chap. 3 for further detail). It is suspected, however, that in a situation involving Police shooting but missing, reputational risk would only arise if someone is, or becomes, aware of the event and makes it public – a journalist, for example. And, given the discretion the Authority has to determine if an investigation is warranted or not, a missed shot(s) may well fall outside an overworked and under-pressure investigative entity's priority list (for further detail refer to Chap. 3).

The scenario raised translates into the reality that over the period 2001–2020, there were 12 instances of Police shooting at a person – what the author considers use of lethal force – that may not have been referred to the Authority, or considered for investigation by the IPCA, because they were missed shots. That equates to 18% of instances where police officers shot at a person, out of the total 66 instances recorded in New Zealand Police statistics for the period. Perhaps, lawmakers in Aotearoa New Zealand never envisaged that Police would miss.

The IPCA legislation does not define lethal force (nor, interestingly, does the *Policing Act 2008* (NZL), or New Zealand Police policy, procedures or instructions); the Act simply speaks of death or serious bodily injury. That, in the author's opinion, is at best an untidy situation, perhaps even unintentional, and should be rectified if the Authority's view of itself and its role is to be fulfilled to the greatest possibly degree regarding such an important issue.

Associated with the situation outlined above is the legislation that covers the activities of the New Zealand Police, and – as will be discussed below in greater detail – the suggested need for a consolidated record of Police uses of lethal force that is comprehensive, up-to-date and easily accessed.

Police Policy, Practice and Governance

The research demonstrates that the New Zealand Police has an extensive ecosystem of policy statements, procedural requirements, instructions concerning the use of lethal force and the deployment of firearms. The rules, while quite wordy and abundant, are also backed up by the two decision-making models – the TENR and TOF assessment tools – both described elsewhere in the book. In effect, the author sees these rules as those that Professor Sarre wrote of when he mentioned "the rules that pertain to the use of lethal force" (Sarre, 2019).

Furthermore, Police, in a democratic, rule-of-law country like Aotearoa New Zealand, are given quite extraordinary powers to enable them to fulfill the functions expected of them under the *Policing Act 2008* (NZL). Those powers include the ability to detain and deprive citizens of their liberty, to use physical force when required, to enter and search premises (in rare instances without first obtaining a warrant from a judicial authority) and to search a person (sometime also without first obtaining a warrant). However, the most extreme power is use of lethal force.

What the author considers lacking in the diverse ecosystem of Police rules is a simple, clear, statement about the use of lethal force and what lethal force is. It is the author's contention that it is almost as if Police wish to avoid the need to confront the issue of taking a life by wrapping the reality in words and phrases such as "active resistance"; "high degree of force"; "firearms and other force with serious implications"; "… cannot reasonably protect themselves, or others, in a less violent manner" or' "incapacitate" and "neutralise" (see Chaps. 5 and 10 for additional commentary).

What is being avoided with such phrases and words is the fact that at one end of the use of force continuum is the use of lethal force.

In the environment of policing, lethal force principally involves the aiming and firing of a Police firearm mostly, but not exclusively. For example, a Police baton could inflict a lethal injury (as tragically shown in the 1990 murder of Senior Constable Peter Umbers), as could a Police vehicle or even a physical hold, such as the "chokehold" or "carotid hold", both of which have come in for commentary concerning use of force that turns lethal. For example, see "Half of the nation's largest police departments have banned or limited neck restraints since June" (Washington Post, 2021).

No doubt, legal minds might argue that the *Crimes Act 1961* (NZL) provides sufficient definition of such force when it comes to determining death, serious injury or grievous bodily harm, for instance. However, from a policing and public perspective, the author contends it would be useful to provide a definition and to link it unmistakably to the oversight role of the IPCA.

It is the author's view that the act of intentionally firing a firearm at another person – given the training police officers get to aim for the centre mass (torso) of a person or to shoot at the head if they desire to inflict an immediate 'incapacitation' injury – confirms the firearm as the most often used, and most likely weapon, to *intentionally* apply lethal force. The substantive and unique issue associated with the use of a Police firearm – regardless of the outcome – is that the intention is to "incapacitate" or "neutralise" (or, put another way, to kill or injure) to such a degree that the person is incapable of posing a threat to the Police, the public or some other person closely involved with the person shot (i.e. a hostage).

That situation leads to the author's suggestion that the Police ecosystem concerning the use of force would benefit from being more explicit about what occurs at the extreme – "last resort" – end of the continuum. Alongside the development and inclusion of a lethal force definition within Police comes a second suggestion concerning the organisation's desired strategic outcome for all situations where use of force is used.

Here the author would suggest something along the lines of modifying the current Police statement "maximise safety; minimise risk" to include the words "for everyone involved". Those words are just a suggestion to illustrate the point and to identify that everyone in a situation where Police resort to the use of force – police officers, the public and the person being policed – deserves maximum safety and minimal risk and that any subsequent review of such engagements should also focus on how well those two maxims were addressed by the officers involved.

What difference would such a statement make and why have one? It is the author's argument that it would set the organisational tone and expectation regarding the use of force. In essence it could be considered the organisational philosophy on use of force.

An international example of such a statement was the one Victorian Police introduced and reproduced here from a report into Victoria Police's use of force by the Office of Police Integrity in Victoria (Australia) *Invalid source specified*:

> [t]he success of an operation will primarily be judged by the extent to which the use of force is avoided or minimised. (ibid., p. 9)

That statement was applied to the Victoria Police after "Project Beacon" which was conducted in 1995, "... following 29 fatal shootings by police between 1987 and

1994"[1] (ibid.) and was described at the time as being "... innovative and nation-leading ..." (ibid.). Unfortunately, Victoria Police were to be described in 2005, during an Office of Police Integrity review of fatal shootings, as having:

> ... lost some of the strategic focus on safety and avoiding the use of force which it developed during Project Beacon .... (ibid.)

Would such a statement stop shootings by Police? No, is the simple answer, but all officers would understand how operational success would be assessed.

Before moving on from this aspect of the broader "rules that apply", as Sarre put it, the author makes one further point. The New Zealand Police, despite being charged with "one of the features that distinguishes policing from other occupations ... [namely] ... the lawful authority ... to apply force when circumstances call for it" *Invalid source specified*, does not formally report or publicly record the number of times it resorts to the use of lethal force, to the Parliament or people of Aotearoa New Zealand.

It is fully acknowledged that the use of force is counted, recorded and published in documents loaded onto the New Zealand Police website in various places and no doubt reviewed and analysed by senior Police and those charged with use of force oversight within the organisation. However, in its formal reporting to Parliament, via the Annual Report, no mention is made of the number of times the organisation uses its power to use force or of its use of lethal force.

In fact, the research revealed there was no consolidated list containing the date, time, location, circumstances and people involved in any Police use of lethal force kept that the author could readily locate. The one exception was an appendix titled "Supplemental Report: Police Shootings 1916 – 2020" at the end of the 2019 Tactical Options Report (New Zealand Police, 2020). So, a list did exist, but it required a hunt.

How are the public of Aotearoa New Zealand to know how often their Police have resorted to the use of lethal force? How are the public expected to keep track of the various occasional reports in the media to the effect that Police have shot someone during a particular encounter? How are the public informed that Police attempted to use lethal force, but missed? Beyond investigative journalistic scrutiny, academic enquiry or the occasional media reports about shootings occurring or an IPCA public report, often months later, there is no one-stop public location for accurate, consolidated and comprehensive data.

Aotearoa New Zealand is not alone in that situation. The author reviewed Annual Reports for the three largest Police organisations in Australia (New South Wales Police Force, Victoria Police and the Queensland Police Service) and found a similar situation. There was no mention of use of lethal force or attempts to use it. There were plenty of data about how much money was spent, what the road toll was and how Police aimed to address it and lots of descriptions about programmes,

[1] By way of comparison, NZP statistics reveal police officers shot 4 people during the corresponding timeframe, 3 fatally and 1 non-fatally (www.police.govt.nz/sites/default/files/publications.annual-tactical-options-research-report-8.pdf).

deliverables and outcomes, but nothing about the use of the most extraordinary power vested in those organisations – the lawful authority to kill if need be. The websites for the three organisations produced similar outcomes when visited in October, 2021. A simple word search on the term "use of lethal force" produced no list or page where lethal force use by police officers in the jurisdiction was provided.

Meanwhile, in Canada, an academic has called for a national database of Police use of force (including shootings by Police) to help better understand what is happening, with commentary from a criminologist stating that the number of shootings remains "too high" and describing as an "unrelenting problem" (Malone, 2021).

Elsewhere, in the USA, the Police Executive Research Forum (comprising senior Police leaders and Justice officials), in 2016, after researching the use of lethal force, issued 30 guiding principles for Police organisations to consider, with number 11 being to "To build understanding and trust, agencies should issue *regular reports to the public* on the use of force" (Police Executive Research Forum, 2021, p. 49). The principle went on to recommend annually published reports that included demographic information, the circumstances and efforts being made to prevent all types of bias (ibid.)

Through undertaking the research, the author developed the view that this aspect of policing, given its seriousness and the impact it has on communities, individuals and society as a whole (e.g., one need only look at the fallout from the death of Steven Wallace), should be recorded and reported by the New Zealand Police on it organisational website and be annually reported to the Parliament via the annual reporting process.

The author's opinion extends to include the number of times police officers kill, wound or miss a citizen they shoot at and the circumstances involved in each case. Furthermore, any other death or serious injury inflicted, or caused, by a police officer in the course of their duty should also be recorded and reported in a similar manner. In essence, if it is right and proper to record and report to the Parliament the expenditure of public funds, it is also right and proper to record and report to the Parliament the death or injury of citizens occasioned through use of those same funds.

What would such a record look like and consist of? Firstly, it is suggested a dedicated page on the organisation's website be created that can easily be found through the site's menu and, secondly, the date, time, location and brief circumstances of each event including the known outcome (fatality, injury, miss), which is routinely updated as and when information is made publicly available by the Police investigative process and/or the IPCA investigative process.

That is not to say that any investigative process or lawful requirement should be overruled by having such a reference point. Information on the page should only be provided (or updated) when lawfully and investigatively appropriate. For example, if the page identified that a person had been seriously injured in a shooting by Police, and the person subsequently dies from that injury, the reference should be updated to reflect the death. Ultimately, when an IPCA public report is completed and released, a link should be provided from the Police site record to that report. Furthermore, all Police and IPCA media releases related to the recorded events should be linked to the relevant event, a one-stop public location for accurate, authoritative, timely and relevant information for all with an interest.

Annually, the relevant details from the site would then go on to form the basis of the information reported to the Parliament, along with any change noted in the number of times lethal force was used across the year in comparison to previous years and previous decades.

As was discussed in Chap. 10, and displayed in Fig. 10.1 (Number of Shootings By Police: By Decade (1916–2020)), the dramatic uplift in the number of Police shootings in the 2011–2020 decade might well result in elected representatives of the Aotearoa New Zealand citizenry asking questions about why and how such a change occurred. Surely, in a democratic, rule-of-law country, such enquiry would be appropriate, particularly if it helps avoid the justification trap and its potential for social unrest alluded to in Chap. 10.

To balance and contrast the information suggested above, Police could also include data from the recently created Gun Safe database to reveal how often officers are confronted with firearms and in what circumstances and concerning the number of officers seriously injured in the line of duty, yet further information noticeably absent from annual parliamentary reporting.

Use of Lethal Force Legal Matters

As summarised and discussed in Chap. 2, various sections of the *Crimes Act 1961* (NZL) address the use of force within Aotearoa New Zealand society. The Act details how force can be used by Police or citizens to defend themselves (s. 48) and what penalties people face when force is used unlawfully.

When researching the cases presented in Chap. 8, and the case studies in Chap. 9, the author was left with an unease by several of them. The unease arose from cases where, while justified in using lethal force in self-defence, police officers had placed themselves into, at best unsatisfactory, at worst dangerous, situations where using lethal force in self-defence was the only realistic tactical option left available to them.

In the cases that left unease, Police had the tactical superiority mentioned in Chap. 10. They had the numbers, the equipment and the training, and yet it all came down to the use of a firearm. When the Police were queried about whether any police officer had been dismissed because of their involvement in a Police shooting, the answer was that none had. Some had "experienced some form of further action " (*n* = 25), with just four facing disciplinary action (see Chap. 8 for additional information).

That left the author with the view that the internal discipline consequence risks police officers faced from making what appeared to be poor tactical decisions were, in reality, quite minor in comparison to the consequences for the person they had engaged with who may be dead. Furthermore, out of 43 cases involving shootings by Police, the IPCA had justified all of them, thus clearing the officer(s) from any criminal liability.

Interestingly, the law makes no distinction regarding the tactical superiority factors, mentioned in Chap. 10, when Police go into situations where they end up killing or injuring a person. The police officer is judged against the very same legal standards as any other citizen who kills or injures another and who then seeks to claim self-defence.

The IPCA, in their public reports, have for some years added a consideration of the tactics and equipment Police can deploy when confronting an armed (or apparently armed) person. Those commentaries are useful and appropriate, given they go someway to providing consideration of the issue of tactical superiority. The Authority also made findings on how well an intervention was conducted and how well, or not, command and control was applied. However, the author's unease remained.

Should the law judge police officers and their superior tactical advantages differently? Perhaps. However, introducing a specific rider or caveat to s. 48 of the *Crimes Act 1961* (NZL) may well result in a public and Police outcry. It appears to the author that the most appropriate mechanism would instead be for the two entities required to investigate the circumstances of a use of lethal force – the Police and the IPCA – to make clear and unambiguous findings about the appropriateness or otherwise of a police officer's tactical decisions once all legal elements have been addressed, possibly added to the previously suggested public record on the use of lethal force. That, no doubt, would raise serious issues if, for example, the IPCA cleared the shooting as justified under s. 48, but reported that it felt the justification only arose because of poor decision-making or the tactics applied by an officer or officers and Police then attempted to apply a sanction (say dismissal).

Whatever the answer to this dilemma is, it is beyond the author's ability to solve it within these pages. Suffice it to say, in the author's view, there have been shootings by Police that, had different tactics, better planning, and tighter command and coordination been applied, *may* not have resulted in a death. But, the fact remains, no officer has lost their job. No officer has been charged with a crime (with the exception of one officer prosecuted by the dead man's family), and no officer has been found to have acted without justification.

Some may argue that all of the above proves that police officers act professionally, appropriately and within the law. The author agrees; the majority do. However, some of the cases reviewed for this work leave an awkward feeling, a feeling that the "system" is structured in such a manner that it would require an extraordinary and outrageous act on the part of a police officer for them to ever face a serious consequence – such as the loss of their employment – for the deadly outcome of their questionable action(s).

Let me use a contemporary and tragic example from a land not far away from Aotearoa New Zealand. A police officer in Western Australian was sent to a call about an armed woman (she had a large knife and a pair of scissors according to media reporting), who had recently been released from prison and was afflicted with mental health and addiction issues. Within moments of his arrival, he had shot and killed her. There were eight police officers present. The case, involving an aboriginal woman, was widely covered by various media outlets, with some using the CCTV footage seized by Police to show the scene as the shooting unfolded.

One of the eight officers was reportedly already engaging the woman in conversation in an attempt to defuse the situation as he had had previous interactions with her when the officer who fired arrived. One had drawn a TASER, but had not activated it. Five remained seated in their Police cars, which CCTV footage showed had parked in the form of a loose cordon around the woman who stood in the roadway. A jury later found the officer not guilty of murder (with which he was charged) or of manslaughter.

Once again, a death. Once again, a person with mental health and addiction issues. Once again, tactical superiority rested with Police (i.e. numbers, equipment, training and options). Once again a rapid resort to a firearm, a claim of self-defence and a jury acceptance of that claim. Once again, outcry from the indigenous community and the woman's family.

In the subsequent court case – the officer had been charged by Police with murder – the prosecution had argued that Police at the scene had what the author described as tactical superiority. The prosecutor drew attention to the officer's length of service, his training, the number of officers who attended and the range of weapons they had available between them (for example, see reporting by McNeill in "WAtoday" on 22 October, 2021). While on behalf of the charged officer, the defence counsel highlighted that the officer had a very short time in which to react given how close the now deceased woman was to him.

The author was left to ponder what part of the officer's training or experience suggested close proximity as a good tactical decision when confronting a disturbed person armed with a knife.

The author was left wondering, as the media coverage did not mention it, what planning the eight officers engaged in over the Police radio about how they were all going to act when they arrived on scene to safely resolve the matter and leverage the advantage that their numbers and various items of equipment (including their motor vehicles) gave them. The author was left wondering who was the person in charge of the response on the ground, as again the media made no reference to a supervisor being present (i.e. a sergeant) or that one of the eight had anointed themselves as 'in charge' given the situation and to coordinate their collective actions, again to leverage their tactical superiority.

The jury's verdict meant it was left to the Western Australian Police to determine, via human resource procedures, what to do next concerning the now acquitted officer.

What did that event highlight? For the author it highlighted that convicting a police officer of a serious crime associated with the taking of a life while they are acting in the line of duty has an extremely high bar attached to it and that claiming self-defence is an almost ironclad guarantee of acquittal, even if multiple unanswered questions are left hanging regarding tactical decisions, taken or not taken; planning, done or not done; and command and coordination, or lack thereof, concerning the actions leading up to a death.

Situations as described above, and in Chaps. 8 and 9, are without doubt dynamic, dangerous and adrenaline-pumping scenarios, but that is precisely why police officers are selected, trained and re-trained to handle them. It is why officers are given a range of tactical tools to help them and have on call other wider-ranging tools to make use of.

This concludes the "soft" side suggestions and commentary arising from the author's research. It is hoped that the chapter and the material contained in Chap. 10 provides readers from all backgrounds with food for thought, discussion and perhaps action concerning some or all of the matters raised.

Bibliography

Independent Police Conduct Authority. (2021, October 25). *Why Police oversight matters.* Retrieved from ipca.govt.nz: https://www.ipca.govt.nz/Site/about-us/Why-Police-oversight-matters.aspx

Malone, K. G. (2021, December 27). *Year in review: Still too many police shootings in Canada, experts say.* Retrieved from cbc.com: https://www.cbc.ca/news/canada/canada-year-end-police-shootings-1.6298888

McNeill, H. (2021, October 22). *Footage of shooting released after police officer acquitted of Geraldton woman's murder.* Retrieved from watoday.com.au: https://www.watoday.com.au/national/western-australia/wa-police-officer-acquitted-of-murder-over-shooting-of-geraldton-woman-20211022-p592g3.html

New Zealand Government. (2021, October 25). *Independent Police Conduct Authority Act 1988.* Retrieved from legislation.govt.nz: https://www.legislation.govt.nz/act/public/1988/0002/latest/DLM126283.html

New Zealand Police. (2020). *Tactical options 2019 annual report.* Retrieved from police.govt.nz: https://www.police.govt.nz/sites/default/files/publications/annual-tactical-options-research-report-8.pdf

New Zealand Police. (2021, November 9). Reference: IR-01-21-30907. In *Official information act request response.* New Zealand Police.

Police Executive Research Forum. (2021, November 25). *Guiding Principles on Use of Force.* Retrieved from policeforum.org: https://www.policeforum.org/assets/30%20guiding%20principles.pdf

Sarre, R. (2019, November 13). *If Australian police officers are allowed to shoot to kill, the should be better trained.* The Conversation. Australia: The Conversation.

The Guardian. (2021, October 23). *Police officer who shot dead indigenous woman in WA street found not guilty of murder.* Retrieved from theguardian.com: https://www.theguardian.com/australia-news/2021/oct/22/police-officer-who-shot-dead-indigenous-woman-on-wa-street-found-not-guilty-of?CMP=Share_iOSApp_Other

Washington Post. (2021, October 25). *Half of the nation's largest police departments have banned or limited neck restraints since June.* Retrieved from washingtonpost.com: https://www.washingtonpost.com/graphics/2020/national/police-use-of-force-chokehold-carotid-ban/

Chapter 12
Conclusion: Where to from Here?

On the one hand – some might argue – the numbers regarding the use of lethal force in Aotearoa New Zealand are cause for celebration. Over the most recent 6 years of available data from New Zealand Police (2014–2019), 28,727 events that were attended by police officers resulted in a choice being made to deploy a tactical option. Out of those events, just 2,076 (less than 10%) involved the choice of arming with a firearm, and, out of those arming events, there were just 30 instances (1.4%) involving lethal force being used (note: using the author's definition of lethal force that includes shots that miss, injure or kill and excluding two events where it could not be determined if Police or self-inflicted gunfire caused the deaths) (see New Zealand Police Tactical Options Reporting 2014–2019).

Alternatively, on the other hand, the numbers could be argued as troubling and a cause for reflection. For example, a near doubling in the use of lethal force (again using the author's definition) from 21 instances between 2000 and 2010 to 41 instances between 2011 and 2019. Across those same two decades, Aotearoa New Zealand is moving ahead of its nearest neighbour Australia in the number of people fatally shot per capita by Police.[1]

Furthermore, between 2000 and 2019, 26 people identified as Māori were the subject of lethal force use by Police, with Māori comprising 16.0% of the population, while 19 people identified as European were the subject of lethal force use while Europeans represented 67.5% of the population (Statistics New Zealand, 2020).

It must also be remembered that for every use of lethal force, there is the impact on the person it was used against and their loved ones and the equally substantial impact on the police officer(s) who used it and their loved ones. Therefore, every instance of lethal force use has *at least* two directly impacted individuals and a much wider group of indirectly impacted lives.

As has been seen in both Australia and the USA, the use of force – particularly lethal force – by Police on First Nations peoples and people of diverse ethnic origins have caused great societal consternation and upheaval in some instances. Aotearoa New Zealand needs to be mindful of this and the figures presented above.

[1] Between 2000 and 2010 it was 0.12 per 100,000 citizens in Aotearoa New Zealand, while Australia recorded 0.19 fatalities. By the 2010–2019 decade, Aotearoa New Zealand was fatally shooting 0.30 people per 100,000 citizens, while Australia was at 0.21.

R. S. Shortt, *Lethal Force and New Zealand Police*,
https://doi.org/10.1007/978-3-031-05269-9_12

As the author has previously commented in this book, the justification trap can spring shut with just one instance of a questionable use of lethal force irrespective of the findings regarding lawfulness. Alternatively, it can reach a tipping point where the number of deaths exceeds the public appetite and the trap springs shut bringing with it demands for review and change (for example, see Project Beacon and the Victoria Police, in Australia).

Where does Aotearoa New Zealand now find itself with regard to the use of lethal force by the New Zealand Police?

First things first, as the saying goes. New Zealand Police have a responsibility to ensure that its members – charged with applying lethal force when absolutely necessary and where alternative options do not exist – understand the law, policies and procedures relevant to that activity. Education, training, practice and testing are necessary to confirm that police officers have the competency to use force lawfully and appropriately on behalf of those they serve.

Furthermore, given the finding in this work that Police enter the vast majority of lethal force use situations with tactical superiority, Police must ensure officers have the knowledge, skills and abilities to maximise that superiority with an overall intention of minimising the number of times that they must resort to the final act of pulling the trigger of a firearm.

For example, one of the findings regarding tactical superiority was that lethal force was used when groups of police officers were present. While current policy and procedure and – no doubt – training emphasises individually based risk and tactical option assessments, teams of officer need to form, in the author's view, team-based risk assessments and tactical option plans. They need to actively coordinate that needs someone to assume a "command" role, be it a ranked officer like a sergeant, or a senior-in-service officer when all involved are of the same rank.

The IPCA has commented on the coordination issue, and it is apparent to the author from the research of shootings in Aotearoa New Zealand and internationally that groups of officers appear to continue to operate as individuals exercising their personal discretion and judgement-based approaches, when in fact the situation they are now confronting has fundamentally changed that equation and requires they now operate as a team with team planning, team assessments and team responses, thus maximising the tactical superiority they bring to the situation.

Also, the research has shown that over 20 years, Police have not had to shoot a person over the extended range that their current Bushmaster rifle provides. Instead, all of the shootings reviewed in the available IPCA reporting involves relatively close ranges far below that delivered by the military-style rifle. Is it still the best longer-range weapon for response officers? Could another weapon provide the accuracy, ease of firing and effectiveness of the Bushmaster, without the potential for the weapon's appearance leading to militarisation concerns? Police would do well, the author suggests, to consider these matters when planning their weapon replacement requirements in the future.

When it comes to specialist teams, it appears to the author that an unintended situation has arisen whereby militarily trained, counterterrorism, specialists are now highly likely to be the first tactical firearms officers to deploy to AOS callouts in

Auckland, Wellington and Christchurch (the country's three major population centres) risking a perception that Police have become militarised by stealth. Furthermore, it is inescapable that those officers bring with them militarised tactics and thinking to their otherwise civilian policing responses.

While that has happened, it appears from the data that the use of the AOS has reduced for emergency callouts – the very reason for which they were created – rendering them more likely to be used for planned operations, a reversal of their use in years gone by. What has instead happened is that the training used to prepare AOS officers has now had to be transmitted across to a much wider (and still expanding) Level 1 group of police officers.

The result is that now several thousand police officers are having to be trained to a much higher level to prepare them to deploy firearms and potentially use lethal force. With greater numbers of firearms being deployed to a wider cohort of officers, the author believes the potential for an increase in lethal force use exists and may well have already been witnessed through the 2011–2019 years as detailed earlier.

The author acknowledges the ill-fated attempt to move AOS into a more proactive Armed Response Vehicle-styled operational role following the Christchurch mass shootings, and that they may well be making a comeback in another form under the recently released shift in tactical response delivery announced by the police commissioner (see "District trial areas announced for Tactical Response Model" www.police.govt.nz, 3 November, 2021). However, it is the author's impression that the unsuccessful ART trial has complicated the waters for Police and while they wish to deliver greater experience and support to operational officers, they are being forced to do so in ways that still do not – in the author's opinion – best utilise the operational knowledge, expertise and options available via AOS teams.

Sadly, if the citizens of Aotearoa New Zealand want less people shot by Police, they need to appreciate that experienced, well-trained AOS police officers, with a wider range of tactical options, such as less-than-lethal munitions, and other alternative equipment are more likely to deliver that outcome than are more Level 1 responders who receive additional training.

Building on from the above commentary, a clearly worded statement from the Police organisation on the outcome it desires from all use of force situations – particularly lethal force situations – would, the author believes, be a good starting point. Such a statement should reinforce the requirement to maximise the safety of *all* involved and to also maximise the tactical superiority that the options police officers bring to a situation gives them. Hendy's research in Scandinavia suggested that organisational polices can indeed have an impact on police officers' decision-making processes, particularly when it comes to making lethal force-related decisions (Hendy, 2014, p. 9).

Linked to the desired outcome and policy statement issue mentioned above is a peripheral matter worthy of comment. That is the apparent need for Police leaders to immediately praise, and almost exonerate officers, involved in the use of lethal force. To not quickly make such statements leaves leaders open to police officer and sometimes other commentator's criticism of "not supporting the troops" (author's experience). Such immediate expressions of support leave the organisation and the subsequent IPCA investigation and findings open to claims of systematic bias. Police leaders must clearly keep an open mind about what has taken place and what may be uncovered during the subsequent investigations. Statements acknowledging the tough decisions taken and the impact on all involved are appropriate; however, anything that suggests a view has been formed on the justification or otherwise of the use of lethal force must surely wait until the facts and findings are in Associated with the above suggestions and comments is the need for the New Zealand Police to constantly monitor and report on its use of lethal force. Great inroads have been made with the Tactical Options Reporting regime and the Gun Safe project, mentioned earlier. However, it remains the author's contention that transparency needs to go further.

The primary suggestion for future consideration is the delivery of a "one-stop-register" of all occasions when police officers use lethal force housed on the New Zealand Police website. Associated with the register concept is the development of an organisational definition about what lethal force is, thus clarifying what needs to be recorded. The author recommends a wide definition as previously detailed in this work that focuses on a police officer's intent, and not on the outcome of the officer's actions.

The ability to use lethal force is the most extreme and defining element of being a constable and working as a police officer in a country that enshrines the right to life, and which has abolished court-imposed death sentences. It is, therefore, worthy of clear definition and of transparent reporting.

If it is felt inappropriate for the suggested lethal force use register to be located on the Police website, then the alternative suggestion is that the IPCA website host the information and that Police link to it when they have information to add.

Finally, with regard to policing, Police must be constantly alert to the risk of allowing a view to form within society that they operate with impunity, under a system that is geared towards justifying their actions and which allows them to be "judge, jury and – in some exceptional cases – executioner" when it comes to how people are dealt with. Being so alert appears to be an implicit requirement of the principles set out for policing under its own Act, which state:

a) **Principled, effective, and efficient policing services are a cornerstone of a free and democratic society under the rule of law**:
b) Effective **policing relies on a wide measure of public support and confidence**:
c) Policing services are provided under a national framework but also have a local community focus:
d) Policing services are **proved in a manner that respects human rights** … (Bold highlight added) (*Policing Act 2008* (NZL), section 8)

Related to the author's above suggestions for New Zealand Police are ones relevant to the Independent Police Conduct Authority and its oversight of lethal force use by Police.

Firstly, adoption of the same wide definition of lethal force use would, either through legislative amendment or via the Memorandum of Understanding (MoU), require the Authority to be informed of and investigate and report on use of lethal force where the shot(s) fired miss.

Furthermore, while the Authority's investigators do consider tactics used, or available but not used, it may well be worth giving consideration to making that element of the independent investigative process as important in every investigation as is the justification question concerning the shooting itself. Importantly, again with a focus on Police tactical superiority, how well have police leveraged that superiority when it comes to resolution of the event.

While on the subject of the IPCA, and from a researcher's perspective and acknowledging that IPCA reports are not produced to satisfy researchers needs, the variety of styles and content of reports is challenging. If Police were to adopt a register of lethal force use as suggested, it would be enhanced by the adoption of standard layouts and content coverage by the IPCA in its reporting to help citizens and researchers fully appreciate all of the dynamics of a shooting event.

For example, what weapon (or weapons) did the person who was shot (or shot at) have access to, use or present? Were they functional? Were they modified? If a firearm, was it loaded? Was it fired? How many shots were fired, if any were by the person? What was the trajectory of those shots? What were the distances involved? Information about the person shot would also be tremendously useful, but it is accepted that privacy issues do exist, particularly when a person survives a lethal force use event.

The final concluding comment regarding the IPCA is timeliness of reporting. It is accepted and acknowledged that the IPCA's investigative work takes place alongside Police investigative work, and the timelines are to some extent dictated by the Police and in some instances the criminal justice process. However, decreasing the delay in producing a public report, and delivering a public report on every use of lethal force event, would help to deliver transparency on this important aspect of policing.

What role does the Government of Aotearoa New Zealand have in this environment? The author believes it has an important one, unsurprisingly, given its funding role and its ability to require and encourage agencies to work collaboratively on complex problems.

Firstly, on the funding side, Police should be funded to deliver the suggestions detailed above, if in fact additional money is required. Included in that is funding of experimental devices and weapons for evaluation which may reduce the need to use firearms. For example, the development and fitting of technology to Police vehicle-mounted gun cabinets to alert the Communications Centres and District Command Centres to the fact firearms have been removed and that officers are now armed (or the weapons have been stolen), independent of the continuing need for officers to verbally acknowledge the fact by radio.

Secondly, because Police lack a scientific research and development capability, the government could make it part of the Environmental Science and Research (ESR) agency's role to deliver science-based evaluation of less-than-lethal equipment developments and to also work with industry to fill gaps in the Police toolkit for less-than-lethal options – appropriately funded, of course. Thirdly, if the IPCA requires additional resources to speed-up and broaden its independent investigative oversight, then the government should provide such funding given the risks – such as civil unrest and reduced confidence in Police – that are at stake.

Finally, given the high percentage of people shot who have mental health issues and substance abuse connections, funding additional crisis response capability to avoid Police having to intervene – sometimes tragically – would seem both a prudent and responsible use of public funds. Other countries and cities are experimenting with combined mental health/Police response units, and some very promising reports are coming out of jurisdictions where they are being trialled. It should not require the justification trap being sprung to embark on such activities in Aotearoa New Zealand. To wait for that motivation places Police reputation and legitimacy at risk.

It was not the author's intention to cover such a wide swath of topics when it came to researching and writing about lethal force use in Aotearoa New Zealand. This work started out with a much narrower scope and expectation. However, as the research progressed, it became evident that a wider-ranging foundation work would provide a springboard for further research and publications on this important and, in the author's view, under-discussed topic.

It should not just be left to occasional news media reports, civil rights advocates, non-governmental groups or people with potentially biased views – both in support and against – regarding Police and policing to be the only commentators. Academics and scholar-practitioners (e.g. the developing discipline of evidence-based policing) also need to focus their attention and efforts on the issue and to provide considered expert input to help deliver sophisticated, and well-informed, public conversations about policing and the use of lethal force. For all its faults, and there are no doubt many, this book is an effort to provide just such an input.

Policing is a challenging occupation. Its most challenging aspect is the decision to use lethal force and to face the consequences – for all involved – of that decision. It is a decision that should never be taken lightly, hurriedly or without the very best funding, research, education, training, equipment and support underpinning it. Society – rightly – expects high standards of police officers, and the vast majority of police officers expect high standards of themselves and their colleagues, based on the author's 34 years of policing experience. It is the author's hope this work will also contribute towards those expectations continuing to be met.

Bibliography

Hendy, R. (2014). Routinely armed and unarmed police: What can the Scandinavian experience teach us? *Policing*, 1–10.

Statistics New Zealand. (2020, September 23). *New Zealand's population nears 5.1 million*. Retrieved from stats.govt.nz: https://www.stats.govt.nz/news/new-zealands-population-nears-5-1-million

Index

A
Active shooter, 59, 94–96, 98
Actual shootings, 218
Adverse commentary, 172
Aggressiveness, 221–223
Aggressive tactics, 221
Allegations, 28
Anti-Terrorist Squad (ATS), 56, 59, 62, 93, 99, 102
AOS officers, 223
AOS rifle, 224
AOS teams, 221, 241
Appropriate Tactical Settings, 205, 214, 216, 217, 223
Aramoana, 53, 58–60
Armed Constabulary (AC), 49, 50, 67
Armed Offender Squads (AOS), 4, 55, 56, 59–62, 65, 68, 70, 71, 97, 147, 210, 214, 216, 217, 220, 221
  activation and deployment, 95
  development, 92
  emergency callouts, 98
  Induction and Qualifying course, 81
  PNT, 93, 101
  pre-planned operations, 98
  responses, 102
  selection event, 97
  squads, 97
  STG, 100
  tactics, 97
  tasks, 98
  units, 97
Armed response teams (ARTs), 68–70, 96, 216
Armed response vehicles (ARVs), 66–69, 113
Arms Amendment Act 1992, 134
Assault Review, 140
Assault Review report, 136
Assault Review's final report, 137
Assault Review snapshot, 148
Australian police, 212, 213
Automatic "pocket pistols", 53

B
Bellingham fatal shooting, 139
Bellingham, Stephen
  aggressive movement, 178
  author's opinion, 180
  authority, 180
  command and control, 179
  cordon and containment approach, 178
  death, 178, 181
  incident, 178
  IPCA report, 180
  justified shooting report, 178
  sawn-off shotgun, 179
  situation, 180
British report, 166
Bushmaster M4 firearms, 86, 90
Bushmaster rifle, 62, 66, 68, 69, 77, 82, 84, 89, 167

C
Carbines, 47, 49–51, 56
Carriage, 80, 85
Case for change, 125
CCTV footage, 237

R. S. Shortt, *Lethal Force and New Zealand Police*,
https://doi.org/10.1007/978-3-031-05269-9

Cerven, David
bank loans, 192
CCTV monitoring equipment, 193
IPCA, 194
scene examination, 193
statements, 192
TASER, 193
Civil policing, 48
Collective goods, 20
Colony, 48–50
Command, 240
Commissioner's Annual Report statement, 120
Contact specialist groups, 95
Coordination, 240
Corruption, 230
Counselling, 173
Covid-19 global health pandemic, 8
Crimes Act 1961, 4, 16, 172
Crimes Act assaults, 122
Criminal investigations, 30
"Critical shot" (head shot), 101

D
Death penalty, 3, 24
Decision-making models, 231
Definition of lethal force, 213, 214
Detective-led investigation, 24
Direct legal authority, 15
Disciplinary actions, 173
District training, 87

E
Emergency callouts, 98, 99
Environmental Science and Research (ESR) agency, 243
Equipment, 84–86
Equipment-related changes, 86
Escape, 15
Ethnicity, 160, 210–212, 239
European ethnicity, 159
Evidenced-Based Policing Centre, 114

F
F061 Use of Firearms by Police, 80, 81
Fatal consequences, 143
Fatal shootings, 143, 210, 213–215, 218
Firearms, 4, 123
access, 60
accessibility, 65, 66
emergencies, 50
firearms-related events, 55
Internet firearms discussion forum, 61
and lethal force, 70
physical injury, 119
Police deployed firearms, 68
possession, deployment and use, 75
protect from Māori, 48
racial stereotyping, 69
recollection, 57
regulation, 52, 60
standards of firearms training, 215–225
strategic policy change, 51
training, 65, 66, 68
unarmed style, 52
use, 48
variety, 48
violence, 119
Firearms shyness, 85
Firearms training, 220
Firearms Training Team, 222
Firehoses, 54
Frontier colony, 48
Fundamental justice, 3
Funding, 243, 244

G
General Instructions, 75, 76, 79, 80, 85
"Generally unarmed" service, 50, 52
Geographic locations, 170
Glock, 218
Glock model 17, 85
Glock pistols, 60, 62, 63, 66, 68, 69, 77, 86, 89–91, 167
Government, 243, 244
Gun culture, 206, 209
Gun Safe, 149

H
Homicide investigation, 23
Homicide/serious injury investigation, 23
Hooper, Astin
AOS, 198
AOS officers, 199, 200
author's view, 200
Authority, 199
confusion, 198
credit union, 197
IPCA, 200
IPCA report, 199
police policy, 198
police vehicles, 198
pursuit, 198

I
Imminence, 18, 19
Incapacitation, 83, 84, 232
Independent investigation, 26
Independent Police Complaints Authority Amendment Bill, 28
Independent Police Conduct Authority (IPCA), 4, 5, 27, 30, 162
  agreement, 34
  briefing paper and website, 31
  evolution, 31
  functions of authority, 229
  functions of the organisation, 30
  investigating teams, 30
  legislated functions, 229, 230
  legislation, 37
  legislative and organisational changes, 30
  lethal force, 231
  ministerial briefing, 31
  policy, 30
  public reports, 234, 236
  public satisfaction with the organisation's work, 42–43
  role, 230
  and role outcome, 230
  shootings, 233, 236
  on shootings by Police, 33–39
  substantial fact, 229
  use of lethal force, 236
Independent review, 43
"In-house" enquiry, 24
Investigation, 35
IPCA public report, 17
IPCA report, 16, 178, 180, 185
IPCA reporting, 240, 243

J
Joint police-military training, 217
Justice system, 30, 36, 42, 43
Justification, 36, 39, 242, 243
Justification trap, 210, 212, 213, 220, 223, 225, 240, 244

K
Kelly-Tumarae, Lachan
  AOS, 188
  Authority's investigation, 187
  incident control, 188
  patrol vehicles, 186
  shooting, 187
  shotgun, 187
  tactical option, 188
Killings, 55, 58, 59, 65

L
Law, 236
Law and morality
  Authority's view, 15
  commissioner of police, 13
  death penalty, 13
  force protections, 16
  IPCA public report, 17
  justification, 14, 20
  legislative parameters, 13
  lethal force, 16
  NZ Police, 14
  police investigation, 18
  police officers, 19
  principles, 21
  protection, 14
Lawful authority, 233, 234
Learning, 205
Legislation, 24, 25, 29, 30, 32, 37
Less-than-lethal equipment developments, 243
Less-than-lethal munitions, 241
Lethal force, 205
  authority, 206
  behaviours, 161
  criminal activities, 161
  data sources, 158
  definition, 157, 213, 214
  development and inclusion, 232
  distances, 167, 168
  eco-system, 214
  encounters, 158
  environment, 157
  environment of policing, 231
  firearms, 213
  force encounters, 166
  independent investigation, 230
  instructions, 231
  IPCA, 229
  mental illness, 162
  non-fatal injuries, 157
  observation, 208
  occasions, 230
  PCA/IPCA reports, 159, 164
  police dog, 161
  Police Executive Research Forum, 234
  Police rules, 231
  Police use, 209, 233
  rules, 206
  in self-defence, 235
  shootings, 157, 159
  use of lethal force legal matters, 235–238
  uses, 163, 210
Level 1 responders, 210, 215, 217–219, 222
Likelihood, 137

M

Māori (tribes), 48, 49, 51, 52, 65, 69
Mass shootings, 205, 206
Memorandum of understanding (MOU), 34
Mental health, 162, 244
Mental illness, 208
  fatal shootings, 162
  lethal force, 162
  SbC, 162
Militarily trained, 240
Militarisation, 240
Militarisation of policing, 217, 220, 222, 223
"Militarised" STG, 220
Militarised tactics, 241
Military-style semi-automatic rifles (MSSAs), 134, 206–207, 217
  ownership, 134
  rules and regulations, 134
  use, 134
Military training, 221
Miller's description, 21
"Minimising risk and maximising safety" goal, 76, 88, 97
Morehu, Adam
  Authority, 191
  confusion, 190
  dog handler, 189
  fatal Police shooting, 191
  IPCA, 189
  motorcycle, 189
  security officer, 190
  TASER, 190
Muzzle-loading Enfield rifles, 49

N

Naitoko, Halatau
  AOS officers, 182, 183
  authority, 184
  death, 185
  drug use, 182
  IPCA, 183, 184
  marksmanship, 184
  pistol, 182
  roadway, 182
  shooting and failure, 184
  shootings, 181
  situation, 185
Necessity, 21
Neutralisation, 83, 84
Newly recruited trainees, 57
New Zealand Bill of Rights Act 1990 (NZL), 3
New Zealand Constabulary Force (NZCF), 50
New Zealand Police, 10, 13, 14, 20, 128, 158
  AK47 style assault rifle, 148
  AOS, 151
  crime, 134
  database, 149
  death and injuries, 145
  decision-making process, 150
  drug methylamphetamine, 144
  environmental context, 137
  fatal shooting, 142
  firearm injury, 136
  firearm licensing system, 135
  firearms deaths, 135
  force, 133
  gun registration, 134
  high-powered rifle, 144
  historical perspective, 133
  history, 47, 52, 58, 67
  legislation, 134
  MSSAs, 134
  non-fatal shootings, 142, 146
  PCA/IPCA, 133, 146
  perception of risk, 149
  police and traffic officers, 141
  Police data, 146
  police officers, 138
  police-specific perspective, 136
  political failure, 134
  resources, 133
  risk management, 143, 147, 149
  risk matrix, 137
  risk police officers, 133
  risk treatments, 138
  routinely unarmed service, 47
  semi-automatic rifles, 135
  sense of security, 135
  substantial threat, 133
  TOR data, 151
  treatments, 138
  24/7 policing, 139
  weapon, 136, 152
New Zealand Police Association, 108, 127, 143
New Zealand Police data, 157
New Zealand Police lethal force environment, 162
Non-fatal injuries, 157
Non-fatal shootings, 158, 210, 213, 214, 218
Non-governmental groups, 244
Northern Communications Centre (NorthComm), 197
Norwegian and Swedish distances, 167
Norwegian Police shootings, 167
NZ Special Air Service (NZSAS), 221, 222

O
Observations, 205, 206, 208, 214, 215, 217, 222, 225
Official Information Act, 8, 125
Operational Safety and Tactical Training (OSTT), 109
Operation Gun Safe, 205
Organisational legitimacy, 26
Organisational structure and operating strategy, 29
Out-gunned, 53, 59, 60

P
Para-militarisation of the police, 217
PCA/IPCA, 177
PCA/IPCA reporting, 8, 159, 173, 177
Perceived Cumulative Assessment (PCA), 149
Philosopher's perspective, 19
Pistols, 48, 53–55, 60, 63, 66
Pocket revolvers, 50
Pocket-sized laminated cards, 81
Police Act 1886 (NZL), 107
Police Annual Report, 119
Police Code of Conduct/employment investigation, 183
Police Complaints Authority (PCA), 5, 17, 43, 157
  Australian data, 158
  and Authority, 25
  decisions regarding shootings, 39–42
  functions of the Authority, 25
  independence and functioning, 27
  IPCA Independent Police Conduct Authority (IPCA)
  legislation, 29
  oversight role, 26
  on shootings by Police, 33–42
  transformational change, 29
  under the legislation, 25
Police Conduct Authority's website, 158
Police data, 159
Police enquiry, 24
Police Executive Committee (PEC), 125
Police executive-level authority, 221
Police Executive Meeting (PEM), 127
Police Executive Research Forum, 234
Police firearms, 3, 127
Police history, 47
Police Integrated Tactical Training (PITT), 78, 89, 91
Police investigations, 16
Police manual, 75
Police militarization, 206
Police Negotiation Team (PNT), 19, 200
Police officers' equipment inventory, 85
Police perspective, 164
Police policy, 229, 231
Police practice, 230
Police services, 47
Police shooting, 4, 32, 167, 212, 222, 223, 230
Police source, 170
Police tactical superiority, 139, 243
Police Technical Support Unit, 144
Police training, 83
Police use of force eco-system, 75, 76, 79
Police vehicles, 198
Police weapons, 168
Policing, 231–234
  in Aotearoa New Zealand, 24, 50
  and British laws, 48
  historical roots, 47
Policing Act 2008, 19, 20
Powers, 231
Pre-planned operations, 98, 99, 103
Preventing escape/rescue, 14
Procedures, 77, 78, 83, 88
Proportionality, 21
Public funds, 244
Publicly available reports, 5–7

R
Reasonable force, 77, 79
Reassurance patrols, 70
Refresher training, 87–91, 94, 97
Relitigate, 8
Remedial training, 173
Replacement satisfaction research programme, 42
Reputational risk, 230
Research, 240
Response and Operations: Research and Evaluation (RORE), 205
Responsibility, 240
Reviews, 25, 27, 29
Revolvers, 48–53, 56–60, 62
Rifles, 49, 53, 56, 59, 60, 62
Right to life, 3, 4
Risk and tactical option assessments, 240
Risk management, 112, 137
Risk matrix process, 137
Routinely unarmed service, 5, 47, 55, 61, 67, 68, 70
Rules, 206, 215

S

Sarre, Rick, 206, 215–217
Satisfaction with the IPCA, 42, 43
Science-based evaluation, 243
Self-defence, 16–19
Semi-automatic pistol, 54, 62
Semi-automatic rifle, 59, 62, 67
Serious crime investigation, 24
Sexual assault, 26
Shootings, 169, 173, 208, 210
  Authority, 224, 225
  culture, 207
  Glock, 218
  research, 240
  review and oversight, 16
Shortest Glock distances, 167
"Skill maintenance" training, 57
Special Air Service (SAS), 100
Specialist, 240
Specialist armed support, 98
Specialist firearm, 99
Specialist firearms response unit, 99, 102
Specialist groups, 97
  AOS Armed Offenders Squad (AOS)
  STG Special Tactics Group (STG)
Specialist role titles, 223
Special operations, 88
Special Tactics Group (STG), 10, 56, 61, 62, 64, 65, 222
  and ATS, 99
  centre-based AOS units, 100
  deployment, 101, 102
  functions and activities, 100
  IPCA, 101
  members, 221
  modern arsenal of weapons, 99
  operators, 102, 222
  police executive, 102
  skills and capabilities, 100
  staffing, 102
  training, 100
  train with the NZSAS, 100
SSTT programme, 116
Staff Safety Project, 107, 112
  anxiety, 108
  assaults, 108
  commissioner, 108
  final report, 137
  police commissioner, 108
  project team, 109
  recommendations, 109, 110
  SSTT programme, 109
  TENR and TOF assessment, 110
  training, 109
  training director, 110
Staff Safety Review, 24
Staff Safety Tactical Training (SSTT) programme, 78, 87–89, 109
Staff Safety Tactical Training (SSTT) refresher programme, 93
Standard AOS activation, 221
Standard Police ranks, 223
Strategic policy, 50, 51, 55, 107
Suicide by cop (SbC), 162, 208
Swedish police's dignitary protection, 163
Swing shift, 91

T

Tactical firearms, 240
Tactical options, 239, 241
Tactical options equipment, 136
Tactical Options Framework (TOF), 78, 79, 82, 109
Tactical Options Reporting (TOR), 146, 148, 212, 213, 242
Tactical response delivery, 241
Tactical response model, 241
Tactical settings, 205, 214, 216, 217, 223
Tactical superiority, 240, 241
Tactics, 243
  AOS, 92
  approach in policing, 92
  ATS, 93
  deployment tactics, 93
  and mindsets, 100
  Norwegian approach, 96
  PITT Police Integrated Tactical Training (PITT)
  PNT, 93
  rifle deployment, 94
  SSTT programme, 76, 78, 87, 88, 93
  STG Special Tactics Group (STG)
  tactical change, 93
  tactical communication, 77
  tactical training, 91
  three-tiered tactical response structure, 90
  TOF, 78, 79, 82
  traditional tactics, 94, 96
  "withdraw, cordon, contain, appeal" approach, 92
Taser, 85, 86, 88, 90, 91
Team, 215, 240
Team-based engagement, 215
Technology-based mechanisms, 214
TENR assessment tools, 231

TENR threat assessment tool, 79
Thorp's report, 111, 134, 135
Threat, Exposure, Necessity and Response (TENR) process, 77, 78, 82
Three-tiered refresher training model, 90
Three-tiered tactical response structure, 90
TOF assessment tools, 231
Toms, Jerrim
  Authority, 196, 197
  first aid, 196
  IPCA investigation, 196
  police car, 195
  shift commander, 197
  spike strip, 195
  unarmed uniformed officer, 195
TOR data, 150
Training, 83, 85, 86, 205, 206, 215, 218, 222
  district training, 87, 88
  enhancements, 89
  firearms and remedial training, 87
  new-style training, 88
  and operational deployment, 90
  PITT Police Integrated Tactical Training (PITT)
  refresher training, 87, 90
  RNZPC training, 88
  SSTT Staff Safety Tactical Training (SSTT)
  three-tiered refresher training model, 90
Training officers, 216
Training recommendation, 83
Training-related observation, 216
Transformational changes, 30
Transparent reporting, 242
Treaty of Waitangi, 48
Trusted justice system, 30, 36, 42

U
Use of firearms, 75, 87, 88, 91, 99
Use of force, 14, 15, 75–77, 79, 82, 83, 88
  AOS, 118
  AOS commander, 116
  ARV deployment, 113
  ARVs, 116
  comparative component, 112
  environmental scan, 115
  firearms deployments, 117
  organisation, 108
  PEC, 126
  recognition, 107
  reviewing policies, 117
  risk management, 112
  shootings, 111
  SSTT programme, 116
  strategic management techniques, 111
  substantial pieces, 107
Use of Force Report, 89, 93, 94
Use of lethal force, 138

V
Vehicle-related shooting events, 169

W
Wallace case, 18
Wallace shooting enquiries, 27, 28
Weapon misfired, 53
Weapon modernisation, 62
Weaponry, 240, 243
Weapons, 163
Wellington-based ATS unit, 59
Wesson revolver, 53, 57, 58, 62